Orissa and Her Remains

Orissa and Her Remains

ANCIENT AND MEDIEVAL
(Puri District)

MONO MOHON GANGULY

WITH AN INTRODUCTION BY
THE HON'BLE MR. JUSTICE J. C. WOODROFFE
WITH NUMEROUS ILLUSTRATIONS

Gian Publishing House
29/6 SHAKTI NAGAR o DELHI-110007 o INDIA

Orissa and her remains

MONO MOHON GANGULY

ISBN : 9788121200646

First Published 1994, reprint 2016 in India by
Gyan Publishing House
5 Ansari Road, Daryaganj,
New Delhi - 110002
Phone : 9811692060

E-mail: books@gyanbooks.com
website: gyanbooks.com

PREFACE.

WHEN some six years ago sitting by the side of Taj one moon-lit night I decided on writing a systematic history of Indian Architecture, I little knew that the first scene of my labour would be enacted in Orissa. I did not know then that the Indo-Aryan style in its purest form was prevalent there only in the whole of India. I was led there by a mysterious dispensation of providence and had accordingly to choose my line of action.

MR. Stirling, the Commissioner of Orissa was the first to write a connected history of the place on which he contributed an article to the Asiatic Researches Vol. XV in 1824. Drs. Mitra and Hunter have in the seventies drawn to a considerable extent upon the materials furnished there. Prinsep and Major Kittoe had in the early thirties done some work in deciphering a few inscriptions. Mr. Bishan Swarüp has recently written a book on Konarka which though published before the present one, is of a contemporaneous nature, for I read a paper in the Albert Hall in 1909 purporting to be a synopsis of the present volume then under preparation.

I have tried in this book to give a scientific exposition of the principles of architecture and sculpture obtaining there. I know full well that the room for difference of opinion on many points of a controversial nature raised in my book is so great that it is impossible to expect that my views will be shared in common by all. I have, however, spared no pains to illustrate my remarks by concrete examples. I ve also aimed at arriving at generalizations without which a treatise of this nature has no abiding value. In the second chapter I have attempted at giving a brief outline of the political history of the province with which its architectural history is intimately connected. The fifth and the sixth chapters form the most important portion of the book as I have enunciated therein the principles of Indo-Aryan architecture and sculpture; the last three chapters are illustrative of these two ; so the reader is requested to go through them very carefully before he reads the description of the temples.

I have to offer an apology to my readers for the use of Indian terms. The students of Indian history and literature are well aware of the difficulties the author has to labour under; he cannot but stick to Indian terms which invariably connote more or less than what their English equivalents do; there are many terms, again, which do not admit of being expressed by English terms at all. To obviate this difficulty I have appended a glossary of Indian terms (Vide Appendix II). There are some terms in the glossary which do not require any explanation, but as the book is intended for both Europeans and Indians, such terms could not be passed over.

The method of transliteration followed in the book for spelling the Indian terms is simple; '*a*' is meant to be pronounced like long 'a' as in far; '*s*' and '*d*' are for শ and ড় of the Indian alphabet; ü is meant to be pronounced like the u in "pulling". I owe an apology to my readers for the following omission which is due to a pure accident over which I had no control. The Plate V. B. referred to in several portions of the book could not be incorporated in this edition as it is reported to me too late that the block with the sketches, both fair and rough, have been missing from the artist's studio, without any chance of recovery; and unless I go over again to Orissa the block cannot be reproduced. I shall, however, insert it in the second edition.

It is my pleasant duty to gratefully acknowledge the help rendered to me by many noble gentlemen, the foremost of whom is the Hon'ble Mr. Justice J. G. Woodroffe who in the midst of his multifarious duties has been pleased to write the introduction for my book. I am also indebted to Prof. S. K. Dutt, M. A., for kindly testing the pieces of iron in the testing laboratory of the Sibpur C. E. College

HOWRAH,

15th June, 1912

INTRODUCTION.

The author has asked me to write these few words of Introduction to his work which I am very pleased to do both because of the evidence it affords of the increasing interest taken by Indians in the Art of their own country as also on account of the intrinsic merits of the book itself.

From 1834 when Ramraz wrote his remarkable Essay on Indian Architecture until the present time no Indian has I believe, with the exception of Dr. Rajendralala Mitra in the seventies, concerned himself with the investigation of those magnficent remains which testified to his country's former greatness. Our own day has witnessed the manifestation of a profound interest of the West in the East which has been in some measure reflected in this country. If the interest here aroused is yet slight it is something that it has arisen at all, oppressed as it is on the one hand by indifference and on the other by the "progressive" hostility of Indian imitators of English industrialism and by others of a similarly narrow outlook. Given this opposition such work either literary or by way of collection as has been recently done by Sj. Purna Chandra Mukherjee of the Archaeological Survey, Sj. Bishan Swarup, Sj. Nagendra Nath Vasu in his valuable "Archaeological Survey of Mourbhunj," Kumar Sarat Kumar Roy, the founder of the Barendra Anushandhana Samiti, Sj. Akshay Kumar Maitra, the Bangiya Sahitya Parishat and by the present author has the greater merit.

But the value of the present book does not consist only in this. It is so far as I am aware the first work by an Indian author in which an attempt has been made to treat the subject from a scientific point of view. Chapters V, VI & VII contain much original matter now published for the first time. Chapter V deals with the main features and subsidiary parts of an Orissan temple, and the relative proportions of the different sections in the general ground plan are shown from measurements taken by the author *in situ* such as the *ratio* of the height of the *vimana* to the length of the base. The direction of the temples which is generally eastward is determined, and the author then deals in detail with plinth, pedestal, wall construction and bonds. The author puts forward formulas for the thickness of the walls relative to the height and proportion of the edifice to be raised and others. Chapter VI classifies Orissan decoration and contains very useful observations as to the Devatas represented in the temple of the Shaiva, Vaishnava and Saurya divisions of Hindu worshippers ; the rhythm of spacing in ornament, and its character, and the relative proportions of the representation of the human body ascertained by actual measurement and compared with those given in the *Sukraniti* of Sukracharya which the author has ascertained to be more in accordance with Orissan sculpture than the Manasara to which Dr. Mitra refers.

In this connection we may again express the wish, which has recently been voiced by others, for a collection and translation of the extant Silpa Shastras and cognate Sanskrit texts such as the works last cited, the Vrihat Sanghita of Varaha mihira and like treatises ; the relevant portions of the Agni,

Matsya and other Puranas, and of the Tantras which though now fragmentary, had the Encyclopædic character of the Pauranic Shastra. It is encouraging therefore to note in a recent number of a magazine distinguished for its right understanding and support of Indian art (The Dawn, April, 1912) that the importance of this matter is being now appreciated. From it we learn that the Visvakarma prokasha has been printed and published, the Bangiya Sahitya Parishat have issued a Vishnumurti parichaya and a work on iconography is in preparation by Sj. Akshay Kumar Maitra.

A tabular statement is given by the author showing with great care the relative proportions for *navatala* and *saptatala* images. He raises an interesting question in his reference to the presence of erotic figures which are so commonly found in Orissan temples and more sparingly, I believe, in those of the Dravidian type. The second, however, of the explanations offered is of that *adhyatmik* character which is so common now-a-days in other departments of enquiry, but is as little convincing as such explanations generally are. Modern sentiments, not to speak of sentimentalities, are of no use for the understanding of ancient realism. Probably it will be found that no one theory will adequately explain the presence of such figures which are found, as Dr. Maeterlinck has recently well shown, on old Gothic cathedrals as on Indian temples, though in the former case the images are not so numerous and are more grotesque.

Chapter VII deals with the building materials used, and the author has made an analysis of these and of the metal beams such as those which are found at Konarak. It has been discovered that whereas only 36 years ago the average tensile strength of wrought iron was in England 23 tons per sq. inch the ancient Orissan metal work shows a strength of 20 tons per sq. inch. The remaining chapters give interesting details verified by the personal examination of the author of the celebrated temples at Bhubanesvara and Puri and the great Sun temple at Konarak in the Arkakshetra, a chief centre of the Saura Brahmanas which excited the wonder of the author of the Ain-i-Akbari. Appendix II contains a very useful glossary of Indian terms.

I desire to take this opportunity to confirm from personal observation the remarks of the author as to the necessity for protecting the Konarak sculptures. I found recently that in the period between my last two visits to the Sun temple some of the smaller figures in the lower friezes had been weathered almost beyond recognition.

The author has done well in commencing his researches with a study of the *punya bhumi* of Orissa, for there it is that we still find some of the finest examples of the subject of which his work so usefully treats.

Calcutta, June 14, 1912. J. G. WOODROFFE.

CONTENTS.

CHAPTER I.

INTRODUCTORY.

PAGE.

CHAPTER II.

HISTORY.

CHAPTER III.

CAVE TEMPLES.

CHAPTER IV.

GRÆCO-ROMAN INFLUENCE ON ORISSAN ARCHITECTURE.

CHAPTER V.

ARCHITECTURE OF THE MEDIÆVAL TIMES.

CHAPTER VI.

SCULPTURE.

CHAPTER VII.

BUILDING MATERIALS.

CHAPTER VIII.

THE TEMPLES OF BHUBANESVARA.

CHAPTER IX.

THE TEMPLE OF JAGANNATH AT PURI.

CHAPTER X.

THE TEMPLE AT KONARKA.

LIST OF PLATES.

ORISSA AND HER REMAINS—ANCIENT AND MEDIÆVAL.

CHAPTER I.

INTRODUCTORY.

I need not make an apology to my readers for taking up Orissa in preference to the other provinces comprising India. It is a patent fact that it has peculiar interests of its own alike from an archæological and architectural point of view, not shared in common by the other Indian provinces. To a student of Architecture, it is important by reason of its being the seat of Indo-Aryan style in its purest form; here we do not notice the least vestige of foreign influence. It has maintained its native purity marvellously, being nurtured and reared on the very soil where it grew, without any extraneous aid. This is really a marvel in the History of Architecture, the like of which we very rarely come across. However advanced we may be in the scale of civilization, our dwelling places, or temples indicate a curious combination of various styles, or no style at all. Here, a bit of Doric entablature with an Ionic shaft, or column and a Corinthian base, or pedestal of irregular intercolumniation, there arcuation replaced by trabeation or corbelling; here, the characteristic Grecian triglyphs, metopes, and cornices, there, a few feet below, an Anglo-Saxon doorway, or a venetian. Here, a few square feet of flat terrace, there, a row of Jack arches with a Mogul dome. Such is our architecture, having no definite system or style to follow. The Orissan style of Architecture indicates a definite style not hampered by any extraneous influence. That the Orissan sub-group of Indo-Aryan style of Architecture presents a continuous series for a period of 5 to 6 centuries lends an additional weight to its study, and renders it very interesting.

The importance of Orissa is also due to its being a pre-eminently sacred country. Reference to its sanctity is noticed in the Mahabharata, Brahma Puranam, Skanda Puranam, &c. However shrouded in comparative obscurity may be its early history, I have traced it clearly since the advent of Gautama Buddha, in the next chapter. In the Mahabharata, it has been described as inhabited by the Rishis*; in the Brahma Puranam it has been spoken of as the country of the "blessed adorned with all the virtues," and as the "bestower of Heaven, and Salvation."† Its sanctity preserved it from an attack by the Moguls, so late as the 16th cent. A. D., and we shall see later on that its sanctity, strangely, was an incentive to the Moslem onset led by **Kalapahar**.

* Vana Parva, Sec. 114, slokas, 4-5.

† Brahma Puranam, 26th Chapter.

In India, Benares and Puri are the two most important places of pilgrimage famous alike for sanctity, and historic associations treasured up in the nation's undying remembrance. It is here that the whole nation's fervent devotion has manifested itself in many a form; it is here that the heart and intellect of the nation have proceeded on parallel lines. Benares, and Puri present paradoxes to the ordinary conception of Hinduism. Here, the lowest of the low will meet on the same platform with the proud Brahmin; they worship the deity standing abreast.

Before the Christian era Buddhism, and Jainism gained ascendency here, and exercised a great influence on Hinduism, or more properly, Brahminism. The union of Brahminism with Buddhism or Jainism is marked by a great upheaval in every department of thought and art; architecture with sculpture could not escape its influence. The cosmopolitan tendency of Buddhism is still traceable at Puri.

After the introduction of Buddhism or Jainism, Tantrism was the order of the day, and rendered the amalgam of Buddhism, and Brahminism a more complex one; the different forms of worship, *Saiva*, Vaishnava, or Saurya were all Tantric in character. Several centuries afterwards, Vedantism raised its voice of protest against Tantrism, but could not gain any permanent footing. The religious climax was reached when

Sri Chaitanya, the Prophet of Nadia, came to Orissa with his band of disciples. This marks a new epoch in the History of India, nay in the history of the world. It is a well-known fact that the popularity of Puri is due to the advent of *Sri* Chaitanya. The Vaishnavas recall to mind with a sense of thrilling joy the victory of love over knowledge in the defeat by Sri Chaitanya, of Pandit Vasudeva Sarbabhauma, a scholar of the orthodox school, and of Ramgiri, a Bauddha *Sramana*. They remember with humility the supremacy of spiritual power over the temporal one, in the conversion of Pratap Rudra Deva to Vaishnavism, and they chant with fervid devotion the couplets from the *Sri* Chaitanya Chandrodaya Mahakavyam by Kavi Karnapur, where the ecstatic dance of the Prophet with Pratap Rudra Deva in the car procession of Jagannath has been so beautifully described.*

Taking everything into consideration, I am inclined to think that Orissa has far more glorious traditions of past history than Bengal may possibly claim, and that she occupied a more prominent place than Bengal in the hierarchy of the Indian nations.

* *Sri* Chaitanya Chandrodaya Mahakavyam by Kavi Karnapur, 16th canto sloka 24.

[illegible]

[illegible]

CHAPTER II.

HISTORY.

My attention was struck by the remark of an English scholar that our sacred dialect Sanskrit had been forged by the wily Brahmins after the fashion of Greek, and that the two great national epics, the Ramayan, and the Mahabharat had been composed on the basis of Homer's Illiad, and Odyssey. I had really to pause awhile before I could proceed any further. In a most inauspicious hour did Sir William Jones make the startling discovery that Sandracottos was Chandragupta, and Palibothra was Pataliputra, or the modern Patna; for, since then, the natural tendency of oriental scholars has been to trace the growth of everything that conduced to our culture and civilization to the Graeco-Roman influence.

Historically speaking, India may be styled the land of paradoxes. To settle the chronology of Indian History, one is lost in the intricate mazes of vain conjectures; and these conjectures have given rise to theories at variance with one another. Before the rise of Buddhism ws have no authentic history worth the name; traditions handed down from generation to generation have taken their place, and the conclusions derived from such traditions or hearsays when carefully analysed, and put to the crucial test of critical examination prove to be erroneous. It is passing strange that no rational vestige, or trace of historical basis was left before the Buddhist period. It is a curious fact that very few architectural remains of the pre-Buddhist period are extant. Some links of the chain of the great Indian synthesis are missing. It is inexplicable why everything has been carefully recorded since the advent of Gautama Buddha, the product of the great Indian synthesis, and that authentic records would be missing previous to this. The religion of Buddha brought about revolutions in Indian history; it permeated every stratum of Indian thought and life; since the advent of that great religious reformer historical data began to be collected to supply the materials for a connected history.

Among the provinces that present stupendous difficulties in deciphering their historic records Orissa stands foremost. It was always a *terra incognita*, by reason of its geographical position, and local circumstances. The whole country was a swamp intersected by a network of rivers with their feeders and tributaries carrying silt to the Bay of Bengal; impassable hilly jungles fringed its borders. The country was in a process of geological formation; there was a perpetual struggle between the different rivers and the sea, for the formation of the deltaic regions. Wh n Orissa first became fit for human habitation it was peopled by a non-Aryan primitive race, probably the Savaras, Mals, Khonds, Pans, &c, the traces of whom are still to be met with; they live up till now in the hilly fastnesses. In the Mahabharata this part of India introduces itself to us under the name of Kalinga.

We read in the Mahabharata that through the grace of Deerghatama (दीर्घतमा) Muni Sudeshna, wife of Bali, bore him five sons, Anga, Vanga, Kalinga, Pündra, and Sümha respectively; and the provinces ruled over by them were called after them.* It is for this reason that the names of Anga, Vanga, and Kalinga are frequently associated together, as sister kingdoms. We find this story narrated also in the Brahma Puranam.† The name of Deerghatama, the son of Utathya is mentioned in the Rig Veda‡; hence we may safely infer that Kalinga must have been well-known in the Vaidic period. Mention is made of Kalinga in the *sutras* of Panini. ǁ

The fame of Kalinga extended far and wide in the time when the Mahabharata was composed. Duryodhana married the daughter of Chitrangada §, the King of Kalinga, whose

* Adi Parva, Sec. CIV.

† Brahma Purânam, chap. 13th, Slokas 29, 30 and 31.

‡ Rig Veda, Mandal, I, 147.

§ Santi Parva, Sec. 4.

capital was R*a*jpur; some are inclined to identify R*a*jpur with the modern R*a*jmahendry. I do not know how far the conjecture based on the accidental coincidence of prefixes may be taken as sound; the geographical position of R*a*jpur can hardly be ascertained with anything approaching accuracy.

It is stated in the Mah*a*bh*a*rata, Van Parva, Sec. 114, that when Yudhisthira reached Kalinga after journeying along the sea-coast from the mouth of the Ganges, he was informed by Lomas Muni that the country through which the Vaitarini flowed was Kalinga, where Dharma, or the god of virtue performed Yajna with the aid of the gods. The modern Y*a*jpura, or Yajnapura is evidently alluded to here.

From the text quoted below,* it appears that Lomas Muni pointed out to Yudhisthira the boundaries of Kalinga from the northern banks of the Vaitarini; and that other provinces had to be traversed by the P*a*ndavas from the mouth

* "ततः समुद्रतीरेण जगाम वसुधाधिपः
भ्रातृभिः सहितो वीरः कलिङ्गान् प्रति भारत।
लोमश उवाच।
एते कलिङ्गाः कौन्तेय यत्र वैतरणी नदी
यत्रायजत धर्मोऽपि देवाञ्छरणमेत्य वै॥
ऋषिभिः समुपायुक्तं यज्ञियं गिरिशोभितं
उत्तरं तीरमेतद्धि सततं द्विजसेवितं॥"

Van Parva, Sec. I

of the Ganges before they reached Kalinga; and these were a portion of Tamralipta, and Utkala.

My reason for fixing the nomenclature of the intervening provinces is clearly explained by reference to the very epic quoted already.

According to the Mahabharata, I assign the following boundaries to Kalinga; on the north, the Vaitarini, on the south the Godavari, on the east, the Bay of Bengal, on the west the tributary states of Orissa. Utkala of the Mahabharata is not the self-same province which bears that name at present. It was bounded on the south by the Vaitarini, and on the north by Tamralipta, or the modern Tamlük. It will at once be apparent to a careless reader of the text of the Mahabharata quoted already that the editor of the Dt. Gazetteer of Puri is obviously wrong in supposing the province of Kalinga to extend from the confluence of the Ganges with the sea.

According to Dr. Fleet the country of Kalinga extended between the rivers Godavari, and the Mahanadi*, and Dr. Bhandarkar, has in his History of the Dekkan made Kalinga correspond with the Northern Sircars†; both these views

* Dr. Fleet, Bombay Gazetteer, Vol. I, Part II, Dynasties of the Kanarese Districts, p. 341.

† Dr. Bhandarkar, History of the Dekkan, p. 139, same.

have been proved to be erroneous. The Northern Sircars was a portion of Kalinga no doubt, but not conterminous with it.

In the age of the Ramayana, and the Mahabharata, Utkala and Kalinga were two distinct provinces independent of each other. After the time of the Mahabharata, and before that of the Puranas, Kalinga extended beyond the Vaitarini up to Tamlük on the north; for, by referring to the Datha Dhatu Vamsam we see that in the time of Gautama Buddha its limit was as far north as Tamralipta.

It is stated in the Datha Dhatu Vamsam describing the legend of Buddha's tooth-relic, that the left canine tooth of Buddha was taken from the funeral pyre by a disciple of his, Kshema by name, who handed it over to Brahmadatta, the king of Kalinga by whom it was enshrined. This tooth-relic gave rise to dissensions between the kings of Kalinga, and Pataliputra, and eventually in the 3rd cent. A. D. was cleverly removed to Ceylon by Dantakumar, Prince of Ojein, and his consort; they weighed anchor in the harbour of Tamralipta, or the modern Tamlük. It can easily be imagined that the prince would not have availed himself of the harbour of Tamlük were it not at a short distance from the seat of that Government by whom the tooth had been enshrined; and it is absurd to imagine that the prince chose the farthest harbour from the capital even though there were intermediate harbours from which it would have been easier to set out on his voyage.

Since the advent of Gautama Buddha, though Utkala used as before to maintain its distinctive character, still the opulence and glory of Kalinga outshone those of Utkala to such an extent that it dwindled into insignificance. Utkala came to be indiscriminately called Kalinga ; it lost its identity gradually, and its existence merged in that of Kalinga.

Megasthenes, the ambassador of Seleucus Nicator came to India in 295 B. C. and lived at the court of Chandragupta for a long time ; he wrote a history of what he saw and heard in India ; but unfortunately that invaluable book is lost, and the fragments of his narratives have been preserved in the writings of others "diligently collected and critically arranged by Schwanbach."*

Pliny has left a record based on the information gathered from the accounts of Megasthenes. This record, however meagre it may be in the description of contemporaneous events, is very important, in as much as it supplies some geographical data upon which the Ancient Geography of India may be roughly based. Pliny has given information regarding the position of Kalinga which unfortunately admits of various

* Sir Walter Elliot, Numismata Orientalia, Vol. 11, Part II, 1886. Coins of Southern India

interpretations to suit the whim, and convenience of students of antiquity. As a typical example, the province of the Malli in Orissa is strangely identified by Parisot, with Multan.*

Kalinga is the *Calingæ proximi mari* of Pliny. To sum up in a few words, that portion of India which, according to Pliny, represented Kalinga, extended from the mouth of the Ganges to the Godavari including the deltaic island formed in the mouth of the Ganges; on the west it was bounded by the hilly fastnesses of the tributary states of Orissa, and on the east by the Bay of Bengal, and the Indian Ocean. It is definitely stated that its northern boundary extended as far as the Ganges.†

Pliny speaks of the three following divisions of the Callingæ:—(*a*) The Gangerides Callingæ, or "the last nation situate on the banks of the Ganges is that of the Gangerides Callingæ,‡" (*b*) The Modo-Callingæ living in the portion called Modo-Galingæ, and (*c*) The Macco-Callingæ.

The country of the Callingæ as mentioned by Pliny was situated below the provinces of the Mandei, and the Malli; the province of the last-named people has been described as containing Mount Maleus. The Mandei are identical

* Dr. Bostock and Riley, Pliny's Natural History, Vol. II, p. 43, foot-note.

† Pliny's Natural History, Vol. II, pp. 42-43

‡ Ibid, p. 44

with the Mundas, an aboriginal tribe inhabiting the southern portion of the Chota Nagpur Division. This view regarding the identity of the Mandei can be borne out by reference to the following passage in Pliny's Natural History, Vol. II :—"Behind these people (the Palibothri) and lying still more in the interior, are Monedes and the Suari, among whom is a mountain known as Maleus".*

Prof. Lassen is correct in assigning to the Sabarai, or the Suarai, the districts of Midnapur, Dhalbhum, Singbhum, Morbhunj and Keonjhar.†

The country of the Malli is identical with the portion of Bengal inhabited by the Mals,or Khonds living in the highlands of the Orissa Tributary States.‡ We encounter a great difficulty in ascertaining the geographical position of Mount Maleus. It is our classical Malya-Vana, or Malay Giri, in the state of Pal Lahara, Lat. 21° 22′ 20″. N, and Long. 25° 18′9″. E.§

Some are inclined to identify Maleus with Mahendra Giri. That it is not so is proved by reference to the 9th Chapter, Visma Parva. where the separate existence of Mahendra, and Malay

* Pliny's Natural History, Vol. II, Book VI., Ch. XXII. p, 46.

† Lassen, Indische Alterthumskunde.

‡ Hunter's Statistical Account of Bengal Vol. XIX p. 209 (1877).

§ Ibid, p 199.

has been established, in addition to the passage quoted from Pliny's Natural History. My view that Maleus is not situated in the Madras Presidency is shared by Hewitt who holds that " Mandar Mountain, mons malleus, and Parisnath are identical with one another".*

According to Pliny, already quoted, the *S*avaras or the Suari inhabited Mount Maleus ; it is too well-known to mention that the *S*avaras live up till now, in the hilly fastnesses of Orissa. Pliny has recorded a natural phenomenon which he may have gathered from dame tradition in respect of Maleus. It is here that "the shadow falls to the north in winter, and to the south in summer in 6 months alternately". This would happen if Maleus be situated due east and west ; and this isolated fact gathered from hearsay may help us in fixing the position of the hill alleged to be on the outskirts of Kəlinga.

The Modo-Galingæ of Pliny seems to me to correspond with the Midnapur District. Modo seems to be a contraction of Madhya or middle. Pliny has described it to be an island in the Ganges‡, and I have noticed the district of Midnapur to look exactly like an island near the confluence of the Rupnərəyan with the Hughli. Hewitt has identified it with Barisal, and

* J. F. Hewitt, History and Chronology of the Myth-making Age.

†Pliny's Natural History, Vol. II. p. 46, translated by Dr. Bostock and Riley.

‡ Pliny's Natural History, Vol. II, p. 45.

the portion of the Presidency Division consisting of the 24-Perganas, and Khulna*

This view will be at once rejected as erroneous when we consider that according to Pliny, "the boundary of this region (Kalinga) is the river Ganges †". The Macco Galingæ is Orissa proper, and a portion of the Madras Presidency near the Godavari, in the Northern Sircars. Macco seems to me a contraction of Mükhya or chief.

Prof. McCrindle has fixed the locale of the capital of the Callingæ, "a great and widely diffused tribe,‡" in the modern Orissa on the Mahanadi, "higher up than the side of Katak," the name of their capital being "Partualis (called by Ptolemy Kalligra)".

It is certain beyond the least shadow of doubt that the whole of Orissa was a part and parcel of Kalinga as described by Pliny. My view is borne out by the following passage from the Cyclopædia of India.

"The Kalinga of Pliny certainly included Orissa, but latterly it seems to have been confined to the Telinga-speaking country, and in the time of Hiwen Thsang (A. D. 630) it was

† J. F. Hewitt, History and Chronology of the Myth-making Age.

‡ Pliny's Natural History Vol. II, pp. 42-43.

¶ J. W. McCrindle, "Ancient India as described by Megasthens and Arrian" p. 63. foot-note.

distinguished on the south and west from Andhra, and on the north from Odra or Orissa."

I accept the above with certain reservations, for it will be apparent on going through the following pages that Orissa continued for a long time after the advent of the Chinese pilgrim to form a part of Kalinga as before. In the poetical works of the great Bengali poet Kavikankan Mukunda Ram who flourished in the 16th century A. D., I have come across several passages in which Kalinga has been made to correspond with Orissa, and that its capital has been described as situated on the Kans or Kansbans in the district of Balasore. The passages referred to unmistakably represent the belief of the age ; so late as the end of the 16th centary, Orissa used to be thought at least a part of, if not conterminous with Kalinga.

Even supposing the locale of the capital of Kalinga as fixed by the poet to be incorrect from the geographical point of view, what he has written receives ample support from the historian. It is stated in Ain-I-Akbari that Orissa formed a part of the Soobah of Bengal and consisted of the six following Sircars, viz, "Jalasor, Buderuck, Cuttack, Kalinga-Dandapaut and Rajmahendri".. From the above it is clearly proved that even in the 16th century. A. D. the southern limit of Orissa was the Sircars, *i. e.* Orissa coincided more or less with the Kalinga of ancient times.

According to Hiuen Tsang Kalinga belonged to Southern India which extended from the mouth of the Mahanadi. General Cunningham has, according to the Chinese traveller, located the site of the capital of the kingdom at Rajmahendri on the Godavari in the Madras Presidency. He has identified Dantapur, the capital of Kalinga with Rajmahendry. Rajmahendry might have been the capital of Kalinga in Hiuen Tsang's time for a short period, but this was not so before the advent of the Chinese pilgrim. This has been already proved by me by referring to the Datha Dhatu Vamsam.

We have reason to believe that Orissa was an important seat of Buddhist and Jain influence from the 3rd century B. C. to the 8th or 9th century A. D. Buddhism began to exercise its influence at the conquest of Kalinga by Asoka, the great Maüryan king in 262 B. C. ; this conquest entailing an inhuman slaughter of men has been immortalised in his Rock Edict XIII ; elements of new civilization began to be henceforth introduced, and Kalinga rose into eminence ; although some stray edicts of Asoka have been discovered farther to the south in the northern frontiers of Mysore, still Dr. Bhandarkar,* Vincent Smith†, etc. consider Kalinga to be the southern limit of his empire.

* Dr. Fleet, Bombay Gazetteer, Vol. I., Part I., History of the Dekkan, by Dr. Bhandarkar, p. 146. † V. Smith, Early History of India, p. 131.

The introduction of Buddhism, and the advantage of being situated on the sea-side, brought Kalinga into contact with many different countries ; it had been a great maritime power for a long time ; new energy and impetus were now imparted, and commerce, and industry began to thrive. In the year 75 B. C. an expedition from Kalinga formed a colony in *Java.**

When Hiuen Tsang visited U-cha or Orissa sometime between 629 and 645 A.D., he saw many towering *saṅghārāmas, stūpas,* etc. indicative of Bauddha influence ; he does not mention the name of any Hindu temple. Outside the town of Che-li-ta-lo-ching, or Charitrapur, or the modern Puri, he saw "five contiguous *stūpas* with towers, and pavilions of great height."† These have been long ago razed to the ground ; but what little vestige of Bauddha influence is still visible in caves and elsewhere, still attests the glory of an almost defunct creed which contributed to a great extent to the civilization of the people. Buddhism has left an indelible impress on the conception of Jagannath so dear to the Hindus. This we shall deal with later on.

The Hati Gümpha inscription as deciphered by Pandit Bhagwanlal Indraji is dated in the middle of the 2nd cent. B. C., and ascribed to Kharvela, the king of Kalinga and a

* Cyclopædia of India, Vol II. (1885.)

† Cunningham, Ancient Geography of India.

patron of Jainism. We know nothing of Kharvela in particular, nor of the dynasty to which he belonged; we come across his wife's name in an inscription in the Swargapuri cave at Udaygiri. These fragmentary evidences tend to prove the existence of an influential Jain dynasty which ruled over Kalinga. The Khandagiri and Udaygiri caves bear visible traces of Jain and Bauddha influence.

Jainism was so deep-rooted in Kalinga that we find traces of it so late as the 16th cent. A. D. Pratap Rudra Deva the king of Orissa, of the Sūrya Vamsa dynasty had a great leaning towards Jainism. The Rev. Long has declared him a Jain*; in an inscription in the Nava Müni cave at Khandagiri we come across the name of a Jain Sramana Sübha Chandra.

From these records scattered here and there we can safely conclude that Jainism gained ascendency here for some time, and was the state religion.

We do not know for certain the definite royal dynasties that ruled over Kalinga in the beginning of the Christian era; but we do know that it was conquered several times by the kings of different provinces in India. The fame of its opulence reached far and wide, and it became an object of ambition to the neighbouring kings to subjugate it. That it was a very

* J. A. S. B. vol. xxviii., Nos. i – v, (1859.)

flourishing kingdom may be easily inferred from the fact of its being one of the nine ***khandas*** or divisions of the known continent, or *Nava-Khanda-Prthivi* referred to by the Tamil lexicons. (Vide Sanderson's Kanarese Dictionary.)

The occasions on which it has been overrun by invading princes since the time of the earliest historic records,—not to speak of the Ramayan and the Mahabharata—are too numerous to mention. I have already referred to its conquest by Asoka in the 3rd cent. B. C. The invasion of Satkarni, probably a king of the Andhra dynasty, is recorded in the Hati Gümpha inscription; he sent "a numerous army of horses and elephants" which was repulsed by Kharvela*.

In the 2nd cent. A.D. Kalinga came under the Andhras; we learn from the pillar inscription of King Mangalesa that Kirtivarman I, the king of the Western Chalükyas of Badami, who reigned from 567-68 A.D. to 597-98 A.D. subdued the king of Kalinga. Pulakesin II. of the same dynasty and son to Kiritvarman I. subjugated it in the 7th cent. A.D. when Harsa Vardhana was reigning in Kanauj.

Kalinga was conquered by Dantidürga, the king of the Rashtrakütas in the middle of the 8th cent. A.D. It was again conquered by Akalvarsa, the great patron of Jainism in the 9th

* V. Smith, Early History of India, p. 185.

† Dr. Fleet, Bombay Gazetteer, Dynasties of the Kanarese Districts, p. 280.

cent. A.D. The Eastern Chalükyas always invaded and overran the country whenever opportunity presented itself. Raj-Raj Deva, the king of the Eastern Chalükyas invaded it in the beginning of the 11th cent. A.D.*

The great Sanskrit poet Kalidas flourished in the 7th cent A. D., and it is natural that he should have placed one of the scenes of Raghu's conquest in Kalinga†. Kalhan Pandit has given an animated description of Lalitaditya's conquest of Kalinga in his RajTarangini, written in the middle of the 12th cent. A.D.‡

To conquer Kalinga became rather fashionable, and the title of "Lord of Kalinga", became a title of distinction ; for, we find the honorific distinction, Trikalingadhipati attached to the names of the kings of the Kosalas and Chalükyas.

The history of Orissa is wrapt up in obscurity till the beginning of the 9th cent. A.D. That there was a powerful dynasty there can not be gainsaid ; but it is difficult to ascertain with accuracy the names of separate kings who ascended the throne in succession, for there is no authentic record that we may fall back upon.

* Dr. E. Hultzsch, South Indian Inscriptions, p. 63.

† स तीर्त्वा कपिशां सैन्यैर्बद्धद्विरदसेतुभिः ।
उत्कलादर्शितपथः कलिङ्गाभिमुखो ययौ ॥

Raghu Vamsam, Canto IV., Sloka, 38.

‡ Raj Tarangini, translated by Dr Stein, vol. I. Sec IV. 147th sloka, p. 134.

The Madla Panji or Temple Archives seem to me a tissue of myths, incorporated complacently by different men in different times; and considering the fact that all the records, and treasures of the Puri temple were seized upon, and destroyed by Kalapahar, we may reject in all propriety the veracity of the Madla Panji chronicles bearing dates prior to the invasion of the Mahomedan iconoclast. That the Madla Panji is not a safe record to rely on can be conclusively proved by reference to the many copper-plate grants which are being unearthed and deciphered from day to day. Although these copper-plate grants have led to different interpretations by different scholars, still they throw a flood of light on Orissan history, which is unerring in the revelation of truth.

The unusually long line of the Kesaris consisting of forty-four kings presents us with a riddle which it is difficult to solve. The view of the old school of scholars headed by Dr. Rajendra Lal, and established by Mr. Stirling according to the Madla Panji, has already lost its hold on our minds; and the arguments brought against it by Dr. Fleet in his "Records of the Somavamsi kings of Katak",* seem to us to be very plausible with certain reservations. It is not our purpose to enter into these questions, but we shall give some broad features of the points at issue according to our own light.

* Epigraphia Indica, Vol. II. pp. 323-59.

We fail to establish with precision the exact date of Yayati Kesari, the so-called founder of the Kesari dynasty; but the approximate date of his reign can be assigned with sufficient accuracy to the period from the middle of the 8th to the beginning of the 9th cent. A.D. That the popular date of his founding the dynasty in 476. A.D. is wrong can be proved by referring to the very source, e.g. the Madla Panji, whence it is derived. It is stated that six kings reigned in Orissa since Vikramaditya, and that their reigns terminated in an invasion of Orissa by the Yavanas. Now, it is well-known that Harsa Vikramaditya reigned about the middle of the 7th cent. A.D.; and this, when added to 180 years, the period covered by their reigns taking 30 years to be the average number of years for which each of the 6 kings reigned, comes up to the first quarter of the 9th cent. A.D.

The Yavanas are supposed to have reigned in Orissa for 146 years; hence the advent of Yayati should, according to the Temple Archives be dated in the last quarter of the 9th cent. A.D. We do not ask our readers to accept this date; this is simp y stated to prove the defect in the views of the old school.

From palæographic considerations, Dr. Fleet agreeing with Prof. Kielhorn, has placed the earliest possible date of the Rajim grant of Indrabala and the Sirpür inscription of his grandson Tivara Deva, in the 8th cent A.D. Tivara Deva, a feudatory prince of the Kosala country is otherwise called Chandragüpta. Harsagüpta, Sivagüpta, Bhavagüpta, and Sivagüpta reigned in succession from Chandragüpta. The last Sivagüpta is identical with Mahasivagüpta, mentioned in the Katak copper-plate grant of the 9th year of Mahasivagüpta, who again was no other than Yayati Kesari. Hence if 720 A.D. be the probable date of Tivara Deva, that of Mahasivagüpta or Yayati Kesari comes up to 720 + 30 × 3 = 810 A. D. or 800 A. D. Thus we are inclined to accept the beginning of the 9th cent. A. D. as the probable period when Yayati flourished.

Yayati or Mahasivagüpta's father was Janmejaya or Mahabhavagüpta I. Hence Janmejaya might have flourished sometime between the middle of the 8th century and the beginning of the 9th cent. A. D.

There is one fact, however, which is rather strange and worth mentioning; Madla Panji mentions the name of Janmejaya as one of the Kesari kings, and Messrs Stirling, and Hunter have, following the temple records, assigned the date of his reign to 754 A. D. The date of this Janmejaya strangely coincides with Janmejaya Mahabhavagüpta I referred to already. This Janmejaya was father to Yayati, whereas that of Madla Panji was a king of Orissa, 13th in succession from Yayati. This reversal of connection and chronology may be ascribed to carelessness of the keepers of of the Archives. Here, however, we notice a reminiscence of authentic history rendered dim by the inadvertence of later chroniclers.

We do not, however, go so far as to make the bold statement like Dr. Bloch that "the long line of Kesari kings...may be regarded as a later fabrication, containing nothing historical, except a dim reminiscence of two actual kings of Orissa, Yayati and Janmejaya"*

The history of Orissa is comparitively obscure till the latter part of the 11th cent. A. D. when Chodaganga ascended the royal throne, and inagurated the Ganga dynasty belonging to the lunar race. Chodaganga was connected with the Chola royal family through his mother Rajsundari, daughter of Rajendra Chola. The installation ceremony of Chodaganga took place, according to Sewell, in 999 Saka-Samvat, or 1078 A. D.†; according to Dr. Hultzsch, his accession to the throne is dated in 1075-76 A. D.; we are inclined to accept the former date, for it is conclusively proved by referring to the "Vizagapatam copper-plate grant of Ananta-Varman issued from Sindurapura‡. We need hardly point out that

* J. A. S. B. Vol. LXVII., 1898, Part. I., p. 377.

† Sewell's Archæological Survey of India, Vol. II., pp. 33-34.

‡ Indian Antiquary, Vol. XVIII., 1899, Sanskrit and Old Kanarese Inscriptions by Dr. Flee

Chodaganga Deva is otherwise called Ananta-Varman, as having a pedigree which is traceable to Ananta or Vishnu.

The list of the kings of Orisas as supplied by the *Madla Panji* and accepted by Messrs Stirling and Hunter is decidedly incorrect; for obviously the chronicler inserted the names of some minor chiefs in the list by mistake; that the list is wrong can be proved by going through the copper-plate grants* of Nrisimha Deva IV. deciphered by Babu Manomohan Chakravarty, and incorporated in the Appendix in Epigraphia Indica, vol. V. by Prof. Kielhorn.

Chodaganga, Ananga Bhim I, and Nrisimha I. were three powerful kings of the Ganga dynasty whose glory and renown are still attested by the architectural monuments left by them. Choda Ganga built the great temple at Puri, Ananga Bhima I built its important appurtenances, and Nrisimha Deva I built the Black Pagoda at Konarka.

Anianka Bhima, otherwise called Ananga Bhima I, reigned from 1170 to 1202 A. D. We learn from the Chatesvar inscription of Ananga Bhima II* that Anianka was the son of Chodaganga. He surveyed the whole of his territory with reeds, measuring 39407 sq. miles yielding an annual revenue of Rs 28,000,000. He extended his kingdom up to Tribeni on the north

* J. A. S. B. 1895, Vol. LXIV, Par I

* J. A. S. B., Vol. LXVII., Part I, 18

in the Hugly District. He spent a large portion of his revenue in aligning new roads, excavating tanks, sinking wells, and erecting bridges, temples, and *ghats* for landing, and bathing purposes. In his time Orissa rose to the pinnacle of prosperity. I have come across an inscription of Ananga Bhima Deva I., or Aniyanka Deva (not yet published) on the left wall of the staircase leading down to the sanctum of the P*a*t*a*les*va*r temple within the precincts of the great temple of Jagann*a*th at Puri.

The Gang*a* dynasty was subverted by Kapilendra Deva in 1435 A. D., who founded the SuryaVamsa dynasty which continued to reign for nearly one hundred years till 1542 A. D. The most powerful kings of this dynasty were Kapilendra Deva the founder, Pürüsottama Deva and Prat*a*p Rüdra Deva. Orissa reached the zenith of fame and prowess in the time of Kapilendra; he extended his territory as far as Nellore in the Madras Presidency; and by many conciliatory measures endeared himself to his subjects. His son, Pürüsottama extended his kingdom still farther to the south. Prat*a*p Rudra Deva was the son and successor of Pürüsottama Deva. The name of Prat*a*p Rudra Deva is fondly cherished by the Gau*a*iya Vaishnavas for the sympathetic support he lent to the propagation of the creed propounded by the Prophet of Nadia. Prat*a*p Rudra has been immortalised in the Vaishnava literature.

The Surya dynasty was replaced by the Bho-I dynasty which continued to reign till 1560; this was subverted by the Telinga dynasty, the founder of which was Mükünda Deva. Müküda Deva was the last independent Hindu king of O rissa.

As a set off against chafing spirit of the Afghans of Bengal who were always looking out for an occasion to throw off the yoke of the emperor of Delhi, Akbar entered into a treaty with Mükünda Deva. When the emperor was busily engaged in warfare in the far west, Süleiman Karrani, the Nawab of Bengal, sent a large force under the command of his general, Kalapahar, a Mahomedan apostate, who forced Mükünda to retreat backwards; at this critical juncture a rebellion broke out among his own feudatory allies, and Mükünda hastened to quell it; he was slain by one of the feudatory chiefs; thus Orissa passed easily into the hands of the Afghans. Kalapahar seized this opportunity, and advanced as far as Puri, the heart of Orissa; when he approached Puri, the priests of the deïty removed the image to Pariküd on the banks of Chilka, and buried it in earth fearing lest it might be defiled by the Mahomedan iconoclast. Kalapahar getting scent of this proceeded there, dug out the idol, and brought it to the banks of the Ganges, and burnt it in a pile of wood set on fire. The charred remains of the idol were, however recovered by the priests.

The vandalism of Kalapahar has become a proverb; and the very mention of his name still strikes terror into the minds of the people. Popular ballads and legends still keep alive the memory of those inhuman and cruel barbarities perpetrated by the Mahomedan general with all the fury of a renegade. His vandalism has obliterated some of the brightest monuments of our architecture, and sculpture. Who can tell, how many temples *he razed to the ground, or how many images he seized, and* trod under feet!

The first Mahomedan invasion of Orissa by Ismail Gazi took place in 1510; but the Mahomedans could not establish their supremacy till Süleiman Karrani, Nawab of Bengal and Behar conquered portions of it in 1567-68.

Daüd Khan the Nawab of Bengal, Behar and Orissa having denied the suzerainty of the emperor of Delhi, Munaim Khan and Todur Mull were sent by Akbar to march into Orissa. The forces of Daüd Khan were routed in battle at Mogul Mari in 1574. This battle transferred Bengal and Behar from the Pathans to the Moguls, and Daüd Khan continued to rule over Orissa only as a vassal of the Mogul emperor. On the death of Münaim Khan, Daüd Khan again raised the standard of revolt. The Afghans were defeated by the Moguls. On the death of Daüd at Rajmahal, Masüm Khan was appointed governor of Orissa by Akbar; he eventually revolted against the emperor of Delhi, and with the aid of the Pathans expelled the Moguls from Orissa ; Katlu Khan now usurped the Orissan throne, and extended his kingdom as far as the Damodar.

Katlu Khan had been seeking for an opportunity to throw off the Mogul yoke. He fought with Man Singh, the governor of Bengal and Behar, in a pitched battle in 1590, in which the Rajput was defeated, and his son, Jagat Singh was taken a captive. On Katlu's death, his two sons Süleiman and Osman seized Puri; the Moguls under the leadership of ManSingh invaded Orissa again. The Afghan forces were completely repulsed, and Cuttack was captured. The Afghans made some futile attempts to drive the Moguls but eventually Orissa was formally annexed to the Mogul dominions in 1592 ; the Pathans, however, temporarily gained possession of Orissa under Osman ; Man Singh was appointed by Akbar, the governor of Bengal, Behar and Orissa.

Nothing of importance happened in the subsequent period till 1741-42 A.D, when the Mahrattas invaded Orissa. Alivardi Khan made many useless efforts to drive them out ; he had practically to surrender the whole of Orissa to the Mahrattas, and to pay, 12 lakhs of rupees as subsidy or *chouth*. The Mahratta rule occupied a brief period of 48 years from 1756 to 1803 when it was overthrown by the British.

CHAPTER III.

CAVE TEMPLES.

Since the introduction of the tooth-relic into Orissa, we notice three following periods of architectural growth.

(1). The Buddhist and Jain period.

(2). The *Saiva* period.

(3). The Vaishnava and Saurya peiod.

The Buddhist and Jain period is characterised by cave temples. The Buddhist influence is noticed from the 5th cent. B. C., down to the 5th or 6th cent. A. D., the *Saiva* from the 5th or 6th cent. A. D. to the 12th cent. A. D., and the Vaishnava from the 12th cent. A. D., downwards.

The history of the caves is wrapt up in obscurity, and the historians have made many useless attempts to lift the veil from this dim and forgotten past.

The group of caves of this part of India has no very intimate connection with those of the western part. The genesis and history of these caves are so very obscure that one is sure to be led astray in solving the difficult problem of their chronology. Happily for us, the inscription in the Hati Gümpha throws a great flood of light on this dark and murky corner of Orissan history. The latest date that we may at all assign to it is the middle of the 2nd cent. B.C., according to the interpretation of the inscription by Pandit Bhagwan Lal Indraji. The Gümpha, according to him, was excavated by Kharvela, a Jain prince. From palæographic considerations it is apparent that many of the caves were excavated in the 2nd and 3rd cent. B C ; and we think we shall not be far from truth in dating some of the caves even in the 4th or 5th cent. B.C.,i.e., before the period of the Hati Gümpha inscription, for the locality where the caves were excavated must have had some sort of "previous sanctity preserved in the eyes of the co-religionists."

It is not the purpose of this book to deal with all the details of the caves, but to give an outline conveying a general idea of their growth and history.

The Khandagiri and Udaygiri hills, otherwise called Khandagiri. (20°16'N. Latitude, and 85°47'E. Longitude) are situated at a distance of about 5 miles to the northwest of Bhubanesvara. These two hillocks or prominences are separated by a ravine forming a continuous line with the road from Bhubanesvara. They form part of a belt of sandstone rock extending from Autgur towards Chilka lake.

These hills are honey-combed with caves or cells inhabited in ancient times by the Buddhist and Jain hermits or Sramanas, many of which belong to the period before the third cent. B.C.

PLATE I

GENERAL DESIGN OF CAVES, KHANDGIRI

Showing the columns and brackets.

Sketch by J. SHOME.

The caves show in a marked way different degrees of architectural perfection; some of them, especially at Khandagiri, are very small like the den of wild beasts, some moderately spacious; ordinary caves are characterised by a chamber shaded by a pillared verandah in front (vide Plate I); in some cases the ante-chamber is divided into two or three cells. More elaborate caves are two-storeyed, the upper storey in some cases receding back from the lower one. They are very simple in design and execution.

The chamber at the rear is often divided into 5 or 6 cells, and there is a long stretch of verandah in front, supported by columns. The peculiarity with almost all the caves is that a bench of stone runs round the three sides of the front verandah, the height varying from 1 ft. to 1′ 6″. The two walls of the verandah are so hollowed out at the top as to present the appearance of cupboards. These were meant to hold the scanty necessaries of lives of the Bauddha or Jain monks. The doors are of very small dimensions; the monks had to crawl into the cells. In the case of so important a cave as the Rani Gümpha, they measure only 3′-11″ x 2′. The jambs of the doorways in many cases slope inwards. The height of the cells is not sufficient for any man to live in at ease; but considering the fact that they were meant for the monks living retired lives in meditation, these were retreats worthy of them.

The cells of the chamber are separated by a thin stone partition wall about 3" thick.

On the walls of the cells are usually carved the sculptured figures of Buddhist legend, and of the Jain Tirthankaras in *basso-relievo*. The columns that support the verandah are mainly primitive in style; they are usually square above and below, and octagonal in the middle (vide Plate I). In very primitive types they are frustums of pyramids having a square section, and resting on a thin base, or without any base at all. Elaborate pillars are noticed in the Jain Gümph*a* on Khandagiri hill. The arrises of the pillars are not straight lines; they are rather gentle curves; stop-chamfering is noticeable where the intermediate octagonal portion ends. From these columns brackets protrude forward, and carry the ceiling. On these brackets are carved the figures of women with "swelling bosoms and retreating heads". The brackets are carved, and hollowed out in the centre, and are at right angles to the façade of the caves. The roof of the verandah is usually lower than that of the ante-chamber.

The caves present a very simple, though massive, face consistent with the lives of their past inmates.

The façade usually shows massive pillars, and plain pilasters without any sculpture on them. The design of these caves has led many to ascribe their origin to wooden models.* The great French architect E. Viollet-Le-Duc calls them an imitation of a wooden structure in stone; but the arguments adduced by him may be applied to any and every structure. Now, if wooden structure be considered the primary source from which the idea of all structures is derived, we shall not raise any serious objection here; but if it holds goods here only, we must reject it with all the scorn it deserves. According to the French architect, "the cylindrical form is the very last a carpenter adopts for vertical supports, the squaring of the wood being of primary necessity in timber framing". This remark supposes the elaborate work of timber framing with squared pieces of wood to precede the excavation of these simple caves which requires only a chisel, and a hammer for its execution. The square vertical supports necessitated the use of saw which is not possible for primitive men to devise. Cylindrical form of support, I think, is the very first form chosen by a primitive carpenter, for the trunk of a tree stripped of its bark naturally presents a cylindrical form, and may be used with advantage without the labour of squaring. Now, supposing for argument's sake that these caves were an "imitation of a wooden structure in stone", why should the Greek temple, according to the architect, form an exception?

If we look at the Lycian Sarcophagus (Tombean Lycien)

* E. Viollet-Le-Duc, Lectures on Architecture, Vol. I, p. 39.

preserved in the British Museum we shall invariably be struck with the joinings and notchings of carpentry work, "framed gables supporting the purlins that carry the roofing"; all these typify a veritable wood-work in stone; but from the above remarkable features the author of "Lectures on Architecture" comes to the conclusion that "the Greek temple is a stone construction, and not the imitation of a construction in wood"; these self-same structural features would lead to a different conclusion in a different country; for judging from the very same elements of construction the author remarks as follows:—"We find in India certain sacred edifices of stone which are singularly suggestive of the wooden pyramid described by Vitruvius";* and according to him, "the temple of Barolli, and the pagoda of Canaruc" (the temple of Kon*a*rka, Plate XXI) are among the sacred edifices referred to. We fail to appreciate the logic of the French architect in the statement reproduced below:—"Why contend that Greeks, the inventors of Logic—men gifted with refined æsthetic sensibility—amused themselves with simulating in stone a construction of wood,—a thing essentially monstrous? That such imitations have occurred among the Hindus, that they have influenced the architecture of the Assyrians, and of the inhabitants of Asia Minor, is

* E. Viollet-Le-Duc, Lectures on Architecture, p. 43.

possible; but to suppose it among the western Greeks is to misunderstand their genius altogether".*

I have made a careful survey of the caves illustrated by plate I (C) showing their relative positions. The result of my survey is given towards the close of this chapter.

The Rani Gumpha.—Vide Plate I (A):—

The caves in the Udaygiri hill are the most important of the caves in Orissa from the point of view of architecture and sculpture; and of them the R*a*ni Gümph*a* is the most well-known. I quote below what Dr. Grünwedel has written in respect of this cave. "Among the oldest sculptures of India are perhaps those of the caves of Udaygiri in the Puri district of Orissa. The most interesting are in the two-storeyed R*a*jr*a*ni or R*a*ni-k*a*-Nür cave. These remarkable reliefs show an uncommonly animated style, little influenced by foreign elements. They form, so to speak, the primitive basis from which issued the purified and refined forms of later times."†

The R*a*ni Gümph*a*, or the R*a*ni Nür is the most important and elaborately carved cave on Udaygiri hill; it is noted for commodious wings, large number of cells, and spacious quadrangle in front. It is the easternmost cave of the Udaygiri group. It consists of two storeys abutting on the three sides of the

* E. Viollet-Le-Duc, Lectures on Architecture, p. 52.

† Dr. Grünwedel, Buddhist Art in India, edited by Jas. Burgess, p. 23.

quadrangle, the south-east side being left open; this is indicative of excellent adaptibility for human habitation. From the main or central wing facing south-east two more wings project forward at the two ends. These wings enclose a court-yard 49′ × 24′. The length of the upper main verandah is 62 ft., that of the lower, 44 ft. The right verandah on the ground floor facing the south-west is 19 ft. long, 6′ – 6″ broad and 7 ft. high; it leads to one room 20′ × 7′ × 7′. The left verandah is 23′ × 9′-6″ and leads to 3 rooms; the northern wing is 44 ft. long, and leads to 3 rooms. The upper storey is not placed directly over the lower one, but recedes back from it. The height of the cells of the lower storey is 3′-9″, and that of the upper storey is 7 ft.

The main or central wing on the first floor contains 4 rooms, the left and the right wings one room respectively. The door openings are very small, some of them measure 3′ – 11″ × 2′. The pillars supporting the verandah are for the most part broken down; atmosphere has done great mischief to the nice carvings by its weathering action.

The Rani Gümpha is characterized by most elaborately carved friezes representing various scenes of human activities; many of these have been well-nigh obliterated. For the explanation of the tableaus, I refer the readers to the memorable works by Drs. Rajendra Lal Mitra and Hunter. Among the

PLATE I(A)

Elevation of Rani Gumpha

Photo by A. Ghose, B. A.

Printed by K. V. Seyne & Bros.

various tableaus, the two depicting the Abduction and Hunt scenes are worth mentioning. The monkey scene is most life-like.

One of the scenes in the friezes is supposed by the editor of the Dt. Gazetteer to have been taken from the life of Parsva Nath, the 23rd Jain Tirthankar. This view seems to us too far-fetched. In the face of the characteristic Bauddha symbols, one is most inclined to accept the view held by me. Buddhist rails have been most abundantly represented in the walls just below the friezes sculptured in low relief. The rails are noticeable in the horizontal bands connecting the arches at the springing points. The Buddhist rails of the right wing consist of three cross-bars tennoned into the uprights bearing a faint resemblance to stone columns. The bars present a curved appearance so as to have lenticular cross-section. They do not contain the figures of circular discs carved with "rosettes or concentric bands of petals" as at Amaravati. Over the rails are noticed human figures carved in low relief and in various postures. The semicircular arch-bands contain the bas-reliefs of scrolls, and various ornamental devices issuing from the mouths of a lion, elephant or deer. The representation of the Bo-tree within the sacred enclosure is clearly indicative of Bauddha influence; in one of the arch-bands in the wing facing the east, we see a small votine *stupa* in front of which a devotee stands with folded hands; the arch above one of the tympana is surmounted by a Bauddha *trisula*; the characteristic *swastika* mark is also noticed here; all these considerations would tend to establish the fact of its being an eminently Buddhistic cave.

Near the right-hand corner of the upper storey is seen the figure of a soldier 4′-6″ high, hewn out of the verandah wall; this figure is dressed in a tight-fitting, flowing garment resembling *chapkan*; a band passes round the waist of the figure, from which is slung a short sword sheathed in a scabbard; a sort of buskin covers the feet and leg to the middle of the calf. This figure has given rise to various theories which I shall deal with in the next chapter.

The interest of this cave is due to the combined action of architecture and sculpture. Great relieving effect is produced by the setting back of the upper storey. I do not agree with Drs. Fergusson and Burgess in their surmise* that the set-back was adopted in order to give the structure a pyramidal form characteristic of the Bauddha Viharas. What have they got to say in the case of the Swaragpüri cave? This artifice on the part of the architects was a forced one, and was demanded by the nature of the rcok. If the upper storey were placed just over the lower one, the

* Fergusson and Burgess, Cave Temples of India, p. 78.

structure would not have stood for centuries; it would, perhaps, have come down in the course of excavation, because the rock is soft and porous in texture. This cave alone justifies the remark of Drs. Fergusson and Burgess in the Cave Temples of India regarding the Katak caves that "the picturesqueness of their forms, the richness of their sculptures and architectural details, connected with their acknowledged antiquity render them one of the most important groups of caves in India.*"

The next in point of importance to the preceding one is the Ganesa Gümpha, so called from a sculpture of Ganesa on the wall of the ante-chamber; it is situated on the highest peak of Udaygiri hill. It is a one-storeyed cave of the ordinary type, with a covered verandah leading to an ante-chamber divided into two cells. Pillars, square above and below, and octagonal in the middle support the verandah; small brackets protrude from the pillars supporting the verandah; a flight of steps leading to the verandah is flanked by two huge elephants nicely carved in stone.

Ganesa Gümpha.

The pillars and pilasters on the right hand side of the verandah are broken; on the left pilaster of the verandah is carved the standing figure of a guard with a spear in hand. Each of the two rooms has two doorways with pilasters; over the doorways are the tympana capped by arch-bands;

* Fergusson and Burgess, Cave Temples of India, p. 55.

from the springing of the arch-bands runs the horizontal band representing the Buddhist rails; this representation of rails consists of a series of a pair of cross-bars mortised into uprights which are placed at regular intervals, and mortised into two continuous, upper and lower pieces meeting the semi-circular arch-bands. The uprights or balusters are octagonal in form, for four vertical ridges are seen in elevation. These resemble the uprights of rails at Sanchi which are octagonal in form ; but the uprights of the Ganesa Gümpha are not embossed with devices representing lotus, snake &c, as at Sanchi.

A bench runs round the three sides of the verandah, and on the walls just above the bench are carved the rails. The face of the wall intervening between the arch-bands is sculptured like the Rani Gümpha with different scenes. In the friezes of the Ganesa cave the same scenes are represented as what we notice in those of the upper storey of the Rani Gümpha. It is not the purpose of this book to give an interpretation of the tableaus for which I refer my readers to the works of Drs. Mitra and Hunter.

From the occurrence of kilted soldiers in the frieze sculpture of this cave like Rani Gümpha, the editor of the Dt. Gazetteer, Puri, comes to the conclusion that this scene refers to the abduction of Prabhabati by the Yavana king of Kalinga, and her subsequent rescue by Parsvanath, the twenty-third Tirthankar of the Jains. I do not agree with the editor in considering the cave a Jain one, for the symbols of Buddhism are seen clearly represented. The sculptures unmistakably indicate a Bauddha origin. At the crown of the arch-band is seen the characteristic Bauddha emblem of *trisūla*; the emblem on the first arch-band is rather elaborate in form, and perhaps represents the Bauddha shield. This shield represents a crown to some extent; the elaborate form is due to the sculptor's attempt at making it look like a veritable crown having due regard to the position of the emblem at the top of the arch-band. I have already referred to the representation of Buddhist rails. Another characteristic Buddhist sculpture noticed here is the *makara* or capricornus represented at the springing of the arch-band, from the mouth of which issues forth a floral device. These floral devices either consist of full-blown lotuses enclosed in beaded panels, or a sort of creeper ending in a full-blown lotus. The jaws of the *makara* are less distended than what we notice on an angle pillar at Amarāvati The creeper referred to above, resembles that represented in the bas-relief on the left-hand pillar, of the northern gateway at Sānchi.

Next in point of importance from the architectural point Jaya-Vijaya cave. of view come the Jaya-Vijaya cave, the Swargapūri cave, the Tiger and Serpent caves.

The Jaya-Vijaya is an upper-storey cave facing the south. Unlike the Rani Gümpha, the upper storey is just over the lower one; the front staircase just leads to it; it contains two rooms of unequal dimensions (7′ × 7′ and 6′ – 6″ × 6′) the height being 4 ft.; a verandah in front leads to them; the rooms are provided with a doorway each, the dimensions being 3′ – 6″ × 1′ – 10″. A bench 1′ – 5″ high surrounds the 3 sides of the verandah; the characteristic cupboards on the two end walls of the verandah are noticeable. The verandah is flanked on the outside by two *dwārpālas* or guards, male and female. This cave is interesting on account of the bas-reliefs which indicate their Buddhist origin. The space between the semicircular arch-bands over the two doorways contains the bas-relief of the worship of a Bodhi-tree overgrown with fruits and fenced by a low gabion showing characteristic Buddhist railings; the two female devotees on the right and left are carrying trays of offerings for the worship of the Bodhi-tree. The horizontal band just below the scene contains the bas-relief of a line of Buddhist rails. This cave differs from the Ananta cave in not having any bas-relief in the tympana which are semi-circular openings; it is similar to Rani Gümpha in some respects, viz. in having the floral devices in the semi-circular arch-bands, and similar dwarfish figures with plaited turban on and carrying trays of offerings and garlands at the two ends of the arch-bands already referred to. This cave is of no historic importance as it contains no inscription. The Jaya-Vijaya cave belongs probably to the period between the 2nd and 1st cent. B. C.

The Swargapuri cave.— This is a two storeyed cave to the west of Rani Nür, and unlike the latter, the upper storey just rests over the lower one. This cave is not of any great importance except indicating the design of a hall on the ground floor and on the right side; this was probably meant as a meeting place for the Buddhist *Sramanas* who used to congregate together for discussion. There are two exquisite bas-reliefs of elephants in the two sides of the arch of the doorway, and just over the horizontal bands commencing from the spring line.

These horizontal bands have on them carved a line of Buddhist rails similar to those already referred to. This cave is an eminently Buddhistic one, and I feel inclined to place it in the same period as the Ganesa Gümpha.

The Tiger Cave. The Tiger cave, on the west of the Hati Gümpha is a small one consisting of a verandah, and a single cell. It is situated higher up the hill than the Ganesa or the Hati Gümpha. The roof of the front verandah is formed by the upper jaw of the animal. In this cave, the eye, nose, and upper jaw of the tiger have been represented; the two canine teeth on the two sides of the incisors have been shown; the number of incisors is greater than what is noticed in the animals of the feline species.

The cell is provided with one door flanked by pilasters resting on raised platforms, and surmounted by a semi-circular arch-band.

This cave is interesting by reason of a small Buddhist inscription engraved on its wall. Dr. Hunter has placed it towards the end of the third cent. B. C. (300 B. C.) I refer my readers to the plate given by Drs. Mitra and Hunter.

The Sarpa or Serpent Cave:— It is a small cave consisting of a single cell, and verandah, the latter having in the front tympanum of the door, the carving of the hood of a three-headed serpent, and hence the name. The level of the verandah is higher than the ground in front. Drs. Fergusson and Burgess have taken the Tiger, and the Serpent Caves to be "the oldest sculptured caves in the hills".* This cave is important for containing an inscription which, however, does not throw any light on the probable date of its construction. From this we learn that it was built by one Chaulakarma or Chaulakamasa, according to Prinsep and Mitra respectively.†

* Fergusson and Burgess, Cave Temples of India, p. 69.

† Mit Antiquities of Orissa, Vol II., p. 31.

The Hati Gümpha, a natural cavern very little improved and enlarged by art although, not important from an artistic, and architectural point of view is the most important of all the caves in the locality by reason of containing a long inscription recording the autobiography of a king of Kalinga "on the overhanging brow of the cavern". This inscription used before Dr. Bhagwan Lal's interpretation, to be considered as the oldest one in India; though this view is no longer held, the importance of the cave has not abated a little.

The Hati Gümpha:—

It was Mr. A. Stirling, who first discovered it, and with the help of Col. Mackenzie took a facsimile of this "interesting monument" in 1820, and published it without translation or transcript, in the Asiatic Researches, Vol. XV., in 1824 with his most valuable article on "An Account, Geographical, Statistical, and Historical of Orissa Proper, or Cuttack". Mr. Stirling was ignorant of deciphering inscriptions, and consequently could not make anything out of it except detecting "the close resemblance of some of the letters to those of the Greek alphabet"*, and "the occurrence of it on sundry ancient monuments situated in widely distant quarters of India".

James Prinsep published the inscription with transcript

* A. Stirling, An Account, Geographical, Statistical, and Historical of Orissa Proper. (Reprinted from the Asiatic Researches, XV), p. 151.

and translation based on the correct facsimile of Lieutenant Kittoe in the Journal of the Asiatic Society, Vol. VI., in 1837. His interpretation drew the attention of the oriental scholars to its importance, and historic worth. Dr. Rajendra Lal revised the inscription, and published it in the Antiquities of Orissa, Vol. II., with some minor changes in 1880.

Prinsep and Mitra ascribed the inscription to Aira, the king of Kalinga, originally a usurper, who distributed largesses, dug tanks, and by many works of public utility endeared himself to his subjects. According to Prinsep the inscription is dated not earlier than 200 B. C. The author of Corpus Inscriptionum Indicarum agreeing with Dr. Prinsep considers the inscription later than the Asoka Edicts, and places it in the last quarter of the second century B. C., "as there is no appearance of heads or *mátrás*, to any of the letters"*. Dr. Mitra, however, has placed it sometime between 416 B. C. and 316 B. C.; his conclusion is based on the reference to king Nanda, one of the nine Nandas of Magadha who reigned from 416 to 316 B. C. I quote below the translattion of the portion (line 6) wherein mention has been made of Nanda.

"Jewel—all equipages—he gives to god. Afterwards

* Corpus Inscriptionum Indicarum, p. 28.

inclining to charity—the hundred houses of Nanda Raja destroyed, and himself expelled, all that was in the city of *Vajapanâdi* he converted the plunder to the charitable purposes alluded to." *

According to Prinsep and Mitra, the cave is a Buddhist one, the inscription containing the characteristic Buddhistic symbols. Dr. Bhagwan Lal Indraji, has, however, proved it to be a Jain one, and ascribed it to Kharvela; Aira of Prinsep has been metamorphosed into Kharvela of Indraji; we come across the name of Kharvela in the 17th or the last line of the inscription. The date of the inscription, according to Pandit Bhagwan Lal, is 165 Mauryan era, or 157 B. C.,† the Mauryan era dating from 321 B. C. Thus the latest possible period that can be assigned to the cave is the second cent. B.C. This has been accepted by the modern school of antiquarians headed by Vincent Smith‡, until recently exploded by Dr. Fleet in a recent issue of the Journal of the Asiatic Society of Great Britain. I do not share the views of the late Pandit, and am inclined to place it towards the close of the 3d cent. B. C., before Asoka came to the throne of Magadha. According to Drs. Burgess and Fergusson "300 B. C., or thereabouts is the most

* J. A. S. B., Vol. VI.

† Actes du Sixieme Congres Or, tome iii. pp. 174-177.

‡ V. Smith, Early History of India, p. 35. (foot-note.)

probable date for the inscription."* They add that "with his (of Asoka) reign the fashion of chiselling cells out of the living rock commenced, and was continued with continually increasing magnificence, and elaboration for nearly 100 years after his time".†

It is stated in the 16th line of this inscription that the king "caused to be constructed subterranean chambers, caves containing a temple and pillars". From this we deduce that there are caves in the locality as old as the H*a*ti Gümph*a*, although, it cannot be ascertained accurately which of the neighbouring caves are so meant; we can also safely conclude that there must have been older caves dated prior to "those containing a chaitya temple and pillars."

Among the Khandagiri caves the S*a*tghar*a* or S*a*tbakhr*a*, Navamüni, and Ananta are the most important. The first two bear evident traces of Jain influence, the latter, of Baüddha. The S*a*tbakhr*a* cave had a pillared verandah projecting in front with seven intercolumniations which do not exist now. It consists of two caves separated by a thin wall; they are otherwise called the Trisula, or B*a*rbhüji caves. The S*a*tghar*a* cave is noted for the figures of Jain Tirthankaras with their characteristic symbols or *lànchhanas* sculptured on the antechamber walls of the southern portion. I give below the

* Fergusson and Burgess, Cave Temples of India p. 67.

† Ibid, p. 68.

description of the figures of the Tirthankaras starting from the left end wall of the ante-chamber.

(1) It is a tall nude figure of Rishava Deva with the bull as his characteristic symbol, and flanked by two attendants overhead holding musical instruments; there are two other attendants on the two sides,—the right one holding *chámar*, or *chouric*, the left holding a tray containing offerings. They stand on a pedestal containing bas-reliefs of two cross-legged figures in deep meditation—the left one with folded hands at the breast, the right one with its left palm placed below the right one. Below these figures are carved two female N*a*ginis (Snake-goddess) worshipping with folded hands, and surmounted by hoods of serpent. Below these is the characteristic symbol, the figure of a bull placed in the centre, and flanked on the left by a watervessel with a spout, and on the right by a conchshell and a lion. The bull is represented most naturally showing the wrinkles on the dewlap.

(2) This is a tall nude figure of Ajitn*a*th. The moon is represented on the top frieze; the top figures are those of two females holding bowls. Among the two intermediate attendant figures, the left one holds a *chámar* and the right one, a fan; the figures at the base resemble those of (1). The symbol in this case is an elephant. At the two ends of the symbol are represented two lions.

(3) This is a figure of Sambhavanath in meditation, and seated on a full-blown lotus with the right palm resting on the left. The attendants at the top hold musical instruments. The intermediate attendant figures are similar to (2). The symbol is a horse; on the left is a water vessel with a spout and at the two ends are two lions.

(4) This is a *Dhyani* figure of Abhinandan Nath similar to (3); the two attendants at the top have been replaced by two lotuses; the symbol is a monkey.

(5) Similar to (3); the left intermediate attendant has one hand on the crown of head. The symbol is a goose. The figure is that of Sümatinath.

(6) Similar to (3); the symbol is a lotus or *padma*; on the right of the lotus is a water vessel as in (3), and on the left a pitcher or *kümbha*. This is the figure of Padma Prabhü.

(7) This is a *Dhyani* figure of Süparsvanath, the top figures of which have been replaced by scroll work. The symbol in this case is a swastika, the branches of which have been so doubled over as to make them appear counter-clockwise.

(8) Similar to (7); but the scroll work at the top differs from the preceding one. The symbol is the crescent moon. This is a figure of Chandra Prabhü.

(9) Similar to (8); the top figures in this case are

lotuses; the symbol is a peacock; this figure cannot be identified, as no Tirthankar has the peacock as his symbol.

(10) This, unlike the preceding one, is a nude standing figure of a Tirthankar; the symbol has been obliterated. The top figures are parrots; the figure cannot be identified.

(11) Similar to (10); but the nude figure is canopied over by a hood of serpent. The top figures are those of two nymphs flying in the air. The symbol is some unknown plant; it is flanked on two sides by two pitchers and griffins. This is probably a figure of Naminath, the twenty-first Tirthankar.

(12) Similar to (10); the symbol is not visible by reason of its being intercepted by a statuette set up in front very recently. This figure cannot be identified.

(13) Similar to (1); the face of the symbol has been broken.

(14). *Dhyani* figure similar to (5); the symbol in this case is a crocodile flanked by two griffins. This is a figure of Sübidhinath, the 9th Tirthankar.

(15) Similar to (14); in this case the symbol is intercepted by a statuette like (12); this figure cannot be identified.

(16) Similar to (15); the attendants have been represented as holding *châmaras*: the face of the symbol has been

broken ; it is probably a deer. This is a figure of *Santinath* the 16th Tirthankar.

(17) It is a *Dhyani* figure ; top figures are those of scroll ; the face of the symbol is broken ; it is probably a sheep ; the figure is that of Künthanath, the 17th Tirthankar.

(18) Similar to (15) ; the symbol is a fish. The figure cannot be identified, and perhaps is imaginary as no Tirthankar has the fish as his symbol.

(19) It is a *Dhyani* figure ; top figures are lotuses ; the symbol is a vase or water jar, and hence it represents Mallinath, the 17th Tirthankar.

(20) This is a *Dhyani* figure similar to (15) ; the symbol is an imaginary plant, and hence it represents Naminath, the 21st Tirthankar.

(21) A *Dhyani* figure similar to (15) ; the symbol is a tortoise, and hence it represents Münisübratanath, the 20th Tirthankar.

(22) This is a *Dhyani* figure ; top figures are those of nymphs ; the symbol is a conchshell, flanked by peacocks, and hence represents Neminath, the 22nd Tirthankar.

(23) This is a nude standing figure ; top figures are lotuses ; two nymphs are represented as holding a pitcher about to pour water over the head of the Tirthankar. The symbol is a rhinoceros. This figure represents *Sreansanath*, the 11th Tirthankar.

(24) This is a standing nude figure; top figures are those of nymphs holding musical instruments similar to (1); the symbol is a lion, and represents the 24th, or the last Jain Tirthankar, Mahavir Swami.

From the following passage* by Hem Chandra, the Jaina lexicon, it will appear that no definite system has been followed in carving the above figures in relief. Some of the figures have been repeated, while some of the Tirthankars have been altogether omitted. The eleventh, and twentieth figures represent Nami Nath, the 21st Tirthankar. There is a regular order based on chronology in the arrangement of the Tirthankars having characteristic symbols referred to by Hem Chandra. This order has been reversed in some cases. The reversal of order in these cases as illustrated above is due to the ignorance and inadvertence of the sculptors. Their ignorance is evidenced by the introduction of imaginary symbols not mentioned in the Jain scriptures, *e. g.* the 9th and 18th figures.

For reference, and comparative study I annex hereto a tabular statement giving the names of the Tirthankars in order, and with their characteristic symbols.

* वृषो गजोऽश्वः प्लवगः क्रौञ्चोऽब्जं स्वस्तिकः शशी ।
मकरः श्रीवत्सः खड्गी महिषः सूकरस्तथा ॥
श्येनो वज्रं मृगश्छागो नन्द्यावर्तो घटोऽपि च ।
कूर्मो नीलोत्पलं शङ्खः फणी सिंहोऽर्हतां ध्वजाः ॥ हेमचन्द्रः ।

Number.	Name.	Symbol.
1	Rishava Deva	Bull.
2	Ajitnath	Elephant.
3	Sambhavanath	Horse.
4	Abhinandannath	Monkey.
5	Sumatinath	Heron.
6	Padma Prabhü	Lotus.
7	Süparsvanath	Swastika.
8	Chandra Prabhü	Moon.
9	Subidhinath	Crocodile.
10	Sitalnath	Sreebatsa (a sort of mark).
11	Sreansanath	Rhinoceros.
12	Sree Vasapüjyanath	Buffalo.
13	Vimalanath	Hog.
14	Anantanath	Eagle.
15	Sree Dharmanath	Vajra or lightning
16	Santinath	Deer.
17	Künthanath	Sheep.
18	Sree Aranath	Nandyavarta (a sort of mark)
19	Mallinath	Water jar.
20	Münisübratanath	Tortoise.
21	Naminath	Aquatic plant or lily.
22	Neminath	Conchshell.
23	Sree Parsvanath	Serpent.
24	Mahavira Swami	Lion.

Ananta Gümpha. The Ananta Gümpha is the most important cave on the Khandagiri hill.

The verandah of the cave commands an open terrace which was probably used as a meeting place of the Buddhist

Sramanas. That this cave was a Buddhist one can be clearly proved by examining the Swastika carved on the back wall of the ante-chamber. It is a veritable Bauddha Swastika, for its vertical and horizontal branches have been doubled over clockwise; in a Jaina Swastika they run in a counter-clockwise direction; representations of Buddhist rails and pyramidal battlements are noticed running over the arches of doorways; in the tympanum of one of the arches is represented the Bo-tree within a sacred enclosure, and worshipped by a male and female accompanied by their attendants; this representation of the Bodhi-drüma is noticed in the Sanchi topes. On the back-wall of the ante-chamber is represented the standing figure of Buddha in low relief. All these things tend to show that this cave was intended for the Buddhists.

The Ananta Gümpha consists of an ante-chamber (24′ × 7′) having a covered verandah (26′ × 7′) in front. The ceiling of the chamber at the rear is curved, the rise of the arch or curve being about a foot; originally there were four doors leading to the room; these have been reduced to two doors, and one window. The doorways are surmounted by circular arches ending in horizontal bands at the springing. The two fillets of the circular band enclose ornamental figures. The horizontal friezes resemble those noticed in Rani Nür and Ganesa Cave. The crown of the arches is formed by the interlaced tails of serpents forming the Buddhist symbol of shield, and the two sides of arches are adorned by the hoods of the serpents projecting forward. Vide Plate I (B.)

A long line of Buddhist rails runs over the arches unlike those in Rani Nür, and Ganesa cave broken at intervals by battlemented pyramids, the like of which we notice in the Bharhüt sculptures. On the back wall of the ante-chamber are carved the characteristic Bauddha symbols of Swastika, Trisula, etc., and also a standing figure of Buddha. The tympana of the arches are carved with representations of various scenes. The scene of Gaja Lakshmi standing on a lotus, with lotus stalks in hand, and flanked by two elephants pouring water over her head from a pitcher held in uplifted trunks is exquisitely beautiful; this is noticed in one of the cross-bars of the rails at Bharhüt. The pilasters by the sides of the doorways have striking features characterised by animal capitals and profusion of sculptures not noticed elsewhere in the locality. The capitals of the pilasters are very striking being formed by pairs of animals in a reclining state; some of the animals are winged. The portion below the capital is formed by representations of overlapping slabs; exception is noticed in only one of the pilasters in which the overlapping slabs have been replaced by a full-blown lotus consisting of two mouldings, *kümüda* or astragal

Plate I.B

Frieze o[illegible]e Ananta Gumpha

or torus, and *padma* or cyma. This indicates a decided development in the principle of a column. The base of this pilaster is also significant. It is made to spring from a vase or jar resting on a pedestal formed by overlapping slabs; all the pilasters are not provided with bases or pedestals. The shaft of all the pilasters except this one is plain. The top and the bottom of the shafts are rectangular, (except that having the lotus capitals) and the arrises in the middle have been chamfered so as to present an octagonal form characteristic of the pillars of the cave temples of Udaygiri. Dr. Burgess has detected "a wooden origin indicative of the early age to which the excavation of this cave must be assigned"*. I fail to appreciate the soundness of the theory of wooden origin, and ascribe the forms of the pilasters to a sense of beauty inherent in man.

We agree with Drs. Fergusson and Burgess in detecting similarity between the sculptures of the Ananta Gümpha and those of the Bharhüt *Stüpa*, built sometime between the 2nd and 3rd cent. B. C. This similarity is based on the architectural ornaments and the character of the sculptures.† The pyramidal battlement, or the pyramid of

* Fergusson, History of Indian and Eastern Architecture, (edited by Dr. Burgess, 1910), Vol. II., p. 16.

† Drs. Fergusson and Burgess. The Cave Temples of India (1880) p. 71.

steps with an intervening lotus referred to already is common to both, and is found nowhere else. This we notice to run round the whole of the coping of the rail of the *stūpa*. We also draw the attention of our readers to the sacred Bo-tree, and Gaja Lakshmi referred to above. From the evidence of style, and the character of the inscription on the back wall of the ante-chamber, I am inclined to think that the probable period of the excavation of the cave cannot be later than the second century B. C. and earlier than the third century B. C., and not second or third century A. D. as fixed by Beglar in the Archæological Survey of India, Vol. XIII*.

On the north of the Trisula cave is the Barabhüji, and next to it is the Nava Müni Cave.

The Nava Müni Cave is an ordinary one consisting of two rooms with a common verandah. This cave is noted for an inscription referring to the Jaina *S*ramana, Sübha Chandra, and dated probably in the 10th century A.D. The editor of the Archæological Survey Report, Vol. XIII is obviously wrong in considering the sculptured figures "to resemble Buddha". They are veritable Tirthankaras with their *Sa*sanadevis.

I may make a passing reference to the Jaina temple built

* Beglar, Archæological Survey of India, Vol. XIII., p. 81. (1875 76)

on the summit of the Khandagiri hill by the *Mahrattas* towards the close of the eighteenth century. Kittoe considers the present temple as occupying "the site of a chaitya" as he noticed "traces of former buildings"*. I did not notice the least trace of any "former building" referred to by Kittoe.

Further to the west of the Jaina temple, and on a comparatively plane ground lie scattered small rectangular pieces of stone standing on their ends representing, according to Cunningham, votine Chaityas†. These form the Deva Sabh*a*, a name popularly given to this plot of ground.

Excavation and Drainage.

It can be easily imagined how tedious a process it was to blow up the rocks before the invention of explosives such as nitro-glycerine, gunpowder, gun-cotton, the Kieselgurh or Nobel dynamite. Happily for the architects, the rocks are of gritty sandstone, soft and porous in texture, and admit of easy excavation. The caves have usually been excavated with a gentle slope away from the main rock, thereby ensuring effective drainage. Weep-holes have been provided in cases where there is a chance of landslip in consequence of the rain water percolating through the surface, and collecting in

* Kittoe, J. A. S. B., Vol. VI., p. 1079.

† Cunningham, Archæological Survey of India, Vol. XIII., p. 80.

the soil below. I need hardly point out that these weep-holes are often seen provided in railway cuttings through rocks. On the whole, drainage arrangement is satisfactory. Prinsep was so much impressed with it that he wrote to the following effect in the Journal of the Asiatic Society, Vol. XVI. p. 1079:—

"………the ingenious method which had been adopted to drain the chamber which from the porous nature of the stone would otherwise have dripped in wet weather, small grooves are cut along the ceilings all verging to one point at the lower corner, where a perforation is made to conduct the water without."

The ceiling of the chambers often presents a gentle curved appearance. I measured the rise and span of the ceiling of the Jaina Gümph*a*, &c., and noticed that the ratio which the rise bears to the span is what will be accepted by any engineer of the modern school.

The so-called evolution of the caves.

It has been already stated that these caves display a marked difference in the excellence of construction; some are spacious for habitable purposes, and some are, in the language of Dr. Hunter, "scarcely larger than a dog's kennel." This fact has led the European scholars, with some Indian scholars in their train, to commit an egregious blunder in thinking that the elaborate ones belong to a comparatively recent period. To quote Dr. Hunter, "these small single cells represent the first human dwellings yet discovered in India". These scholars discover the process of evolution in the origin, and gradual growth of the caves. The term Evolution, I am sorry to remark, has acquired some sort of notoriety by reason of its application in and out of season. The historian, sociologist, and cosmologist all cut their Gordian knots at one stroke, and it is evolution. Most aptly did Prof. Huxley remark in his "Science and Culture" that "some truths begin as heresies, and end as superstitions". The theory of evolution is an apt illustration of this wise apothegm.

The ulterior object in discovering gradual growth, or the process of evolution in the caves at Udaygiri is, I apprehend, to place the elaborately carved ones at a comparatively recent period, and to prove conveniently that they are the products of extraneous influence, and that stone architecture proper was introduced by the Greeks.

Udaygiri, and Khandagiri were holy places of pilgrimage, inhabited by the Buddhist *Sramanas*; the kings of Kalinga at different times had the caves excavated for these *Sramanas*, and for other religious purposes. It was a natural outcome of a deep-seated religious instinct that people, rich and poor alike, would resort to these places, and excavate caves for the *Sramanas*; and these caves must necessarily have been spacious, or "small as a dog's kennel", according as they owed their origin to the rich or the poor. If we notice a towering castle of a landlord to stand side by side with a miserable abode of a street beggar, will it not be illogical to infer that the latter must in strict conformity with the principles of evolution have been built at a period prior to that of the former?

We may consider it from another stand-point. Religious zeal first manifests itself in charitable works, and in the process of its transmission to posterity it becomes evanescent, or conventional; hence mere conventional religious spirit must manifest itself in conventional works of art, and accordingly some of the caves became nothing more than "dog's kennels".

There are vivid traces of Jaina influence in some of the caves, especially the Jaina Gümph*a*, Nava Müni Gümph*a*, &c. In the bas-reliefs on the walls are noticed the figures of Jaina Tirthankaras. Dr. R*a*jendra L*a*l has erroneously taken them for the figures of Buddha. In the caves taken together the number of nude figures of Jaina Tirthankaras is far greater than those of Buddha. Even in the famous inscription on the H*a*ti Gümph*a* there are traces of Jaina influence. In that inscription what Dr. R*a*jendra takes for a Bauddha Swastika is, in reality, a Jaina one. The inscription also begins with a salutation which is characteristic of both Jaina and Bauddha scriptures. Hence we come to the conclusion that the caves at Udaygiri and Khandagiri bear evident traces of Jaina and Bauddha influence. The Bauddha and Jaina influences are often noticed associated together. At Benares near the Sarnath Stūpa we notice a Jaina temple; at Buddhagaya there is also a Jaina temple close by.

Sculpture.

The sculptures of the caves on Udaygiri hill are eminently Buddhistic; but unfortunately they do not describe so vividly the manners and customs of the people who carved them as is the case with the Bharhūt or Sanchi sculptures. The discovery of the Bharhūt sculptures by Cunningham marks a new epoch in the history of Indian Archæology, and introduces a new era of its systematic study, for it has since then thrown a great flood of light on an otherwise dark chapter of Buddhist history. The discovery of the sculptures of the cave temples of Orissa by Stirling has furnished some data which strengthen the generalisations arrived at by the discoveries of the remains at Bharhūt, or Sanchi; the intrinsic value of the Buddhist remains at Udaygiri is not so much as is that of their sisters in Central India.

I have remarked that the sculptures at Udaygiri are

Buddhistic; but I searched in vain for sculptures describing the Jataka or birth-stories of Buddha similar to those noticed at Bharhüt or Sanchi, e.g. the Sama Jataka at Sanchi, the Yava-Majhakiya Jataka at Bharhüt.

The well-known scenes engraved in the friezes of Rani and Ganesa Gümphas are evidently not derived from the Jatakas, as far as I am aware. They have been drawn from the rich imagination of the sculptors having very little to do with the Buddhist legends. In view of the striking Buddhist features, I am not at one with the editor of the District Gazetteer, Puri, in thinking that they represent the scene of abduction of Prabhabati, the would-be wife of Parsva Nath, by the Yavanas; nor do they represent the abduction of Sita Devi by Ravana, as some would have us believe.

I have already drawn the attention of the readers to a very close similarity existing between the Bharhüt pillars, and a pilaster of the Ananta Cave, and a general one between the former and all the pilasters of Ananta. The capitals are strikingly similar: unlike those of Bharhüt, some of the couchant figures of the capitals of Ananta, Jaya-Vijaya are winged thus bearing some resemblance to Mathura sculptures. This winged form of the capitals is noticed since the era of the great Mauryan king Asoka who may appropriately be called the father of Buddhist architecture and sculpture.

The sculpture of the running figure in a frieze in the upper verandah of Rani Gümpha carrying a tray containing fruits and flowers meant as an offering, and having his right hand encircled by stalks of full-blown lotuses and lotus buds interlaced with each other, is clearly indicative of the warmth of fervour characterising a devotee. The head-dress is most elaborately carved. The artist's skill is displayed in the garland hanging from the tray, folds of the scarf and cloth, and the interweaving of lotus stalks. Elsewhere is seen another such running figure holding a nicely carved garland much obliterated by the weathering action of the atmosphere. A similar running figure in a frieze of the Jaya-Vijaya cave is not so beautiful as its counterpart in the Rani Gümpha. The representation of a half-opened doorway with a semi-circular arch-band in one of the friezes of Rani Gümpha illustrates the artistic skill of the sculptor.

The figures of the cave temples are full of animation and liveliness, and have been portrayed so as to indicate human activities either in the scenes of abduction, or of elephant hunt, or of drinking bouts represented in the friezes of Rani Gümpha. The female figures are equally muscular as the male ones, and are strangely lacking in feminine effeminacy as is noticed in later sculptures. In one of the friezes of Rani Gümpha is noticed a combat scene between two male and female figures holding swords, and oblong shields having the figures of Buddhist conventional chields attached to them. The masculine character of the female figures has led Fergusson to take them for Yakshinis.

It is very curious to note that the lotus had already, in that early age, become the national form of floral device throughout the whole of India. At Bharhüt, Sanchi, and in Orissa, the lotus is seen in that early period of history in various forms of decoration, as buds, full-blown flower, in garlands, rosettes, half-discs, etc. This device had been so abundantly worked out that it had already become conventional, as the representation of rows of lotus stalks terminating in a full-blown flower sculptured in the arch-bands indicates. We notice, however, a faithful accuracy in the delineation of this floral design; as an illustration of this, lots of instances may be cited in the Rani, Ganesa, J[illegible] Vijaya caves. I have already referred to the lotus buds with the parent stalk in the scene of the running figure of the Rani Gümpha.

The representation of vegetable or floral design is not poor; creepers of graceful curves with buds or full-blown flowers have been largely depicted in the arch-bands surmounting the door openings. In the curves of continuous and contrary flexures the principle of gradation and contrast has been skilfully illustrated. In many instances however, the creepers have been conventionally represented, the idea being derived from the Buddhist emblem of *tristila*. As an illustration of this, I may refer my readers to the arch-bands of Jaya-Vijaya, and Rani Gümpha. This conventionalism is noticed in the carvings at Sanchi, c. f., the northern gateway at Sanchi.

The trees, the representations of which occur frequently in the friezes, have usually been delineated as laden with fruits, but their branches are not so natural as the trunks which are noticed in some cases as knotty and shaky as obtain in nature. The fruits with which the trees are laden have been most unnaturally depicted, and this defect is not only noticeable here, but is flagrant in almost all Buddhist representations either in stone, or on canvas. This has become rather conventional.

The creepers represented in the arch-bands referred to above are also in many cases laden with fruits which are often plantain and mango; the former is noticed largely represented. The delineations of fruits representing custard-apples, and jack-fruits or pine-apples (?) are noticeable in the friezes depicting the hunt of wild elephants in the Rani Gümpha. A somewhat similar delineation of fruits is noticed at Sanchi. A tree laden with custard-apples is represented in plate IX of "Sanchi and its Remains" by General Maisey.

The mark of Buddha's feet bearing characteristic mystical emblems especially the *Chakra* or the wheel of Law is one of the well-known subjects of Buddhist sculptures usually noticed in the old remains. This mark is noticed at Buddha Gaya, Sanchi, Mathura, Savatthi, &c. The foot-prints of Buddha are not to be seen in any of the sculptured bas-reliefs of the friezes or arch-bands of the Orissan caves.

The images of Buddha as classified in the foot-note below* either in *basso-relievo* or *alto-relievo* are noticeable in the architectural monuments of the Buddhist period; detached images are also noticed in the niches. The latter form of decoration is not possible with the cave temples. The Ananta Gümpha, I think, forms the only solitary exception where the sculpture of Buddha is met with; on the back wall of the ante-chamber is noticed a figure of Buddha carved in low relief. I have not seen anywhere

* The sculptured images of Buddha are usually classified under the following five heads :—

(a) The *Dhyâni* Buddha or Buddha in meditation.

(b) The *Samâhita* Buddha or Buddha in a state of super-consciousness.

(c) Buddha as a teacher.

(d) Buddha as a *Parivrâjaka* or pilgrim.

(e) Buddha in *Mahâparinirvâna* or on his death-bed.

else in the Udaygiri caves any image of Buddha in any of the postures stated below.

It is also worthy of note that the images of the Bodhisattvas, e.g. Padmapani or Vajrapani, &c., are also wanting here.

The Bodhi tree (*Ficus bengalensis*) with a sacred enclosure or a gabion is a very important feature of Buddhist sculpture, and is noticeable in the Orissan caves, e. g. the tympanum of the Ananta Gümpha, and frieze of *Jaya*-Vijaya. The tree is held in great sanctity by the Buddhist, and in its sculptural representation devotees are made to worship or stand by it with trays containing offerings to the holy tree. The Bodhi tree is usually flanked by two umbrellas on two sides from which garlands are made to hang. This form of representing the Bodhi tree is common at Sanchi, Bharhüt, Mathura, and Amaravati. In Orissa we have a very simple representation of the tree laden with fruits, and fenced in by elaborat ' ddhist railing, or a simple one as in the tympanum of Ananta.

In some cases, however, semi-ophide human figures (*Nágas*) are represented as worshipping the Bodhi tree. The semi-ophide figures are the Nagas, one of the eight classe of demi-gods mentioned in the Buddhist scriptures*.

* Grunwedel, Buddhist Art in India, p. 43.

The Naga is supposed to reside "under the Triküta rocks supporting Mount Merü, and also in the water of springs, lakes, rivers, &c., watches over great treasures, causing rain, and certain maladies.*"

I did not notice the figure of a Naga in any of the friezes, or pilaster of the Buddhist caves here. I have, however, noticed one in the Jaina Gümpha on the Khandagiri hill; this is probably a *Mahoraga*, one of the following eight classes of Jaina demi-gods mentioned in the Jaina scriptures, viz—*Pisâchas, Bhûtas, Yakshas, Râkshasas, Kinnaras, Kimpürüshas, Mahoragas*, and *Gandharvas*.

I have already referred to the frequency of occurrence of the Buddhist symbols of *trisüla*, shield, lotus, in the sculpture of the cave temples; but I have nowhere met with the mystical *Chakra*, or the Wheel of Law. It is very curious that no representation of the Chakra or Dharma-chakra is noticeable, which, according to Dr. Mitra, "was the most ancient emblem of Buddhism," and which "as the emblem of religion, was first taken up for lithic representation.†" Buddha turned the Wheel of Law at Benares whither he repaired from Urüvilva after attaining perfect knowledge under the Bodhi-drüma, I give below in the foot-note an extract from the Lalita

* Ibid, p. 43.

† Rajendra Lal Mitra, Buddha Gaya, p. 127.

Vistara† translated by Dr. Mitra, wherein reference is made of the Dharma-chakra in the conversation at Gaya between Tathagata and Ajivaka, a hermit.

The representation of *Apsarâs* is a characteristic feature of Buddhist sculpture. The dance of the *Apsarâs* has been depicted in bas-relief on the gateways of Bharhüt and Sanchi. The two scenes of dance of a similar nature by the *Apsarâs* have been sculptured in the frieze of the Rani Gümpha, one of which has been so badly obliterated that it does not admit of being interpreted clearly; the other, however, is distinct. The frieze is surmounted by a line of stepped pyramids representing *Chaityas*, and is bounded at the base by representations of Buddhist rails. The movements of the dancing *Apsarâ* are exactly similar to those of an ordinary dancing girl of the present day. I may mention incidentally that one of the group is playing without a plectrum on a harp, the shape of which is not similar to that noticed at Sanchi, or Amaravati.

Zoology of the Caves.

Even to a careless observer of the caves it will be at once apparent that the ancient sculptors had a knowledge of the physiognomy of a large variety of animals some of which are quite unknown in Orissa.

† "Ajivaka asked :—"Where are you going to?"

Tathagata replied :—"I shall repair to Varanasi, and, arriving at the city of Kasi, make refulgent the world immersed in darkness. I shall repair to Varanasi, and, arriving at the city of Kasi rouse the mute world with the blast of the immortal

This knowledge was based partly on an actual and keen observation of animals, and partly on convention. Orissa had been noted from time immemorial for elephants, and hence we find them abundantly sculptured. Reference to it is found in the Mahabharata; the reputation of the place for the rearing of elephants reached even Kashmere, and the farthest limits of India. I have come across a reference to it in the Rajtarangini, a book of the twelfth century.

The representation of the elephant in the caves is far more numerous than that of any other animal. The huge tusker has been depicted in various positions—crouching, standing with uplifted trunks, carrying lotuses in the trunks, &c. Crouching elephants in the caves of a hill are seen represented both in the right and left wings of the Rani Gumpha. The figures of stray elephants (and not calves, as described by Dr. Mitra) taking shelter in a cave sculptured in the space between the arch-bands of the upper storey of the central wing of the Rani Gümpha are very significant. The scene describes the fight of an elephant with a man and a set of women with clubs or bludgeons. The two elephants by which Lakshmi in the tympanum of Ananta Gümpha is flanked are nicely sculptured and deserve special notice. The figures

trumpet. I shall repair to Varanasi, and, arriving at the city of Kasi, turn the wheel of the law in this world". Dr. Mitra, Buddha Gaya, p. 47.

* Rajtarangini translated by Dr. Stein, Vol. I, Sloka 147, p. 134.

of elephants holding garlands of lotus or rather bunches of lotus buds with stalks, and a central full-blown lotus, on the two sides of the flight of steps leading to the verandah of the Ganesa Gümpha seem to have been copied from nature. The bas-reliefs of elephant scenes of the Ganesa cave are important; three warriors, two males and one amazon, riding on an elephant followed by four kilted warriors are sure to strike the attention of an observer.

It has been already stated that the tops of the doorways are seen in many cases provided with semi-circular arch-bands; these are connected together by horizontal friezes starting from the springing points where are usually noticed the figures of elephants, lions, and deer from the mouth of which issue the scrollworks (c. f. Rani Gümpha) decorating the semi-circular arch-bands.

The monkey was a very favourite subject with the Buddhist sculptors; we come across representations of it in the Rani Gümpha; two monkeys have been represented as looking at a snake, pursuing them. The monkey scenes sculptured in the stüpa of Bharhüt are more numerous than those noticed here. "The representations" at Bharhüt, according to Cunningham "are in various aspects, both serious and humorous"*; and in this connection, the capture of elephants

* Stüpa of Bharhüt by Cunningham.

by monkeys leading them in triumphal procession, and the turning of a monkey into an ascetic are worth noticing.

The horse has not been lost sight of by the sculptors. A well-caparisoned horse provided with a saddle is noticed over the horizontal band, and the interval between the semi-circular arch-bands of the lower storey of the central wing of the R*a*ni Gümph*a*. The horse is without stirrup; it has been very faithfully sculptured. The horse of the hunter, probably a king, in the well-known Hunt-scene may be mentioned here; it is also represented as an emblem of Sambhavan*a*th in the cave of S*a*tbakhr*a*. I have already made a reference to the deer. The flying buck or fallow-deer with her fawns, struck with an arrow still sticking to her side is, nicely depicted in the famous Hunt-scene of the upper storey of the R*a*ni Gümph*a*. At Amar*a*vati too are noticed figures of spotted deer worshipping the sacred Bo-tree.* The bull is noticed as an emblem of Rishava Deva, the first Tirthankara of the Jainas, in the S*a*tbakhr*a* cave on the Khandagiri hill. In the R*a*ni Gümph*a* is seen a female figure, probably a guard, bestriding a bull. Dogs have also been noticed in the bas-relief of the Abduction-scene sculptured in the R*a*ni Gümph*a*. I give below the list of other animal figures that I have come across in the caves on the Khandagiri hill:—The lion, goose,

* Burgess, The Buddhist Stupa of Amaravati and Jaggyyapeta, p 50, fig. 13.

peacock, sheep, fish, tortoise ; all these are emblems of the Jaina Tirthankaras represented in the Jaina Gümphas of the Khandagiri hill. The *Makara* or the mythological monster called capricornus as commonly noticed in the Buddhist stūpas of Bharhüt and Amaravati is also noticed in the horizontal portion of the bands in which the semi-circular arch-bands surmounting the tympana terminate (cf. Ganesa Gümpha).

Chronology. It is almost a hopeless task to fix with anything like certainty the chronology of the caves ; and the intermingling of Buddhist and Jaina influences has rendered it more so. This is evidenced by the wide divergence in the chronological order fixed by different scholars. As an illustration I may cite the instance of Ananta Gümpha, the date of which covers a period of four centuries according to different texts. The authors of the Cave Temples of India have placed it sometime between 200 and 150 B. C*. Cunningham has placed it in the second or third century A.D.† The inscriptions that are engraved on the walls of the caves do not furnish the surest key to unravel this mystery of chronology, for they are not of a very decisive character ; they can be interpreted either way ; and even nearly the same interpretations lead to different conclusions in respect of chronology. In the case of the Hati Gümpha, for instance,

* Fergusson and Burgess, Cave Temples of India, (1880), p. 70.

† Cunningham, Archæological Survey of India, Vol. XIII (1875-76), p. 81.

Dr. Mitra has placed the date of inscription sometime between 316, and 416 B. C.; and Prinsep has decided it to be of later date than the Asoka edicts. The author of Corpus Inscriptionum Indicarum agreeing generally with Prinsep, has placed it sometime between 175 and 200 B. C. *

Pandit Bhagw*a*n L*a*l Indraji has, however, upset all the interpretations offered up till then by Prinsep, Mitra, &c., and has substituted a new one, according to which the inscription, in question, is dated sometime between 158 and 153 B. C. ‡; this interpretation has again been called into question by Dr. Fleet in a recent article in the Journal of the Royal Asiatic Society; thus it is seen that the interpretation is undergoing changes according as it is handled by different scholars. This difficulty is aggravated by the present indistinct nature of the characters inscribed on the wall, caused by the weathering action of the atmosphere. I have accordingly tried to fix the dates on principles based on architectural and sculptural considerations.

The Ananta Gümph*a* seems to be contemporaneous with the remains at Bh*a*rhüt, for there is a great similarity existing between the nature of the sculptures, and the mode of execution. The stepped pyramid is a very striking feature of both, and this is very significant. Gaja-Lakshmi, the serpent, the

‡ Corpus Inscriptionum Indicarum, p. 28.

* Actes du Sixieme Congres' Or, tome iii pp. 174-177.

Buddhist rails, the Bodhi tree within an enclosure of rails are noticeable both in the Ananta Gümpha and Bharhüt sculptures. The capital of the pilasters of Ananta is formed by recumbent animals, and this is also noticed at Bharhüt. It is only in a pilaster of Ananta, and in no other Orissan caves, that rosettes, or bosses, and half-discs of full-blown lotuses are noticed, and we notice them at Bharhüt also; and the lower echinus or the capital of this pilaster only bears a resemblance to that of the Bharhüt pillar. The flying figures of nymphs flanking the tympanum of the doorway containing the figure of Gaja-Lakshmi, and carrying offerings in their left hands are very similar to the Bharhut figures. The representation of *hamsa* or goose is noticeable in both. From these considerations I am inclined to place the Ananta Gümpha sometime between 250 and 200 B. C.

The Rani Gümpha, Jaya-Vijaya, Ganesa, and Swargapüri caves form a continuous series from the chronological point of view. The first two, however, are chronologically intermediate between the Bharhüt and Sanchi remains, and are hence placed in the period dating from 200 to 100 B. C. Ganesa, Swargapüri and some other minor caves are contemporaneous with the Sanchi remains, and I am inclined to place them in the first century B. C.

The intermediate uprights of the Buddhist rails sculptured in the caves, and into which the cross-bars have been tennoned are usually provided with four vertical ridges to make them look like the uprights at Sanchi which present a decided semi-octagonal appearance; these ridges also end at top and bottom in small plane faces. I have already referred to the representation of *makara* or capricornus near the springing points of the arch-bands, e. g. of Rani, Jaya-Vijaya, and Ganesa Gümphas.

The sculptures of these caves are very similar. The floral devices sculptured in the arch-bands bear a striking resemblance to those of the right-hand pillar of the northern gateway at Bharhüt. The representation of a creeper ending in a full-blown lotus in the arch-bands of Ganesa and Rani Gümpha bears a close affinity to its counterpart at Sanchi.

I have already remarked that Rani Gümpha and Jaya-Vijaya are similar in many respects; both are two-storeyed. The stepped pyramids representing *Chaityas* are noticeable in both these caves, as in Ananta, and the Bharhüt remains. The representations of the running figures carrying trays containing offerings are similar in both. The sculptures of Rani Gümpha, however, resemble those of Bharhüt more than of Jaya-Vijaya; the representations of *hamsa* (goose), monkey and jack-fruit are met with both at Bharhüt and in Rani Gümpha.

I give below a chronological table showing the probable dates of excavating the important caves.

No.	Caves.	Date.
1	Hati Gümpha ...	300 B. C.
2	Ananta Gümpha ...	250 to 200 B. C.
3	Rani Gümpha ...	200 „ 100 „
4	Jaya-Vijaya ...	200 „ 100 „
5	Ganesa Gümpha ...	100 „ 1 „
6	Swargapüri Cave ...	100 „ 1 „
7	Jaina Gümphas such as Satbakhra Navamüni.	50 B. C. to 100 A. D.

Much difficulty is experienced in ascertaining the age of the Jaina Gümphas on the Khandagiri hill. From the elaborate character of the pillars and the images of the Jaina Tirthankaras it is obvious that the caves are later than the Buddhist ones; it can also be stated that the Jaina caves are decidedly much older than the Jaina temple at Gaya supposed to have been built by Amara Sinha, the great Sanskrit lexicographer, in the 6th century A.D., for we come across references of a powerful

Jaina dynasty of kings represented by Kharvela, in the Hati Gümpha inscription the latest possible date of which is the middle of the second century B. C. From this consideration alone we may surmise, in propriety, that there must have been caves excavated for the Jaina Sramanas in the · hood of the Hati Gümpha ; and the Udaygiri hill being already honey-combed with Buddhist caves, and in order to keep themselves rather aloof from the Buddhists, the Jaina hermits chose the Khandagiri hill for their habitations ; and this may be assigned to the period from the first century B. C. to the first century A. D.

In the Nava Müni cave, however, is noticed an inscription referring to Udyata Kesari who, as I have proved at great length in Chapter VIII, flourished in the first quarter of the tenth century A.D. In this cave a disciple of Küla Chandra, a Jaina Sramana, is supposed to have lived. From this inscription the inevitable conclusion is arrived at that the cave, in question, must have been excavated sometime in the tenth century A.D. ; but the conclusion loses its force when we see the figure of Ganesa carved on the ante-wall of the Ganesa Gümpha evidently a Bauddha cave of the first century B.C., or the figure of the Hindu goddess Dürga in a Jaina cave on the Khandagiri hill. It will be absurd to conclude that the Ganesa Gümpha or the Jaina Gümpha is a Brahminical one in as much as the images of the Hindu pantheon are noticeable there. The figures, in question, were evident interpolations. By a parity of reasoning, and in view of the fact that Udyata Kesari was a great patron of Jainism it is probable that the inscription referred to is a spurious one not contemporaneous with the cave, and engraved simply as a mark of respect for one who was so noted for the catholicity of his views.

Survey of the caves.

The survey of the caves to determine their relative positions in respect of the road leading from Bhubanesvara, and passing through the two hills was made at my instance by some of my engineer friends who accompanied me during my brief sojourn in Orissa. The Plate I (C) clearly shows in plan the position of the caves. I have given below a serial list of them the numbering of which corresponds to that given in the plan. Some of the caves have been designated as nameless, for I could not either determine their names, or different names being offered by different guides they have been so styled; some of the names, I have found, have no significance either etymologically, or historically; hence I have been careful to attach more importance to their relative positions which are far more significant than meaningless uncorroborated names.

No.	Khandagiri Caves.	Udaygiri Caves.
1	Nameless	Rani Gümpha.
2	Nava Müni Cave ...	Nameless.
3	Satbakhra or Satghara Cave consisting of the Barbhüji, and Trisüla Caves.	"
4	Supposed grave of Lalatendü (only a bare wall is visible).	"
5	*Akasaganga* ...	Swargapüri or Alakapüri.
6	Deva Sabha ...	Jaya-Vijaya Cave.
7	Jaina temple on the summit.	Nameless.
8	Ananta Gümpha ...	"
9	Nameless	Vaikanthapüra & Patalpüri Caves.
10	"	Manchapüri.
11	"	Ganesa.
12	"	Nameless.
13	... .	Hati Gümpha.
14	... .	Sarpa Gümpha or Serpent Cave.
15	... .	Tiger Cave or Byaghra Gümpha.
16	... .	Nameless.
17	... .	"
18	... .	Jagannath Gümpha.
19	... .	Haridas Gümpha.

Dhauli Inscription.

It will not be out of place to make a passing reference to the inscription on the Dhauli hill or Dhavala-giri, a group of three hills or prominences to the south-east of Bhubanesvara. This portion of Orissa was held in great sanctity by the Buddhists, for the tooth-relic of Gautama Buddha had been preserved here for several centuries before it was removed to Ceylon in the beginning of the fourth century A. D.

It has been stated in the second chapter that Asoka conquered Kalinga which became the eastern limit of his vast empire. King Piyadasi Asoka caused his edicts to be engraved on a prominence of Dhavalagiri, called Asvatth*ama* rock in the middle of the third century B. C. Though not very important from an architectural point of view, this rock is most well-known for the invaluable treasure it contains. This inscription throws a great flood of light on some obscure corners of Orissan history of which no other authentic record is available.

The inscription consists of eleven edicts, preceded and followed by two minor ones unlike those found elsewhere except at Jauga*da* in the Dt. of Ganj*a*m. Dr. Hunter doubts the authenticity of the two minor edicts already referred to, and considers them as "added by the local Prince of Orissa."*

* Orissa, vol. I. p. 192.

This inscription has been edited by Prinsep, Wilson, Bühler, Senart, etc. Dr. Burgess has published in parallel columns the transcripts and translations of the Dhauli and Jaugada versions of Asoka's edicts by Dr. Bühler in "The Buddhist stüpas of Amaravati and Jaggayyapeta." In the summary given below I have followed all these versions of different scholars as far as practicable.

The first edict begins with the prohibition of the slaughter of animals for religious sacrifice, or food. The second describes his organization of systematic medical aid in his own kingdom, and that of "Antiochus, the Yona (or Yavana) Raja," and other kingdoms from the Himalayas to Tambapanni or Ceylon. The third enjoins a "public humiliation......for the confirmation of virtue, and for the suppression of disgraceful acts"*; it also describes the duties to our parents, kinsfolks, Brahmins, and Sramanas. The fourth one amplifies the third. The fifth is with regard to the appointment of missionaries for "intermingling among all unbelievers with the inundation of religion, and with the abundance of the sacred doctrines"†. The sixth one is with reference to the appointment of instructors or Pativedakas to impart instructions having a bearing on the minutest details of our domestic lives. The seventh

* Prinsep's Translation.

† Same.

enjoins on the necessity of repentance, peace of mind and "undistinguishing charity." The eighth describes the duties of a king as compared with the practices of old. The ninth insists on the value of "the happiness of virtue." The tenth is a statement of Piyadasi's ideas of glory and reputation "for enforcing conformity among a people praiseworthy for following the four rules of virtue, and pious"*. The eleventh edict describes the manner in which the edicts have been composed and the purpose for which they have been incised, i. e. "with the intention that the people may act thus."†

* Prinsep's Translation.

† The Buddhist Stupas of Amaravati and Jaggyyapeta, p. 125

CHAPTER IV.

Græco-Roman Influence on Orissan Architecture.

Let us now turn our attention to the Græco-Roman theory propounded by the European scholars. In front of the Rani Gümpha is seen the figure of a guard of *Dwârpâla* wearing boots reaching up to the knee, and dressed in a flowing garment like a *châpkân* of the present day. The wearing of boots has led the scholars to think that there must have been European influence, or else how could the boots be represented; from this has sprung up a tissue of myths which, if analysed, would prove to be utterly baseless. That we had our national boots has been conclusively proved by Dr. Mitra in his Indo-Aryans, vol I. Even if we suppose that the boots were not Indian in origin there is no absolute certainty that they were introduced by the Greeks or Romans. Mr. Pococke has proved conclusively in his book entitled "India in Greece," by adducing a long chain of evidence that there was colonisation in Greece in pre-historic times, and that Indian thought and dialect had left an indelible impress on those of the Greeks. Pythagoras is believed to have come to *Sakya* Müni in India, and in the language of the author of the "History of Science*," "to the Indians he was perhaps indebted for his theology." From such intercommunion existing between the Greeks and Indians it can not safely be ascertained which of the two nations copied from the other. If we admit that the Indians copied the boots from the Greeks, what avails it to prove that the Greeks necessarily influenced the architecture of Orissa ?

That the Greeks never exercised any influence on the Orissan architecture will be evident from the following considerations. There is a great deal of difference between the Indo-Aryan and Greek columns as far as outward shape is concerned. The Greek columns are invariably cylindrical, or circular in cross section, whereas those of the Indo-Aryan type may be circular, square, pentagonal, hexagonal, octagonal or even 16-sided in cross section. Different technical terms have been coined in M*a*nas*a*ra to designate the different forms.

Square—Brahma K*a*nda (ब्रह्मकाण्ड)

Pentagonal—*S*iva K*a*nda (शिवकाण्ड)

Hexagonal—Skanda K*a*nda (स्कन्दकाण्ड)

Octagonal—Vishnü K*a*nda (विष्णुकाण्ड)

16-sided—Rüdra K*a*nda (रुद्रकाण्ड)

The monolithic column that is standing in front of the temple of Jagann*a*th at Püri is Rüdra K*a*nda.

* The History of Science, p. 12. (edited by Routledge.)

The Indo-Aryan columns have their characteristic cornice, frieze, architrave, capital, shaft, base, and pedestal. These features do not mainly correspond to those of the Greek or Roman type. The entablature, pedestal, plinth, and capital of Greek or Roman technology have their Indo-Aryan equivalents in our Prast*a*ra or Uttira (पस्तार वा उत्तिरा). Upapitha (उपपीठ), Up*a*na (उपान) and Bodhik*a* (बोधिका) respectively. The details of these parts of a column do not tally with Greek features. Far greater diversity of forms is noticeable in the Indo-Aryan capitals of columns, than we come across in the Doric, Ionic and Corinthian orders.

As the Greeks or Romans represent acanthus in the capitals of a particular order of columns, so do the Hindus represent lotus and *âmalaki* or phyllanthus emblica.

There are some who complain that the entablature of Indo-Aryan columns is narrow ; this is not generally the case ; there are instances of columns with narrow entablature and long-drawn shafts even in the edifices erected under the Emperor Augustus down to the time of Diocletian.

In M*a*ns*a*ra 64 different types of the base of a column are mentioned ; no nation in the world, not to speak of the Greeks or Romans, has so many different modifications of column base.

In M*a*ns*a*ra, columns have been classified according to the ratio the diameter bears to the height, and certain rules have been enunciated to determine the slope in the case of tapering columns. During my brief sojourn in Orissa, I carefully studied the columns specially of the rock-cut caves at Udayagiri or Khandagiri, and I have noticed with wonder that this rule of proportion has strictly been followed. I cannot resist the temptation of citing the case of a tapering octagonal column in one of the caves at Khandagiri. I made a pencil sketch of it, and measured its height *in situ*, and applied the rule of Manasara to the measurements taken. I see that the rule of slope has been followed with almost mathematical precision, the discrepancy being ½". I quote the rule below. The diameter at the top of a column below the moulding is the diameter of the base minus that at the base multiplied by the ratio which it bears to the height of the column. The Greek or Roman architects were guided by altogether different rules to determine the slope.

All these things tend to show that the Orissan architects had in view purely Indo-Aryan style in executing their works of architecture, or else the very formulæ or the rules enunciated in our Indian architectural treatises would not have been so rigidly followed.

The European scholars headed by Dr. Fergusson, Vincent Smith, etc. assert that the introduction of stone architecture in India is traced to the advent of the Greeks in India after its conquest by Alexander. Vincent Smith has written as follows in an article on "Græco-Roman Influence on the civilization of India" in the Journal of the Asiatic Society. "No Indian example in stone either of architecture or sculpture earlier than the reign of Asoka (B.C. 260-232), has yet been discovered, and the well-known theory of Mr. Fergusson, that the sudden introduction of the use of stone instead of wood for the purposes both of architecture and sculpture in India was the result of communication between the empire of Alexander, and his successor and that of the Maurya dynasty of Chandra Güpta and Asoka, is, in my opinion, certainly correct."*

We quote the following from the Encyclopædia Britannica.

"Certain pillars erected by him (i. e. Asoka) and inscribed with his edicts are the earliest extant architectural remains of India."

Sir George Birdwood has struck the same chord in his "Industrial Arts of India" from which we quote the following :—

"The architecture of India begins with a strong admixture of Greek Art, the effects of which we are able to trace for centuries in the architecture of the valleys of Cashmere and Cabul."*

Let us consider the above remarks ; the invasion of India by Alexander is dated in the first quarter of the fourth century

* J. A. S. B. Vol. LVIII, Part I. p. 108.

B. C.; the invasion was of a very short duration and was confined to the north-western limits of the Indian province. It was more of a formal nature than of an actual one. Considering the time, extent and situation we may consider the invasion of very little consequence, as not having affected the internal condition, much less the art of the Indians. In this advanced age of civilization, this short invasion affecting a small fraction of the whole area inhabited at present by a far more homogeneous race would hardly leave any impression worth the name. How infinitesimal would its effect be in those days of most inadequate means of communication when the country was parcelled out into small divisions inhabited by alien races, and ruled over by different kings having no community of interest to unite them into action against a common foe. This would have been more impossible in case of Orissa which is situated on the farthest east of India, and surrounded on all sides by trackless forests, and hilly fastnesses.

To influence the art and architecture of an invaded province it is necessary that the invaders should live among the conquered people for a very long time. We have been under the British rule for more than a century and a half in intimate terms of fellowship with the British people; but the amount of influence exercised on our art is quite incommensurate with it; this is very natural, for the art of a nation is an index to its genius moulded to its present shape being worked for centuries. Hence it is absurd to imagine that the brief invasion by Alexander could possibly influence forthwith the art and architecture of even the portion of India invaded, much less of Orissa. Following the parity of reasoning it will be equally absurd to consider for a moment that the expedition led by Col. Younghusband in Tibet has produced results similar to those estimated by Fergusson and others in respect of India. There is another thing to consider in this connection. Some of the caves of Orissa are at least as old as the invasion by Alexander, and some elaborate ones are little later than it. If it be possible for the ancient Indians to build cave temples approaching in arrangement and elevation a domestic building of no mean order (c. f. R*a*ni Gümph*a*) would it be impossible for them to build the buildings themselves which are easier in execution than these elaborate cave temples. It cannot be questioned that the excavation of a cave temple requires greater care, skill and experience than the construction of a building entailing a manipulation of isolated stone blocks.

One of the main reasons leading the European scholars to uphold the Græco-Roman theory is the absence of any extant old stone building. I must admit that this fact presents a difficulty which it is apparently impossible to tide over; but a moment's consideration, and comparative study would obviate the difficulty. I think no evidence is to be adduced to prove that the kings of Orissa, or of any other Indian province had palaces with commodious chambers even in the mediæval times, if not in the period anterior to Alexander's invasion ; but how many palaces or chambers are still extant to prove their existence? It is needless to point out that mighty lines of kings ascended the Orissa throne ; but curiously, there is not the least vestige of their palaces, except perhaps a few foundations densely covered with jungles, as at Bhubanesvara. This last vestige may in course of time disappear altogether from the face of the earth to afford a suitable theme for archæological research to future generations as to whether the mediæval Orissan architects were conversant with the principles of building dwelling houses of stone.

Dr. Burgess and others, however, concede that the only uses of stone that the Indians were conversant with, anterior to the invasion by Alexander are for constructing bridges, foundations and boundary walls which like the Druidical Cromlechs, Cyclopic walls, and Cloaca-maxima have no part in the history of Indian architecture. I do not know on what data is the above conclusion based. If the foundations extant of pre-historic buildings lead to it, the foundations extant of the mediæval times as noticed by me at Bhubanesvara may point to the same conclusion ; again, if the knowledge of boundary walls be conceded to them what logical inaccuracy is there in allowing that they used stone in building the external walls of a building? The durability, and efficiency as a building material of stone should have naturally impressed them with its significance, and should have naturally led them to reject wood, bamboo, or reed ; it does not stand to reason that the chain of reasoning followed by them in constructing boundary walls was different from that followed in the case of building the external walls of a structure which obviously demanded greater care and skill. By conceding to them the knowledge of stone as a suitable material for building bridges they make their position very untenable ; for, the construction of bridges is no easier task than that of domestic buildings.

Let me now consider it from another stand-point. It is stated in the temple archives at Puri that the Yavanas ruled in Orissa for 146 years. To the European scholars these Yavanas are synonymous with the Asiatic Greeks, and that they taught the children of the soil all the fine arts. Let us briefly analyse the premises on which this conclusion is based. The temple archives do not at all indicate who these Yavanas were ; the assertion in the archives is based on mere hearsays, and the conclusion which has drawn its vital principle from some incoherent hearsays cannot pass for truth ; even if we admit that the Yavanas retained possession of Orissa for about a century and a half, there is no absolute certainty that the Asiatic Greeks are to be meant by this term.

The term Yavana connotes the Turks, Persians, Arabs, Sakas, Hüns, Magas, etc. There is no definite proof that the Greeks are to be meant. It is stated in Harivamsam that in order to carry out the orders of his preceptor, and to keep his vow, Prince Sagara enjoined on the Yavanas prohibition from the study of the Vedas, and the practice of the Vedic rituals; according to Smarta Baudhayana they have been termed Mlechchas for giving up their religious rites. Ordinarily the two terms Mlechchas and Yavanas are synonymous. In the Matsya Puranam the Mlechchas have been described as dark-complexioned like black collyrium—कृष्णाञ्जन सम प्रभाः. The Greeks were never dark-complexioned, not to speak of their resemblance in colour to collyrium. In the Ramayana the Yavana soldiers of Vasistha arrayed against those of Visvamitra have been described as "dressed in flaming yellow robes." The Greeks were never so attired. In this connection reference may be made to the satirical composition of Aristophanes meant against Euripides.

Moreover, to establish the Yavana theory we need not go beyond the confines of India. The Mlechchas or Yavanas lived both inside and outside India, and hence by the term

Yavana some non-Aryan primitive Indian race may be understood. We come across the following couplet in Brihat Parasara Samhita.

"हिमपर्व्वत विन्ध्याद्री विनाशन प्रयागयोः ।
मध्ये तु पावनो देशो म्लेच्छदेशस्ततःपरम् ॥"

The holy land or Pünya Bhümi is surrounded on all sides by the Himalayas, the Vindhyas, the Saraswati and Prayag ; and beyond these is the land assigned to the Mlechchas

Hence we see that the major portion of India was the land of the Mlechahas. The Persians have been styled the Yavanas by the great Sanskrit poet, Kalidasa. In the fourth canto of Raghu Vamsam we come accross the following two couplets regarding Raghu's conquest.

"पारसिकांस्ततो जेतुं प्रतस्थे स्थलवर्त्मना ।
इन्द्रियाख्यानिव रिपूं स्तत्त्वज्ञानेन संयमी ।
यवनीमुखपद्मानां सेहे मधुमदं न सः ।
बालातपमिवाब्जानामकालजलदोदयः ॥"

What we aim at by the preceding remarks is to prove that we come across instances after instances in which the Yavanas have connoted races other than the Greeks. We cannot establish in the face of the above references that the Ionian or Asiatic Greeks ever came to settle in Orissa. We can, however, solve this enigma of the introduction of the Yavana element in Orissa by reference to a passage in the *Samba*

Pūraṇam in which the sun-god is stated to have instructed *Sa*mba to introduce the Magas, M*a*magas, and others from *Sa*kadvipa to perform the religious rites of the deity in the temple at Kon*a*rka.

"न योग्यः परिचर्यायां जम्बुद्वीपे ममानघ ।
मम पूजापरान् कृत्वा शाकद्वीपादिहानय ॥
मगश्च मामगाश्चैव मानसा मन्दगास्तथा ।
तस्मात् मत्पूजार्थं शाकद्वीपादिहानय ॥"

Hence from Orissan temples it is conclusively proved that the theory of the introduction of stone architecture by the Greeks is utterly erroneous. If it be possible in Orissa why should it not be in other parts of India equally advanced as Orissa.

We can judge the merits of the Græco-Roman theory by considerations based on general principles. It is a natural law that man at the early dawn of history must have recourse to such building materials as are easily accessible, and have sufficient durability. John Ruskin, the able critic of arts understood fully the significance of this first canon of architecture; he has written to the following effect in his "Seven Lamps of Architecture."

"Its first existence and its earliest laws must therefore depend upon the use of material accessible in quantity, and on the surface of the earth; that is to say, clay, wood, or stone."

India abounds in various stones adapted for building purposes, and also easily accessible ; hence it is inexplicable why should India furnish an exception to this fundamental canon of architecture. Professor Fletcher has also said to the same effect in his "History of Architecture."

"The centre of the Peninsula, and the hill country generally abound in excellent building stone which had considerable influence on Indian Architecture from the earliest times."*

General Cunningham recognises the existence of stone architecture in a period anterior to Alexander's invasion. We quote the following from the Archæological Survey Report Vol. III., pp. 142-143.

"As the city of Girivraja or old Rajgriha was built by Bimbisara, the contemporary of Buddha, we have another still existing example of Indian stone building at least 250 years older than the date of Asoka."

We may pertinently quote here the observations of Dr. Lübke from his "History of Art" relating to the origin and growth of Indian Architecture. The learned doctor, while referring to the fact that the Indian style began with forms borrowed from other nations, observes, "If this, however, be the case still in the earlier Indian civilization, of which undoubtedly there is no certain knowledge, distinct national

* Professor Fletcher, History of Architecture. p. 606.

forms of art must have been already developed (i. e. before Alexander's conquest) and these Buddhism developed into monumental importance."

Dr. Sturgis has also taken a somewhat similar view of the case in his Dictionary of Architecture. He says that "Inspite of these exterior influences the architecture of India is pre-eminently original, unlike that of any other land."*

In Fa Hian's Travels translated by Giles, I have come across a tediously long list of architectural examples, evidently of stone, which are dated as far back as the time of Bimbisara, Buddha, and even older than that, many of which Fa Hian saw in actual existence.

(1) "The pagoda of Fang-Kung-Chung at Pi-she-li or Baishali standing by which Buddha is stated to have said to Ananda that he would enter Nirvana very soon."

(2) In Chapter XXVIII, p. 66,

"From this point going south-east nine yu-yen, the pilgrims arrived at a small Ku-shi hill, on the top of which there was a stone chamber facing the south. When Buddha was seated within, the heavenly ruler Shih on this spot edified him with celestial music."

(3) In Chapter XXX, p. 72,

* Dr. Sturgis, Dictionary of Architecture, p. 461

"Six li further west, on the north side of the hill, and (consequently) in the shade there is a chamber called Chüti, where after the Nirvana of Buddha, the 500 Lo-hans compiled the Ching."

I need hardly point out that a stone chamber to accommodate 500 men is sufficiently spacious, and not a mere cave or cell excavated by primitive men simply to protect the body against elemental warfare.

That we had our indigenous stone architecture will be evident by reference to Manasara, MayaMata, Casyapa. In Agni Püranam rules of architecture have been enunciated. In the Matsya Püranam we come across the following,

"शिलान्यासस्तु कर्तव्यः प्रासादे तु शिलामये ।
इष्टकानान्तु विन्यासः प्रासादे चेष्टकामये ॥"

In another passage we have the following,

"प्रासादार्थं समासेन शिलान्यासमथोत्तमं ।
शिलान्यास विधानञ्च प्रोच्यते तदनन्तरं ।
शिला वा चेष्टका वापि चतस्रो लक्षणान्विताः ।
प्रासादादौ शिलाभिन्न मसृणाः समकोष्ठकाः ॥"

The two foregoing couplets refer to the selection of stone blocks of a superior quality, and the laying of well-dressed cubical stone blocks.

In the *Sreematbhagabatam*, I have come across the following passage referring to buildings and propylons built of stone.

सरत्कुमसतोद्यान विचित्रोपवनान्वितं ।
हेमरत्नैर्द्दिविस्तम्भैः स्फाटिकाट्टाल गोपुरैः ॥५१

दशमस्कन्धे पञ्चाशदध्याये ।

In Bhabisya Püranam, Mahanirvanatantram, are found references to stone buildings which are quoted below.

कोटिकोटि गुणं पुण्यं फलं स्यादिष्टकालये ।
द्विपरार्द्धगुणं पुण्यं शैलजे तु विदुर्बुधाः ॥

भविष्यपुराणे ।

मृत्तिकामयदाने तु तस्माच्छतगुणं भवेत् ।
ततोऽयुतगुणं पुण्यं शिलागेहप्रदानतः ॥२५

महानिर्व्वाणतन्त्रे त्रयोदशोल्लासे ।

The last couplet speaks of the free gift of a stone building as more meritorious than that of a brick-built one.

Raghunandan, the great Indian jurist and lawgiver (स्मार्त) of the fifteenth century A.D. has quoted in his Mathapratisthaditattvam (मठप्रतिष्ठादितत्त्वम्) a passage from the Vrihatdharmottara, a book not extant now, referring to a stone temple. The passage quoted below describes the construction of a stone temple as more meritorious than that of a brick-built one.

दशकाष्ठमये पुण्यं मयैतत् कथितं द्विजाः ।
तस्माद्दशगुणं पुण्यं त्वैष्टकमये भवेत् ।
तस्माद्दशगुणञ्चापि निर्मिते शैलमन्दिरे ।

In the Agni Püranam, I have come across numerous passages graphically describing the details of stone architecture; from the above considerations it is clear that India had her own stone architecture uninfluenced by any foreign example, and thriving under purely Indian auspices. In this respect the Indians followed their own traditions as did the builders of the palace of Osymandyas at Thebes, the temple at Karnak, or the pyramids at Gizeh. I quote below what Bury has said regarding the Indian styles of Architecture.

"The Indian styles, whatever their defects may be, have at least the merit of being original; for there can be little doubt but that they were invented in the country where we find them."*

Lieutenant Cole has expressed a similar opinion regarding Indian Architecture, which is quoted below.

"The Indian Architecture, like that of Egypt, Assyria, Greece, &c, is an important part of the History of the World's Art of Building, and that a student of architecture cannot complete his studies without the acquirement of, at least, some knowledge of Indian modes of building and decoration, and from these reproductions, which can be studied in his own country, he is able to derive a large number of suggestive principles. ....The people of India have for centuries been very considerable builders in ornamental styles of unusual purity."†

* T. Bury, The Styles of Various Countries and Periods (Rudimentary Architecture), p. 58.

† Lieut. Cole. R. E., The Architecture of Ancient Delhi (1872), p. 8.

CHAPTER V.

ARCHITECTURE OF THE MEDIÆVAL TIMES.

Architecture, as classified by John Ruskin, the able critic of arts, arranges itself under the following five different heads:—Devotional, Memorial, Civil, Military and Domestic.

The above five classes can be well illustrated by Indian examples.

Devotional—Such as the temples at Püri, Bhubanesvara, Jumma Musjid, &c.

Memorial—The Taj Mahal, Itimuddowla.

Civil—Dewani Khas, Dewani Am.

Military—The forts of Delhi, Chunar, &c.

Domestic—Sishmahal, or every rank and kind of dwelling place.

In Orissa we come across the first type of Architecture i.e. Devotional. The other types have disappeared with the rise and fall of different dynasties that ascended the Orissan throne. There is no vestige left of the palaces, fortresses, moats, &c., of the powerful monarchs of the Lion or Gangetic dynasties, but the temples built by them still rear their soaring heads high up in the air. A few examples of the Memorial type are still extant by reason of their association with the Devotional one.

The principal Br*a*hminical styles of Architecture are the Dr*a*vidian, the Ch*a*lükyan, and the Indo-Aryan. Their characteristic features are the following. In the Dr*a*vidian, the ground-plan is rectangular, and the superstructure is pyramidal; in the Ch*a*lükyan, the ground-plan is star-like, and the superstructure is pyramidal, and in the Indo-Aryan, the ground-plan is square, and the superstructure is curvilinear. The Ch*a*lükyan form seems to me an improvement on the Dr*a*vidian one by the addition of pilasters and buttresses to the structure. The Dr*a*vidian, and the Ch*a*lükyan styles are extant in the Decc*a*n, and the Indo-Aryan, in Hindoostan proper, or Upper India (आर्य्यावर्त्त). In Orissa the Indo-Aryan style prevails.

Dh*a*rw*a*r, and Orissa are the ancient seats of Indo-Aryan style of architecture. The Dr*a*vidian style crept into, and hence adulterated the architecture of Dh*a*rw*a*r; but that of Orissa is still in its native purity, unadulterated, and unfettered by the conventional formulæ of other styles. To whichever part of India may we turn our attention, *e. g.* Ben*a*res, Mathur*a*, Brind*a*ban, &c., we notice a curious mixture of the Indo-Aryan, Saracenic, and other styles. Orissa towers above all in solitary grandeur; this significant fact has raised it in the estimation of those who study the genesis and evolution of architecture in India from a scientific stand-point.

The Orissan style of temple architecture has two main features similar in many respects (vide plates—II, III) :—(1) the 'Vimana' (विमान') or Bara Dewl, i.e. the towered sanctuary, or the sanctum or cella where the idol is enshrined. (ii) The 'Jagamohan' (जगमोहन') or the Audience Chamber for the pilgrims. The Vimana and Jagamohan are both square in plan ; the former is a cube or a rectangular parallelopiped, surmounted by a curvilinear tower ; the latter, the same, but surmounted by a pyramidal tower. This, I shall try to illustrate later on.

In the Dravidian, and Chalükyan styles the tower is many-storied, whereas in the Indo-Aryan one it is single-storied.

In very important temples, such as those at Püri and Bhubanesvara, two more features are added to the two already mentioned. (Vide Plate—XX.)

(1) The Nat Mandir—Festive Hall.

(2) The Bhoga Mandir—Hall of offerings.

In ordinary temples of Orissa the plinth does not exist ; the structure rises at once from the ground level ; but in important temples, it rises from the plinth which often presents an elegantly artistic appearance. I may refer to the plinth of the temple at Konarka which is pre-eminently beautiful. (Vide Plate—XXIII.)

The constructive peculiarities of the temple are very simple. The walls rise straight up till a cube or a rectangular paralellopiped is described. From this height horizontal courses of stone project or bracket inwards ; this is called corbelling. The Uriya architects had recourse to this method of horizontal projection to reduce the internal dimensions of the room for roofing ; this method involves necessarily the construction of the sanctuary to a great height, thereby adding grandeur, and solemnity to the outward appearance. The horizontal projection, or corbelling continues till the internal dimensions contract to a reasonable proportion where the horizontal flags of stone cover the opening below, being supported on iron beams.

I do not think that the Uriya architects were ignorant of the principles of a radiating arch which is an assemblage of wedge-shaped voussoirs covering a space, and supported intermediately by their mutual pressure on each other caused by gravity, and ultimately by their pressure against the abutment or pier. The pressure on the abutment which is inclined, necessitates the construction of the walls to a great width in order to keep the line of thrust within the central third of the base for ensuring the stability of the structure. Thus the Uriya architects were wise in preferring the horizontal arch to the radiating one. "An arch never sleeps" says the proverb; this is indicative of distrust of the arch as a constructive element in ensuring permanency to any structure. This belief has a greater hold on the oriental mind than on the European one, and has consequently led our architects to have recourse to the trabeated style in preference to the arcual one in covering large spaces. Cole has detected this instinctive distrust, or rather horror cherished by the Hindus for an arch, in the temple of Hardeo Jee at Goverdhan. The following extract from his work, "Buildings in the Neighbourhood of Agra" will bear me out. "The eastern entrance to the 'mantapa' or porch is peculiarly characteristic of the horror which the Hindus had for a true arch."*

That the Uriyas were actuated by this belief will be evident from the following consideration. If we admit that the Uriyas were unacquainted with the principles of an arch there is no gainsaying the fact that they do not know its use now, at this stage of civilization; but they will invariably set it aside as a principle of construction in constructing temples. In this case, the present is an index to the past; the past will be best explained by studying the present. The sense of effecting permanency was so deep-rooted in their minds as to make them ignore the arch altogether as an essential principle of construction. This sense led the Egyptians, according to Barry,

* Archæological Survey of India, Buildings in the Neighbourhood of Agra by Cole, p. 34.

to deliberately "set it aside as a principle of construction"* This sense of permanency coupled with that of convenience made the Orissan architects prefer the trabeated style all the more. There is another fact, in this connection, which is worth considering; an arch is usually employed as a constructive element where the building materials do not admit of being used in large blocks; this depends upon the geological formation of the country, and the skill of the architects in manipulating huge blocks. Professor Fletcher has laid stress on this point in his "Influence of Material on Architecture."†

The horizontal courses of stone that project inwards give to the inner face of the temple the unsightly appearance of a flight of inverted steps. The topmost courses are surmounted by an assemblage of sectoral slabs of stone, having, when put together, the appearance of an oblate spheroid with ribbed or denticulated surface. This is called *A*malaka Sil*a* (आमलक शिला) for bearing resemblance to *Amalaka* or phyllanthus emblica. (vide plate—III). Dr. Fergusson considers this resemblance a mistaken one, it being according to him an "insignificant berry"; hence "it could hardly ever have been adopted as an architectural pattern." Probably the learned doctor was ignorant of the significant fact that *A*malaki and Haritaki formed as it

* E. M. Barry. R. A. Lecture on Architecture, p. 18.

† B. F. Fletcher, Influence of Material on Architecture, p. 8.

Plate II

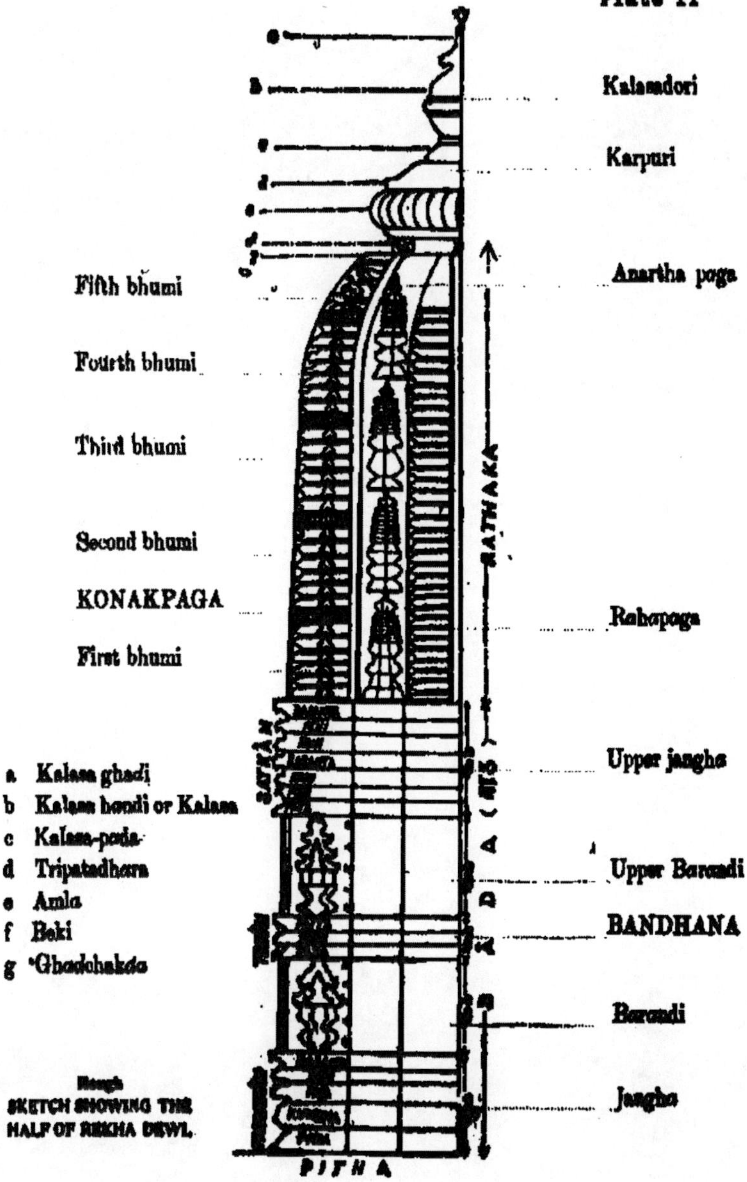

Rough
SKETCH SHOWING THE
HALF OF REKHA DEWL

were the staple food of some of the ancient *rishis*, and are from time immemorial associated with ideas of sanctity and spiritual culture. "The melon or gourd" of the doctor, from which the idea is said to have been taken is far more insignificant to us than Amalaka was to him, and we see no reason why this Amalaka should not furnish the architectural pattern.

There is an intervening recess between the *Amalaka Silâ*, and the lower horizontal course referred to already. This is, as it were, the neck of the Vimana, and is technically called Beki (बेकि), and contains at definite intervals figures of lion, and fantastic dwarfish monsters. The *Amla* is capped by a flat dome having some resemblance to an unfolded umbrella which is technically called Karpuri (कर्पुरि) ; over this is placed the artistically carved Kalasa Prastara which serves the purpose of a finial, or pinnacle. (vide plate—II). Over the Kalasa is placed the trident, or discus, according as the temple is dedicated to Siva, or Vishnü.

These are the main features of an Orissa temple. I shall now dwell at greater length on the essential and subsidiary parts of a temple.

The Orissan temples are characterized by pilasters which are technically called *pâga* (पाग) ; the classification of the Orissan temple is based on the number of pilasters used. The central, end, and intermediate pilasters are technically called Rahapaga (राहापाग), Konakapaga (कोणकपाग), and Anarthapaga. (Vide plate—IV).

The following are the different classes into which an Orissan temple is divided.

1. Ekaratha (एकरथ) Dewl, or an edifice having no pilas ter; it is a plain square in general ground plan.

2. Triratha (त्रिरथ) having one central pilaster or Rahapaga, and two Konaka pagas, or end pilasters.

3. Pancharatha (पञ्चरथ), having one Rahapaga, two Konakpagas and two Anarthapagas or intermediate pilasters. (Vide Plate IV.)

4. Saptaratha (सप्तरथ) having two Konakpagas, 4 Anarthapagas, and one Rahapaga. Out of the four Anarthapagas, two are called Parianarthapagas.

5. Navaratha (नवरथ), having 4 Konakapagas, 4 Anarthapagas, and one Rahapaga; out of the 4 Konakapagas, 2 are Parikonakapagas.

The Brahmins, Kshatriyas, Vaisyas, and Südras have the following classes assigned to them respectively—Navaratha, Saptaratha, Pancharatha, and Triratha. The Ekaratha temple is of no classic importance. I have not come across any temple of the Navaratha type either at Bhubanesvara or at Püri. I might have noticed a Navaratha temple showing false pilasters; this is like a pseudo-alum in Chemistry.

PLATE III.

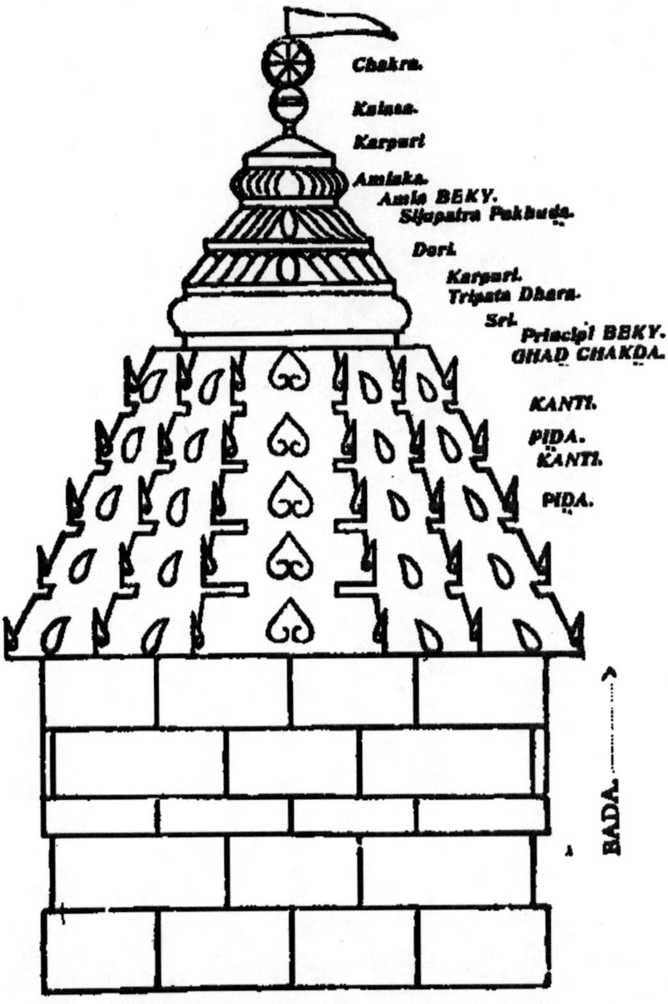

ELEVATION OF PIDA DEWL

Sketch by M. Ganguly.

I give below illustrations of the different classes into which an Orissan temple is divided.

Ekaratha :—The Vim*a*na of Vait*a*l Dewl, the Jagamohanas of Vait*a*l Dewl, and the temple of Para*s*ür*a*me*s*vara.

Triratha :—The Vim*a*na of the temple of Para*s*ür*a*me*s*vara.

Pancharatha :—The Vim*a*nas of Lingar*a*ja, Ananta Vasüdeva, R*a*jar*a*ni, Brahme*s*vara, Bhaskare*s*vara, Meghe*s*vara, R*a*me*s*vara, Siddhe*s*vara, Ked*a*re*s*vara, Yükti-Ked*a*re*s*vara, Gauri, Yame*s*vara, etc.

Saptaratha :—The Vim*a*na and the Jagamohana of S*a*ri Dewl.

The Orissan temple is also divided into two classes based on the nature of the tower over the cube. The tower may be either curvilinear or pyramidal. The former is called the Rekha Dewl (रेख देउल), (Vide Plate II), the latter, the Pi*d*a Dewl (पीड़ देउल), (Vide Plate III). Hence the actual number of classes into which an Orissan temple can be divided is the number 10 derived from the simple mathematical process of combination of 5 things taken 2 at a time. To be more explicit, we have Rekha Saptaratha Dewl, Pi*d*a Saptaratha Dewl, Rekha Navaratha Dewl, Pi*d*a Navaratha Dewl, etc.

The Jagamohana or the Audience Chamber is always a Pi*d*a Dewl.

In a Pi*d*a Dewl, horizontal slabs of stone with their ends

turned up project forward; these are called Pi*d*as, and hence the name of the edifice. There is a recess between the horizontal courses of stone and the Pi*d*as; this is technically called Kanti (काँटि). *There are often deep and large* recesses after an odd number of Pi*d*as, say 3,5,7,9, etc. These are called P*ara* Ghar or Pigeon nooks.

The Pi*d*a Dewl is again subdivided into 2 classes based on the height of the tower, e. g.,

(*a*) K*a*th Ch*a*li*a*.

(*b*) N*a*h*a* Ch*a*li*a*.

The superstructure below the pyramid in a K*a*th Ch*a*li*a* is a perfect cube or a rectangular parallelopiped, and that in a N*a*h*a* Ch*a*li*a* is invariably a rectangular parallelopiped.

In a K*a*th Ch*a*li*a* Pi*d*a Dewl the height of the pyramidal tower is usually two-thirds of the cube over which it rests; in a N*a*h*a* Ch*a*li*a* tower, the height of the pyramid is equal to, or five-sixths that of the cube or बाढ़.

We come across the N*a*h*a* Ch*a*li*a* type of Pi*d*a Dewl in the Jagamohana of the Müktesvara temple, the Bhogaman*d*apa of Kapiles*v*ara; and the K*a*th Ch*a*li*a* type in the Jagamohanas of the great Lingar*a*ja, Ananta V*a*südeva temples, etc.

The Mohana is always a Pi*d*a Dewl, and is divided into the three following classes:—(*a*) *Ghantā Sree Mohana*, (*b*) *Nadti Mohana*, (*c*) *Pida Mohana*. The former is an ordi-

PLATE IV

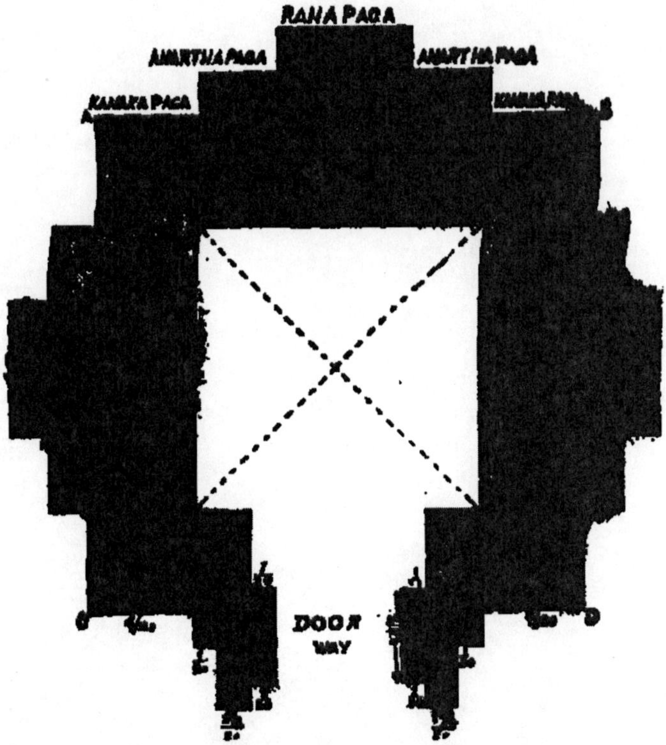

General Ground Plan of Pancharatha Dewl showing the proportion of the pilasters or *Pagas*

Sketch by M. Ganguly

Printed by K. V. Seyne & Bros.

nary Pida Dewl containing *Amlâ*, *Sree*, *Tripatadhâra*, *Kalasa*, (vide plate II.); this is well illustrated in the Jagamohana of the great Lingaraja at Bhubanesvara, (vide plate XVII). The *Nadü Mohana* is a *Pida Dewl*, the *pidas* of which coalesce, so that no recess or *Kânti* is visible. A *Nadü Mohana* does not usually contain *Sree*, *Amlâ*, &c, but it contains only the *Kalasa*. The Jagamohanas of Müktesvara. Siddhesvara, Rajarani belong to this type (vide plate XIV). Deviations from the standard type of a *Nadü Mohana* are often noticed, e. g. the Jagamohana of the Kedaresvara temple containing 6 ordinary *pidas*, and 6 *Nadus* or *Pidas* having no recesses; this Jagamohana, again, contains the *Sree*, *Amlâ*, *Tripatadhara*, *Kalasa*. The *Pida Mohana* is a distinct type of *Pida Dewl* consisting of ordinary *pidas*, and no *Amla*, *Kalasa*, etc. This/type of structures usually ends in a flat terrace surmounted by battlemented or crest tiles. The best examples of this type are the Natmandirs of the temples of Jagannath (vide plate XX.), and the great Lingaraja at Bhubanesvara.

I shall now attempt to show the relative proportions of the different parts in the general ground plan of an Orissan temple taking up a *Pancharatha* by way of illustration.

Divide the side of the square A B C D (vide plate—IV) into 20 equal parts, and take 4 parts for Konakapagas or end pilasters, 3 parts for Anarthapaga, and 6 parts for Rahapaga. The thickness of walls should be thc same as the length of the Konakapaga.

The *Rekka Dewl* contains the following important features. (vide plate. II.)

1. Pavement or *Talapattana.*
2. Plinth or *Pitha.*
3. Cube or *Bâda.*
4. Curvilinear tower or *Rekha* or *Rathaka.*
5. Neck or the recess just below the *Amlaka Silâ* called *Beki* corresponding to (f) of the plate.
6. Denticulated blocks of stone or *Amlaka Silâ.* (e) of the plate.
7. Stone cap resembling an unfolded umbrella or *karpûri.* (d) of the plate.
8. Finial or *kalasa.* (b) of the plate.
9. Trident or discus.

In a *Rekka Dewl*, the cube or *Bâda* consists of five distinct divisions, each division being subdivided into several others. I give below the parts from below upwards *ad seriatim.*

1. *Janghâ*, otherwise called *Panchakarma*, or a work of five parts.
2. *Sâkkar* or *Bârândi*, i,e. the portion, above *Janghâ*, and below *Tinkarma* or *Tinkâma.*

3. *Tinkarma*, or a work of 3 parts, otherwise called *Bandhanâ*.

4. *Sikkar*, othewise called the second *Bârândi*; it is evidently a contraction of *Sikhar*.

5. *Saptakâma*, or a work of 7 parts, otherwise called the second *Janghâ*, or upper *Janghâ*.

Generally speaking, the *janghâs*, upper and lower, are equal to each other; so are the *Bârândis*; but the *Bârândi*, as a rule, is a little less than the *Janghâ* in height; the *Bandhanâ* is one-third of the *Janghâ* or *Bârândi*. The following dimensions taken by me *in situ* will bear me out.

Siddhesvara temple :—

Jangh*a*	...	...	...	3′–11′
B*a*r*a*ndi	...	...	...	3′–5½″
Bandhan*a*	...	...	...	1′–3″
Upper B*a*r*a*ndi		...	...	3′–5″
Upper Jangh*a*		...	...	3′–9½″

Ananta Vasüdeva temple :—

(*a*) Jagamohana :—

Jangh*a*	...	...	...	3′– ½″
B*a*r*a*ndi	...	..	...	2′–6″
Bandhan*a*	...		...	0′–11½″
Upper B*a*r*a*ndi		..	...	2′–6″
Upper Jangh*a*		..	...	3′– ½″

(b) Vimana or Sanctum :—

Jangha ... ... 4′– ⅛″

Barandi ... . 3′–4″

Bandhana ... ... 1′–4″

Upper Barandi ... ... 3′–4″

Upper Jangha ... ... 4′– ⅛″

Lingaraja temple :—

(a) Vimana or Sanctum :—

Jangha ... ... 10′–4½″

Barandi ... ... 9′–10″

Bandhana ... ... 3′–0″

Upper Barandi ... ... 9′–3″

Upper Jangha ... ... 11′–0″

(b) Jagamohana :—

Jangha ... ... 7′–0″

Barandi ... ... 6′–6″

Bandhana ... 2′–0″

Upper Barandi ... ... 6′–1½″

Upper Jangha ... ... 7′–1″

(c) Natmandir :—

Jangha ... . 4′—11″

Barandi ... . 4′—1″

Bandhana ... . 1′—1″

Upper Barandi . ... 4′—1″

Upper Jangha .. .. 4′—11

I have taken many such measurements; from these I have worked out the following proportions for the component parts of a Bada.

Lower Jangha : Barandi : Bandhana : Upper Barandi : Upper Jangha : : 1 : 5/6 : ⅓ : 5/6 : 1; in some cases the proportions are 1 : ⅞ : ⅓ : ⅞ : 1. In the generality of cases, the former proportions prevail. In the majority of cases the sum of the Janghas, upper and lower, is equal to that of the Barandis and Bandhana.

I may mention here that the *badas* of all the Rekha Dewls do not contain the usual five elements already mentioned; as illustrations, I may cite the cases of the temples of Müktesvara, and Parasüramesvara which do not contain the last three component parts from below upwards. It is a very curious fact that the most picturesque temple of Müktesvara, very reasonably styled, "the gem of Orissan Architecture," is provided with an ordinary plain *bâda* having very few mouldings to adorn its surface.

Janghâ consists of the following subdivisions (vide plate-IV. A.),—

(*a*) ***Pâda***
(*b*) ***Kümbha***
(*c*) ***Patâ***
(*d*) ***Kani***
(*e*) ***Basanta.***

In some *janghás* I have noticed the omission or the repetition of some of the elements; as an example, in the temple of Müktesvara, some of the *janghás* of the Vimana or sanctum have the *Kani* wanting; it has been replaced by a *Patá*; again, in the temple of Parasüramesvara, *Patá* and *Kani* are altogether wanting; the *Janghá* consists of 3 elements only, viz, *Kumbha*, and *Basanta*; I may mention, here, incidentally that the second element of the *Janghás* of Parasüramesvara is again, not a *kümbha* at all; it shows a bold departure from the usual practice; it resembles a *kümüda* or an astragal, which is a semi-circle projecting from a vertical diameter. The *Janghá* of Parasüramesvara is technically called Trikarmajangha; it is a non-descript.

The *Páda* (Vide plate—IV. A.) consists of a fillet supporting a cyma reversa not deeply flected; this is technically called *Márani* (मारणी); the inflection of the convex element of the cyma is rather sharp; the cyma ends in a cavetto of gentle curvature; the cavetto terminates in either a recess or a small bead.

The idea of *Kümbha* is derived from a vase or urn; and is invariably represented in almost all the temples; it is an ovalo of gentle inflection, surmounted by a scotia; the ovalo is often provided with an intermediate bead.

The *Patá* consists of a cyma recta supporting a fillet ending in a cyma reversa.

PLATE IV(A

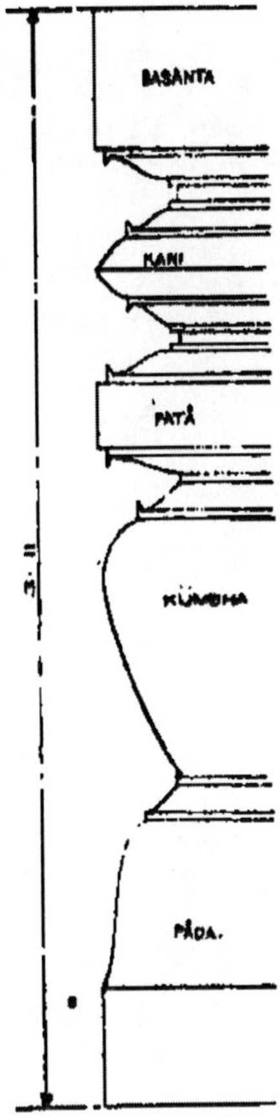

JANGHA
OR
PÂNCH KÂMA.
FIG. I.

SANDHANÂ
OR
TINKÂMA.
FIG II.

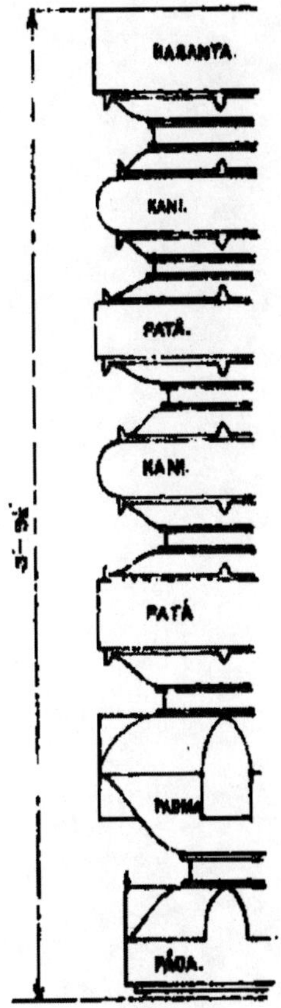

UPPER JANGHÂ
OR
SAPTAKÂMA
FIG III

THE BADA MOULDINGS OF THE TEMPLE OF SIDDHESVARA.

The *Kani* is like the *Patâ* except that the fillet is replaced by two sloped lines. The *Kani* ends in a groove or recess, and over it rests the *Basanta* which is a veritable cyma recta supporting a fillet.

The following measurements taken down by me *in situ* at the Brahmesvara temple at Bhubanesvara will convey some idea as to the relative proportions of the above five elements of *Panchakarma* or *Janghâ*.

The height of *Janghâ*	„	3′-9¾″
The height of *Pâda*	„	1′-4″
„ „ „ *Kûmbha*	„	1′-⅛″
„ „ „ *Patâ*	„	0′-8⅛″
„ „ „ *Kani*	„	0′-4⅛″
„ „ „ *Basanta*	„	0′-4¼″

From the above data we may safely fix the following proportions of the elements. *Pâda* : *Kûmbha* : *Patâ* : *Kani* : *Basanta* :: 4A : 4A : 2A : A : A, where A is some constant.

I draw the reader's attention to the proportions in Plate IV. A. taken from the temple of Siddhesvara.

The *Bârândi* is a recess between the *Janghâ* and *Bandhanâ* (Vide plate.—XV). It is meant to contain human figures in *alto-relievo*; the *Bârândi* contains niches at regular intervals for Dikpalas or the presiding deities of the cardinal points of compass (Vide plates, VII, X). The niche portion of the

Bárându usually consists of the *bâda* or the rectangular recess for the figure, *châla* or a forward projection resembling an awning, and the *mastaka* or the moulding at the top. (Vide plate X). In very elaborate *Bârândıs* the niched portion consists of the following four parts from below :—

(*a*) *Khür Pristha*

(*b*) *Bâda*

(*c*) *Châla*

(*d*) *Mastaka.*

Khür Pristha is like the *patâ* of the *janghâ* having a bead in the centre, instead of a fillet or horizontal projection ; this is surmounted by a moulding resembling a cornice in miniature.

Bâda is rather recessed, and presents a plain surface. In the *Bâda* referred to are placed small statuettes. *Mastaka* rests upon the awning and lends a special charm to the awning below by the distribution of light and shade.

In an ordinary *Pida Dewl,* the *Bâda* or cube has the following three parts :—

(*a*) *Janghâ*, worked or plain.

(*b*) *Bârândi.*

(*c*) Upper *Janghâ*,

In important ones, the *Bâda* consists of the usual parts as in a *rekha dewl,* e.g. the Jagamohanas of Lingaraja, Ananta-Vasüdeva, &c.

The walls of the *Báda* rise straight up, and from the *Báda* rises the curvilinear tower. The walls of the Dorians used to be built with a slight inward slant; the Uriyas resembled the Ionians in this respect, who made their walls perfectly vertical.

I have dwelt at great length on the details of a *Báda* or cube of an Orissa, temple. I shall now pass on to the tower.

In a Rekha Dewl, as I have already stated, the tower is curvilinear, and in Piḍa Dewl, it is pyramidal.

In an ordinary temple, the tower rises from the edge of the *Báda*, but in large ones there is a recess or set back of about two inches. The tower rising in courses slopes upwards very gradually by an imperceptible diminution of projections. The last course of stones is called the *Ghád Chakdá*, (Plate. II) or the shoulder course. The curvilinear tower just below the shoulder course has half the width of the *Báda*. The pyramidal tower of a Pi*d*a Dewl has also the shoulder course; over it is the cylindrical portion called Beki or neck.

The plate. II. illustrates in detail the different parts from *Ghád Chakdá* to the top of the pinnacle.

The Beki is the cylindrical portion just above the shoulder course resembling the neck of human physiognomy. The portion above the Beki resembles the head of a human body, and that below reaching up to the *Báda* is, as it were, the trunk of the temple. Above the Beki is the *Amlá Sree*, resembling *Amlaki*, as far as its ribbed surface is concerned, but more flattened than the natural berry.

In the space between the *Amlá Sree* and shoulder course are placed at regular intervals four female figures called Dewl Charani or the mistress, or custodian of the temple. These are placed just over the R*ahapagas* or central pilasters, and hence point to the four cardinal points of the compass. In the four corners of this recess are placed the figures of lions. The haunches of two lions placed back to back meeting in each corner end in a single head; these are technically called Düpichh*a* Sinha.

Over the *Amlá* rests a short cylindrical portion called Tripatadh*ara*, supporting the Karpüri, the outlines of which resemble an umbrella. A vertical section drawn through Karpüri would look like a trapezium with the slant sides replaced by cyma reversa, the curvature of which is much flattened.

From the top of Karpüri commences the Kalasa with its pedestal.

I give below *ad seriatim* the details of Kalasa from Kalasa-p*a*da or base of finial upwards.

(1) Kalasap*a*da—a cylindrical portion surmounted by a segment of sphere having a short height. (c of plate III).

(2) Kalasap*a*da Dori—It is a moulding separating the Kalasap*a*da from the Kalasa proper.

(3) Kalasa—with a moulding in the centre resembling a bead and running round it. (b of plate III).

(4) Kalasa Beki—the neck of Kalasa.

(5) Tripatadh*ara*.

(6) Kalasa Karpüri.

(7) Gha*di*—resembling a pitcher. (a of plate III).

Over the Ghadi is the trident or the discus as the case may be.

I give below the proportions of the above in case of a *Pida dewl*.

The diameter of Beki is half the maximum breadth of Gh*ad* Chak*da*. The diameter of the moulding above it is that of the Beki added to ¼ its height (i. e. of Beki).

The diameter of the *S*ree must be ascertained by drawing lines ftom the extreme ends of the *pidas* to the *kalasapāda* (vide plate III). The diameter of *kalasa* in the centre should be equal to the height of the *kalasa* measured from its base to the bottom of the *karpüri* above it.

The diameter of *karpüri* above *kalasa* should be half of the height of *kalasa* from its base to the bottom of *karpüri*.

The height of the *pidas* depends upon the number chosen; an odd number of them is usually employed as 3, 5, 7, etc.; I have, however, noticed deviations in several cases.

The height of the *pidas* taken together including the *ghâdchakdâ* and forming a frustum of pyramid is usually ¾ the height of the *bâda*; the height of the portion from the top of *ghâdchakdâ* to the base of *kalasa* or finial is usually ¾ the frustum of pyramid already referred to.

(*a*) The *Beki* = ½ the last *pida* with *ghâdchakdâ*.

(*b*) The *Sree* = 1½ *Beki*

(*c*) The *Tripataahâra* = ¼ *Sree*

(*d*) The *Karpüri* above *Sree* = ¾ *Sree*

(*e*) The *dori* above *karpuri* = *Tripatadhâra*

(*f*) The *Sejüpatrapâkhudâ* = ¾ *Sree*

(*g*) The *Beki* below *Amlâ* = ¼ of (*f*)

(*h*) The *Amlâ* = ¾ (*f*)

(*i*) The *Karpüri* of *Amlâ* = ½ of (*h*)

(*j*) The *Kalasapâda* = ½ (*i*)

(*k*) The *dori* in the middle of *kalasa* should be as high as the base of the *kalasa*.

The breadth of the *ghâdchakdâ* should be equal to the height of the *pidas* taken together.

The *pida* should project beyond the *bâda* or the cubical portion by a length equal to half the height of the upper *Janghâ*.

The proportions are a little different in a Rekha dewl, and are as follow.

The height of the *Amlá* should be twice that of *Beki*; the height of *karpüri* above *Amlá* should be the same as that of *Beki*; that of *Kalaspáda* is ⅛ of *karpüri*; the *kalasa* should be the same as in the case of a *Pida dewl.* I have fixed the above proportions by studying numerous cases; the above proportions are tabulated in the following list.

Beki = *Amlaka Silá*

Tripatadhára = ⅓ *Amlaka Silá.*

Amlaka Silá = *Amlá karpüri.*

Kalasapáda-dori = ⅛ *kalasa-handi.*

Kalasa dori = ¼ *kalasa-handi.*

Kalasa Beki = ¼ *kalasa-handi.*

Tripatadhára = *kalasa beki.*

Kalasa (including *dori* but including *ghadi*) = 1¾ Amlá.

The maximum width of the *kalasa-handi* = ½ the height of *kalasa* including *páda* and *dori.*

On referring to Plate II. it will be seen that the portion of the Rekha in the prolongation of the *konakapága* is divided into certain portions separated from one another by *Amlaka Silá*; these divisions are called *Bhümis* or planes; in the sketch referred to, I have shown five *bhümis*; a temple having some pretension to importance usually contains ten such *bhümis* (vide plate—XVII); the heights of these divisions are not equal; their relative proportions are given below.

First *Bhūmi* = ¾ the width or length of *konakapāga*
Second „ = ¾ of the first *bhūmi*.
Third „ = ¾ of the second *bhūmi*.
Fourth „ = ¾ of the third *bhūmi*.
&c, &c, &c.

Thus we see that the heights of the *Bhūmis* form a geometrical series, having ¾ as the common multiple.

In the *Anarthapāga* above the *bāda* are (usually) seen representations of *rekhadewl* with intervening projections of *kani*, and *basanta*, the *rekhadewls* diminishing in size as the *ghādchakdā* or the topping course is reached (vide plate II.); exceptions are, however, noticed in the temples of Muktesvara, Parasūramesvara, Vaital. There are deep vertical recesses noticeable between the *pāgas*; but in some cases, as in the temple of Muktesvara, the recess between the *konakapāga* and *anarthapāga* is carved with panels at regular intervals containing female figures.

The *rāhāpāga* above *bāda* consists of plain horizontal projections, the face of which is usually carved; just above the *bāda*, the figure of lion projects, and over this is noticed an ornamental device consisting of concentric circles, the outermost member of which has the curve divided and the ends turned up into spirals; these circles are often flattened, and are hence more or less elliptical, and they are in many cases found to be eccentric. These circles are flanked by reclining human figures, and resemble, when taken together, a representation of the armorial insignia. The whole ornamental device is technically called Bho or भो, and is classified as per the details in the innermost circle; as an illustration, if it contains the figure of lotus, it is called Padma Bho (पद्म भो), if that of Narayana, it is called Narayana Bho, as on the eastern face of the Vaital dewl, etc. The height of the Bho is nearly equal to the *janghâ*, or the first element of the *bâda*; over the Bho, is noticed the figure of lion resting on an elephant on a slab of stone and projecting from the *râhâpâga*; higher up on the *râhâpâga* on the side facing the Jagamohana is seen a huge lion projecting from the *rekha*, and floating, as it were, in the mid-air; it is situated at half the height of the *rekha* from the *bâda* to the *kalasa* or finial.

In some cases, the *râhâpâga* is formed by representations of *rekha dewls* receding back from one another, and at different heights; the Rajarani temple is a nice illustration of this (vide plate XIV); in these cases the *dewl* is called a *rekhà pancha-mundi dewl*, or a *rekha dewl* having five pinnacles, viz., one central and four on the sides.

The height of a *rekha dewl* is generally 2⅙ the length of

Height. the *bâda* measured between the *râhâpâgas* or central pilasters. In very few cases, however, the height becomes three times the length. I have carefully measured the heights of several temples promiscuously, and have deduced therefrom the following proportions. The measurements are given below in round numbers.

	Length.	Height.	Proportion.
Müktesvara temple ...	15′	34′	2·3
Rajarani temple ...	17′	46′	2·7
Temple of Jagannath at Puri.	80′	209′*	2·6
Ananta Vasüdeva temple	22′	60′	2·7

In the case of the temple of Siddhesvara the proportion rises to 3; and strangely, in the case of the great Lingaraja, at Bhubanesvara, the proportion becomes less than 2.

Generally speaking, it may be asserted that in the case of Orissan temples, the height of the Vimana bears a ratio of 2·5 to the length of the base; this ratio has been recommended in the Agni Puranam; there the ratio has been made to range between 2 and 3.†

It may be mentioned here that the classification of the temples into five classes as quoted by Ram Raz from Kasyapa in his treatise on the "Architecture of the Hindus" does not

* This height is recorded with reference to the ground level of the Uttara Parsva Math on the courtyard of which the theodolite was set up. This is at a lower level than the quadrangle of the temple, which again starts from a plinth; hence the proportion in column 4 comes down to 2·5.

† Agni Puranam, 225th Chapter.

hold good in this part of India ; that classification is, I believe, applicable in the Deccan.*

The rules of the Agni Pur*a*nam were followed in Orissa as far as practicable in those days. In the Brihat Samhit*a*, the ratio has been fixed at 2. This ratio is not found to obtain in practice in Orissa in the Mediæval times.

I have already remarked that the *bâda* of a *rekha dewl* is either a cube or a rectangular parallelopiped. The temple of Siddhe*s*vara may be cited as an example of the first case ; for the length, breadth, and height of the *bâda* are 16 feet each, and hence it is a veritable cube. On working out the ratio borne by the height to the length of the *bâda* in many cases, I have seen that it ranges between ·65 to ·72. I give below the following figures in a tabular form.

	Length of *bâda.*	Height of *bâda.*	Ratio.
Ananta V*â*südeva ...	22′-1″	16′-1″	·72
Para*s*ür*a*me*s*vara ...	19′-9″	14′-3″	·72
Mükte*s*vara ...	15′	10′-9″	·71
Vait*a*l	20′	13′-11″	·70
Vim*a*na of Lingar*a*ja ...	66′	43′-5⅝″	·66

* It may be mentioned here incidentally that on referring to the book by Ram Raz, it appears that the proportions quoted by Dr. Mitra in the foot-note of page 57 Indo-Aryans, Vol. I. are incorrect. Dr. Rajendra Lal, I believe, took those proportions from General Cunningham, and not from the text itself.

It may be stated here that by the term "height of the *bâda*" he external height is meant; the internal height of a *bâda* is ess than the external one, for internal corbelling or bracketting commences at a less height inside than outside.

The height of a *rekha dewl* exclusive of the *kalasa* or finial is usually three times the height of the *bâda*.

Names.	Height of *bâda.*	Height of the Rekha dewl exclusive of Kalasa.	Ratio.
Müktesvara temple	10′-9″	31′	3 (app.)
Siddhesvara temple	16′	47′	3 "
Lingaraja at Bhubanesvara.	43′-5″	127′-1	3 "

Regarding the height of the Lingaraja without the *kalasa* it may be stated that the theodolite was set up in the compound of the local school to the south of the temple; the height of the temple may, for all practical purposes, be taken as three times the height of the *bâda*, for there is a discrepancy of 2 or 3 ft. only in respect of the calculated height according to the Brihat Samhita. From my professional experience of buildings in Calcutta, I have carefully noticed that in 95 per cent. of cases the deviation in height from the sanctioned plans is about 1 ft in an average two-storeyed building of 24 ft. in height: according to this rate the modern architects in constructing a building as high as the temple at Bhubanesvara would have a tendency to exceed the theoretical height by about 5'-6"; this difficulty will be aggravated in a building which is curvilinear in section, has constructive peculiarities, and in which stone is used as the building material; hence it may be reasonably stated that in the case of the temple of Lingar*a*ja, the modern architects would exceed the height by 10 to 11 ft.; and this will happen in an age when harsh Municipal laws act in all their rigour to enforce conformity to sanctioned plans.

The rule laid down in Brihat Samhit*a* is that the height of a temple should be three times the perpendicular height of the rectangular portion*; and the above figures in the tabular form will prove that the rule of Brihat Samhit*a* has been strictly followed.

There is another style prevalent in the Puri district which

Vait*a*l Dewl. is distinctly exotic in origin; a temple of this style is called a Vait*a*l Dewl (Vide plates XVIII, XIX). This style was imported from the south, and it is rather difficult to detect the exact type of which it forms the counterpart. On a careful examination of this style, I have come to the conclusion

* "उच्छ्रायाद्यस्तृतीयोंऽशस्तेन तुल्या कटिर्भवेत्" ॥ ११

वराहसंहितायां प्रासादलक्षणं नाम षट्पञ्चाशत्तमोऽध्यायः ॥

that it bears a close affinity to the *ratkas* of Mahavellipore, the earliest date of which can be assigned to the fourth century A. D. The crowning member, at least, of the Vaital bears a resemblance to the latter in a remarkable degree. On referring to plate XVIII. it will be seen that the top of the temple is a semi-cylinder showing a semi-ellipse in end elevation; this is surmounted by three crowning elements consisting of *Amlaka*, *Karpuri*, *Kalasa*, &c. as in the case of an ordinary *Rekha Dewl.* The plates XVIII & XIX clearly indicate that there is a break in the continuity of the *rekha* portion of the tower effected by means of a recess which resembles the neck of human physiognomy, and hence the semi-cylindrical crowning member has been styled *mastaka* or head of the structure; it is solid in construction. The portion below the recess referred to does not resemble exactly the *rekha* ending in *ghâd chakdâ* already explained. The *rekha* of plate XIX is nearly similar to the *mastaka* in general appearance. The *mastaka* (Plate XIX) is technically called *Vaitâ*, and hence the name of the *dewl.* The term *Vaitâ* is probably a contraction of the Sanskrit word Vahitra which means a sea-going vessel or a ship. The external appearance of the *mastaka* is similar to the hull of a ship reversed, and with the ends removed by planes at right angles to the longitudinal axis. The three crowning members resemble the masts of a ship. The *rathas* of Mahavellipore from which this style, has been derived are also provided with similar finials crowning the main structure.

The *mastaka* might probably have been derived from the fruit *Vaitâ*, a sort of pumpkin gourd, or more properly *Vaitâ—kakhâru*, much relished by the people of Orissa as is evidenced by the adage quoted below *. Whatever be the derivation of the term there is not the least doubt that this style is indicative of a decided Dravidian origin manifested in the general outline and sculpture of the structure, described in Chapter VIII. In this style the *pâgas* or pilasters are not prominent, and the temple described in chapter VIII is, therefore, *Ekaratha* or *Chaurasa* or square or rectangular in ground plan.

There is, however, still another class of Orissan style which is rather a non-descript. I have explained its details in chapter VIII; it is called *Gaurichâra*, the name being evidently derived from Gauri, a goddess enshrined in a temple of this style; the plate XI, however, shows the present temple of Gauri Devi after the restoration of the roof which was in a dilapidated condition.

Gauri Chara Dewl.

The selection of site is a very important item in the construction of temples; the soil is very carefully examined before the site is approved of. In the Agni-Puranam,

Selection of site.

* बैता कखारु भजा खाविबि पखाल

240th. chapter, I have come across a few rules to be observed in the selection of a site. The soil, according to its quality is assigned to the Brahmins, Kshatriyas, Vaisyas, and Sūdras respectively; and this classification is based on the colour of the soil, and the scent emitted by it; from the description given, I judge the soil assigned to the Brahmins to be loamy in character, those to the Kshatriyas and Vaisyas to be ferruginous, that of the former being evidently more rocky; the soil assigned to the Sūdras is the worst of all, being black cotton soil, perhaps oozy, and "emitting the smell of wine". In the Agni-Puranam, the soil filled up with bones, ashes has been forbidden to be selected as a suitable site for a building. The reason is not far to seek; for a soil made up of these things never attains the solidity or homogeneity necessary for the base of a structure; I have seen the tanks filled up by ashes or some such things when dug up after 30 years of their filling in present the same original condition of the contents without any consolidation or homogeneity being effected. The Agni-Puranam has prescribed many religious ceremonies to be performed at the time of selecting a site with which we are not concerned.

Ram Raz has quoted a rule from the Kasyapa which is very ingenious in ascertaining the suitability of the ground to be used as a site. I quote the rule below. "Having dug a pit a *hasta* (cubit) in depth, in the middle of the ground return the earth into it, and according to the space which the latter may now take up with reference to that which it occupied before the digging of the pit, whether more, less, or the same, the ground should be considered as good, bad, or indifferent; the good and indifferent sorts are acceptable, but the bad should by all means be avoided." *

I have come across an exactly similar passage in the Matsya Pur*a*nam.

The rule quoted above does not require any elucidation; it has been observed by all that the earth taken out of a solid and homogeneous plot of land has greater cubical contents than the pit or hole from which it is dug out; the prohibition by the Agni Pur*a*nam of the soil filled up with ashes, &c. is noticed in this text in a nut-shell.

The next point in the Architecture of the Orissan temples is the determination of the cardinal points of the compass. The temples of Orissâ usually face the east, so that the observer looking at the image will have his face turned towards the west. There are some temples, however, which form exceptions to the general rule, *e.g.*, Mükte*s*vara, Parasur*a*me*s*vara, etc. The builders of the temple are found to punctiliously observe the rule regarding direction. I have seen

Direction.

* Ram Raz, The Architecture of the Hindus, p. 17.

that this practice is often followed now; while at Konarka, I made a careful survey of the temple with the prismatic compass, and theodolite, and found that the direction from the true north is so very slight that it may be neglected. A greater error is nowadays committed by a practical surveyor having accurate mathematical instruments to work with. I give below the data collected by me.

The magnetic bearing of the eastern doorway of the Jagamohana determined several times lies between 1°30′ and 1°15′; it may fairly accurately be taken as 1°22′30″. The magnetic bearing of the southern doorway running from east to west, determined several times lies between 271°15′ and 271° 30′; hence it may fairly be taken to be 271° 22′ 30″.

On referring to the Surveyor General, India, I am informed that the magnetic north at present is 1° 16′ east of the true north at the town of Puri; but as the village of Konarka is about 20 miles distant from the town of Puri as the crow flies, the magnetic direction may be taken as the same at both the places; hence the deviation from the true north of the north line determined by the Orissan architects amounts only to 6′ 30″ which is negligible; this receives additional weight from the consideration that the magnetic deflection *at present*, is 1° 16′ and nothing is recorded as to what was the case so many centuries ago; it might have been 1° 22′ 30″

From the above it is apparent that the directions used to be ascertained carefully before laying out the foundation. By reference to the ceremony of Dikpati Yaga mentioned in Chapter VI, it will be seen than an accurate determination of the points of the compass was an important part of the duties of an architect.

The directions used to be determined, and are so done at present in many parts of India, by the method of Gnomon or *Sanku*. This method, though not very accurate in ascertaining the true direction, is enough for all practical purposes, and hence a method exactly similar to this one has been invented in modern treatises on surveying, viz., Roorkee Treatise on Surveying. I quote below this rough method as described in the Sūrya Siddhanta.* I may mention incidentally that the accurate method of ascertaining the directions was well-known to the Indian astronomers. The principle of the gnomon or *Sankū* is as follows. The gnomon of a definite height is to be erected on a plot of land, the level of which is to be tested

* शिलातलेऽम्बुसंशुद्धे वज्रलेपेऽपि वा समे ।
तत्र शङ्क्वङ्गुलैरिष्टैः समं मण्डलमालिखेत् ॥
तन्मध्ये स्थापयेच्छङ्कुं कल्पनाद्वादशाङ्गुलम् ।
तच्छायाग्रं स्पृशेद्यत्र वृत्ते पूर्वापरार्धयोः ॥
तत्र बिन्दू विधायोभौ वृत्ते पूर्वापराभिधौ ।
तन्मध्ये तिमिना रेखा कर्तव्या दक्षिणोत्तरा ॥
याम्योत्तरदिशोर्मध्ये तिमिना पूर्वपश्चिमा ।
दिङ्मध्यमत्स्यैः संसाध्या विदिशस्तद्वदेव हि ॥
इति सूर्यसिद्धान्ते तृतीयोऽध्यायः त्रिप्रश्नाधिकारः ।

by water; describe a circle of a definite diameter with the foot of this gnomon as centre. On the circumference of this circle the gnomon casts its shadow which moves along as the Sun moves in its diurnal course. Mark on the circumference the shadow cast by the gnomon just a definite period after and before sunrise and sunset; the extremities of the line joining the above two marks will roughly indicate the east and west, the former being represented by the shadow of the gnomon in the afternoon. Describe two more circles with these two points as centres, and the length of the line joining them as diameter. The straight line joining the points of intersection of these two circles points towards the north and south.

The soil of Orissa has a hard substratum of laterite a few feet below the surface; unlike other buildings trenches for

Foundation:—

foundation were not dug, but the whole surface proposed to be covered used to be excavated till the hard substratum was reached; the whole surface was then built up with stone, and from the plinth level the walls were to be raised.

The temples of any importance are generally provided with a plinth; but there are many important temples which have no

Plinth or *Upanam* (उपानं):—

plinth at all; as a typical case the temple of Lingar*a*ja at Bhubane*s*vara may be cited as an example; it can therefore be expected that the small temples scattered here and there at Bhubane*s*vara should show no plinth, and should therefore start at once from the pavement or *tala-pattana.*

The plinth in the case of some temples is very high (Vide Plates XV. A, XXII, XXV); the plinth in many cases consists of two tiers; and in only one instance I have noticed it to consist of 3 tiers as in the Bhogamandapa of the temple at Konarka.

In the case of a plinth consisting of two elements, the upper one is called the *Khür Pristha*, and the lower, the *Tala-Pristha;* the former recedes back from the latter by several inches. In a temple dedicated to Vishnu, the Khür Pristha is carved with the petals of lotus, and in a *S*aiva temple, no such carving is noticeable; a temple dedicated to *S*iva does not usually consist of the two elements noticed above. It may be mentioned here that this *Khür Pristha* is higher than the *Talapristha*; the following figures will convey some idea as to their dimensions.

(1) Ananta Vasüdeva temple :—

Bhogamandapa :—

(*a*) Tala Pristha...........2′—3⅝″

(*b*) Khür Pristha..........3′—1¼″

Jagamohana :—

(*a*) Tala Pristha..... ......1′—1″

(*b*) Khür Pristha..........3′—11″

(2) Rajarani temple :—

(*a*) Tala Pristha.........8..1′—11″

(*b*) Khür Pristha..........2′—7″

(3) Bhogamandapa at Konarka :—

(*a*) Tala Pristha............2′—1″

(*b*) Khür Pristha.........9′—7″

(*c*) Upper Khür Pristha...4′—5″

The Khür Pristha of Rajarani temple is very beautiful by reason of the mouldings shown on the face. (Vide Plate XV). It consists of *Pâda*, *Kani*, and *Basanta*, and the intervening narrow recesses are carved with *jâli* or lattice work. The Tala Pristha usually presents a plain face.

The Indo-Aryan style is eminently astylar; its very form does not admit of the introduction of pillars or columns for external decoration. In *S*ukra Niti, too, I have come across the passage* quoted in the foot-note, prohibiting the use of columns in a building or a temple surmounted by a spire; columns are, however, used inside the structure in some cases, not of course, in a Vimana or sanctum; they are used mainly as props for the ceiling, and not for any ornamental purpose, and from these

Pedestal or *Upapitha* (उपपीठ) :—

* प्रासादे मण्डपे वापि शिखरं यदि चाचरेत् ।
[illegible] न चालंकारविधिविधान शुभप्रदा ॥ १११ ॥
शुक्रनीतिसारे [illegible] चतुर्थप्रकरणम् ।

columns foiled arches spring to carry the roofing. I may mention here that the arches referred to are formed by horizontal corbelling.

Column.

In Orissa we do not find the principle of column much developed; and even those met with in very important temples are without any ornamental pedestal as we come across in the southern part of India. The columns here rest on plain rectangular pedestals; I may, as a typical illustration, cite the case of the Bhogamandapa at Konarka; such an elaborately carved structure standing on three tiers of plinth receding from one another is provided with four columns inside, standing on pedestals 2′—10″ high presenting a bare appearance and having not a single carving, or a moulding including a fillet or a bead to decorate their surfaces. The bases of the columns in the Bhogmanadapa of the great Lingaraja temple are most disgusting; these have been rendered all the more so by the way in which the plaster coat has been applied. The artistic taste of even a connoisseur of art receives a rude shock at the bareness of the pedestals. Not to speak of carvings or mouldings, we do not even notice the necessary offset given to the column at the top of the pedestal in order to present an appearance of stability.

There is another defect in the construction of columns in Orissa. The column as a structural whole has definite component parts, e.g., the pedestal, base, shaft and entablature; the columns here have no shaft or entablature clearly defined; from the pedestal rises the column showing the characteristic mouldings of the outer wall of the *bâda*; then the purely rectangular portion continues till the springing line is reached; exception is, however, furnished by the *Arûna Stambha* standing in front of the eastern gateway of the temple of Jagannath at Puri (vide Plate XX); in that case, I may say, exception proves the rule.

A later development in the principle of columns is, however, noticed in the pillars of the cook-room to the southeast of the Jagamohana at Konarka; the structure does not exist, nor is there any trace of it except a few columns scattered here and there; in this case we notice a definite column base, a shaft, and an entablature; the columns are octagonal and tapering from below upwards; stop-chamfering is noticeable in the base of the column to make the shaft more sharply defined; the entablature has a distinct abacus.

Construction of walls :—

The walls of the temples are made wholly of stones; they are not hollow. Great care has been taken in building the two faces of the wall, and the interior filling in of walls with rubble stones does not appear to have been neglected by the Uriya architects. I have studied this with advantage in the walls of the sanctum at Konarka.

The interior of the wall is solidly packed with horizontal blocks of stone laid in courses; I have noticed the introduction of wedge-shaped blocks of stone in the interior; this is calculated to ensure the solidity and stability of the interior to a great extent; these blocks of stone have been evenly laid and connected together with iron cramps. The Uriya architects were perfectly aware that a careless filling in of the interior would effect an unequal settlement of the wall, and would accordingly hasten its collapse. This care on their part made them dispense with the use of thorough bond stones at regular intervals. The walls present ashlar faces consisting of carefully dressed blocks of stone. The treatises on Hindu Architecture, and the Puranas lay particular stress on the use of well-dressed cubical or rectangular blocks of stone. I have already quoted a passage page 102) from the Matsya Puranam directing the use of such stones.

A conscious attempt is noticed at breaking the vertical joints, or in other words, preventing a vertical joint between any two blocks of stone in one course from being in a continuous line with that between any other two in a course above or below the one already mentioned. Their attempt, however, is not successful, and the breaking of joints is not what is expected; in some cases the joints have not been broken at all, and in some, the lap

Bonds :—

between two contiguous vertical joints is so small that they form for all practical purposes a continuous vertical joint; in many cases I have noticed the masons to be very careful in maintaining bonds, and in many others, to be very careless; for instance, I have noticed the blocks of stone of the Konak-paga in many cases, to be inserted skilfully into spaces for the Anartha-paga, while in others I have observed very fearful gaping, and continuous vertical openings between the Konaka and Anartha pagas. It may be mentioned here that this disregard or rather want of thorough regard for the bond as an effective means of ensuring the stability of a structure has brought about the collapse of many temples; this is due to water gaining access through the interstices, and reaching the the iron cramps which are oxidised by the combined action of water and air, swell in volume, and thereby cause a great strain, too great for the stone blocks to resist; and they have a tendency to splinter off accordingly. Stone dowels, if used instead of cramps, would have rendered the structures more lasting; and the engineers of the P. W. D. have acted very wisely in using stone dowels for connecting the blocks of stone together in the works of restoration and repair.

We can not blame the Orissan architects for the use of iron cramps; for their use is noticeable from very ancient times.

The Persians also used to have recourse to this device in connecting together huge blocks of stone.*

I have already remarked that the blocks of stone are noticed to have been laid horizontally; I have in many cases tested the perpendicularity of the walls with a plumb bob; the walls are true to the plumb line; to this fact coupled with that of perfect horizontality of courses is mainly due the stability of the edifice.

Plumb :—

The thickness of walls is guided by the proportion and height of the edifice to be raised. I have tried to fix a definite formula for the thickness of walls; I am glad to be able to say that my efforts have been partially crowned with success in case of a *Pida Dewl.* I have been able to determine an equation which will yield fairly accurate results. It is as follows :—

Thickness of walls :—

The thickness of the wall of a *Pida Dewl* = $\frac{1}{2}x.A$, where x = distance between the R*a*h*a*p*a*gas; A varies from $\frac{6}{14}$ to $\frac{6}{21}$ or $\frac{3}{7}$ to $\frac{2}{7}$.

Let me verify the accuracy of the equation by citing the following cases.

Müktesvara temple :—

Length of the Jagamohana between the R*a*h*a*p*a*gas = 26′

Theoretical thickness according to the above equation should be $= \frac{1}{2} \times 26 \times \frac{6}{15} = \frac{78}{15} = 5'\text{-}2\frac{2}{5}''$

It is curious to note that discrepancy is nil in this case.

* Perrot and Chipiez, History of Art in Persia.

Ananta Vasudeva temple :— (*a*) The length of the Jagamohana between the R*a*h*a*p*a*gas = 33′.

Theoretical thickness $= \frac{1}{2} \times 33 \times \frac{6}{14} = \frac{99}{14} \doteq 7\frac{1}{14} = 7'$ (say)

Actual maximum thickness $= \frac{33-19}{2} = 7'$

Discrepancy is nil.

(*b*) The length of the N*a*tmandir = 24′

Theoretical thickness $= \frac{1}{2} \times 24 \times \frac{6}{21} = \frac{24}{7} = 3' - 5^{1}/_{7}''$

Actual maximum thickness $= \frac{24' - (17' - 4'')}{2} = 3' - 4''$

Discrepancy = 1 inch which may be neglected.

(*c*) The length of the N*a*tmandir = 29′

Theoretical thickness $= \frac{1}{2} \times 29 \times \frac{6}{17} = \frac{87}{17} = 5' - 1\frac{1}{2}''$

Actual maximun thickness $= \frac{29 - (18' - 9'')}{2} = \frac{10' - 3''}{2} = 5' - 1\frac{1}{2}''$

Discrepancy is nil.

Doors, windows and niches. The doorways of the temple have square perpendicular sides; the jambs are not splayed or chamfered so as to make the entrance look wider. On referring to plate IV. illustrating the plan of a Pancharatha Dewl it will be clear that the jambs are too thick to render splaying effective in any way; besides, the width of the doorway of important temples is usually so great as to dispense with splaying as an effective means of facilitating ingress and egress; for the friction caused by the rush of pilgrims for so many centuries has not been so much as to make the arrises lose their straight outline.

Only one doorway leads from the Jagamohana to the *dewl* which is not provided with any side-doorway, Side-doors are noticeable in the Jagamohana, Natmandira, and Bhogamandira. I may state here incidentally that the arrangements for the introduction of light and air in an Orissan temple, nay in one of the Indo-Aryan style are most unsatisfactory. The reason of it has been clearly stated in the next chapter.

The Dewl is not provided with any window or any other opening either for light, air or outlook. The Jagamohana, however, is often provided with side-windows consisting of balusters (vide plate XIV), as in the Lingaraja, Rajarani, Siddhesvara temples, or windows containing perforations, rectangular, or diamonded as in Müktesvara, Parasürامesvara temples. Vide plate IX.

There is, however, noticed an exotic style of window opening or more properly inlet windows technically called clerestory windows, as in the Jagamohana of Parasürameşvara, Vaital (vide plates XII, XVIII). The clerestory may be likened to a sky-light, and is formed by a small upper storey perforated with small windows, and surmounting the main lower storey. The upper storey is formed by a sloping roof supported on wedge-shaped uprights the intervals between which form the clerestory windows.

Non-provision of window openings is a characteristic defect

of the Orissan, nay of the Indo-Aryan style of Architecture.

Niches. Niches occupy the position of the windows. These serving no purpose for the provision of light and air are simply meant to decorate the outer faces of the temple. These niches contain images of gods or goddesses described at great length in the sixth chapter. They are surmounted by a canopy or tiers of canopies (vide plates VII, XIII) receding back from each other, and nicely decorated with carvings. These canopies crown the niche proper or the recess (vide plates VII, X) or the entire width made up of the recess and the two pilasters flanking it (vide plate XIII) as in the cases of Müktesvara and Brahmesvara. In cases where the canopies surmount the recess only they are usually topped by a sort of dripstone moulding (vide plate VII) resembling *Pâda*.

This arrangement of protecting the niches by canopies is at once simple, and elegant. The Gothic gable with side pinnacles, as is noticed in the Cathedral of Florence*, or the Renaissance front or upholstery replacing the former as in the porch of the church of St. Appollinare, would be but poor substitutes for this simple contrivance.

It is a matter of great wonder as to how could so very

Hoisting of stone blocks and iron beams. heavy stones and iron beams be raised to such a great height before the invention of steam engine,

* Ruskin, The Stones of Venice, vol. I., p. 175 (edited by L. March. Phillips.)

wirerope, derrick or pulley block. Our imagination is raised to its highest pitch in trying to discover the contrivances that the Hindu architects had recourse to in raising, fitting and fixing these heavy beams and blocks of stone. The huge stone figure of the lion meant for the Vimana at Konarka was raised to a height of about 100 ft., and was brought from a quarry at a distance of many miles from the actual site of work across forests, swamps and rivers with inadequate means of communication.

It is still a problem for the modern engineers to ascertain the method used by the ancient school of architects; they explain away the difficulty by assuming that the Orissan architects resorted to the contrivance of the inclined plane made of sand, as a statical machine, and that the blocks had to be dragged along the line of the greatest slope; even if we admit the possibility of an inclined plane the question may still be asked as to how they could manipulate such huge blocks at all. There is another difficulty in the assumption of the inclined plane; as the structure increases in height the line of slope changes, and hence this contrivance of the inclined plane is to be adjusted at every step of progress by changing the base and height of the plane, and the difficulty is all the more aggravated if the plane be made up of heaps of sand.

A moment's reflection would make us convince how absurd must be the supposition that the structures were covered with sand both inside and outside as they increased in height, and that the blocks of stone used to be dragged to the required height and position along inclined planes or ramps made of sand. The absence of sand in the locality of Bhubanesvara would be a damaging proof against the accepted supposition; although we cannot exactly determine the contrivances or methods used by them, it can safely be asserted that some sort of staging used to be made certainly over which the blocks of stone used to be hoisted by means of winches; it is not unlikely the case that the Hindus were acquainted with the use of some sort of pulley, however crude it might have been in design; I must admit here that I have gone through the *Sukra Niti* Brihat Samhita, Agni Puranam, and many other treatises on Arts and Architecture very carefully, but nowhere I have come across any technical term for a pulley, or a winch, or a description thereof.

Iron beams. The following fact which I noticed at Konarka, clearly indicative of great engineering skill is worth mentioning. I noticed several beams at Konarka not of uniform cross section, the dimensions of which are quoted below.

Length taken along the centre	...	23′
Thickness at the end	... ...	9¼″
centre	... ...	11″

The above dimensions are of a lintel over the southern

doorway of the Jagamohana; from them it is atonce apparent that the longitudinal section of the lintel presents the form of a parabola. It is a fundamental rule of Applied Mechanics that if a beam be supported at both ends, and uniformly loaded, the maximum bending moment occurs at the centre of the beam, and that the locus of bending moments is a parabola. Hence it follows, that for a beam of uniform strength the breadth is constant, and depth is varied to suit the varying stresses. This principle has exactly been followed in forging these huge iron beams. This reflects a great credit on the architects.

By applying the usual Deflection formula, and taking the usual value of the Modulus of Elasticity of wrought iron, I have tested the stiffness of these beams; and I am very glad to be able to state that the beams are within the prescribed safe limits; stiffness has been secured without any unnecessary waste of material.

Very seldom have I seen the beams or lintels to sag. One memorable example is, however, noticed in the lintels over the southern doorway of the Jagamohana of Lakshmi's temple within the precincts of the temple of Jagannath. This is not probably due to the insufficiency of the section chosen, for the lintel over the eastern doorway has not sagged at all, although it has nearly the same section; the sagging is explained by the fact of the architects having inadvertently placed the lintels along the depth and not along the width, and also having chosen a less number than what would have been sufficient.

The aim of Architecture should, mainly speaking, be fitness, stability and beauty. It should present a harmonious development of these three principles. The Orissan Architecture is pre-eminently a religious one, and as such, its fitness will be dealt with later on; we should always bear in mind that the structures, in question, were not dwelling houses, but places of worship. By its constructive peculiarities, stability has been much more ensured in Orissan Architecture than in other forms; but this has been effected at the sacrifice of economy which, according to Vitruvius, was one of the seven principles of Greek Architecture.

Aim of Architecture.

The style of Orissan temple building rendered economy impossible; this, I have already stated, derives its vital principle from the deeply ingrained sense of permanency. The trabeated style resorted to by the architects ensured stability of the temples, for no inclined thrust is called into play here. It is too obvious to state that the manipulation or statical adjustment of an inclined pressure is very difficult; and the occurrence of unknown agencies renders these inclined thrusts very complex, and hence the equilibrium of the edifice becomes a matter of theoretical speculation which does not invariably obtain in practice. Economy has no doubt

System of forces called into play.

been sacrificed, but with the compensating advantage of stability. The statical equilibrium in an Orissan temple is simply due to the combined action of the simple vertical action and reaction.

The only break in the uniformity of statical design of compression is caused by the use of the architraves where cross strain is called into play. The principle of subjecting materials to cross strain introduces a weak element in the whole system; for the sake of permanency, this weak element involves a waste of materials. It causes a certain amount of uncertainty in permanency so fondly sought to be ensured. The Orissan architects had accordingly to use iron lintels or beams as supports for the stone architraves. Most of the forces affecting the equilibrium of the structure are those of compression. A cross strain calls into play the forces of tension and compression; hence I may say that the Orissan style of construction is a combined one of tension and compression. I call it a Tensio-compressile system.

The durability of the temples is mainly due to the way in which the thrusts are exerted, and to the hugeness and horizontality of the blocks used. The thrusts are

Durability :—

not only perpendicular to the bearing surfaces, but also vertical. This is a great source of strength and durability. The use of vertically perpendicular thrusts, and the elimination of inclined ones may be considered the chief causes to which their durability may be ascribed. The system of trabeation or corbelling entailed to some extent the use of massive blocks. This method of construction gave the walls a tendency to be thrust inwards, and introduced, by its very nature, a weak element. This tendency has been counteracted by the huge topping courses, the Beki, and *A*mlaka ; it is too obvious to explain how the counteraction is effected. By the above remark, I do not mean that the walls would instantly be thrust inwards as soon as the capping or topping course is removed. I have noticed several instances in which the temples are still standing *in situ* although the *A*mlaka has been removed.

The durability of an Orissan temple is mainly due to the factors to which reference has been made ; it is also due to the nature, both chemical and physical, of the component stone blocks of which it is made. The stones principally used are different varieties of sandstone mentioned in the seventh chapter. Stones brought from the locality of Khandgiri hills are coarse-grained, and easily liable to the disintegrating influence of the atmosphere, and as such they easily crumble into pieces.

The durability of stone is also due to the nature of the cementing material of the grains of which it is composed. I have noticed in the seventh chapter that the matrix of some varieties of sandstone employed is calcium carbonate which renders them susceptible to the destroying influence of the atmosphere. Except in the town of Puri, the atmosphere of the place does not fortunately contain any deleterious substance that might hasten the disintegration of the stones. The Rangd*a*lim*a* variety of sandstone containing ferric oxide and fine grains of quartz or silica is very durable, and the temples built of them do not show the least trace of disintegration anywhere.

The temples on the sea-side, and in tracts containing sand dunes as at Puri, Kon*a*raka, are less durable than those in the interior. The drift sand being blown by high wind against the face of the temples gradually grinds it away; and so we notice a marked difference in the relative durability of temples built of the same variety of sandstone in the interior and near sea-side respectively. There is another source affecting the durability of the structure to a considerable extent. The stone blocks are noticed to have been connected together by iron cramps doubled over; when rain water gains access to them through the interstices between the blocks, they invariably become oxidised, swell in volume, and cause an unusual strain; and thus the stone blocks are sometimes detached or displaced from their initial position. I have seen such displacement in many cases.

CHAPTER VI.

Very aptly has Fergusson remarked regarding the Linga-Raj temple, Bhubanesvara that "if it would take a sum—say a lakh of rupees or pounds—to erect such a building as this, it would take three lakhs to carve it as this one is carved."* There is a great truth underlying the above statement. It is an unmistakable indication of their earnestness to make such an expensive outlay; for there was nothing which they prized so highly as religion. It was the be-all and end-all of their lives. Every thing they did was ascribable to this instinct. Religion was the mainspring of their activities. It was not an excrescence, but a vital part of the system. Hence it is natural that their architecture which was an outcome of their deep-seated religious instinct should be pervaded by a sense of earnestness. In this respect they were even superior to the Greeks, not to speak of the Romans. The religion of the Romans was borrowed from the Greeks, and was a matter of form, and hence lacked in earnestness. The Greeks somewhat attempted at self-glorification; the ideal of the Hindus was self-abnegation.

The Spiritual basis of Orissan decoration.

* Fergusson, History of Indian and Eastern Architecture (1876), pp. 421-22

The Temple-Architecture of Orissa was as it were an offering presented to the deity. To the architects, the building for the deity to live in must be worthy of him ; hence from the pavement to the pinnacle, it is full of exquisite carvings feasting the eye and soul of the devotee from a distance. The little temple of Müktesvara, or Parvati is an apt illustration of the above remark. One is sure to feel a sense of rapturous delight at the sight of Müktesvara in front of the *torana* or gateway. How exquisitely beautiful ! The architects must have poured forth the full exuberance of their hearts in designing the ornaments. We notice everywhere a conscious attempt to reach a consummation of the decorative art.

Spirit of self-sacrifice.

A building decorated with beautiful devices and designs shows the spirit of self-sacrifice pervading it ; all the lines of the design unmistakably illustrate the noble self. A building devoid of ornamentation looks ugly for two reasons ; firstly, it does not appeal to the senses inherent in man, secondly, it exercises a definite psychological effect ; it is purely mental. The structure, referred to, bespeaks the selfishness of the designer, or rather the deadening effect of the idealisation of utility. Everything in the world is seen and felt ; this is/more so particularly with a building or structure which presents an organic combination of different forms. Now, if the spirit of selfishness so manifest in an ordinary, undecorated or unarchitectural building offends us so clearly, how much more would it do in the case of a temple or a shrine. Here we are to sink our petty jealousies, and differences, settle our disputes, in fact we are to rise above every little thing of the world, and to be with the gods ; and as such, want of decoration, the concrete expression of gross selfishness, becomes very offensive to the eye, as well as to the soul. I should remark incidentally that as the very existence of society demands of every individual unit to perform his duties, so is it equally incumbent on every builder or designer to make his building architectural. I think it is a part of our rights to expect every building to fulfil all the necessary conditions of architecture ; it should not be allowed to offend the sense of sight as a return for our allowing it to intercept our air, light, view of the azure sky, and bounteous nature.

The decorative idea has been manifesting itself since the dawn of history ; this sense actuated the primitive man in his humble sphere of life with the crude means of satisfying the wants to which he used to attach the same amount of importance as we do to ours in this advanced age of civilization.

It is natural that this idea of decoration should be applied to architecture which is the concrete expression of a nation's genius, foibles and wants ; we need not even be astonished at the conflict between the decorative

Architecture and Decoration.

idea carried to the extreme, and the constructive idea which lays, as it were, the foundation for the former. Architecture without decoration is not worth the name ; it is not construction ; the one must not be taken for the other. The latter is a part of the former. Architecture is the index to the nation's life and sentiment. It is complex in nature, and this complexity increases in accordance with the nation creating it. The nation which has imbibed the spirit of beauty to a great extent, has its architecture commensurate with it. This spirit becomes reflected on the works of art that the nation produces. History bears testimony to it. When the nation degenerates its architecture also deteriorates.

Some are inclined to attach no value to decoration, and would condemn it as superfluous, serving no end. We need not wonder at it, for this is the spirit of rank utilitarianism ; everything that falls short of this standard is rejected as useless. Utilitarianism has, I am sorry to remark, divested life of half of its pleasures, and has rendered it dull and insipid. Now, huge mounds of brick or stone, wood or iron are considered as good specimens of architecture. These, fortunately, do not at all come under this category. They may contain good illustrations of the Principle of Least Resistance as propounded by Moseley, or of Gordon's formula ; but do they appeal to eye, intellect, and the noble sentiments inherent in man? Do they produce that harmony or repose which is caused by the proper adjustment or balancing of parts appealing to the different senses?

The structures of the present age betray a sad want of the application of this fundamental canon of Architecture. As opposed to the decorative idea carried to the extreme in the past, a retrogressive reaction has already begun to set in; since then the constructive idea has eclipsed the decorative one, and and we have come to the other end of the diameter. This is the true nemesis action. The present tendency of the age is to confine what remains of architecture within the narrow compass of set formulæ. There is a marked tendency of having the style stereotyped, which is not uniform in all ages and climé, but varies under different conditions. We can not reasonably expect a uniformity of style in all countries; we can not even expect it in all the different provinces of India. The pediment, metopes triglyphs of the Grecian temple, would be very poor substitutes in an Indian one, or, the *kalasa*, *karpuri*, and *amla* of an Orissan temple would spoil the beauty of a cathedral. It has been very wisely remarked by E. Viollet-Le-Duc that, "if the Parthenon is in its place at Athens, it is but an absurdity at Edinburgh, where the Sun prevails over the mists only for some days in the year....Art therefore does not reside in this or that form, but

Nemesis in modern Architecture.

in a principle, a logical method."* "It is barbarous to reproduce the Greek temples in the streets of London or Paris."†

The Orissan decoration is of three kinds, (a) Constructive, (b) Representative, and (c) purely Ornamental or Decorative.

Classification of Orissan Decoration.

The pilasters containing statuettes in their niches, and ornamented with an infinite variety of scrolls mainly come under this head. The tiers of cornice noticed in the Jagamohana of the temple at Konarka are particularly picturesque. By their constructive peculiarities, beauty has been ensured to a great extent. The protruding brackets of the caves, and temples have added much to the grace of the structures. The Representative class admits of two subheads, (a) Natural, and (b) Conventional. As an illustration of the Natural type I may refer to the leaves of plants with their radiating veins represented in the centre of the main pilasters of almost all the temples (c. f. *Rajrani*, Konarka). The full-blown lotuses with their stalks as noticed at Konarka have been most faithfully copied from nature. The life-like representations of monkeys as seen on the Muktesvara temple (Vide plate IX), or the elephants as seen at Konarka, or on the temple of Ananta Vasüdeva may be referred to as instances of their excellence in imitating nature.

* E. Viollet-Le-Duc. Lectures on Architecture, Vol I. p. 56.

† p. 57, Ibid.

The towering lions over crouchant elephants placed in the recesses between the pilasters may be cited as the best example of the conventional class of the Representative type.

The Orissan temples furnish good specimens of the purely Decorative type of ornament; of this, they have an infinite variety of patterns both geometrical, and asymmetrical. This type of ornaments consists of various scrolls, beads, tassels, or geometrical patterns. The scrolls on the surface of Muktesvara (Plate-X) are specially noteworthy; in them the transitions from the curves to the straight lines are very gradual, and not sharp so as to produce an irritating effect on the retina; curves of double flexure are so designed as to make one merge into the other.

Æsthetic or purely Decorative type.

The representative or symbolic ornament directly appeals to our intellect, whereas the purely decorative or æsthetic type, to our feelings. The æsthetic has no special purpose to serve except appealing to our sense of the beautiful based on gradation, contrast, symmetry, distribution or arrangement, radiation, continuity, colour and such other cognate ideas inherent in man; I shall try in the following pages to explain and describe the above principles of the Orissan style of decoration.

The symbolic and Æsthetic types.

In Orissan Architecture, the superstructure of the sanctum is curvilinear; this is more beautiful than a pyramidal one, as

Plastic from ensures grace.

is noticed in the temples of Upper India, or in structures, of the Dravidian style. By the adoption of this plastic form the possibility of ornamentation has been more ensured than it would have been in flat, inclined surfaces. In a pyramidal tower the geometrical, or rather the mechanical impression effected by a straight contour is offensive from an æsthetic point of view. This has been successfully avoided by the selection of a curvilinear form.

By the introduction of pilasters or *pâgas* the beauty of the structure is enhanced remarkably ; but the plastic and curvi-

Pilasters and Pinnacles :

linear form of the pilasters renders impossible the surmounting of them by pinnacles as in Gothic structures. This is also due to the rather large forward projection of the *Amlaka Sila.* As the tendency of the walls is to be thrust inwards, it is desirable for the sake of strength that the pilasters should project from the main walls rather within, than without. This is usually noticed in some French churches, as the cathedral at Amiens. In Orissân Architecture the pilasters have been intended more for beauty of design, and play of light and shade than for strength.

Making allowance for the doorway an Orissan temple is of the equifacial type ; it presents the same face in all directions.

Equifacial type and its defects.

The architect has not to experience much difficulty in designing structures of an equifacia type. The statical adjustment of the forces called into play becomes far easier than in the trifacial, or multifacial structures This is more so in a trabeated style ; it must be admitted here that the beauty caused by a rich variety of forces entailing a complicated design is sadly wanting in the Orissan style. This is an inherent defect of the Indo-Aryan school or rather the Indian school of Architecture. This defect has been aggravated by the astylar form. The architecture of Orissa is eminently astylar ; its very form renders columniation impossible ; hence we do not come across that sublimity resulting from the perspective effect as is noticed in the temples of R*a*mesv*s*ra, or M*a*düra (c. f. Tirumalla N*a*yak's Choultrie, M*a*dür*a*).

Effect of Astylar form.

The artistic effect produced by collonading or arcuation or a combination of both cannot be sought in an astylar form or a trabeated one. The effect is due to perspective, and a play of light and shade caused by a multiplicity of plane or curved surfaces. This is an inherent defect of the Indo-Aryan school ; and the style became so stereotyped that no attempt is noticed to have been made at making a departure, however slight, from the established one. There is, however, noticed an attempt at making good the above defect by the provision of most elaborate details ; this can be likened to an endeavour to improve the component parts without attaching any importance to the beauty or propriety of the whole. To study these details one must be a connoisseur of art, but to study the whole no such qualification is necessary. He must be provided with a heart; this is all that is demanded of him; he cannot but be affected by the sublimity of conception. He will pause and think, and if he has time and competence he will try to analyse the beauty of details.

There are two distinct mental processes of appreciating the beauty of the two systems just described—Synthetic and Analytic. The mind will have to go through the analytic process (mainly) in recognising the artistic merits of the Indo-Aryan school, and a synthetic one in that of the collonaded, arcuated or arcaded type.

It is curious to note that the synthetic effect of ensemble has been neglected as compared with that of the other method.

Neglect of Ensemble.

This seems to be against the genius of the nation. For, the Hindus always aim at generalisation, and at discovering unity in variety. The synthetic method is typical of this discovery of unity in diversity. In this connection it must be admitted that the Greeks were far superior in this respect to those who inaugurated the Indo-Aryan school of Architecture.

In Orissa the device of Fenestration was unknown as in

all Indian temples; I have stated the reason briefly. This method of Fenestration in addition to the sufficient supply of light and air renders ornamental treatment possible in a remarkable degree; the ancient builders of the rock-cut temples understood fully the value of it at such an early age. This is evidenced by nice carvings on the vertical and horizontal bands round doorways and in the tympana; there is another pleasing effect brought about by the use of this device. It affords spots of darkness as contrasted with the lighted surface of the wall. It is too obvious to mention that a bare surface, however lighted, is not half so beautiful as that showing a play of light and darkness.

Fenestration.

The defect of the Orissan Architecture due to the absence of the device of Fenestration was made good by the introduction of niches referred to already, containing the images of the P*a*rsva Devat*as*, Dikpatis, Asta Sakhis etc. (Vide plates—VII, X, XIII). These niches admit of nice decoration illustrating exquisite symmetry, fine proportion, and a grandeur of outlines.

Niches.

The niches are designed in the S*a*kkar or *Barandi* portion of the B*a*da; (vide plate X); and all the *pâgas* are provided with them. The niches in the *Râhâbâgas* or central pilasters are the most important, and largest of all. The sides of niches are usually very exquisitely carved with floral devices and scrolls, and are flanked by columns usually ending in panels containing human figures, or dwarfs. The niches are capped by tiers of awning, or hood showing elegant carvings (Vide plate—X); these projecting pieces are surmounted by an ornamental device containing a medallion enclosing the lotus, or the head of a human figure (Vide plate—X). I may refer my readers to the central niches of the Rajarani temple by way of illustration.

Central Niches

The images placed in the central niches are called Parsva Devatas, or side deities (vide plate—XIII). I have tried to come to a generalisation in respect of the Parsva Devatas; but unfortunately the images have been removed from most of the niches.

Parsva Devatas in the central niches.

The Parsva Devatas are not the same in all the temples, but differ according to the deities enshrined therein; thus they are not the same in the *S*aiva, Vaishnava and Saurya temples. In a temple dedicated to *S*iva, Kartic or war-god is placed in the niche on the back wall of the sanctum, Ganesa and Parvati, in those on the right and left walls, respectively, the position of the observer being at the rear of the sanctum.

Parsva Devatas for temples of different sects.

In a Vaishnava temple, (c.f. Puri temple) Kartic, Parvaty and Ganesa are replaced by Nrisinha, Vamana and Kalki respectively, these three being the three incarnations of Vishnü. In a *S*akta or Saurya temple, the arrangements are different. In the three niches of the temple at Konarka, the only Saurya temple worth the name, we find three figures of the Sun in different postures representing perhaps the Sun in different positions of its diurnal course in the heavens. In a *Sakta* temple the three different forms of the goddess *Sakti* are noticed. I may cite the case of the Vaital Dewl which is a veritable *Sakta* temple, it being dedicated to Kapal Mochani, another name of the goddess *Sakti*. In this temple, which, I have already noticed, is a departure from the usual type, the central niche on the back wall contains the dual image of Hara Gauri, the other two on the side walls containing the images of Dürga and Vairavi. In this connection, I may mention that the positions of Ganesa and Parvati have been reversed in the temples of Parasüramesvara and Bhaskaressvara. This is certainly due to the inadvertence of the P. W. D. in fitting the images in their respective niches after the restoration of the temples; the engineers, in charge of the restoration work, might have been ignorant of the definite order in which the images should be placed in the niches.

Niches for the deities of the different points of the compass

I have already referred to the niches in the pilasters containing statuettes; eight of such niches in the *Sâkkar* or the lower *Bârându* in the eight Anarthapagas contain the images of Dikpalas, or the presiding deities of the different points of the compass. Every Orissan temple of any importance is invariably provided with the niches containing images. I quote below the following passage* from the Agni-Pür*a*nam wherein the particular directions are assigned to the respective Dikp*a*las in the ceremony of Dikpati-y*a*ga to be performed at the installation

* कुम्भेष्वावाह्य शक्रादीन् पूर्वादौ पूजयेत् क्रमात्
इन्द्रागच्छ देवराज वज्रहस्त गजस्थित
पूर्वद्वारञ्च मे रक्ष देवैः सह नमोऽस्तु ते
त्रातारमिन्द्रमन्त्रेण अर्चयित्वा यजेद्बुधः ॥
आगच्छाग्ने शक्तियुत छागस्थ बलसंयुत ।
पाह्याग्नेयीं दिशं देवैः पूजां गृह्ण नमोऽस्तु ते ॥
अग्निर्मूर्द्धेति मन्त्रेण यजेत् अग्नये नमः ।
महिषस्थ समागच्छ दण्डहस्त महाबल ॥
रक्ष त्वं दक्षिणद्वारं वैवस्वत नमोऽस्तु ते ।
वैवस्वतं सङ्गमनमित्यनेन यजेद् यमम् ॥
नैरृतं गच्छ खड्गाढ्य बलवाहन संयुत ।
इदमर्घ्यमिदं पाद्यं रक्ष त्वं नैरृतीं दिशम् ॥
एष ते नैरृतं ... यजेदर्घ्यादिभिर्गुरुः ।
मकरारूढ वरुण पाशहस्त महाबल ॥
आगच्छ पश्चिमं द्वारं रक्ष रक्ष नमोऽस्तु ते ।
उरुं हि राजा वरुणं यजेदर्घ्यादिभिर्गुरुः ॥
आगच्छ वायो सबल ध्वजहस्त सवाहन ।
वायव्यं रक्ष देवैस्त्वं समरुद्भिर्नमोऽस्तु ते ॥
वात इत्यादिभिश्चार्चेदों नमो वायवेऽपि वा
आगच्छ सोम सबल गदाहस्त सवाहन ॥

ceremony of an image enshrined in a temple, I have carefully observed that the positions of the Dikpalas described in the passage quoted have not been deviated from in the case of Orissan temples; not only do their respective positions, or directions coincide with those fixed in the text, but the characteristic symbols and accessories have also been followed. Starting from the northern face we come across Küvera, or the god of wealth with the characteristic vehicle of seven jars in the north-eastern niche, and Pavana or the god of the winds with stag or deer as his vehicle in the north-western one. Varüna or the god of water with *makara* (capricornus) as his vehicle, is noticed in the north-western niche of the western face, and Nirita with a human figure as his symbol, in the south-western one. Yama, or the god of the nether regions with buffalo as his vehicle is seen in the south-eastern niche of the southern face, and Agni sitting on a ram is placed in the south-eastern one. Indra, or the king of the gods with an elephant or Airabata as his vehicle, is seen in the south-eastern niche of the eastern face, and Isana or Mahadeva with the bull as his vehicle is noticed in

रथस्थमुत्तरस्यां तु कुबेरं मध्येऽस्तुतं ।
सोमं राजानमिति वा यजेन् नैशाय वै नमः ॥
चतस्रो याम्य यमस्य मूलमन्त्र प्रकल्पिताः ।
पञ्चमन्त्रपदं प्राग्नी दिशं रक्ष मध्येऽस्तुते ॥
अग्निपुराणे दिक्पालयागो नाम षट्पञ्चाशोऽध्यायः ॥

the north-eastern one. Out of the eight Dikpalas four preside over the cardinal points of the compass, and these four with the rest are arranged according to a regular system. The figures on the left of the observer looking at a face represent the presiding deity for that face. I did not notice the least deviation anywhere, and this coincides exactly with the Agni-Püranam.

Comparison with the Chalukyan Dikpatis.

In the Chalükyan Architecture, too, I have noticed the introduction of the *Dikpatis* mounted on their respective vehicles; but these vehicles do not tally with those of the Indo-Aryan style as noticed in Orissa, which, I have remarked above, are true to the text of the Agni-Püranam. In the Chalükyan Architecture again, uniformity has not been maintained in respect of the vehicles; a great difference is noticed on studying the *dikpatis* represented in the panels of the flat ceiling of the *Antarála mandapa* of Harihareswara temple in Maisur territory, and those in the ceiling of the Kallesvara temple at Bagali*. The vehicles assigned by Ziegenbalg to the regents of the points of the compass in Southern India are very different from all those noticed above. I give below a tabular statement of all the different varieties of vehicles.

* Archæological Survey of Southern India, Vol XXI. p. 32.

Dikpatis	Regent of	Vehicle of Orissan or Indo-Aryan style.	Vehicle. A.	Vehicle. B.	Vehicle according to Ziegenbalg
Indra	East	Elephant	Elephant	Elephant	Elephant
Agni	South-east	Goat or ram	Gray goat	Horse	Gray goat
Yama	South	Buffalo	Black Buffalo	Black Bufialo	Black Buffalo
Nirita	South-west	Human figure	Bhüta	Bhüta	Crocodile
Varüna	West	Makara	Crocodile	Crocodile	Stag
Vayü	North-west	Stag	Stag	Stag	Bhüta
Küvera	North	Seven jars	Horse	Gray goat	Chariot
Isana	North-east	Bull	Bull	Bull	Bull

A = Harihareśvara temple in Maisur.
B = Kalleśvara temple in Bagali.

I may mention here incidentally a peculiarity noticed by me in respect of the Dikp*a*las; the niches in the lower B*ara*ndis of the Anarthap*a*gas contain the Dikpatis or Dikp*a*las with their characteristic vehicles; but the upper B*ara*ndis of some temples, *e.g.* Ananta V*a*südeva, S*a*ri Dewl, Sapta-m*a*trik*a*, etc. are also found to contain the consort of the Dikpatis, having exactly similar features and vehicles.

Besides the eight *Dikpatis* stated above, two subsidiary ones are noticed in the Agni-Pür*a*nam meant for the upper and lower regions; they are Brahm*a* and Ananta respectively. A serpent either of gold, or silver is placed in the foundation before laying the courses of

Subsidiary Dikpatis.

stone. This procedure was strictly followed in Orissa, and is still so done in the construction of temples. A block of stone carved with the lotus flower is placed on the topmost course of corbels as a representative of Brahma, or of the Sun above. This piece of stone is called the Garbha-Müdra. The stone block above the Garbha-Müdra contains a hole as a receptacle for grains, and is accordingly called Dhan-Müdra; over this comes the Bali-Müdra, and the topmost one is called the Ratna-Müdra; on this rests the Beki. It is stated that the Ratna-Müdra is meant to contain the jewels, or treasures belonging to the temple. It is surmised accordingly that the broken dilapidated condition of many a temple is due to the attempts of the vandals in quest of the much spoken of treasures, at removing the Beki, or a portion thereof, which hastened their collapse.

Ashta Sakhis.

I have already referred to the Ashta-sakhis which are analogous in character to the Ashta Dikpatis in the outer decoration of an Orissan temple. These *sakhis* or maidens, eight in number, occupy the niches in the *Bárdndi* portion of the Anarthapaga, or they are seen to project from the *Barandis* themselves in *alto-relievo.* These *sakhis* are female figures standing in artistic and graceful poses under the shade of umbrageous trees, these forming the background of the figures.

It is very difficult to trace clearly the genesis of the *sakhis* or maidens mentioned above. They are not probably derived from the Vishnuvite idea of the Ashta-sakhis; they seem to me to represent the eight *Saktis*, or female energies mentioned in the Agni-Püranam. In the 262nd Chapter of the Agni-Püranam, I have come across a reference to the Ashta-saktis, each of them again representing an octave, or a set of eight. Each of these different sets, or octaves confers when propitiated, a boon on the devotee; these are technically called *Ashtáshtaka-Sakti* (अष्टाष्टकशक्ति). Representation of Ashta-saktis has also been noticed in a piece of Buddhist sculpture discovered by General Cunnigham at Sarnath sometime between 1835 and 1836.*

The Naga and Nagini, or snake-god and goddess play an important part in the temple Architecture of Orissa; although primarily based on Brahminical mythology, these are evidently Buddhistic. This will be proved by reference to page 312, Lalita Vistara, edited by Dr. Rajendra Lal Mitra.

Naga & Nagini.

The Naga and Nagini ornaments are represented in pilasters in the recesses between the Konaka and Anarthapagas (vide plate -X); the Naga and Nagani pilasters are often noticed to flank the main doorway, or the balustraded windows

* Dr. Anderson, Catalogue and Hand-book of the Archæological Collection in the Indian Museum, Part II, pp. 30-31.

of the Jagamohana, as in the case of the temple of R*a*jar*a*ni (vide plate XIV). The pilasters, rather the shafts thereof, in which they are carved, are cylindrical outwardly, and show the figures of N*a*ga with a hood of snakes, and a tail encircling the shaft, and with its end turned up. The N*a*ga column rests upon a rectangular portion showing representations of rampant lions supported on crouchant elephants, or without them. The snake surmounting the god, or goddess may be three-hooded, five-hooded (vide plate X) and even seven-hooded.

I have come across a reference in the *A*di Parva of the Mah*a*bh*a*rata to the genesis of these *nâgas*; they are described as descended from Ka*s*yapa, and one thousand in number. According to Hindu theogony, the N*a*gas form one of the classes of demi-gods, being associated with the Yakshas, R*a*kshasas, &c. The principal N*a*gas, according to the Agni-Pür*a*nam, are eight in number, and the Hindus while worshipping Manas*a*, the presiding deity of the N*a*gas, recite the following couplet referring to the eight principal N*a*gas,

अनन्तो वासुकिः पद्मो महापद्मश्च तक्षकः।
कुलीर कर्कटः शङ्खो ह्यष्टौ नागाः प्रकीर्तिताः॥

Though chiefly derived from the Br*a*hminical mythology, the idea of the N*a*gas was much developed in the Buddhist period, and we accordingly come across numerous references of this in the Buddhist literature, and find abundant representations in the extant Buddhist remains at Bharhüt, Ajanta, the cave temples of Orissa, &c.

The Nagas, according to Buddhist theogony, are one of the eight classes of demi-gods mentioned in the Buddhist scriptures in the following order,—Devas, Nagas, Rakshasas, Gandharvas, Asüras, Garüdas, Kinnaras, and Mahoragas.* The Nagas are said to have the power of assuming human forms, and are spoken of as residing under the Triküta rocks supporting mount Merü.

I have already referred to this in pp. 71-72; the Nagas of the old Buddhist school are very similar to those of the later Brahminical period; this will also be evident on comparing the Nagas and Naginis of the Vidhüra-Panakaya Jataka in the scene of the "worship of the Blessed One by Airapata, the serpent-king" sculptured at Bharhüt; the sculptures of the Nagas of the Gandhara school bear a close affinity to those of the Mediæval Orissan group. In the very early Buddhistic representations, the Nagini is single-hooded; she eventually becomes many-hooded like her consort†; so the Nagini, or

* Grünwedel, Buddhist Art in India, p. 43.

† Dr. Mitra, Buddha Gaya, p. 44

Nagakanya is noticed to be many-hooded at Buddha-Gaya *; accordingly, the Nagini of the mediæval Orissan school is represented as many-hooded like the Naga ; this is the case not only in Orissa but in all parts of India where they are met with. The Naga and Nagini carved in strong relief in the slab discovered† in the Gond country on the Narbada, and presented to the Asiatic Society of Bengal by the Hon'ble Mr. F. Shore in 1827 show unmistakable affinity to those of the Orissan school.

Another representative decoration of the conventional type is the Sardüla. It, I may mention in passing, has three

Sardüla

distinct varieties with different characteristics and different situations. They are the following :—*(a)* The Ulta-Gaja-viraja-Sinha, (*b*) the Ulta-Gaja-Sinha, (*c*) the Chhida-uda-Gaja-Sinha. The first variety is a rampant lion with pointed ears, leafy horns standing on a crouching elephant, and with its face turned back ; it is met with in the recesses between Konaka and Anartha Pagas. The second variety is a rampant lion with an elephant's head turned back holding a human figure, male, or female (a deman) in its trunk ; this variety of Sardüla is noticed in the recess between the

* Dr. Mitra, Buddha-Gaya, Plate XXI, Fig. II.

† Anderson, Catalogue and Hand-book of the Archæological collections in the Indian Museum, Part II. pp. 308-309.

Anartha and Raha pagas. The third variety is a rampant lion standing on an elephant, and mounted by a male, or female figure holding the reins passing through the mouth of the lion from which a beaded tassel dangles. This variety is never met with on the surface of the Vimana, or Jagamohana, but in the recess of the portion separating the two.

Carvings lining the doorway. The carvings that decorate and line the front doorway are three in number, and are invariably the same with all the ordinary Orissan temples. They are called Dali, Gelbai, and Bara-Jhanji respectively in order of distance from the door-sill or jamb (Plate V (A), fig. II, 6, 4, 3). The Dali (Plate V (A). fig. II, 6) is a sort of scroll-work ; the intermediate one, i.e. the Gelbai (Plate V (A), fig. II, 4) is a sort of arabesque worked in low relief consisting of fanciful human, or animal figures combined with floral forms. The third, or the farthest one is called Bara-Jhanji. (Plates V, fig, 5. and V (A) fig, II, 3). The Bara-Jhanii is a sort of weed growing in tanks. In big temples the above carvings are five or six in number. (Vide plate V (A), fig. II). The doorway of the Jagamohana at Konarka may by cited as a typical illustration of this. The deep recesses between the carvings already referred to are also nicely carved, generally with Jali, or lattice, or wicker work.

The door carvings appear incased in frames ; these

frames with the carvings go round the three sides of the doorway, the bottom sill being excepted, which, again, is intercepted b; a carved stepping stone; in the top sill, the *dáli* and *barajhánji* are repeated, whereas a change in the *gelbái* scenes is often introduced. In the top sill, the floral portion of the arabesque is often omitted, as in the case of Müktesvara temple, where the fanciful human scenes have been changed into one of rows of flying nymphs following close upon one another.

It may be noted here that the *barajhánji* mentioned above is noticed in a door-sill exhumed from the remains at Buddha Gaya*; the *Barajhânji* of the mediæval Orissan school is exactly similar to that of the Buddhist remains assigned by Dr. Mitra to a period between the first century B. C. and the first century A. D.† It is curious to note that the floral device resorted to by the Buddhists at such an early age has been incorporated in the Hindu sculpture of mediæval Orissa, and its exact form and situation have been strictly followed; among the broad and varied succession of door carvings, *barajhánji* occupies the position farthest from the door opening.

Barajhanji, a Buddhist sculpture.

From the centre of the top sill projects a block of stone

* Vide Plate XLVIII, Fig. 3, Buddha Gaya by Dr. Rajendra Lal Mitra.

† Ibid, p. 247.

containing the figure of Lakshmi in relief. The figure of Lakshmi is noticed in two situations, and is accordingly called Gaja-Lakshmi and Mah*a*lakshmi.

Lakshmi carved on the topsill.

The Gaja-Lakshmi is represented as sitting on a full-blown lotus with one leg hanging down; she is flanked by two elephants, the trunks of which are raised over the head of the goddess, and are about to pour water over her head. The Gaja-Lakshmi is usually noticed in the top sill of the doorway; the second variety is not so frequently met with. The Mah*a*lakshmi is a figure of Lakshmi seated on a lotus without the attendant elephants; the front entrance of the temple of Müktes*v*ara shows the figure of Mah*a*lakshmi carved on the door-sill.

The jamb carvings.

The jamb carvings, already referred to, do not start from the level of the door-sill, but from a portion a little higher up; this portion of the jamb on each side of the doorway contains a representation of a *pida-dewl*, and a panel containing the figures of Gang*a*, Yamün*a*, Mah*a*k*a*la and Nandi. In the left panel are Yamün*a* and Nandi, and in the right one, are carved Gang*a* and Mah*a*-k*a*la, Gang*a* and Yamün*a* being on the extreme left of their respective panels. Gang*a* and Yamün*a* are represented with their characteristic vehicles; Gang*a* stands on a Makara or capricornus, and Yamün*a*, on a tortoise. In some temples the figures of Gang*a* and Yamün*a* are omitted.

The occurrence of Ganga, Yamüna, and the arabesque containing human figures in the jambs of doorways is traceable in the Güpta style of architecture, the latest example of which is found extant sometime between the 6th and 7th centuries A. D. The doorway discovered by Beglar* in Buxar in the district of Sahabad in Bihar, and belonging to the sixth century A. D. bears a very close resemblance to the door frame of the Orissan style ; there we come across the "rich arabesque with human figures", the goddesses Ganga and Yamüna with their respective vehicles ; the figures of Nandi and Mahakala, hawever, are not met with there.

I do not understand why the figures of Ganga and Yamüna have been carved in the panels of ths jambs, nor do I discover any reason of their association with Nandi and Mahakala ; for, on going through some of the Püranas and the two most important lexicons Vachaspatya, and Savdakalpadrüma, I do not anywhere find any reference to these associations.

I really doubt as to whether the male figure in the left panel is that of Nandi at all, although there is a hint in the 221st chapter of the Agni-Püranam of the services of Nandi as a guard or *dwàrpàla.* In the Kalika-Püranam, I have

* Anderson, Catalogue and Hand-book of the Archæological collections in the Indian Museum, Part II, p. 269.

come across several passages narrating the posting of Bhringi and Mahakala as sentries* at the entrance; so the figure of Bhringi really passes for that of Nandi; the figures may probably be those of Vetala and Bhairava, for these were no other than Bhringi and Mahakala, as is borne out by the passage from the Kalika-Püranam quoted in the foot-note†.

Nava-Graha or nine planets.

The architrave in front of the entrance is carved with the seated human figures of the planets, nine in number, according to Hindu astrologers. The architrave is often divided into panels for containing the figures mentioned above; these panels have often the trefoiled arches surmounting them. The architrave has often at the two ends two additional panels for the *dwarpâlas*, or guards, or for the conventional dwarfish figures, or Vetalas, as they are called. This *Navagraha* architrave is also seen in front of the doorway separatig the sanctum from the Jagamohana.

* "भृङ्गीशो मया तौ द्वारौ द्वारि महोत्सवम् ॥"

कालिकापुराणे ४५ अध्यायः ।

"यदा सा पार्वती बाला गौरी चारुहासिनम् ।

तदा भृङ्गिमहाकालौ द्वास्थौ द्वारि प्रतिष्ठितौ ॥"

कालिकापुराणे ४६ अध्यायः ।

† "भृङ्गी गतौ महाकालौ मानुषत्वं च धरिष्यथ ।

वेताल भैरवाख्यौ च तथाभूतौ द्विजोत्तमाः ॥"

कालिकापुराणे ५३ अध्यायः ।

The names of the planets are given below *ad seriatim*: e.g. the Sun (रविः), the Moon (चन्द्रः), Mars (मङ्गलः), Mercury (बुधः), Jupiter (बृहस्पति), Venus (शुक्रः), Saturn (शनिः), the Ascending Node (राहु), and the Descending Node (केतु). I need hardly mention that the Sun, Moon and the nodes are not planets, and it is out of place here to offer an explanation from their stand-point. These planets, however, are supposed to govern the destinies of mankind, and to exercise a great influence over anything connected with the human race; and hence hymns to the Navagrahas are repeated every morning by the orthodox Hindus to propitiate them, and to invoke their blessings for granting them health, wealth and prosperity in their daily pursuits. The introduction of the Navagraha figures, hence, was invariably meant to ensure prosperity to the persons who built the temples, and to prevent any evil happening to the temples themselves.

Indo-Aryan and Chalukyan doorways compared.

The Chalükyan doorways are similar to the Indo-Aryan ones as far as the wide succession of richly carved jamb mouldings is concerned; the usual order or succession in which the mouldings or carvings in an elaborately worked doorway are noticed is the following, viz.,—two mouldings, one slender well-carved pilaster, two mouldings, one slender well-carved pilaster, a carved recess, a big pilaster plainly carved. The carvings showing fanciful human figures, or *gelbdi* or Manusya Kautük' (मनुष्य कौतुक), in Orissan technology, are noticed here; the *dâli* or scrollwork is also noticeable. The figures of Bhairava like Nandi, Mah*a*k*a*la of an Orissan doorway are seen near the base of the pilasters referred to above. Gaja-Lakshmi is prominent in the centre of the top-sill or lintel of the doorway, as we see here, but the *Navagraha* architrave is not met with. The *Navagraha* figures are noticed in the panels of ceilings.

I have already remarked that the Representative type is an important feature of the Orissan school of sculpture. I cited several instances to illustrate this. I give below a few more examples of the Representative type. These are so commonly met with that they may be considered as important accessories to temple decoration.

Vet*a*l

The Vet*a*l is a pot-bellied, sitting, human figure with raised hands struggling to uplift the structure. This figure is sunk in bas-relief in panels surmounting the pilasters nearly at the top of the *bâda* (Vide plates VI, VII); these are also sunk in small pilasters flanking the niches (vide plate X), or the doorway. The *Vetâl* is noticed in Ch*a*lükyan Architecture also ; there it is called by the name of Bhüta, or demon. I think that the *Vetâl* has a distinct Buddhistic origin, and is probably derived from one of the eight Buddhistic demi-gods.

The Kirttimükha is a sort of conventional decoration generally found with arabesque on the face of pilasters, or at the

Kirttimukha.

top of statuettes placed in the niches. It is the mouth of a horned lion from which issue beaded tassels, which in the cases of statuettes form an ornament of the foiled arches surmounting the figures. The Kirttimükha with the beaded tassel dangling from it is technically called *Râhür Mükher mâlâ* (राहुर मुखेर माला). I have noticed this ornamental decoration in Chalükyan Architecture. A distinctly pronounced type of Kirttimükha is noticeable in Buddhist sculpture at Buddha Gaya.*

Floriage rather than foliage was a prominent characteristic

Lotus as an ornamental device.

of the mediæval Orissan school as it was in the early Greek period, or Doric age before the Alexandrian era. Orissan sculpture is very rich in flowers of various stages of growth; and among the flowers, the lotus was selected to be the choicest floral device; it became pre-eminently the national form of floral decoration. As the early Egyptians took a great fancy to lotus and papyrus, the Greeks to anthemion or palmette, the early Christians to the lily (the fleur-de-lis), the Indians are noticed to do the same to lotus from the earliest dawn of history. The lotus has a pan-Indian interest from the decorative

* Dr. Mitra, Buddha Gaya, Plate XLIX, figs. 4 and 5.

point of view. In India this floral device is resorted to in decorating the base, pedestal, and capital of columns. In the magnificent *torana* or gateway (Vide Plate VIII) in front of the temple of Müktesvara, the lotus leaves have been very nicely depicted ; the lotus has also been used as a pendant hanging from the ceiling ; as instances, I refer the reader to the Jagamohanas of Müktesvara, Brahmesvara. The gods of the Hindu Pantheon are made to hold full-blown lotus, or lotus-buds in their hands ; they are made to sit on lotus thrones, or to stand on lotus pedestals, or to rest their feet on lotus footstools.

The curvature of the petals of a full-blown lotus has been selected to designate the *cyma reversa* and *cyma recta*, for these two curves are technically called *Padma* (पद्म), or lotus. The outer faces of the Orissan temples are decorated with discs, or half-discs of lotus ; the *Bhos* (भो), I have already described in the last chapter, contain insets of lotus.

Contrast.

The fundamental idea on which the sense of decoration, or ornamentation is based, is contrast either in the domain of the flat, or the relieved. In the former, there is a contrast between light and darkness, and in the latter, between light and shade ; in the former, the play of lines is the characteristic feature, and in the latter, the play of masses ; in the latter case, colour may or may not be used. The Orissan decoration belongs to the class of the relieved in which colour has not been used.

I shall briefly dwell on the different forms of carvings used, and the plates illustrating them will convey a rough idea as to the curves of various degrees of flexure resorted to in designing the ornamental devices.

The carvings illustrate both the principles of Gradation, and Contrast, but never a compromise between the two principles which is positively injurious from an æsthetic point of view. I need hardly point out that the purpose sought to be served is never so done by introducing a compromise which invariably impairs the beauty meant to be enhanced. The Orissan architects were fully conscious of this, and owing to this consciousness, is never seen an attempt at rounding off the corners, or angles, which are kept perfectly rectangular, and not curved in the least.

Contrast and Gradation compared.

The contrast afforded by angularity has a definite psychological effect; apart from the stand-point of light and shade, it has a sense of severity and strength attached to it. This angularity, let it be rectangular, has a decided tendency te excite, and the curvature illustrating gradation exercises a pleasing effect. The skill of an architect lies in effecting a happy combination of contrast and gradation, not in a particular portion of the form, but in different parts of it. On a careful examination of the mouldings, and the pilasters, it will be apparent that the severity of form has been best ensured by maintaining an angular character as far as practicable under the circumstances. This, I have remarked, is an effect of contrast. As far as the decoration of the main form is concerned, it may be said that the Orissan architects were consummate masters of this art of carefully selecting forms illustrative both of contrast and gradation.

Contrast afforded by uniformity of halves.

As a good illustration of the principle of contrast and gradation, I may refer to the ornamental decorations on the Rekha surface just over the R*ahapaga* of the Müktesvara temple (vide plate VI). Straight lines running vertically are noticed to divide the decorated surface, and on both sides of the straight lines as chords, are placed successively pairs of semicircles, or segments of circles having the springing point of one as the centre of its counterpart. The semicircles have also been so nicely arranged about the consecutive straight lines or directrices that the lower element of one pair is placed adjacent to the upper one of another pair in respect of the next directrix; in this way, a nice contrast illustrating the principle of Uniformity of Halves has been effected. This design is so exquisitely beautiful that it hardly fails to exact the admiration of a passing observer.

PLATE V

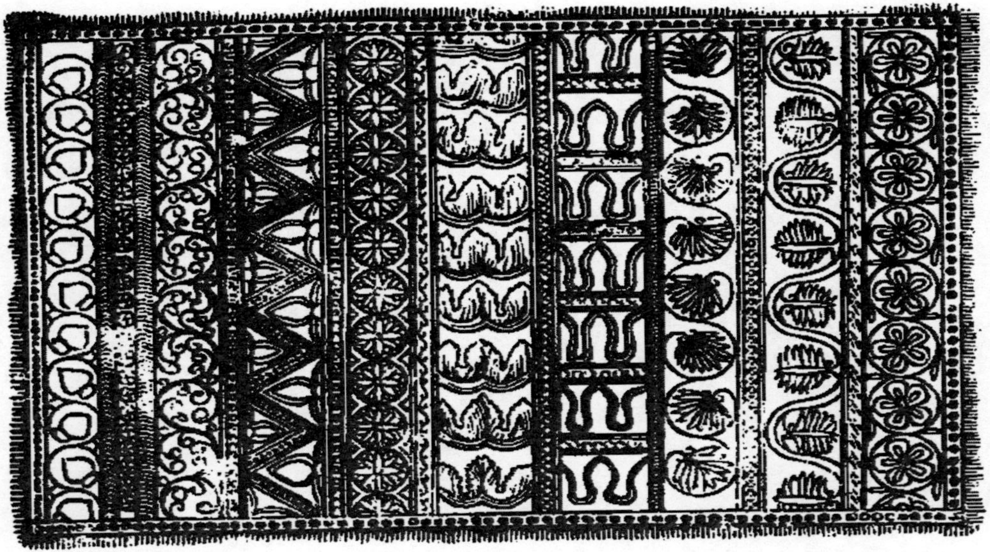

Ornamental Ca: ngs and Floral :es of the temples of Orissa

Sketch by M. Ganguly

Printed by K. V. Sayne & Bros.

In Orissa, as in Moresque Architecture, harmony of form has been brought about by the proper gradation and contrast of straight and curved lines.

The Orissan sculpture is very rich in scrolls and arabesques, and different technical terms have been coined to designate the different varieties. The scroll and the arabesque are combinations of the two following types of decoration, *e. g.*, (1) the Representative or Symbolical, (2) the Æsthetic, or purely Decorative; both the scroll and the arabesque show the conventional representation of the Representative type. The scroll, I have noticed in Chapter III, has been resorted to as an ornamental device from the remotest historic period we are familiar with; it is noticeable in the ancient Egyptian and Greek works of art.

Scroll and Arabesque.

The scroll that we come across in the Orissan school of sculpture, is derived from the idea of a creeping plant with its tendrils, leaves and flowers; the Orissan technics are based on the inclusion or exclusion of any one of the above three elements in or from the main stem. Thus on referring to plates V(A) and V(B), it will be seen how the different varieties of scrolls have been represented*. The following classification is given.

* Of course, all the figures on the plates are not scrolls.

(*a*) *Phūl latā* (फुललता).

(*b*) *Nati latā* (नटोलता).

(*c*) *Patra latā* (पत्रलता).

(*d*) *Vana latā* (वनलता).

Phūl latā is a scroll work enclosing flowers; this device may be with, or without tendrils. The first, second, third and the sixth rows on Plate V are examples of *Phūl latā*; in the first one, tendrils are noticeable, and two scrolls cross each other so as to form definite contignous circles. The eighth row is an illustration of *Nati Latā* which is a scroll work of a creeping plant with a luxuriant growth of tendrils. The ninth or the last row is an example of *Patra latā* showing a creeping plant and the leaves thereof. For the *Vana latā*, the reader is referred to Plate VII; the carving in the *Bārāndi* portion of the second pilaster on the left shows the densely-foliaged *Vana latā*. An illustration of *Patra latā* is given below.

The fifth row on Plate V, is an example of *Barajhānji* described at great length already. The seventh row is technically called *Māli-phūl-phādikā*. (*Phādikā* means a triangle; *Māli* = beaded).

The ordinary scroll work is called *Dâli*; it shows several convolutions in the centre; this is like a succession of spirals reversed alternately. This is technically called *Sâdâ-dâli* [Vide Plates V(A), & V(B).]; a rich variety of the same may exhibit flowers, leaves, tendrils, etc.

The Orissan architects were superior to their Greek or Roman brothers in the different types of ornament used. The Greek ornament was neither constructive, nor symbolical or representative, but it was a purely decorative one. Their ornaments were something like an excrescence which, if removed, would not affect the constructive peculiarity of the temple; nor do their decorations convey any sense of pleasure and pain except that due to geometrical symmetry; in this respect the ornaments of the Orissan school resemble those of the Egyptian one.

I must admit that, generally speaking, an attempt is noticeable in Orissan Architecture to make the ornaments outshine the constructive grace; this sense, when carried to an excess, has caused them to create in some cases an "over-decorated ugliness."

Rhythm of spacing. On referring to the plates that follow, it will be apparent that the surface has often been decorated with the repetitions of the same ornamental device placed at regular intervals; by this rhythm of spacing, the sense of monotony or weariness is much relieved, and a sense of ocular pleasure, though not a purely mental one, is aroused. This spacing is like the rhythm of the waves of sound, or cadence in music, and has an equally pleasing effect.

Music and Decoration are analogous in character; rhythm is noticeable in both; in the former, the rhythm is in respect of time, in the latter, of spacing; as rhythm of time plays an important part in the sweetness of a tune, so does that of spacing in case of ornament; in fine, art itself is a rhythmical expression; nay it is more. As music is a combination of rhythmic sounds, so is decoration one of measured or well-balanced forms, or details. Hence, it is necessary for the efficiency of expression of a piece of decoration that, not only should the details be artistic but that they should also be artistically arranged; however natural your details may be, if the arrangement be defective, the whole effect is lost; and even if the individual, or component parts be executed inartistically their artistic arrangement may be very impressive.

Rhythm of time and spacing.

The above effect has been sought to be ensured by the introduction of various geometric figures, or patterns including zigzag, diaper, *jáli*, or lattice or wicker work and various sorts of scrolls. I refer my readers to plates V, V(A), V(B), and VI.

The diaper work is noticed to have been resorted to in decorating the external faces of temples. I refer the rea-

Plate VI.

Southern Facade of Mukteswara.

Photo by A. Ghose F. C. S, F. G. S.

Printed by K. V. Sayan t

ders to plates VI, VII and X; the diaper work on the face of the *vimâna* of Müktesvara, (vide plates VI, VII and X) is technically called *Phând-granthi* (फांदग्रंथि); it has been described on page 190; it differs from that noticed on the *pâgas* of the Lingaraja temple at Bhübanesvara. This is a geometric diaper, and has a very pleasing effect. In this case, however, the patterns are not sunk below the general surface; and the workmanship is called *cameo* as opposed to *Cavo-Relievo*, or *Intaglio relievato*.

Diapers.

The diaper as I have noticed above is a sort of combination or a repetition of geometric patterns; equal-spaced repetition in sculpture can be skilfully effected by curves of contrary flexure as the sine curve symbolical of the propagation of sound and light waves; this has been largely used in the Buddhistic and mediæval decorations. This repetition can also be brought about in various rectangular forms of which the zigzag, the fret, etc. are examples.

Geometric Figures.

The zigzag is a simple variety and combination of lines; the fret, either carved in stone or painted on canvas, serves as a nice ornamental device very simple in design requiring only little geometrical accuracy in execution. I have not noticed anywhere in Orissan sculpture the fret as an ornamental form except in the temple of Parasüramesvara, and that too as a solitary instance in the third

Fret

panel from below upwards in the recess between the Konak and Anarth pagas at the south-west corner of the *vimâna*.

Jali or wicker work

Repetition can also be effected by a definite arrangement of geometric figures such as rectangles, parallelograms, etc; these are illustrated by the *Jâlis* of the Orissan school; the *jâli* resembles a lattice or wicker work; the retiform character of the *jâli* varies in different forms; the reticulation may either be formed by small horizontal squares, or squares with the diagonals vertical. In the former case, the *jâli* is called a *Patâ jâli*, and in the latter, *Bânkâ Jâli* where the reticulation is said to be diamonded. The *Jâli* represented in the window of the Jagamohana of Müktesvara (vide plate IX) is an instance of this form. There are yet two more forms of *Jâli*, e.g, the *Bilkhüjâ Jâli*, and the *Phül Jâli*. In the former, the small squares are arranged so as to form parallelograms, or rectangles, the interior filling in of which is effected by graceful carvings of single leaves or petals [vide plate V. (B)]. In the latter case, the small squares form triangles, or other rectangular figures, the inset being carved with flowers, petals, &c.

Orissan and Saracenic sculptures compared.

The Orissan sculpture is superior to the Saracenic or Moresque one by reason of having the representative, or symbolic form of treatment in addition to the purely æsthetic one resorted to by the latter school; but it should be borne in mind that the Saracens had a rich variety of curves, tracery, interlacings having inscriptions elaborated into them. The Orissan inscriptions are noticed to be usually incised on the jambs of doorways, or some obscure portions of the temples, or on slabs inserted in the compound walls. As illustrations of these, I may cite the case of the temples of Lingar*a*ja, Ked*a*re*s*vara, P*a*t*a*le*s*vara (Puri), Ananta V*a*südeva, &c.

The Saracenic inscriptions entail a nice design showing exquisite symmetry, elaborate and well-balanced details, viz, tracery, interlacings, &c. We do not notice a rich variety of interlacings in Orissan sculpture; but the one resembling the tail of a snake and found round doorways, as at the Bhogamandapa of Puri, or the Jagamohana at Kon*a*rka is exquisitely beautiful, and is not in any way inferior to the guilloche of the Greek, or any interlacing of the Saracenic school, or that of the comparatively modern Cinquecento as noticed on the face of Santa Maria de' Miracoli, Brescia.* This Orissan carving bears some resemblance to the rope ornament of the Egyptians; another type of interlacing noticed by me is worth mentioning in this connection. It was noticed round a niche on the northern face of the Vim*a*na of Para*s*ür*a*me*s*vara. This is

* R. N. Wornum, Analysis of Ornaments, The Characteristics of Styles, Plate on p. 97.

a very ingenious device showing the appearance and disappearance of the parent stem of a plant at regular intervals.

Interior decoration.

The interior of an Orissan temple is never decorated with the exception of Müktesvara, Brahmesvara and the Vaitala Dewl. The reason is not far to seek. The design of the temple is such as not to afford sufficient air and light inside it. The interior is purposely meant to be shrouded in mystic darkness. It is to be rendered solemn in keeping with the solemn occasion of communion of the devotee's soul with the deity; here, the soul must rise above the trifles of the world; hence the necessity of decoration is dispensed with; to this is due the entire absence of ornamentation inside as contrasted with the profusion of outside decoration. The remarks of M. Paoul Rochette* with regard to this in the case of Gothic Architecture do not hold good here at all; it is neither "a striking defect," nor "a veritable absurdity," as observed by him in the case of Gothic Architecture, but absolutely necessary.

The Hindu temples are not halls of congregational worship like the Christian churches, or Mahomedan mosques; hence the amount of diffused light streaming through the entrance leading to the Jagamohana is considered as sufficient for the purpose;

* E. Viollet-Le-duc, Lectures on Architecture, p. 414.

† Dr. Sturgis, Dictionary of Architecture and Building.

if the windows were considered superfluous in Grecian temples which were also "not halls of worship, but shrines for the protection of the statue of a divinity, and for the deposit of votive offerings",† and if in them the sun-light streaming through the entrance doorway was considered sufficient, how much more should light be reasonably dispensed with in a temple of the Indo-Aryan style.

I have already remarked that Architecture was a veritable "petrified religion" to the people of Orissa ; as religion degenerates into cant and hypocrisy, architecture shows signs of convention, deceit or falsehood. Architectural Deceits, according to Ruskin, are threefold, (1) Constructive or Structural Deceit, (2) Colour Deceit, (3) Deceit by reason of "the use of cast or machine made ornaments of any kind". The last kind of Deceit is not noticed in Orissan Architecture, and was obviously not possible considering the situation, fitness, and the time when it flourished ; the second form is noticed to some extent, and more at Puri than at Bhübanesvara. The main temple at Puri is covered with stucco plaster, and coloured with different pigments ; by this method, all that is unworkmanlike has been concealed from the public view ; moreover, this gave them an incentive to execute works badly, and in haste ; hence this had a decided tendency to debase them as architects. The stone blocks have, in many cases, been dyed in red ochre

Architectural Deceit.

in such a way as to make the grey or yellow stone blocks look like red sand stones, a variety not to be found in the locality. This artifice of painting or dyeing has made many with Dr. Mitra as one of them, commit the grave blunder of taking them for red sandstones. I should admit here that this device of stucco plaster resorted to by the architects was necessary in some cases, e.g, at Puri. By concealing the stone surface it has effectively prevented the weathering action of the stone over which it has been applied. At any rate the second form of Deceit is not so objectionable as the first one, for it is not very assertive, or constructive in character, though it is objectionable by reason of its very existence ; for though a greyish variety may pass for a red one, the structural design is not affected in the least. This practice of stucco is noticeable in the pre-historic, Grecian and Mycenæan structures. At Ninevh, a sort of stucco used to be applied as an external coating to the clay walls. In Chaldæa, the walls used to be "faced with a skin of glazed and coloured brickwork of many colours."*

Deceit in Orissan Architecture.

The spirit of simulation or dissimulation is notoriously flagrant in the first form ; for here the very soul of the edifice is roughly handled. Let us see how we can justly detect any such Deceit in the case of the Temple Architecture of Orissa. This we can best

* Fletcher, Influence of Materials on Architecture, p. 8.

ascertain by standing outside a temple and looking at it. The temple looks like a curvilinear tower surmounted by a rather flat dome; and the immediate inference that the observer makes is that the inside must necessarily present the form of a vaulted ceiling, or some such thing. When he goes in and looks up, his expectation is at once frustrated; instead of a high vault his vision is intercepted by a low flat roof formed by flags of stone. His architectural taste, however imperceptible it may be, receives a rude shock at once. This is the result of Architectural Deceit or falsehood; the uniformity or unity of form could not be maintained both inside and outside; though the outward form has been introduced out of a particular motive, the same motive should have been kept in view inside too. The observer is not bound to consider that the dome-shaped stone at the top is a solid block, or a combination of blocks meant to keep the four walls from being thrust inwards; nor should he think that a trabeated style does not admit of a vaulted ceiling as is the case with an arcual one. He would simply seek for a uniformity, or a continuity of the same both inside and outside.

In architecture we have an experience of two distinct and contrary mental states, viz, Æsthetic comfort and discomfort.

Æsthetic comfort and discomfort.

The string courses, pillars, buttresses or pilasters, and architraves, or a combination thereof afford a sense of satisfaction and repose or relief by disclosing the reasons of their introduction. An Orissan temple affords in an eminent degree this relief or æsthetic comfort. In some case, however, a contrary effect is noticeable. On looking at the huge lion projecting from the *vimâna* so as to look floating in the mid-air, one is sure to think more or less that the figure is threatening to come down and to crush him ; this sense of the danger of being crushed produces a sense of discomfort which is termed æsthetic discomfort.

Zoology of the temples :—

The zoology of the temples is varied and indicates a decided improvement on what is noticed in the Buddhist period. The animals that are found abundantly represented are the lion and the elephant ; they are often found together, the former standing over the latter in the crouching state. This, according to some, is representative of the ascendency of Brahminism over Buddhism, the votaries of which held the elephant in great sanctity. This is probably indicative of the ascendency of one dynasty, the Kesaris, over another. The Kesaris came to power before the Gangas ; but it is difficult to ascertain the dynasty supplanted by the Kesaris. The lion was the emblem of the Kesaris, whence the name of the dynasty is derived, and the elephant was that of the unknown dynasty referred to. This ascendency has been signalised by the efforts of art. Instead of any graphic account, or even mention of this fact in any historic document, or legend we have a symbolic representation of it in the recesses of temples.

The Sardūla

The victory by the Kesaris must have been an epoch-making event, or else its representation would not have influenced the architecture of Orissa in such a remarkable degree, for almost all the temples of mediæval times in the Puri district are invariably found to contain in the narrow recesses between the pilasters representations of a lion standing over a crouchant elephant. These lions are, as a matter of fact, fantastic monsters having leafy horns, pointed ears, elaborate manes and a beaded tassel dangling from the mouth. This is the sculptor's Sardūla which does not obtain in nature. In this connection I may invite the reader's attention to a somewhat similar representation of huge rampant horses in the Dravidian style of Architecture, e. g. the Vellore temple. From this conventional representation of Sardūla we should not come to the conclusion that the Uriyas had no knowledge of the physiognomy of a lion ; in support of the above remark, the lion on the Jagamohana of the Mūktesvara temple may be cited by way of illustration.

Different varieties of the lion.

The lion has been represented in various situations. It is seen on both sides of the main entrance as a guard, or a *dwârpâla*, and towering over a crouchant elephant. It is seen in a similar posture projecting from the Rekha of the sanctum at a definite height. It is also placed on the roof of the Jagamohana, and is invariably found in one of the three following postures,e. g. (1) *Udâ-sinha*, or flying lion, as in the temple of Yukti-Ked*a*resvara, (2) *Jhâppâ-sinha*, or rampant lion, as in Ked*a*res*v*ara, (3) *Kshepâ-sinha*, or mad lion, as in the temple of Müktes*v*ara. The lion is also noticed in the intervening space below the Amlaka *Sila* referred to already. This representation of the lion is called *Dupichchâ-sinha*, or two lions placed back to back.

The elephant

I have dwelt at some length on the abundant representation of the elephant in chapter II; the importance of Orissa as the breeding place of elephants reached the farthest limits of India, and it is no wonder to see it so largely represented. The most natural, life-like carvings of elephants are noticed in the temples of Ananta V*a*südeva, S*a*ri Dewl, Kon*a*rka, &c. Elephants in procession, following close upon one another are noticed usually on the face of the Basanta, and P*a*da portions of the Jangh*a*; they are also noticed on the faces of the Pi*d*as of the Jagamohana, e. g. Kon*a*rka. The artists of the Buddhist period far excelled those of the later times in depicting the elephant in various scenes.

The huge monolithic elephant at Kon*a*rka carved out of a

single block is worth mentioning (vide Plate XXVI). It may be said to have been copied from nature; and in consequence of this, it has exacted the unstinted admiration from the most captious critics of art.

The elephant of the temple at Konarka

The horse

The horse is noticed to be too frequently represented; but unlike the mediæval sculpture of Europe it is far less met with than the lion, or the elephant. It is often seen enclosed in panels with beaded borders on the face of the *pidas*, or the *Basanta* of the *Janghá*. At Konarka it has been abundantly represented; and the huge one in front of the Jagamohana at Konarka may be considered a masterpiece, the like of which we very rarely come across, and it may reasonably be "the pride of some metropolitan museum in Europe and America."* We may pertinently quote the following observations of Prof. Havell in respect of this magnificent work of art. "The superbly monumental war-horse in its massive strength, and vigour is not unworthy of comparison with Verocchio's famous masterpiece at Venice."† This horse, or the elephant already referred to, may appropriately figure well if inserted in the hunting sculpture of the Lombards, and may compare favourably with the noblest examples of sculptural treatment in Europe, e. g.

* Havell, Indian sculptures and Painting, p. 146. † Ibid, p. 147.

"the lions of Egypt, the Ninevite bulls, and the mediæval griffins." ‡

Other animals

Among the animals that I have observed in Orissan temples, the following are worth mentioning :—the lion, elephant, horse, boar, duck, peacock, pigeon, crocodile, bull, cow, deer, hare, monkey, goose ; the tiger, owl and crow have not been noticed by me. These animals have no classical sanctity attached to them, and to this perhaps, is due their omission from the temple zoology of Orissa.

The Monkey

The monkey (*Macacus Rhesus*) in various scenes of life, as in the Buddhist period, (vide Chap. III) was a favourite subject with the artists from the remotest antiquity down to the middle ages. I have described at great length the famous monkey scene noticed in the window moulding of the Jagamohana of the Müktesvara temple (Vide Chapter VIII and Plate IX). The agility and playfulness characteristic of the monkey coupled with motherly tenderness have been so very graphically described that they leave a very deep and lasting impression on the mind of a most casual observer.

The Bull.

The bull is seen represented in an Orissan temple, more especially in those belonging to the *Saiva* sect. It is observed in the Jaina Gümpha at Khandagiri as the Vahana of Rishava Deva, the first Tirthankara of the

‡ Ruskin, The Stones of Venice, Vol. I., p. 208 (edited by L. March Phillips).

Jainas; in a *S*aiva temple it is represented as the V*a*hana or carrier of *S*iva. The huge bull carved out of a single block and placed in a small temple abutting on the north side of the N*a*t-Mandira within the precincts of the Linga R*a*j temple, Bhūbanesvara, may be cited as a well-proportioned and nicely carved example of the animal.

The Makara or capricornus.

The *Makara* like the lotus is an ornamental device which can be traced from the earliest Buddhist period down to the Mediæval times, and which is met with in all the Indian styles of architecture and sculpture. In chapter III, the *makara* or *capricornus* has been noticed as an ornament in the arch-springing from the distended jaws of which floral devices have been made to issue; it is also noticed at S*a*nchi, Bh*a*rhūt, Amar*a*vati, etc. In the Mediæval Orissan sculpture the *makara* is seen as a gargoyle, or long projecting spout through which rain water, or temple washings are meant to be discharged clear of the wall; it is also noticed at the springing of the arched gateway or *torana* in front of the temple; the *torana* of the temple of Mūktesvara may be cited as an example (vide plate VIII).

The most elaborately and artistically worked gargoyle of R*a*ma Chandra's temple at Kon*a*rka may be cited as a fine specimen of this decorative form. This gargoyle compares favourably with those in the Meaux Cathedral, Eglise d' Eu or the bell-tower, Toulouse, restored by Viollet-le-duc.

The Makara is represented in various forms, with huge distended jaws set with teeth, with a short, or elongated curling snout, or trunk, and magnificently carved fins and tail.

It may be mentioned that this representation is conventional, and the reason is not far to seek ; for the animal is a purely mythical one not found in nature ; but there is a uniformity in this conventional representation throughout India as is borne out by the study of the Chalükyan sculpture of the Kanarese districts,

Proportions of the limbs of a human body

On going through the *S*ilpa *S*astras to ascertain the relative proportions of the different limbs of the body of an image, be it human or divine, I have carefully noticed that no mere convention having no scientific basis has been resorted to by the Indian sculptors. A comparative study of the proportions used by them, and an actual measurement taken of human limbs would convince one of the fact that they studied human physiognomy thoroughly ; of course, the relative proportions recorded by different Indian schools do not strictly tally with one another, but the discrepancy is ordinarily of such a trifling nature that it may safely be neglected, and the figures belonging to the different schools may for all practical purposes be considered the same

I have worked out the relative proportions of the Orissan school of sculpture from measurements taken by me *in situ*, and compared them with those given in *S*ükra-Niti, a text ascribed to Sükr*a*ch*a*rya. I have found the text of Sükr*a*ch*a*rya to suit Orissan sculpture more than M*a*nas*a*ra quoted by Dr. R*a*jendra L*a*l Mitra.* Before I submit the tabular statement for the consideration of my readers, I should make a few prefatory observations explaining briefly the general principle, and the technics followed by the Indian sculptors. The images are classified according to the ratio the head from crown to chin bears to the whole body. Thus they are called Pancha T*a*la, Sha*d*a T*a*la, Sapta T*a*la, Asta T*a*la, Nava T*a*la, according as the ratios are $\frac{1}{5}$, $\frac{1}{6}$, $\frac{1}{7}$, $\frac{1}{8}$ and $\frac{1}{9}$ respectively.

The term "T*a*la" has been clearly defined in *S*ükraniti thus,

स्वस्वमुष्टेश्चतुर्थांशो ह्यङ्गुलं परिकीर्त्तितम् ।
तदङ्गुलैर्द्वादशभिर्भवेत् तालस्य दीर्घता ॥

82 Sloka, 4th ch, 4th Prakaranam.

i.e. 12 *angülas* make one T*a*la, an *angüla* being ¼th the width of the fist.

T*a*la is a standard of lineal measurement in sculpture, meaning a span, or the distance from the tip of the thumb to that of the middle finger.

* Mitra, Indo-Aryans, vol. I, pp. 136-37

The images are Sapta T*a*la, Nava T*a*la, &c., according as they are found in different climes; the images of gods, or goddesses with a few exceptions are usually made Sapta T*a*la. I shall presently show that the images in Orissa have been made Sapta T*a*la from the Buddhist period down to the mediæval times. The author of *S*ukraniti recommends Sapta T*a*la images for the Kali Yuga, or the present age†. *Sükra*-ch*a*rya has, however, laid down the proportions for Nava T*a*la, and has instructed to reduce them to Sapta T*a*la, Asta T*a*la, &., by the simple mathematical process of the Rule of Three.

In the tabular statement (A) given below, I have given the measurements of a Nava T*a*la image in a separate column, and have deduced therefrom those for a Sapta T*a*la one by the process stated above, and also the relative proportions in decimals taking the whole body as the unit, or standard of measurement. To test the accuracy of the relative proportions as fixed by the Indian school of sculptors is given below the statement (B) showing the measurements of different limbs of a full-grown adult taken by me personally.

* सप्ततालाद्युक्ता या मूर्तीनां देशभेदतः ।
सदैव स्त्री सप्तताला सप्ततालश्च वामनः ॥
84 Sloka, 4th Ch, Sukraniti.

† दशताला कृतयुगे त्रेतायां नवतालिका ।
अष्टताला द्वापरे तु सप्तताला कलौ स्मृता ॥
Ibid, 89th Sloka.

Tabular Statement—(A), showing the relative proportions for a Sapta Tâla image.

Limb of the body.	Nava Tala Angülas.	Sapta Tala Angülas.	Relative Proportions in Decimals.
Height of man ...	108	108	1
Head (from crown to chin) ...	12	$12\times\frac{9}{7}$	·142
Forehead ...	4	$4\times\frac{9}{7}$	·047
Nose ...	4	$4\times\frac{9}{7}$	·047
Nose to chin ...	4	$4\times\frac{9}{7}$	·047
Neck ...	4	$4\times\frac{9}{7}$	·047
Neck or shoulder to Breast ...	12	$12\times\frac{9}{7}$	·142
Breast to Navel ..	12	$12\times\frac{9}{7}$	·142
Navel to Penis ...	12	$12\times\frac{9}{7}$	·142
Thigh ...	24	$24\times\frac{9}{7}$	·284
Knee ...	4	$4\times\frac{9}{7}$	·047
Leg ...	24	$24\times\frac{9}{7}$	·284
Heel ...	4	$4\times\frac{9}{7}$	·047
Arm up to the finger ends ...	48	$48\times\frac{9}{7}$	·568
Arm from shoulder to elbow ...	20	$20\times\frac{9}{7}$	·238
Arm from armpit to elbow ...	13	$13\times\frac{9}{7}$	·120
Arm from armpit to the end of middle finger	28	$28\times\frac{9}{7}$	·259
Palm ...	7	$7\times\frac{9}{7}$	·064
Middle finger ...	5	$5\times\frac{9}{7}$	·046
Thumb ...	3½	$\frac{7}{2}\times\frac{9}{7}$	·032
Index finger ...	3	$3\times\frac{9}{7}$	·0377

Tabular Statement—(A), showing the relative proportions for a Sapta Tâla image—contd.

Limb of the body.	Nava Tala Angülas.	Sapta Tala Angülas.	Relative Proportions in Decimals.
Ring finger ...	3	$3\times\frac{9}{7}$	·0277
Little finger ...	2	$2\times\frac{9}{7}$	·018
Foot ...	14	$14\times\frac{9}{7}$	·129
Great toe ...	2	$2\times\frac{9}{7}$	·018
Ankle ...	2½	$\frac{5}{2}\times\frac{9}{7}$	·023
2nd toe ...	2½	$\frac{5}{2}\times\frac{9}{7}$	·023
3rd toe ...	1½	$\frac{3}{2}\times\frac{9}{7}$	·013
4th toe ...	1½	$\frac{3}{2}\times\frac{9}{7}$	·013
Forehead (length) ...	8	$8\times\frac{9}{7}$	·074
Eyebrow (end to end) ...	8	$8\times\frac{9}{7}$	·074
Space between eyebrows ...	½	$\frac{1}{2}\times\frac{9}{7}$	·004
Eye (length) ...	3	$3\times\frac{9}{7}$	·0277
„ (width) ...	2	$2\times\frac{9}{7}$	·018
Pupil of the eye ...	1	$1\times\frac{9}{7}$	·009
The root of the nose ...	1	$1\times\frac{9}{7}$	·009
The tip of the nose ...	2	$2\times\frac{9}{7}$	·018
Ear (Length) ...	4	$4\times\frac{9}{7}$	·037
„ (Breadth) ...	3	$3\times\frac{9}{7}$	·0277
„ Thickness ...	½	$\frac{1}{2}\times\frac{9}{7}$	·004
The Bridge of the nose ...	3	$3\times\frac{9}{7}$	·0277
Height of nose ...	1½	$\frac{3}{2}\times\frac{9}{7}$	·013

Tabular Statement—(A), showing the relative proportions for a Sapta Tála image—contd.

Limb of the body.		Nava Tala Angülas.	Sapta Tala Angülas.	Relative Proportions in Decimals
From neck to shoulder	...	8	$8\times\frac{7}{9}$	·074
Breast between arms	...	24	$24\times\frac{7}{9}$	·222
„ „ teats	...	12	$12\times\frac{7}{9}$	·111
Face between ears (curved length)	...	16	$16\times\frac{7}{9}$	·148
Ear to chin (curved length)	...	8	$8\times\frac{7}{9}$	·074
Ear to nose	...	8	$8\times\frac{7}{9}$	·074
„ „ eye	...	4	$4\times\frac{7}{9}$	·037
Face	...	4	$4\times\frac{7}{9}$	·037
Lip	...	½	$\frac{1}{2}\times\frac{7}{9}$	·004
Circumference of head	...	32	$32\times\frac{7}{9}$	·296
Width of head	...	10	$10\times\frac{7}{9}$	·092
Length of head	...	12	$12\times\frac{7}{9}$	·111
Circumference of neck	...	22	$22\times\frac{7}{9}$	·203
„ „ chest	...	54	$54\times\frac{7}{9}$	·500
„ „ „	...	47	$47\times\frac{7}{9}$	·435
Thickness of chest near breast	...	12	$12\times\frac{7}{9}$	·111
Circumference of waist	...	44	$44\times\frac{7}{9}$	·407
Height of do	...	4	$4\times\frac{7}{9}$	·1039
Width „ do	...	6	$6\times\frac{7}{9}$	·055
Circumference of hip of female figure	...	43	$43\times\frac{7}{9}$	·435
Do. do male figure	...	42	$42\times\frac{7}{9}$	·388

Tabular Statement—(A), showing the relative proportions for a Sapta Tála image—contd.

Limb of the body.				Nava Tala Angülas.	Sapta Tala Angülas.	Relative Proportions in Decimals.
Circumference of arm near armpit			...	18	18×$\frac{7}{9}$	·166
Do	do	elbow	...	16	16×$\frac{7}{9}$	·148
Circumference of head near elbow			...	14	14×$\frac{7}{9}$	·129
Do	do	wrist	...	10	10×$\frac{7}{9}$	·092
Width of palm			...	5	5×$\frac{7}{9}$	·046
"	"	Meta-tarsus	...	5	5×$\frac{7}{9}$	·046
Circumference of thigh near hip			...	32	32×$\frac{7}{9}$	·296
Do		knee	...	29	29×$\frac{7}{9}$	·268
Do		leg near knee	...	16	16×$\frac{7}{9}$	·148
Do		ankle	...	12	12×$\frac{7}{9}$	·111
Do		middle finger (near root)	...	4	4×$\frac{7}{9}$	·037
Do		middle toe (near root)	...	5	5×$\frac{7}{9}$	·046

I give below the text in original from which the above proportions have been taken.

नवताल प्रमाणे तु मुखं तालमितं स्मृतम् ।
चतुरङ्गुलं ललाटं स्यादधो नासा तथैव च ॥८०
नासिकाधश्च वक्त्रं चतुरङ्गुलमीरितम् ।
चतुरङ्गुला भवेद् ग्रीवा तालेन हृदयं पुनः ॥८१
नाभिस्तस्मादधः कार्या तालेनैकेन शोभिता ।

नाभ्यधश्च भवेन्मेढ्रं भागेनैकेन वा पुनः ॥९२

स्थितावूरू आयतावुरू जानुनी चतुरङ्गुले।

जङ्घे चारुसमे कार्ये गुल्फाविव चतुरङ्गुलम् ॥९३

नवतालात्मकमिदम्मूर्त्तिमानं बुधैः स्मृतम् ॥९४

शिखामपि तु केशान्तं त्र्यङ्गुलं सर्वमानतः।

द्विमानया च विभजेत् सप्ताष्टदशतालिकाम् ॥९५

चतुस्तालात्मकौ बाहू स्कन्धान्तावुदाहृतौ।

स्कन्धादि कूर्परान्तं च विंशत्यङ्गुलमुत्तमम् ॥९६

त्रयोदशाङ्गुलं बाहुः कलायाः कूर्परान्तकाम्।

अष्टाविंशत्यंगुलस्तु मध्यमान्तः करः स्मृतः ॥९७

सप्ताङ्गुलं करतलं मध्या पञ्चाङ्गुला मता।

सार्धत्र्याङ्गुलोऽङ्गुष्ठस्तर्जनीमूलपर्वभाक् ॥९८

पर्वत्रयात्मकोऽन्यासां पर्वाणि त्रीणि त्रीणि तु।

अर्धाङ्गुलेनाङ्गुलेन हीनानामा च तर्जनी।

कनिष्ठिकानामिकातोऽङ्गुलोना च प्रकीर्त्तिता ॥९९

चतुर्दशाङ्गुलौ पादौ अङ्गुष्ठो द्व्यङ्गुलो मतः।

सार्धत्र्याङ्गुलोऽङ्गुष्ठसम्मिता वा प्रदेशिनी।

प्रदेशिनी द्व्यङ्गुला तु सार्धाङ्गुलसमेतरा ॥१००

शिरोन्नतौ पाणिपादौ गूढगुल्फौ प्रकीर्त्तितौ ॥१०१

* * * *

* * * *

शास्त्रमानविहीनं यदङ्गं तद्विपश्चिताम्।

षडङ्गुलं ललाटं स्यात् तावन्मात्रौ भ्रुवौ मतौ ॥१०६

अर्धाङ्गुला भ्रुवोर्लेखा मध्ये धनुरिवायता।

नेत्रे च त्र्यङ्गुला यामे द्व्यङ्गुले विस्तृते शुभे ॥१०७
तारका तत्तृतीयांशा नेत्रयोः कृष्णरूपिणी ।
द्व्यङ्गुलं तु भ्रुवोर्मध्यं नासामूलसमयाङ्गुलम् ॥१०८
नासाग्रविस्तारं तद्वद् द्व्यङ्गुलं तत्त्रितयम् ।
शुकनासाकृतिर्नासा पुष्पवद् द्विविधा शुभा ॥१०९
निष्पावसदृशं नासापुटयुग्मं सुशोभनम् ॥११०
कर्णौ च भ्रूसमौ ज्ञेयौ दीर्घौ च चतुरङ्गुलौ ।
कर्णपालीत्र्यङ्गुला स्यात् स्थूला चार्द्धाङ्गुला मता ॥१११
नासावंशोऽर्द्धाङ्गुलस्तु स्वस्थः सार्द्धाङ्गुलोन्नतः ॥११२
ग्रीवामूलाच्च स्कन्धान्तमष्टाङ्गुलमुदाहृतम् ।
बाह्वन्तरं द्वितालं स्यात् तालमात्रं स्तनान्तरम् ॥११३
षोड़शाङ्गुलमानं तु कर्णयोरन्तरं स्मृतम् ।
कर्णस्कन्धाग्रान्तरं तु सदैवाष्टाङ्गुलं मतम् ॥११४
नासा कर्णान्तरं तद्वत् तदर्द्धं कर्णनेत्रयोः ।
मुखं तालतृतीयांशमोष्ठावर्द्धाङ्गुलौ मतौ ॥११५
द्वात्रिंशदङ्गुलः प्रोक्तः परिधिर्मस्तकस्य च ।
दशाङ्गुला विस्तृतिस्तद्द्वादशाङ्गुलदीर्घता ॥११६
ग्रीवामूलस्य परिधिर्द्वाविंशत्यङ्गुलात्मकः ।
स्कन्धमध्यपरिधिर्यच्चतुःपञ्चाशदङ्गुलः ॥११७
हीनाङ्गुल चतुस्ताल परिधिर्हृदयस्य च ।
आस्तनात् पृष्ठदेशान्ता प्रसृता द्वादशाङ्गुला ॥११८
सार्द्धत्रितालपरिधिः कट्याश्च द्व्यङ्गुलाधिकः ।
चतुरङ्गुल उत्सेधो विस्तारः स्यात् षडङ्गुलः ॥११९
पञ्चाशांशं नितम्बस्य श्रोण्यामङ्गुलतोऽधिकः ।

धात्रयमूलपरिधिः षोडशाष्टादशाङ्गुलः ॥१२०
हस्तमूलाग्र परिधिश्चतुर्दशदशाङ्गुलः ।
पञ्चाङ्गुला पादकरतलयोर्विस्तृतिः स्मृता ॥१२१
अङ्गमूलस्य परिधिर्द्वात्रिंशदङ्गुलात्मकः ।
अनविंशत्यङ्गुलः स्यादूर्ध्वाग्रपरिधिः स्मृतः ॥१२२
जङ्घामूलाग्रपरिधिः षोडश द्वादशाङ्गुलः ।
मध्यमामूलपरिधिर्विंशं यवचतुरङ्गुलः ॥१२३
तर्जन्यनामिकामूलपरिधिः सार्द्धत्र्यङ्गुलः ।
कनिष्ठिकायाः परिधिर्मूले त्र्यङ्गुल एव हि ॥१२४
स्वमूलपरिधेः पादहीनोऽग्रे परिधिः स्मृतः ।
हस्तपादाङ्गुष्ठयोश्च चतुःपञ्चाङ्गुलं क्रमात् ॥१२५
शुक्रनीतिसारे चतुर्थाध्यायस्य चतुर्थप्रकरणम् ।

Tabular Statement—(B), showing the measurements of a full-grown adult as compared with Sapta Tâla proportions.

Limbs of the body.	Measurements taken	Relative proportions deduced	Relative proportions for a Sapta Tala image.
Height of the full-grown adult ...	5'—6½"	1	1
Head ...	9½"	·142	·111
Forehead ...	2½"	·037	·037
Nose ...	2½"	·037	·037
Nose to chin ...	2¾"	·041	·037
Neck to breast ...	9½"	·142	·111
Breast to navel ...	10"	·150	·111
Knee ...	2½"	·037	·222
Arm up to the finger ends ...	2'-6"	·451	·444
Arm from shoulder to elbow ...	1'-1"	·195	·185
Arm from armpit to elbow ...	10"	·150	·120

Limb of the body.	Measurements taken	Relative proportions deduced	Relative proportions for a Sapta Tala image.
Palm ...	4⅛"	·061	'064
Middle finger ...	3¼"	'048	·046
Thumb ...	2½"	'037	'032
Index finger ...	2¾"	'041	'0277
Ring finger ...	2⅝"	.043	'0277
Little finger ...	2⅛"	'033	'018
Foot ...	10¼"	'154	'129
Great toe ...	2	'03	'018
Forehead (length) ...	5¼	'078	'074
Eyebrows (end to end) ...	5¼"	'078	'074
Eye (length) ...	6½"	'022	'0277
" (width) ...	6¾"	'011	'018
Ear (length) ...	2½"	'037	'037
" (breadth) ...	1¾"	'026	.0277
Neck to shoulder ...	5¼"	'070	'074
Breast between arms ...	1'-2"	'21	'222
" " teats ...	9"	'135	'111
Face between ears ...	9"	'135	'148
Ear to chin (curved length) ...	5¼"	'078	'074
Ear to nose (do) ...	5"	'075	'074
Ear to eye ...	2⅝"	'039	'037
Circumference of head ...	1'	'33	'296

Height of the body		Measurements taken	Relative proportions deduced	Relative proportions for a Sapta Tala image
Width of head	...	6¼	·093	·092
Length of head	...	9½"	·14	·142
Circumference of neck	...	1'-½"	·222	·203
Circumference of chest	...	3'-2"	·571	·500
Thickness of chest near breast	...	9¼"	·139	·111
Circumference of waist	...	3'-1"	·556	·407
Circumference of arm near armpit	...	1"	·180	·166
,, ,, near elbow	...	10"	·150	·148
,, ,, hand near elbow	...	10"	·150	·129
,, ,, ,, ,, wrist	...	7"	·10	·092
Width of palm	...	3⅛"	·046	·046
,, ,, Meta-tarsus	...	3⅞	·058	·046
Circumference of thigh near hip	...	1'-9"	·315	·296
,, ,, ,, near knee	...	1'-4"	·240	·268
,, ,, leg near knee	...	1'	·180	·148
,, ,, ,, ankle	...	0-8½"	·122	·111

Tabular Statement C showing the measurements of the different limbs of Statuettes found in the temples.

Particulars	Dimensions.	Relative proportions deduced	Relative proportions for a Sapta Tala image
(1).—FIG I, ON THE LEFT END WALL OF SATBAKHRA CAVE ON THE KHANDAGIRI HILL :—			
Total height from crown to feet ...	3′—3½″	1	1
Head from crown to chin ...	5¾″	·146	·142
Hand from wrist to the tip of middle finger ...	5¾″	·146	·142
Shoulder to tip of middle finger ...	1′—11½″	·594	·568
Arm from shoulder to elbow ...	10″	·253	·238
(2).—FIG II, ON THE LEFT END WALL OF SATBAKHRA CAVE ON THE KHANDAGIRI HILL :—			
Total height from crown to feet ...	2′—1″	1	1
Head from crown to chin ...	3½″	·140	·142
Hand from wrist to middle finger end ...	3⅝″	·144	·142
Arm from shoulder to tip of middle finger ...	1′—2″	·560	·568
Forearm from shoulder to elbow ...	6¼″	·250	·238
Leg up to knee cap ...	7″	·280	·284
(3).—FIG X, (COUNTING FROM THE END WALL) ON THE BACK WALL OF THE ANTE-CHAMBER OF SATBAKHRA CAVE :—			
Total height from crown to feet ...	2′—5¾″	1	1
Head from crown to chin ...	4⅜″	·148	·142

Particulars.	Measurements of the limbs.	Relative proportions deduced.	Relative proportions for a Sapta Tala image.
Arm from shoulder to the tip of middle finger	1′—4″	·542	·568
Leg ...	8¼″	·279	·284
Forearm from shoulder to elbow ...	7¼″	·245	·238
(4) A small female figure on the southern face of the Rajarani temple. ...			
Total height ...	9½″	1	1
Head from crown to chin ...	1⅜″	·144	·142
(5) A small female figure on the southern face of the Rajarani tenple ...			
Total height ...	9⅝″	1	1
Head from crown to chin ...	1⅜″	·142	·142
(6) A small statuette on the north-western pillar by the side of the niche on the western face of the Rajarani temple :— ...			
Total height ...	10¼″	1	1
Head from crown to chin ...	1½″	·146	·142
(7) A small female figure on the north face of the temple of Müktesvara :— ...			
Total height ...	1′-2½″	1	1
Head from crown to chin ...	2⅛″	·146	·142
(8) A very small statuette which is the right hand attendant of a female figure probably a goddess, or a queen on the western enclosure wall of the temple of Müktesvara :— ...			
Total height ...	6¼″	1	1

Particulars.	Measurements of the limbs.	Relative proportions deduced.	Relative proportions for a Sapta Tala image.
Head from crown to chin ...	1⅛"	·149	·142
(9) The main figure of Sürya, or sun-god found on the Bhoga-Mandapa of the temple at Konarka ...			
Total height from crown to feet ...	4'-4"	1	1
Foot to knee ...	1'-1¼"	·255	·284
From navel to breast ...	7⅜"	·141	·142
From extremities of eye to eye ...	4¼"	·081	·082

An examination of the Statement C as compared with A would at once clearly show that the images of the Orissan school were made according to Sapta T*a*la proportions as laid down by Sükr*a*ch*a*rya. The data were very carefully collected by me, and the images were chosen at haphazard so as to verify the theory that Sapta T*a*la proportions have been generally followed.

European artists and art critics condemn Indian art as not faithfully expressive of nature; they seek in vain for an accurate imitation of what they see in nature. It is apparently a difficult task to answer this charge brought against the Indian artists; but a moment's consideration of the nation's genius would at once make us tide over the difficulty. The plea of ethnic peculiarities* set up by Dr. Mitra in his Indo-Aryans is absurd. India is inhabjted by diverse races with various shades of ethnic peculiarities ; but the artistic representation is everywhere the same ; the same disregard, or rather want of regard for the natural is patent everywhere. It is idle to suppose that the artists whose imagination soared so high, could not possibly excel, if they willed, in a work of easy plodding industry, a work which has been felicitously expressed by Burne-Jones as a "direct transcript from nature."* An Indian artist would say with Burne-Jones, "Transcripts from Nature, what do I want with transcripts ? I prefer her own signature ; I don't want forgeries more or less skilful . . . . It is the message, the 'burden' of a picture that makes its real value."

Stand-point of Indian Art.

Indian artists have not thought it worth their while to copy from the life ; art was to them a means of removing the veil surrounding nature, or apparent reality. To copy from a living model, they knew to be a very easy task not worth pursuing ; in this, they could have easily excelled if they would, and this is borne out by reference to the magnificent war-horse led by a warrior, or the huge elephant lying within the compound of the temple at Konarka, or the huge bull within the precincts of the temple of Lingaraja at Bhubanesvara.

* A. K. Coomarswamy, D. Sc. Essays in National Idealism, p. 25.

I quote below the remarks of no less an authority on Indian Art than Prof. Havell in respect of the war-horse referred to above. He says, "Had it by chance been labelled "Roman" or "Greek", this magnificent work of Art would now be the pride of some great metropolitan museum in Europe and America"; again, "Here Indian sculptors have shown that they can express with as much fire and passion as the greatest European art the pride and the glory of triumphant warfare; for not even the Homeric grandeur of the Elgin marbles surpasses the magnificent movement and modelling of this Indian Achilles, and the superbly monumental war-horse in its massive strength and vigour is not unworthy of comparsion with Verocchio's famous masterpiecc at Venice. *"

The Indo-Aryan Art compared with the Greek or Roman Art.

The Indo-Aryan and the Greek or Roman artists had altogether different starting points. The Greek or Roman school is imitative, the other suggestive, creative, and idealistic. From the earthly point of view ours did not aim at perfection, and from the point of view of the eternal hereafter, of which the present is a glaring mockery, the art of the Greek or Roman school is a miserable failure.

According to the German philosopher Hegel, † "the Divine

* Prof. Havell, Indian Sculpture and Painting, p. 146.

† Ibid, p. 147.

is the centre of the representations of Art." This principle has been followed by the Indian artists. The Greek or Roman artists strive after representing a gross anatomical form, whereas an Indian tries to represent the ultra-physical form of which the physical form is a sheath, so to speak. Our ideal is abstraction, that of the Greeks is concretisation. The artistic expression of the Indo-Aryans is confined to the *Sukshma-sarira* or the ethereal body, whereas that of the Greek or Roman school is to its gross counterpart, the physical body. *

The European artists represent realism to the last dregs of reality. With us art is idealistic ; it has a deeper meaning. Is it not an outward expression of our effort to solve the enigmas of the world ? From outward visible nature we go deeper down to the very essence, the substratum of reality. Our artistic expressions are an outcome of the effort of the human mind to go beyond the apparent and to reach the transcendental. In our art the divinity unconsciously manifests itself even when the artist strives after representing human action and passion. The representations of Kali, Dürga, or Asurmardini may be cited to illustrate my remark. I quote below what Hegel has remarked as to how "the Divine principle shows itself, also in the forms of human activity, in the endeavour to realise the moral and social ideal, and all the display of

* Kedney, Hegel's Æsthetics, p. 60.

action, and passion exhibited in the endeavour Art may represent."

"And even when the gods are represented in their activity, they need not, however, descend from the dignity of their immutable character and their inviolable majesty; for Jupiter, Apollo, Mars, although determined forces, are yet firm and unagitated at the base, preserving their independence even when their activity is outwardly exercised." *

Oriental art based on idealisation and not imitation.

Idealisation and not imitation is an idea deeply ingrained in the minds of the oriental people. Though Assyria is situated on the farthest limits of Asia, this sense of idealization is noticeable in her sculpture. The Assyrian sculpture shows no doubt a decided tendency in imitating nature as indicated by an attempt at expressing the muscles of the limbs; this is due to the close proximity of Assyria to the European continent; but the sense of idealization is patent in the conventional "arrangement of the subject and the pose of the single figure.†" To understand rightly the Indian Art one must attach importance to this trait of national character. Subjectivity is the corner-stone of Indian Art, and objectivity, that of the European classic; to understand the true import of our

* Kedney, Hegel's Æsthetics, p. 62.

† Owen James, Grammar of Ornament, p. 29.

art one must not lose sight of the significance of this important principle. To this underlying principle are due the zoomorphic, or grotesque forms of our deities.

Representation of the divinity within.

I have already remarked that the Indian Art is based on the representation of the divinity. This is one of the main reasons which led our artists to draw their inspiration from the ideal lives of the saints, or from the deities of the Hindu, or for the matter of that, Aryan Pantheon. Our saints are not characterised by muscular development; this is natural. Live as they on vegetarian diet, and practise as they absolute control of the senses, the contours of their body become divested of sharp edges or muscular outlines, and they assume a general rotundity of form spiritually graceful. I need not go back to remote antiquity to prove my point; if we look at the photo or portrait of Paramhansa Ramakrishna, or Pawhari Baba we shall invariably see that the temporal or physical bodies of the saints were living illustrations of the validity of my assertion. We cannot reasonably expect the sharp muscular outlines in the artistic representations of the temporal lives of a Buddha, or a Chaitanya which we notice in those of a Hercules, or a dying gladiator.

One of the most perplexing features of Orissan Architecture and Sculpture is the presence of indecent figures defiling the sacred walls of the Jagamohana, N*a*t mandira, &c., except those of the sanctum. The sight of such figures representing various scenes of voluptuousness is puzzling, and nauseating. One is at a loss to understand why they have a place at all within the sacred enclosure. Not being able to account for this anomaly one is surely to be led into the pitfall of an erroneous conclusion that the artists who designed these ornaments to decorate the outer walls of a temple must have belonged to a race most morally depraved, and vicious. I enquired of the local pandits for a reasonable explanation who could offer none; I came to learn afterwards that such indecent figures are prevalent not only in Orissa, but in other parts of India as well. As an illustration, I may cite the case of the temple of the Kandarya Mahadeva at Khajuraho in Bundelkhand.

Indecent figures.

From the occurrence of such figures extending over a vast area the charge of voluptuousness brought against a whole nation does not stand to reason. There must be a deeper meaning underlying this apparent anomaly.

In the case of a building under construction when the uprights for the scaffolding have just been set up, we notice that a basket, or a broomstick, an old rejected shoe, and such other filthy things are tied to the end of a scaffolding pole so as to attract the notice of a passer-by. They are meant to withstand the evil effects of the jealous gaze of the observers, and to ward off the evil spirits that may possess the building under construction, hamper its progress by causing a catastrophe to befall it. This superstition of the twentieth century furnishes the key to unravel the mystery of indecent figures of the mediæval times, and this view of mine has been corroborated by the Uriya architects and artists of the present day. They cited from their *Silpa Sastras* to bear me out, and there is a definite plan, or arrangement recommended for the relative position of such figures in respect of the structure.* The Uriya artists say that the introduction of such obscene figures is not only to ward off the evil spirits, but to protect the structure against lightning, cyclone or other dire visitations of nature. The pinnacle of the temple ending in a pointed metallic trident or discus, the visitation of it by lightning was a phenomenon of usual occurrence, and the people of those days being unacquainted with the principle of a lightning conductor resorted to this superstition as an effective means of protection. This seems to be a rational explanation of the anomaly perplexing the intellect of not only the students of architecture, but of an ordinary pilgrim.

I may mention here incidentally an explanation which is

* I have very recently secured an old palm leaf manuscript of *Silpa Sastra* with several illustrations. I have not found time as yet to decipher it, but hope to do so very soon.

offered from a spiritual stand-point. The obscene figures are symbolical, or representative of the frailties of the world that flesh is heir to, and unless a spiritual aspirant rises superior to these frailties, he cannot attain the absolute truth, or reality represented by the deity enshrined in the sanctum; a pilgrim whose mind does not become affected at the sight of these obscene figures is spiritually fitted to enter into the sanctum, and to see the image of the deity.

Different theories are advanced as to the way in which the carving work has been executed. The theory supported

Carving in situ.

by Dr. Mitra in Indo-Aryans, Vol. I * is that the Orissan artists followed the Assyrian plan of carving *in situ*. Alex. Rea has advanced a similar theory in the case of Chalükyan Architecture.† I do not understand whence they deduced this theory. According to them, blocks of stone used first to be dressed to the requisite shape, fixed in their respective positions, and then carved *in situ*. I studied this point very carefully in Orissa, and I had ample opportunities afforded to me to do the same. I carefully observed the thorough reconstruction, or construction of the Jagamohana of Gauri's temple going on very near the *bunglow* I used to live in. The stone blocks, I noticed, were carved near the site of work and

* Dr. Rajendra Lal Mitra, Indo-Aryans, Vol. I, p. 150.

† Archæological Survey of Southern India, Vol. XXI, p. 5.

not *in situ* before they were fitted and fixed; and these carved blocks were arranged in heights of 4 to 5 ft. to see that the continuity, or the relative position of the figures carved was carefully maintained. The stone blocks were then numbered, and fixed in their respective positions; the artists seemed to manipulate the blocks with such dexterity and carefulness as to leave very little chance of breaking which was naturally apprehended. Only those blocks which had some chance of breaking, viz. those which had thin edges at the top, or side for the panels sunk in them, were carved *in situ*.

Some more grounds against the principle of carving *in Situ*.

On studying the carvings of old existing temples, this view of mine will commend itself to acceptance. I have noticed in many cases that the figures carved on two contiguous blocks of stone do not exactly form one symmetrical whole; this would never have happened had they been carved *in situ*. There is another important fact in this connection which should not be lost sight of. The work of carving *in situ* does not ensure the speedy completion of the work as it does not permit the working of many artists simultaneously on one particular spot; and in view of the fact that every inch of the face of the temple is carved, it is presumed that the theory of carving *in situ* would involve an unnecessarily long time. This will receive additional weight from the following consideration.

A good artist, I have seen in Orissa, can carve on an average on an area of 4 sq. inches fetching an income of eight annas per diem ; and the amount of work executed will be less if the work be of a superior quality. This fact coupled with that of the physical impossibility of allowing many artists to work together in one particular portion of the face would delay the completion of the work, and would at once lead us to reject the theory as not practicable. The existence of tracings on the temple walls (Rajarani, &c) cannot possibly lead to the conclusion of carving *in situ* ; it is probably the case that such temples had to be completed without waiting for the completion of the carving work ; perhaps it was thought necessary that the remaining works of carving might conveniently be taken up *in situ* gradually after the completion, as we complete many of our buildings of the present day leaving the ornamental work to be taken up at our convenience.

The Architecture of Orissa is defective in one respect viz, that it does not make any attempt at producing colour

Colour. decorations which are as important as sculpture. Very apposite is the remark of Barry that "the architect must go hand in hand with the sculptor, and painter."* The sphere of Architecture is narrowed down by doing away with painting. The importance of colour in the produc-

* Edward. M. Barry, R. A. Lectures on Architecture, p. 24.

tion of a perfect art cannot be overrated. As fine proportions, and a grandeur of lines are very important factors in producing an artistic effect in Architecture, so is harmony of colours a powerful agent in bringing about the desired end. The influence exercised by it is greater than harmony of vibrations in Acoustics ; it is distinctly sensuous and psychological in nature ; here also we notice an illustration of the principle of contrast.

The provision of colour decoration in addition to that of sculpture would have rendered the structures infinitely more beautiful than what they are at present. Though the interior of the temple is dark, yet there is ample room left for the application of colour. The inside walls and ceiling of the Jagamohana, the deep and narrow recesses between the pilasters, for instance, could have been painted effectively so as to withstand the action of the atmosphere. The frescoe paintings of the Chaitya caves at Ajanta are still as fresh as anything, as is evidenced by the copies thereof by Griffiths ; I am struck with the brightness of colour of a copy of a piece of Ajanta wall painting recently made by an amateur artist. Hence it may be reasonably concluded that there is nothing to apprehend in respect of the durability of wall paintings.

It is not the purpose of this chapter to describe, or classify the drapery, ornaments, utensils, furniture, arms and musical instruments of the inhabitants of Orissa as represented in their sculpture. They have been passingly referred to in the last few chapters in describing the different temples or figures.

In the fore-going pages I have dealt exhaustively with the nature and different types of Orissan form of sculpture with various sub-heads. The sculpture of Orissa is purely Indo-Aryan, and I have sought to elucidate it by quoting numerous passages from the Agni-Puranam, Sukra Niti, Brihat Samhita, &c. The details and arrangements of the texts have been faithfully observed. I have shown the points of resemblance to other styles prevailing in the southern part of India. I have also passingly referred to the points of excellence and defects from the stand-point of European classic. There are, however, a few points which I may briefly mention before the next chapter is commenced.

Natural disadvantage of Orissan Sculpture.

Unlike the sculptors of Greece and Rome, those of Orissa, nay of India in general, had to labour under a natural disadvantage of showing off their talents in a remarkable degree; a sort of impenetrable barrier was interposed as it were between their genius and excellence in execution; and this was afforded by 'the nature of the material on which they carved. The partiality of nature in this direction may explain the diminution of effect sought to be increased by their laborious attempts; genius could not override this inherent natural defect. We can well imagine the bright and chastening effect of these very figures were they executed in marble. It requires also much plodding industry to polish the rough gritty sandstone. The huge elephant and horse (vide plate XXVI) of Konarka, the statuettes Rajarani and Brahmesvara, the scrollwork, arabesque, and foliage of Müktesvara and Saridewl, if executed in marble, would have been considered as the brightest monuments of sculpture reaching its culminating point.

I have referred to a decided Buddhist reminiscence noticed in the Brahminical sculpture of Orissa; I have shown in the second chapter that Orissa at one time was a seat of Buddhism, and as an offshoot of Brahminism, it was slowly assimilated by the former throughout the length and breadth of India, and formed an integral part of it. The religious rites of the parent stock and the branch got nicely commingled together; without referring to any particular text such as that of the Mahayana Tantrika school, this can be clearly proved by making a comparative study of the Buddhistic and Brahminical iconography. I have already mentioned in this chapter some of the allied features. The figure III, Plate V (A) illustrating floral devices issuing out of a vase or urn is a distinct piece of Buddhist sculpture noticed on some of the extant Buddbist remains.

Buddhist reminiscence in Orissan Sculpture.

This is met with in the temples of Parasūramesvara, and Vaital at Bhubanesvara. This ornamental device is noticed in the Buddhist and Brahminical caves at Elura;* it has also been used in Chalukyan Architecture where its position is exactly the same as in the Indo-Aryan style. I may refer my reader to the jamb mouldings of the Kattesvara temple, Hirahadagalli.† The representations of pyramidal battlements in the frieze of the *bāda* of Parasūramesvara show decided Buddhist influence on the temple architecture of Orissa. I have also referred to the Chalukyan and Gupta influences; it may be mentioned here incidentally that the Indo-Aryan style has also reciprocally influenced the Chalukyan architecture in a very remote period (*circa* 6th century A.D.). This will be evident on examining the architecture and sculpture of the temples of Dūrga, Meguti, Huchchimalligudi at and near Aihole in the district of Bijapur. Huchchimalligudi temple near Aihole is similar to that of Parasūramesvara; this is older than the Meguti temple at Aihole dated in the first half of the seventh century A.D. (Saka 556 or, 634 A.D.) as appears from a long well-engraved inscription of Pulakeshin II.‡

We have seen already that the half-discs or insets of lotus

* Burgess, Report on the Elura Cave Temples (Archæological Survey of India, Vol. V), Plates.

† Archæological Survey of Southern India, Vol. XXI Plate XXXVI.

‡ Archæological Survey of India, 1907-08.

as noticed in Vaital, Parasūramesvara and many other temples are distinctly Buddhistic in origin. I have mentioned at great length how *Barājhānji* and several other ornaments have been borrowed from Buddhist sculpture. Reference has been made to the Naga and Vetal ornaments; the latter are dwarfish monsters struggling to raise the structure; this representation has been noticed by me in Buddhist sculpture, as in the capital of the gate of the Buddhist tope at Sanchi.*

Classes of Orissan ornaments.

The ornaments of Orissan Architecture are mainly of two kinds, (*a*) Face, or Panel ornament, (*b*) Free ornament. I have described the first sub-head at great length; the following among others come under the second sub-head. (1) Kalasa, or finial, (2) gargoyle, (3) vase or urn, (5) Lotus pendant, (5) Projecting lion, (6) Sardula, (7) Naga or Nagini column, (8) Dewl Charani.

Orissan Kalasa or finial.

The graceful and gradual curvature of the *Kalasa*, and the agreeable proportion between the height and the width render it a beautiful accessory to the temple which, if divested of it, would lose much of its beauty. The *Kalasa* of the Orissan school, simple as it is, is in no way inferior to the French or Italian Gothic. I am at a loss to understand how could Dr. Mitra detect a

* W. Griggs, Preservation of National Monuments in India, Plates, 46, 47 and 48.

† Dr. Mitra, Indo-Aryans, Vol. I (1881), p. 66.

resemblance of it to a Grecian amphora† which, for the matter of that, was invariably pointed at the base so that it could be stuck in the ground*, and which had a narrow elongated neck having a handle on each side. The design is evidently derived from a water jar.

The plate V (B) illustrates the *Kalasa*, or a finial surmounting the temples of Orissa. I have on pages 124-25 exhaustively dealt with the seven parts of a *Kalasa*.

I have dwelt upon all the sub-heads except the third. Vase ornament, or a sort of *Kalasa* is usually noticed, as is the case with Müktesvara at the top of the *bāda* just where the *rekha* commences; it is also found at different heights in Gauri's temple.

Lotus pendant.

In the ornament of the lotus pendant both the flower and the geometrical motives are apparent. The growth is nicely depicted from the centre, whence it is called a radial growth. The lotus pendants of Müktesvara and Brahmesvara are well-known, and have been already referred to by me. I may mention also that I saw beautiful fragments of a lotus pendant scattered near the Bhogamandapa of the temple at Konarka.

[1] Fairholt, A Dictionary of terms in Art, p. 22.

CHAPTER VII.

BUILDING MATERIALS.

Stone has been chiefly used as a building material in Orissan temples; although the localities where the temples abound do not yield an outcrop of building stones of good quality, still the sense of ensuring permanency was so deep-rooted in their minds that it led them to quarry them at some distant hills, and to bring them to the worksite. This fact makes us consider the contrivances that the architects devised for bringing the huge blocks of stone from many scores of miles across trackless forests and swamps to the actual site of work.

Use of stone as a building material.

The principal stones that have been utilized for building purposes in Orissa are sandstone, laterite, chlorite, and granitic gneiss.

The province of Orissa consists geologically of two very distinct portions,—the one near the coastal region, a belt of nearly flat alluvial formations varying from 15 to 40 miles in breadth, and the other, an undulating area studded with numerous hills; the latter is mainly composed of the crystalline or metamorphic series consist-

The Geology of Orissa.

ing of rocks of very ancient date so completely altered and crystallised by metamorphic action that all traces of their original structure are lost.*

Rock system of Orissa.

The following is a list, in descending order, of the rock systems occurring in Orissa :—

8. Blown sand.
7. Alluvium.
   (*b*) River delta deposits.
   (*a*) Older alluvium of coast plain.
6. Laterite.
5. Katak or Atgarh sandstones.
4. Mah*a*deva or P*a*nchet sandstones and grits.
3. D*a*mud*a* sandstones, shales and coal.
2. T*a*lcher sandstones, shales, silt and boulder-bed.
1. Metamorphic, or crystalline rocks.

Rock systems yielding building stones.

Out of the list given above, the rock systems Nos. 2, 3 and 4 are not found to be utilised for temple building in the districts of Cuttack and Puri; and the

* I may refer my readers to the following articles from which I have gathered the informations regarding the Geology of Orissa.

(1) A sketch on the Geology of Orissa by W. Blanford, F. G. S. (Records of the G. S. I. Vol. V).

(2) Physical features of the districts of Bankura, Midnapur and Orissa (Memoirs of the G. S. I. Vol. I).

I am also indebted to my friend A. Ghose, Esqr., F. C. S., F. G. S. for supplying me with some valuable informations on the subject.

systems Nos. 7 and 8 are suited for building purposes. The metamorphic rocks are chiefly found in the Nilgiri hills near Balasore, and in the locality at a distance of a few miles W. S. W. of Jajpur near the village Paikpada ; they are also met with in the tract between the Brahmani and the Mahanadi.

Katak or Atgarh group.

South-west of the town of Cuttack is a considerable area occupied by grits, sandstone and conglomerates with one or more beds of white or pinkish clay. The beds show certain similarity of character with the Mahadeva group.

Laterite.

Of the two kinds of laterite, the high level and the low level, we find only the latter type in Orissa. These are chiefly composed of hydrated oxide of iron and quartz sand. The rock occurs either in a vesicular, or in a loose gravelly condition. This is of detrital origin as proved by the occurrence of pebbles and boulders in the immediate neighbourhood of hills. From the Brahmani to the Chilka Lake, laterite forms raised terrace-like plains around nearly all the hills excepting those few which occur far out in the alluvium.

Geology of the district of Puri.

The country near the coast and a broad tract on the north-east of the district are alluvial, but the western parts of the area are composed of laterite, sandstone, and metamorphic rocks. There is a very small extent of the older undulating alluvium ; and almost all the eastern parts of the district and the country extending from the Mahanadi to the Chilka Lake is perfectly flat, and consists of the newer, or delta alluvium. Hills of blown sand extend along the whole coast, and are frequently arranged in two or three principal ranges—the first close to the shore, the second from one or two miles inland, and occasionally there is another still farther from the sea. South-west of the sandstone country, and west of Khurdah, there is a band of undulating plain partly covered with laterite through which gneiss rises at intervals. On the extreme west of the district, there are two very barren ranges of no great height running east and west, and formed of compact, rather granitoid gneiss. From this point whence the boundary of the district turns eastward as far as the Chilka Lake, only detached hills occur, all of gneiss, with intervening plains of laterite and alluvium.

Geology of the district of Cuttack.

The district of Cuttack is mainly composed of older alluvium, the newer one forming the flat delta of the Mahanadi, and the Brahmani ; blown sand occurs along the coast. There are numerous hills more or less isolated and composed of gneiss.

Geology of the district of Balasore.

The district of Balasore is almost alluvial, the greater portion being of older type with metamorphic rocks in the Nilgiri hills. Laterite forms a narrow fringe to the hills in places. A few sand hills extend towards the coast. The newer alluvium is formed by the deposits of the Vaitarini, Brahmani, Subarnarekha, etc.

Geological Features of the Bhubanesvara area.

The temples of Bhubanesvara are situated in an undulating country in which flats of laterite and alluvium alternate with each other. The basement bed on which these superficial formations rest is entirely obscured, and whether it is composed of metamorphic rocks, or of later sedimentary series cannot be determined. But judging by the enormous outcrops of sandstone-forming hills known as Khandagiri and Udaygiri and of the low-lying beds of the same rock not far from the outskirts of the Bhubanesvara area, it is presumed that the superficial lateritic beds and associated alluvium were formed on the eroded surface of rocks of the Atgarh basin. The gneissose hills which crop out near Khurda probably indicate the floor on which the sedimentary beds of the Atgarh basin were deposited.

The area rich in Building stones

In an area abounding in such excellent building stones such as laterite and sandstone, it is natural that utmost advantage has been taken to turn to account such materials. Although the deposits of laterite are very extensive and more accessible, the beds of sandstone also attain great proportions, and the importance of the latter is comparatively reduced owing to the great ease with which blocks of laterite can be excavated and shaped. It is significant that inspite of this fact the ancient master-builders of Bhubanesvar selected the more difficultly quarried and dressed sandstone in preference to laterite. Their choice could not have been based on the comparative action of weathering on the two rocks, for surely the ancient workers knew well that laterite withstands climatic action as well, if not better than many rocks, and exposure to atmospheric influences only enhances its hardness. The explanation for the preference of sandstone to laterite is to be sought for in the superior resistance which a compact and homogeneous rock like sandstone offers to great superincumbent and lateral pressure—a factor of utmost importance where the great elevation of the temples was concerned. Besides, from the artist's point of view, the texture of the sandstones was far more adaptable to receive the impressions of the sculptor's chisel and to display it to utmost advantage.

The sandstone used in the building of the temples at Bhubanesvara shows compact texture in a marked degree. The rock is usually very fine-grained, and combined with this, its hardness is such that it is susceptible of a fine artistic treatment which would have been out of the question if it had been too soft, too fragile or too hard. The sandstone beds in the vicinity of the Khanda-

Character of the sandstone.

giri and Udaygiri hills attain great development. The quarries are situated in the plains. The bedding planes and the joints substantially reduced the labour of quarrying. The beds of sandstone do not preserve a uniform character over long distances. Fine-grained sandstone, coarse grits and even conglomerate composed of large translucent pebbles of quartz, merge into one another. Such gradations are at times noticeable within a very small area as in parts of Udaygiri hill. The colour of the sandstone also varies, but sandstone of a greyish white and buff colour predominates. Ferruginous infiltrations due to the decomposition of contained iron minerals have often imparted a rich red colour to layers of the sandstone. The blocks of sandstone used in the Müktesvara, Brahmesvara and Rajarani temples show a pleasing dark brick-red colour which appears to be due to artificial colouring which did not penetrate far into the interior of the rock, as the original natural buff colour is clearly visible in the portion where the stone shows a fractured face,

Weathering of the sandstone.

The effect of weathering as seen in the majority of the temples is small. Portions of the Great Temple, of the temples of Parvati, Ananta Vasudeva, Parasüramesvara and Meghesvara exhibit marked signs of weathering so much so that some of the carvings have been partially obliterated. Signs of disintegration by atmospheric influences are clearly shown by some perforated panels. But the extreme effect of weathering are nowhere seen so conspicuously as in Bhaskaresvara Temple. The blocks of sandstone on the exterior face of this temple have been deeply eroded showing in many places spheroidal and conchoidal weathering Apart from the nature of the rocks, if the degree of weathering be accepted as any key to the age of the temples, then the temple of Bhaskaresvara ranks among the oldest, those of Meghesvara, Ananta Vasüdeva, Bhubanesvara Muktesvara, Brahmesvara and Rajarani being of subsequent date.

Other kinds of Stones.

Laterite has been chiefly used in building the outerwalls and enclosures of temples. The later additions to the porch of the Great Temple, Bhubanesvara are partly or entirely built of this rock. They are evidently of more recent date. Dr. R. L. Mitra has stated that the temple of Bhaskaresvara is built of blocks of basalt. This statement is entirely erroneous as that temple is exclusively built of sandstone. The great Lingam in this temple is probably of sandstone. It would be interesting if it were possible to find out to what depth it extends underground and whether there are any inscriptions in the buried portion. The stone has become so discoloured by the offerings of countless pilgrims for ages that it is not easy to ascertain its petrological character. Preparation of a microscopic section is out of the question as it will be an act of sacrilege to secure chips from this Lingam. This very reason also stands in the way of ascertaining the exact nature of the rocks employed in the sc uring of various deities. Such are the great statues of Nisa Parvati, Ganesa and Kartika. Although no definite identification of the material of these huge monoliths is possible under present conditions, it is almost certain that the rock is not chlorite as has been stated by more than one writer. The hardness far exceeds that of chlorite. The rock which is dark greenish is apparently serpentinous. The statues in the niches of the temples of Ananta Vasudeva and Bhashkaresvara are sculptured out of a dense serpentinous or hornblendic rock. This rock was probably brought from the quarries in the Nilgiri hills (of Orissa) near the villages of Santragodia and Goojadeeha.

Chemical and Petrographical examination of the so-called chlorite.

I got a sample of this rock, commonly called chlorite, analysed both chemically and petrographically by a friend* of mine in the Presidency College laboratory, Calcutta. On chemical analysis, the rock was found to contain silica, magnesia, oxide of iron, water and a small quantity of alumina. It is evidently a hydrous ferro-magnesian rock. The hardness of the sample

* Babu Nani Lal Datta, B. Sc.

ranged between 3 and 4; the white streaks noticed suggest the rock to be serpentinous; but it has not the characteristic colour of serpentine; this is due to its admixture with clay or some other rock, and also to subsequent metamorphism.

In thin sections, it was found to include iron ores. The arrangement of the iron ores points to its being derived from some pyroxenic rock, and suggests that it may be serpentine; but the polarisation colour is against its being so; between crossed nicols some talclike mineral is found included within a somewhat brilliantly polarising mineral. I feel inclined to think therefore that the rock may be some intermediate variety between serpentine and potstone, probably an impure variety of massive talc.

The chlorite or *mugni*, in common parlance, is hydrous silicate of alumina, ferrous oxide and magnesia, and is very tough and compact in texture. This stone has been used for moulding, architrave, and for lining the jambs and intrados of door openings. The sculptures carved out of chlorite blocks admit of very fine polish and artistic finish. The monolithic stone pillar in front of the temple at Puri is made of chlorite. The slabs of chlorite that decorate and line the jambs and outer faces of the doorway of the Jagamohana at Konaraka are so exquisitely and artistically carved that they still excite the wonder of the most fastidious critics of sculpture. I quote below what Mr. Stirling wrote about it in 1824 in the Asiatic Researches, Vol. XV.

"The whole of the sculptures on these figures comparing men and animals, foliage and arabesque patterns, is executed with a degree of taste, propriety, and freedom which could stand a comparison with some of our be... ...mens of Gothic architectural ornaments. The workmanship remains, too, as perfect as if it had just come from the chisel of the sculptor, owing to the extreme hardness and durability of the stone."

It has been remarked that the principal building stones are sandstone, laterite, and chlorite and granitic gneiss. Granitic gneiss has been used in many cases in carving sculptured figures.

Varieties of stones and their names in the local tongue

The different technical terms, in the local tongue, of the different varieties of the above stones are given below with the names of temples where they are met with.

Sandstone.

(*a*) Bog*da* Kand*a* (बोगड़ा काखा) is a coarse-grained white or yellowish sandstone, found at Khandagiri ; the deep yellow variety is hard, and that of fainter colour represents soft stuff. Bog*da* Kand*a* has the two following varieties, (1) Nar*a*j Bog*da* (नराज बोगड़ा), (2) Mot*a* Bog*da* Kand*a* (मोटा बोगड़ा काखा) ; the former is harder and more fine-grained than the latter, and is met with in the temples of Lingaraja, Brahmesvara, Yamesvara ; the latter has been used in the temples of Siddhesvara, and Nayakesvara.

(*b*) Raja Rania Kanda (राज राणिया कण्डा) is a fine-grained yellowish (generally) sandstone. Raja-Rania has the following sub-classes :—(1) Lal Raja-Rania, or the reddish variety, (2) Haludia Raja-Rania, or the yellowish variety, (3) Dhala-misa Raja-Rania, or whitish variety, (4) Kaya Raja-Rania, or the hard variety. Lal Raj-Rania Kanda has been used in the temples of Muktesvara, Gauri, and very sparingly in Rajarani. The second variety has been largely used in the temples of Rajarani, and also used in the temples of Gauri and Muktesvara. The third variety is noticed in Muktesvara, Gauri, Rajarani ; lintels, architrave, &c. requiring hardness and great strength are usually made of this variety. The fourth variety is met with in the temples of Rajarani and Brahmesvara. This class of stone is hard, and is used for works requiring strength and toughness, such as lintels, architrave, &c.

(*c*) Khadia Kanda (खड़िया कण्डा) is a white sandstone resembling chalk ; this variety has been noticed in the temples of Ananta Vasudeva, Parvati, Parasuramesvara, &c. It is divided into the following classes, (1) Sapha Khadia Kanda noticed in the temples of Parasuramesvara and Vaital, (2) Phül Khadia Kanda used in Sari-dewl, and the temples of Ananta Vasudeva and Parvati, (2) Balia Khadia noticed in the Sari-dewl and the temple of Ananta Vasudeva. The Phül Khadia variety is soft and admits of fine sculptural works. It is made of grains of silica cemented by a matrix of calcium oxide

The softness of Khadia Kanda is due to the cementing material, and not due to the grains of silica themselves embedded in the matrix. The specific gravity of a sample brought from Konarka was strangely 1·861 (C. F. the table annexed).

(*a*) Rang Dalima :—It is a reddish white sandstone resembling Dalima or Dadimba, or pomegranate. The reddish tinge is due to its containing an admixture of iron oxide; this stone is rather hard for dressing. The main temple of Lingaraja at Bhubanesvara is partly built of this variety of sandstone ; it is also noticed in the Vaitala temple.

The Rangdalima is divided into the following classes :—(1) Sapha Rangdalima or white Rangdalima noticed in the temples of Parasürameśvara, and Vaitala, (2) Matia Rangdalima, a greyish variety met with in the above temples, (3) Rangdalima-misrita-Khadiakanda noticed in the temples of Parasürameśvara, Vaitala, and in small quantities in Siddhesvara.

2. Laterite or Makda :—This variety of stone is called Makda in common parlance ; it is found as a superficial formation, or just below a flat alluvium ; when this alluvium is

denuded, the formation below of laterite is exposed to the surface.

The boundary walls have been invariably built of laterite ; in these unimportant cases the whole structure has been built of this stone and has stood well ; blocks of laterite have in numerous has been placed side by side with sandstone blocks. The weathering action on laterite has caused unsightly stains on the neighbouring sandstone blocks and has accelerated in turn their disintegration ; moreover, these blocks by reason of their crumbling into pieces have helped in the consequent loosening and detachment of sandstone blocks. This stone does not admit of any fine or ornamental work. The peculiar quality of this rock is that it is easy to cut and shape it when first dug, but it becomes hard and tough after exposure to the air.

3. The Khadi Prastara :—It is a red and tough variety of quartz found as an inclusion in a particular variety of sandstone. It is not used as a building material, nor for sculptor's work. The architects avoid it as much as possible. The mortar, pestle, stone for grinding spices, &c. are made of it.

I give below the table showing the chemical and physical properties of various classes of sandstone used in the temples of Orissa with their names in local tongue.

Number	Names in local parlance	Petrographic Character	Action of Hydrochloric Acid	Specific Gravity
(1)	*Lal Raja-Rania*	Sandstone ; with minute flakes of white mica		2·3
(2)	Haludia Raja-Rania	Ferruginous sandstone, occasionally with mica	nil	2·5
(3)	Dhala-misa Raja-Rania	Sandstone with particles of mica	very very slight	2·31
(4)	Kaya-Raja-Rania	Contains only silica ; coarse-grained sandstone	nil	2·28
(5)	Sapha Rang-Dalima	Ferruginous sandstone	nil	2·43
(6)	Matia Rang-Dalima	Ordinary sandstone	nil	2·3
(7)	Rang-Dalima-Misrita-Khadia Kanda	Sandstone with mica	nil	2·35
(8)	Sapha Khadia Kanda	Fine-grained sandstone occasionally with big grains of quartz	nil	2·23
(9)	Phul Khadia	Sandstone with mica	nil	2·28
(10)	Balia Khadia Kanda	Fine-grained sandstone	nil	2·3
(11)	Naraj-Bogda Kanda	Contains only silica ; coarse-grained sandstone	nil	2·3
(12)	Mota-Bogda-Kanda	Highly decomposed granite	nil	2·41

Many Orissan temples present a red appearance by reason of having the stone blocks dyed with a pigment. Although the appearance is deceptive as leading many to take the stone for a red variety of sandstone, the importance from a utilitarian point of view is very great, for it effectively retards the weathering action of the atmosphere. The paint does not seem to be a simple compound but a complex composition of several ones in definite proportions. I have come across a reference to it in the Brihat Samhita which is quoted in the foot-note. The 4th couplet of the text quoted below enjoins on the application of the paste on the palace and temple walls, the well lining, Siva lingam, etc. Roughly speaking, the paste is a composition of the precipitate of unripe *tindük* fruits, *kapiththaka (kat bela* in common

Red appearance of some temples

* आमं तिन्दुकमामं कपित्थकं पुष्पमपि च शाल्मल्याः।
बीजानि शल्लकीनां धन्वनवल्को वचा चेति॥
एतैः सलिलद्रोणः क्वाथयितव्योऽष्टभागशेषश्च।
अवतार्योऽस्य च कल्को द्रव्यैरेतैः समनुयोज्यः॥
श्रीवासकरसगुग्गुलुभल्लातककुन्दुरुकसर्जरसैः।
अतसीबिल्वैश्च युतः कल्कोऽयं वज्रलेपाख्यः॥
प्रासादहर्म्यवलभीलिङ्गप्रतिमासु कुड्यकूपेषु।
सन्तप्तो दातव्यो वर्षसहस्रायुतस्थायी॥
लाक्षाकुन्दुरुगुग्गुलुगृहधूमकपित्थबिल्वमध्यानि।
नागबलाफलतिन्दुकमदनफलमधूकमञ्जिष्ठाः॥
सर्जरसरसामलकानि चेति कल्कः कृतो द्वितीयोऽयम्।
वज्राख्यः प्रथमगुणैरयमपि तेष्वेव कार्येषु॥
इति श्रीवराहमिहिरकृतौ बृहत्संहितायां वज्रलेपो
नाम सप्तपञ्चाशोऽध्यायः।

Edited by Jivananda Vidyasagara.

parlance), blossoms of *sâlmali* (silk-cotton) etc. boiled in a definite quantity of water, and mixed finally with exudation of *sarja* tree, or turpentine, resin, linseed. etc. Another sort of paste mentioned in couplets 5 and 6 consists of Laksha (lac), a sort of resin, the kernel of the Bael fruit (बिल्वफलानि), turpentine, myrobalan, etc.

Wood. From the nature of door openings it appears without a shadow of doubt that wood must have been used as one of the building materials. I could not find out the least trace of wood anywhere although I searched for it very carefully. A few instances of old, worn out doors that I came across are evidently two to three hundred years old, and do not belong to the Mediæval times when the temples themselves came into existence.

Brick. Brick seems to have been occasionally used in the construction of minor appurtenances of temples; at Konarka recent excavations by the P. W. D. have exposed to the surface the remnant of a small temple entirely made of bricks which lay buried in heaps of sand. During my brief sojourn I came across it; on close examination, it seemed to me that the temple was never finished, for the architects might have apprehended that the brick basement would not be able to bear the superstructure.

The rare occurrence of bricks is due to the unsuitableness of the local earth for brick-making; the earth of the locality generally contains an excess of silica and an insufficient proportion of alumina; the bricks are necessarily rather brittle and soft. I took more than a dozen samples of bricks at Konarka, and all of them crumpled into pieces when pressed between the fingers; they could be easily scratched with nails. The bricks that I came across at Konarka seemed to me not sufficiently burnt; they belong to the third class as defined by the P.W.D.

I could with much difficulty secure whole bricks when detached from their original position; in the very process of detaching they invariably gave way, although the mortar between the different courses was not very adhesive; they seemed to me to be set in sandy clay.

The bricks referred to already, are very regular in shape; but the dimensions are not uniform throughout. I give below the average dimensions:—

Length = 1′ – 1½″ = 13½″
Breadth = 10½″
Thickness = 2½″ to 3″

The bricks in old days used to be made of larger dimensions than what obtain in practice at present; they resemble modern tiles. The average superficial area of a brick = 140 sq. inches; that of the bricks at Budh-Gaya described by Dr. Mitra is about 140 sq. inches on an average. The bricks of the Chaldæans and Assyrians measure 15¾ inches square. Here I may refer to the unusual size of bricks that I came across at Sabour in the District of Bhagalpur while digging trenches in a mound probably the seat of an old colony of jewellers.

I have already stated that the bricks have been rather underburnt; this is probabiy due to the necessity of their being dressed for ornamental surface.

The bricks are soft and porous in texture, and the fractured surface presents a honey-combed appearance due to the cavities of the husks of paddy with which the brick-earth was mixed before the bricks were moulded. In many specimens the charred husks are perceptible even now; these were added to the clay which was well kneaded by being trodden under feet. The admixture of the chaff, or husk rendered the under-burnt bricks capable of offering greater resistance and having greater body than would have been otherwise possible. This method was followed by the Egyptians, Chaldæans, and Assyrians. They used to mix clay with "chopped or rather pulverized straw, a proceeding, which was thought to give it greater body and resistance"

Mortar has not been used to set the blocks of stone; fairly

Mortar. dressed stones have been placed on their natural beds. As the force of compression is mainly called into play in an Orissan temple the use of mortar as a means of aggregation has been judiciously dispensed with. The statical equilibrium of the structures is due to the vertical action and reaction, and as such the Uriya architects, unlike the Romans, rejected mortar as useless for the transmission of pressure from one point to the other; stability was ensured by fairly dressed and huge blocks of stone and by a careful adjustment of the centre of gravity. The massive stone blocks had to be connected together by iron cramps doubled over and inserted in holes. The stone blocks have been so accurately dressed in many cases as to make the joints look like hair-cracks. Perfectly horizontal courses of stone have been laid; the architects are noticed to be very careful even in the interior filling in of huge walls. Care has been taken to see that the walls rise perfectly straight up, not a bit out of plumb; but for so much care and skill, the structure would not have withstood the ravages of time so successfully.

Another contrivance which I noticed at Konarka is worth mentioning.

Iron cramps and their effects

Wedge-shaped blocks of stone are noticed to have been fitted in the interior of the walls to ensure stability. Although iron-cramps helped a great deal in keeping the stones in their proper position, yet they have been a great menace to their stability in another way. The iron-cramps have by oxidation swelled in volume and have effected cracks in them by causing a great strain.

The temples were often plastered; this is indicative of a degenerated taste; at the same time this was meant to hide any bad workmanship from the public view; this gave them a tendency to execute bad work. The interior was often plastered; I scraped off the plaster applied to the three tiers of cornice projecting from the inside wall of the cella at Konarka, the lowest one being at a height of 4'-10" above the pavement. There are 2 coats of plaster; the lower coat serves the body over which the upper coat presenting a polished surface is applied. The total thickness of the two coats is $\frac{5}{16}$", the upper coat is $\frac{1}{16}$" and lower coat is $\frac{4}{16}$" or ¼". On being examined with a magnifying glass, the upper coat seems to contain very minute grains of sand; the lower coat is seen with the naked eye to contain large grains of sand. The upper coat resembles the modern stucco plaster and presents a perfectly polished and glistening surface. The lower or the first coat has been applied after filling in the depressions or irregularities of the surface by a reddish mortar, probably powdered laterite.

Plaster work

Iron has been largely used in Orissan temples as architraves or lintels over door-ways, as beams to support the false ceiling, as cramps to connect

Metal

together the blocks of stone, or as door-hinges. It has been already stated that the method of corbelling or horizontal projection was used to reduce the internal space for roofing purposes, and over the topmost course were laid the flags of stone. This was the case with small temples; but this method could not be used with advantage where a large space was to be covered; the Aryan architects were fully conversant with the statical principle that to ensure the stability of a structure the vertical line drawn from the centre of gravity must be within its base. Therefore where large spaces were to be covered, the Uriya architects had to stop corbelling at a reasonable height where the internal area was sufficiently reduced and covered by flags of stone supported on wrought iron joists.

Iron lintels are largely noticed in Puri and Bhubanesvara temples. I shall only deal with the iron-beams of the temple at Konarka. The floor area of the Jagamohana is 40 ft. square; the walls rise straight up to the height of 40 ft, whence bracketting inwards commences till the length and breadth contract to 20 ft; here the joists have been laid with flags of stone on them. The beams and lintels are of high class wrought iron. The maximum length of the beams of Konarka is 35′-9″, and cross section 7″ square.

Iron beams of Konarka

The beams or lintels consist of thin laminæ welded together forming a rectangular piece. I had opportunities afforded to me to study this at Puri and Konarka. The rejected iron lintel placed on the court-yard by the Putalesvara temple within the precincts of the temple of Jagannath is found to be made up of welded pieces of iron, thickness of them varying from [illegible]″ to ⅛″. These laminæ or strips run both in the horizontal and vertical directions. The cross-section of the broken beams scattered near the Jagamohona at Konarka present the same appearance.

Various theories are advanced as to the manufacture of iron beams. I agree with some in thinking that the beam consists of individual laminæ put together and welded by molten iron poured on the surface. It fills up the interstices, and forms them into one mass. This is borne by the fact that gaps or cavities are often visible when these iron-beams are broken cross-wise; this is due to the fact of the molten iron not reaching the interior completely; the following fact also bears out the theory; the intervening pieces of iron do not resemble the laminæ they connect; they look like foreign matter introduced by some mechanical means. This would never happen in case of ordinary welding. These pieces have been the first things to give way to the action of the atmosphere, and they have scaled off in many cases, while the independent laminæ are kept intact.

Theory of iron manufacture

However plausible the above arguments may be, it is still a matter of great wonder how could such huge joists of wrought iron be forged, and the difficulty is aggravated by the curvilinear form that has been imparted to the surface. Those who have studied Metallurgy know full well how tedious and difficult a process it is to extract iron by smelting the ores. The engineers of those days were not conversant with the fourfold principles of Refining, Puddling, Shingling, and Rolling, nor with the modern methods of preparing platemetal, puddleballs, and blooms, nor had they the appliances and machinery that modern science has contrived after the lapse of many centuries ; the Aryan engineers even did not know how to prepare hot blast. All these considerations should make us pause awhile before sweeping remarks of reproach and contumely are levelled against them.

It is a matter of great regret that these beams or lintels are not painted now by the P. W. D. so as to withstand the oxidising influence of the atmosphere. The Mahomedan historian Abul Fazl saw them painted by the forefathers of those who have been branded "enfeebled and degraded" by the writer of the article quoted on page 265.

I secured with great difficulty a very small piece of wrought iron from an iron beam at Bhubanesvara ; coupled with the disadvantage of its being small in dimensions, it was not a sample of good quality, it being full of flaws, and the proportion of carbon and other foreign materials being rather excessive. I sent it to Prof. Dutt* of the Engineering college, Sibpur, who kindly took the trouble of getting it tested for me in the Testing Laboratory.

Test of a sample of iron

He got a small test piece made of it of cross section ·27" x ·415" ; this broke at 1.6 tons. The breaking strength accordingly comes to about 14.3 tons per square inch. Prof. Dutt wrote to me to say that "unfortunately the sample was not without flaws, and the test piece broke at one of these. You can see this very well at the place of rupture. If it had been possible to obtain a decent sample of the iron, I believe, a strength of 20 tons per square inch could be easily attained." The sample sent was of the worst quality, and hence the ultimate tensile stress was less than the usually accepted average of 25 tons per sq. inch.

The assurance of Prof. Dutt that a decent sample of this iron could easily show a strength of 20 tons per sq. inch reflects great credit on the Orissan metallurgists of a by-gone age, for the average tensile strength of wrought iron was 23 tons per sq. inch in England only 36 years ago ; the following is quoted from Prof. Anderson's Strength of Materials and Structures (1874). "The ultimate tensile strength of wrought iron

* Prof. S. K. Dutt, M. A., Professor of Electrical and Mechanical Engineering.

is usually set down as 25 tons per square inch, but this is above the present general average, 23 tons being nearer as an approximate round number."† I believe that the Orissan metallurgists could also have effected an increase in the strength of wrought iron if they willed ; they did not do so, for the nature of forging the beams by the method of welding described above demanded of them to make the iron rather weaker (from the modern standard) in strength. The following lines quoted from Prof. Anderson's work will bear me out : "...but weaker iron is not inferior for some purposes ; such iron frequently has the welding property in a marked degree, and is preferred in consequence, wherever welding has to be extensively resorted to, in converting wrought iron into the required articles."

I may mention incidentally that I have come across numerous instances of wrought iron beams of a quality far superior to the one subjected to tensile stress as stated above.

Iron Pillar at Delhi

In India, we have instances of iron manufacture existing for a long time. The iron pillar at Delhi is more wonderful than the beams of Orissa. I quote below what an eminent engineer wrote in a first class engineering journal of England in 1871 on our Indian Iron manufacture.

† John Anderson, C. E., L. L. D., F. R. S. E. "The strength of Materials and Structures" (1874), p. 49.

"Nothing heretofore brought to light in the History of Metallurgy seems more striking to the reason as well as the imagination, than this fact that from the remote time when Hengist was ruling Kent, and Cerdic landing to plunder our barbarous ancestors in Sussex, down to that of our third Henry, while all Europe was in the worst darkness, and confusion of the Middle Ages—when the largest and best forging producible in Christendom was an axe or a sword-blade—these ancient peoples of India, the forerunners of those now so enfeebled and degraded, possessed a great iron manufacture, whose products Europe even half a century ago could not have equalled."

I quote the following from the address delivered on the 13th April, 1905, by the President of the Institute of Mechanical Engineers, England, on the effects the manufacture of iron and steel has had on the promotion of comfort and well-being of the world.

"While considering forging of large masses of iron and steel, it is not easy to forget the impression caused by first seeing the Iron Pillar at Delhi. This column of wrought iron, which is 16 inches in diameter, of which 22 feet are above the ground, and which is said to be 50 feet long* and weighing about 18 tons, is finished perfectly round and smooth, with an ornamental top, and was made many centuries ago from iron

* The pillar is not 50 feet long.

produced direct from the ore, and built up piece by piece. Remembering the lack of facilities men had in those days for first forging and then welding together such an enormous mass makes one wonder at the iron worker of those days, who must have possessed engineering ability claiming the admiration of our times. It is questionable whether the whole of the iron works of Europe and America could have produced a similar column of wrought iron so short a time ago as the Exhibition of 1851."

CHAPTER VIII.

The Temples of Bhubanesvara.

The temples of the locality in and near Bhubanesvara are older than those at Puri or Konarka; and those at Bhubanesvara belong to various stages extending over several centuries; hence they can be divided into several classes or groups based on their chronological order. They can, however, be classified as per their constructive peculiarities, or the particular localities where they appear. The latter classification has no scientific value, but is greatly helpful in distinguishing them from one another; this method has been resorted to by the Editor of the District Gazetteer, Puri. The basis of his classification is the tank or *sarovara* around which the temples are noticed to cluster; but the temples clustering round a particular tank show various shades of constructive peculiarities having, in fact, very little in common between them. I shall show later on that the temples of Muktesvara, Kedaresvara, Gauri, and Parasuramesvara situated near the Kedara-Gauri tank

Classification of the temples.

at Bhubanesvara are so divergent from one another from the point of view of construction and chronology that they cannot be, properly speaking, classed under one group; but this method avoids the difficulty of classification involved in other methods. This is like a geographical division, and the intermediate tanks scattered here and there like permanent bench marks in surveying serve to fix the *locale* of the temples; but there are some temples still which are not situated by any tank at all, such as Ramesvara, Bhaskaresvara, &c.; so this method of classification does not seem to be exhaustive. The grouping followed by me on page 113 is exhaustive and scientific as it is based on the peculiarity of construction. I have also referred to another classification of the Orissan temples in Chapter V, having an indirect bearing on the constructive peculiarities like the former but from a different stand-point. They are recapitulated below:—Rekha, Pida, Vaitala and Gauri Chara.

There are several tanks or *saravaras*, more or less important, in Bhubanesvara, and they are given below *ad serialim*.

Tanks of Bhubanesvara.

1. Sahasralinga tank or Devipadahara:—

This is situated on the east of the temple of Lingaraja; it has rows of small temples, 100 in number, situated by its four sides; out of these, 77 are in good order, and 23, more or less damaged and dilapidated; the tank has flights of stone steps.

2. Vindüsagara, or Vindüsarovara :—

It is a very big tank measuring 1300 feet by 700 feet, and situated on the north side of the Lingaraja temple ; all the four sides were originally lined with blocks of laterite forming flights of steps ; those on the south only are in good order. In the centre of the tank there is an island measuring 100 feet by 60 feet on which there is a small temple with a terrace in front of it. This island is protected by a revetment wall running all round. At the time of the *Snâna Yâtrâ*, or bathing festival an image of Vishnü is taken there ; a great sanctity attaches to the water of the tank as drops from all the sacred tanks of the world and heaven are supposed to have formed this vast quantity of water ; but it is very impure as a green, slimy mass of cryptogamic organism is seen floating perceptibly on the surface.

3. Papanasini tank :—

It is to the east of the Yamesvara temple, and has flights of stone steps.

4. Ramakunda :—

It is to the west of the temple of Ramesvara.

5. Gauria Kunda :—

It is a very sacred pool to the east of Gauri's temple ; the water of the tank is very pure and is used for drinking purposes. There are two more pools near Gauri Kunda and within the precincts of the temples of Kedaresvara and Gauri on the east and west of Kedaresvara respectively; the one on the west is called Chal-dhua Kunda, and its water is very pure; that on the east is nameless and is overgrown with weeds and aquatic plants.

6. The temples of Muktesvara (Vide Plate-VI. A), Brahmesvara, &c, have their respective tanks attached to each of them. There is a small pool of water called Marichi Kunda just to the south of the temple of Muktesvara; the water of this pool is supposed to remove the sterility of a barren woman, and it sells accordingly at fancy prices during the month of Chaitra corresponding to March.

The names of the temples near and round the tanks are given towards the end of the chapter.

The Chronology of the temples of Orissa.

The student of Orissan history has to experience a great difficulty which is almost insuperable in ascertaining the chronology of the ruins that he comes across. I have shown in the second chapter that the Madla Panji, or the Temple Archives is not an authentic record that may be referred to in precisely fixing the dates and the names of kings who ruled over Orissa. We may, however, gather some information which may be of immense service in this direction. There is a mention in the Madla Panji hallowed by the acquiescence of ages that Yayati Kesari, the founder of the Kesari dynasty built the temple of Lingaraja, Bhubanesvara.

I have sought to prove in the second chapter that Yay*a*ti flourished sometime in the beginning of the 9th century A. D.; hence the earliest date that can be assigned to this temple is the beginning of the 9th century, and not the middle of the fifth century as some would have us believe. I should mention here that the Indo-Aryan art of temple building reached its culminating point in Orissa long before that remote period; and there are temples even now extant testifying to this fact. Although the temples of Parasür*a*mesvara, Uttaresvara show marked influence of the Dravidian or Ch*a*lukyan style, they are eminently Indo-Aryan in design and execution.

Indo Aryan influence in the temples of the Deccan

In the Deccan, are noticed several temples which are distinctly Indo-Aryan and of the Orissan type. The temples of Durg*a* and Huchchimalligudi at Aihole in the district of Bijapur bear a striking resemblance to the temple of Parasur*a*mesvara. The temple of Durg*a* is dated, according to Cousens, within a century before the date of the cave at Badami; from an inscription of Pulakeshin II, the date of the temple of Meguti at Aihole which, according to Cousens, "is an advance upon the Durg*a* temple," has been fixed in 536 *Sa*ka, or 634 A. D; the temple of Huchchimalligudi is even older than the temple of Meguti. Mr. Cousens considers* that the earliest possible date that can be

* Archæological Survey of India, 1907-08.

assigned to the temples at Aihole is the fifth century A. D. From the above consideration it is deduced that the Orissan art of temple building was transplanted in the Deccan so early as the fifth century A. D. at the latest.

I have already referred to the Gupta influence noticed in Orissan sculpture. The Gupta dynasty reigned from the first

Gupta Influence. quarter of the fourth century to the middle of the fifth century A. D ; hence Orissan style must have been in existence in that period also. Orissa was conquered by Samudra Gupta when the great Gupta monarch subjugated south Kosala in the valley of the Mahanadi ; his dominion extended up to the Narmada on the south. Samudra Gupta reigned from 326 A. D. to 375. A. D. (*circa*). Orissan architecture was evidently influenced during his reign, i.e. in the fourth century A. D.

It is reasonable to suppose that a considerable length of time most have elapsed since the art began to be first practised in Orissa, for I have already drawn the reader's attention to definite and stereotyped system of technics followed in Orissan architecture and sculpture. I may accordingly safely conclude that the Orissan style of temple building was much developed in the beginning of the Christian era and even before that.

It is almost a hopeless task to fix with anything like precision the exact dates when the temples were first constructed, but by a careful sifting of evidences, both external and internal, we may arrive at conclusions which would indicate the nearest approach to the exact dates.

Probable dates of the temples.

I have proved above that the temple of Parasürâmesvara is probably dated in the 5th, or 6th century A. D. at the latest. I shall show later on that the temple of Müktesvara is an advance on the temple of Parasürâmesvara; both these temples have striking points of resemblance and difference; this temple may fairly be taken to have been constructed in the sixth, or seventh century A. D. The temple of Lingarâja has been proved to have been built in the beginning of the ninth century A. D. Fortunately the dates of Ananta Vâsüdeva and Meghesvara have been ascertained with accuracy with the help of two inscriptions engraved on slabs of stone now stuck in the compound wall of the temple of Ananta Vâsüdevâ. I shall show later on that they belong to the twelfth century A. D. It can be surmised that the important temples of Bhubanesvara belong generally to a period extending from the 10th to the 12th centuries A. D.

There are some five hundred temples scattered here and there in and near Bhubanesvara, and it is impossible to describe them within a small compass of this book. I give below the names of many such out of which the important ones only will be described. It is also not necessary to describe all of them, for no variation is noticed in the peculiarities of construction and decoration. I shall therefore content myself with the description of a few only out of the list given below.

Muktesvara, Kedaresvara, Siddhesvara, Parasuramesvara, Gauri, Uttaresvara, Bhaskaresvara Rajarani, Nayakesvara, Brahmesvara, Meghesvara, Ananta Vasudeva, Gopalini, Savitri, Lingaraja Saridewl, Somesvara, Yamesvara, Kotitirthesvara, Hatakesvara, Kapalamochani, Ramesvara, Gosahasresvara, Sisiresvara, Kapilesvara, Varunesvara, Chakresvara and many others.

Muktesvara Temple.

The temple of Muktesvara is half a mile to the north-east of the Lingaraja temple, and is situated in the Siddharanya, or the forest of the perfect. The place is picturesque by shady trees with their overhanging branches presenting a sombre appearance ; this forest, or garden has on its outskirts vast expanse of paddy fields interspersed here and there by umbrageous trees towering in solitary grandeur and affording shade and shelter to the peasants and cattle. Here, there is a natural spring bubbling up continually and yielding a perennial supply of water to the sacred *Kundas*, or tanks, the water of which is held in great sanctity by those who frequent them. It is in the fitness of things that this temple of Muktesvara so aptly styled, "the gem of Orissan

PLATE VI(A)

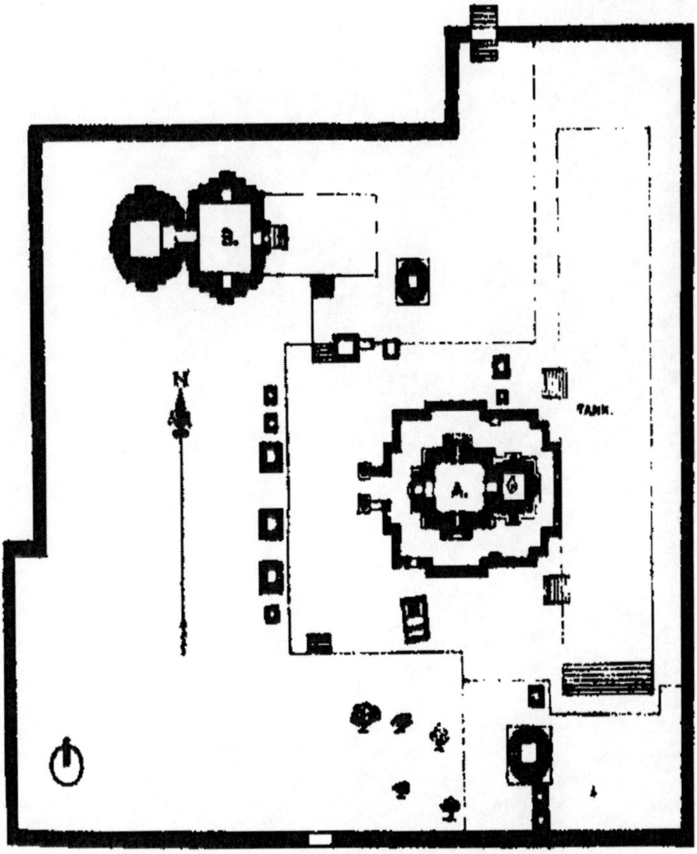

SITE PLAN OF MUKTESVARA & SIDDHESVARA.

SCALE 50' = 1"

PLAN OF PARASURÂMESVARA.

PLAN OF RÂJARÂNI.

SURVD & LITHD BY A.L.

Architecture"*, should be situated here, the veritable "garden of the perfect" where boon Nature has contributed not a little to make it picturesque and charming. I spent several days in the Siddharanya on six occasions, and bear testimony to the genial effect of the natural scenery.

It reflects great credit on Dr. Fergusson to recognise the artistic merits of the temple more than half a century ago when it was in a dilapidated state and overgrown with weeds. We should express our gratitude to Sir John Woodburn, the late Lieutenant Governor of Bengal and to the P. W. Department for restoring the temple to its original condition to enable us to study it with advantage.

The temple of Muktesvara may be styled the epitome of Orissan Architecture showing all that is best in it. It may appropriately be called a dream in sandstone adapting the immortal phraseology of Colonel Sleeman regarding Taj Mehal. It seems that the artist must have bestowed all his care and skill to make it a perfect, well-proportioned model of Orissan architecture.

Site of the Temple.

The site where the temple is situated was originally a low mound little higher than the surrounding land; the temple of Siddhesvara was built on it; and the site for Muktesvara had to be prepared by scooping

* P. 419, History of Indiann and Easter Architecture (1876) by Fergusson.

out and dressing the central and eastern portion of the mound.

The paved quadrangle of the temple commands a terrace in front 3′-9″ high containing the temple of Siddhesvara and many small ones. The quadrangle measures 77′-4″ from north to south, and 32′-6″ from east to west, the measurements being taken from the Torana (Vide plate-VI. A). Unlike most Orissan temples, it faces the west, and consists of the Vimana and Jagamohana ; it is surrounded by a low enclosure wall 4′-4″ high with battlemented copings carved in front of the topping course ; this wall presents a very nice appearance by having carved on it small panels, or niches with nicely worked brackets having ornamental hoods over them (Vide plate-VIII). The hoods contain small medallions in the centre. The portion of the wall on the west is not one continuous straight line, but has been doubled over so as to make one portion recede back from the other and to cause thereby a pleasing effect of light and shade. Some of the figures in the panels stated above are very artistic. I may mention here the curious figures of four men with 2 heads represented in a panel near the south-west entrance of the low enclosure wall.

A few feet apart from the enclosure wall, and just in front of the Jagamohana entrance stands the graceful Torana, or gateway on a low platform rising from the paved quadrangle

PLATE VIII

The western facade of Muktesvara showing the Torana and enclosure wall with panels.

in front (Vide plate-VIII). The Torana is probably the miniature model from which the magnificent one appertaining to the temple of Kon*a*rka referred to by Abul Fazl is probably derived. This was meant for swinging the idol on a particular sacred occasion, or Dol J*atra.* It is about 15 ft high.

The Torana or gateway.

The Torana consists of two pillars rising from a raised pavement ; the square pedestals support the 16- sided shafts surmounted by Amlaka *Sila* capped by an exquisitely carved full-blown lotus ; here the arch commences. The petals of the lotus have been faithfully and nicely represented, their edges being carved. The pedestal and a portion of the shaft show the models of an Orissan temple with characteristic pilaster, *a*ml*a* and kalasa carved on them. The shaft is encircled at the top by representations of beaded tassels placed side by side and occupying one course of stone blocks ; over this is the scroll work having ornamental studs projecting from the centre ; over the scroll work is the Aml*a*, and on it rests the base for the lotus already referred to. This base presents a simple and graceful appearance and is made up of a fillet, (अन्तरित and कम्प :—Antarita and Kampa), a cyma recta, or Padma (पद्म). The arch has three big ornamental scroll works at the two ends and centre showing heads of human figures. In the intervening spaces between the scroll works are seen two recumbent female figures in graceful pose and symmetrically placed. Two exquisitely carved mouths of Makara project outwards from the springing of the arch.

Style of Muktesvara.

The temple of Muktesvara is a Pancharatha Dewl having five *bhümis*; there are three courses of stone between the *amlas* of each *bhümi*. It is made of fine-grained sandstone called Rajarania. The style of Muktesvara indicates a slight departure from the ordinary one; and this departure is noticed in the cases of Parasuramesvara, Uttaresvara and Muktesvara. In this case, the pilaster for the Dikpalas does not consist of the usual five elements, but only Jangha and Barandi surmounted by a representation of Rekha Dewl containing eleven ordinary plain projections; or, in other words, the Barandi forms the Bada of the representation of Rekha Dewl referred to. The end pilaster, or Konak Paga consists of Jangha and a plain face containing a standing female figure in *alto-relievo*, having a tree as her background. The Jangha portion of this pilaster does not contain Kani, or the 4th element. The topmost portion of it is provided with a panel enclosing the rotund figures of dwarfs struggling to uplift the structure. The central vertical band of the Jangha presents the usual leafy representation.

I measured the different parts of the temple very carefully; they are given below *ad seriatim*.

Vimana of Müktesvara :—

The inside height of *the bâda* of *vimâna*	...	10′-8
Inside dimensions of *vimâna* from north to south	...	7′-6″
" " " " " east to west	...	7′-2″
The area of the door leading to the cella		4′-9½″ × 2′-4″

The Jagamohana :—

Inside length from north to south	...	12′-1″
" " " east to west	...	15′-3″
" height of *bâda*	...	8′-8″
Outside height of *bâda*	...	8′-8″

The height of the Dewl :—

Trisula	...	1′-8″
Kalasa Ghadi	...	0-4″
Kalasa Karpuri	...	0-7″
Kalasa handi (diameter = 1′-6″)	...	1′-5″
Kalasa pada (including dori)	...	0-10″
Amla Karpuri	...	0-7″
Tripata dhara	...	0-4″
Amla	...	1′-6″
Rekha including Ghada chakda	...	15′-3″
Bâda	...	10′-9″
Plinth, or Upana	...	1′-1″
TOTAL	...	34′-4″

The height of the Jagamohana :—

Kalasa	...	2′-0″
Height of the pidas	...	8′-9½″
Bâda	...	8′-9″
Plinth	...	1′-1″
Total	...	20′-6½″

The Jagamohana and the Vimana measure 26 ft. and 15 ft. square respectively on the outside; the inside dimensions of the sanctum are only 7′-6″ square. The plinth of the temple is very low, being only 1′-1″.

Window of the Jagamohana.

Arrangements for introducing light and air into the Jagamohana have been made by providing two lattice windows on the north and south walls. The windows (vide plate IX) are unique, diamond-shaped perforations made in stone slab surrounded by three frames of moulding. The first, or innermost one displays scrolls of various degrees of flexure; the 2nd, or middle one shows rows of four-petalled lotuses, the 3rd outer frame shows a peculiar plant device often used in decorating the jambs of Orissan temples. The latticed windows with three frames of moulding are encased within a wide band of moulding showing the famous monkey scene to be described later on.

The entrance of the Jagamohana is flanked by three tiers of

Southern Fac·de of the Jagamohan of Muktesvara showing lattice window.

Photo by A. Ghose, F. C. S. F. G. S.

Printed by K. V. Sayne & Bros.

characteristic moulding. There is a finely carved slab of stone just in front of the door sill, and in the same level with it. The

Entrance

architrave over the doorway is not carved with the characteristic figures of the nine planets; and the figure of Maha-lakshmi is seen below it carved in a panel and seated on a lotus with two attendants (mutilated) in a kneeling posture. The two upper cornices contain flying Gandharvas with wreaths. The characteristic figures of Ganga and Yamuna, Nandi and Mahakala (vide pp. 182-183) decorating the sides of doorways are noticed both in the Jagamohana and Vimana.

Each of the corner pilastars of the doorway, besides ample scroll work, beaded tassels, and lotus borders (partially uncarved on the right pilasters) bears three figures,—a bas-relief of a very small female figure which is at the bottom, a statuette of a female (on the right pilaster) in artistic pose standing under a tree, the leaves of which are drooping by the weight of two monkeys. This is a plantain tree. The pilasters have panels at the top, containing figures of rotund dwarfs struggling to uplift the superstructure.

On either side of the exterior face of the jamb, is shown

Sardula.

the usual emblematic representation of a human figure riding on a maned *Sârdula*, or lion towering above a crouching elephant. The protruding tongue of the griffin has

36

a three-rowed beaded tassel attached to it. The elephant faces the *Sârdula*.

The *Sârdula* has peculiar eyes about to jut forward out of the socket ; it has leafy ears and horns ; the tail passes between the hind legs ; the saddle of the reined *Sârdula* on which the male, or female figure sits has distinct pommel and cantle ; the feet of the rider are inserted in the stirrup.

Starting from the right hand side of the Jagamohana, the second pilaster bears ornamental designs with a few small elephants, all kneeling on the fourth moulding of the jangha. The topmost portion contains a dwarf, and the lowest, two female figures. The third pilaster is in a recess ; it is not wide, and it bears a panel containing a female figure standing in front of an open door. Next to it, there is an extremely small seated figure. This is followed by two griffins standing on a pair of elephants bearing a column with a Nagini (five-hooded) having its tail entwined upwards round the shaft. This Naga column is repeated 27 times. Fourteen of these are Nagas, and the rest, Naginis. The Nagas bear in their hands either a garland, or a lotus, or a casket, or a long stringed instrument, with a single exception where the Naga is seen with folded hands. The Naginis bear in their hands either a lotus and a conch shell, or a long casket covered with hanging beaded tassels or a *chowrie* and a casket, or a lotus and a casket.

I may mention here that a definite plan has been followed in the arrangement of the Naga figures in the case of the *vimâna*; on looking at any face of the *vimâna*, the column for a Naga would invariably be seen in the right hand recess between the Konaka and Anartha pagas, and that for a Nagini, in the left hand recess; no deviation is noticed. In the Jagamohana, however, no definite order has been followed.

Arrangement of the Naga Column:—

The fourth pilaster is a repetition of the second, and the fifth one, that of the third. The sixth pilaster, or the corner one contains three repetitions of itself. The centre of this contains a hanging piece of scroll work carved on the *kümbha*, or ovalo of the pedestal; the *kümbha* repeats itself thrice and bears an ornament with an enclosed medallion. The sixth pilaster (on the southern face) bears, (1) a female figure in a small panel, (2) the figure of Ganesa in a panel, (3) the mutilated figure of a standing female holding a branch of a tree, (4) a seated rotund dwarf.

South face:
- 7th pilaster—Naga column.
- 8th pilaster—Similar to the 2nd.
- 9th pilaster—Nagini column.
- 10th pilaster—same as the 2nd.
- 11th pilaster—Nagini column

The twelfth pilaster contains (1) diminutive fighting griffins,

(2) an unknown statuette, (3) beaded tassel work, (4) a diminutive deer seated under a tree, (5) a small female figure.

Next comes the lattice window which has already been described. I have also made a passing reference to the monkey scenes. (Vide plate IX).

A crab holds a monkey and drags it down ; another monkey hanging down from a neighbouring tree sees this sorrowful plight, and catching hold of its brother makes strenuous efforts to save it from its assailant ; another big monkey is entwining one of its arms round the second monkey to prevent it from falling down. In another scene, two monkeys have been depicted as annoying a crocodile. In the next scene, a monkey is represented as sitting on a crocodile, and two other monkeys are climbing up two trees on the two sides. The above three scenes are repeated on the right side of the window with variations. In the topmost portion of the frame containing the above scenes are depicted the monkeys at home ; this has been obliterated to some extent. The last piece at the right corner shows an erect monkey passing its fingers through the hair of another in search of insects. On the top of this, there is a bas-relief with one Makara head at each end, and eight groups of flying Gandharvas, each Gandharva carrying a garland in both hands and supporting a nymph, or Apsara on the left leg which is outstretched with bent knee.

On the top are represented two female figures playing on a musical instrument with parrots perching on them.

The temple, or the Vimana contains the figures of ascetics in meditation, or preaching to the disciples in the topmost recesses of the B*ada*. Starting from the southern to the northern face one comes across the figures of an emaciated ascetic and his disciple bathing a *lingam* with water passing through a piece of cloth; the figure of an emaciated ascetic in trance with a plaited turban on is very significant; women have been represented as kneeling before him and the musicians as playing on tomtoms. The third figure represents a disciple offering seat to an ascetic *guru*. The fourth is the repetition of the first, the fifth one is a devotee pouring water on a *lingam* from a pot; another devotee is bringing two pots of water, the sixth one is an unimportant figure; the seventh one, that of a sage in the act of writing while two of his disciples are standing with folded hands; the eighth one is that of a man bathing a *Siva lingam* with water from a rinsed cloth. The ninth one represents the worship of Siva; one of the figures here is mutilated. The tenth scene represents a *guru* reading from a book supported on a trestle, and tarbaned disciples are listening; the eleventh one is a *guru* discoursing to tarbaned disciples while another disciple is reading apart.

The peculiarity with this temple is that there is no projecting lion visible on the sanctum, and there are no Dewl-charanis, nor griffins in the recess below the *Amla*. The lion over the portico of the Jagamohan is of the type called Khepa-Sinha, or mad lion.

I should invite the reader's attention to the stag hunt scene depicted most naturally and artistically in the frieze of the southern *rahapaga*; stags have been represented as flying close upon one another, while some of them are looking back to ascertain if the archer is still aiming his arrow; a beautiful elephant scene has been depicted on the northern face.

The attention of a most casual observer is struck by the carvings of the Anartha and Rahapagas of the *rekha* portion of the *dewl* (vide plates VI, VII and X). I have referred to this ornament on pages 190 and 195 while illustrating the principle of diapers and contrast afforded by a uniformity of halves. The observer does not fail to notice the female figures carved in the panels just above the tail of the Naga column and the medallion surmounting it; the figures are represented as standing in a graceful pose in front of an opened doorway. The Sardula is noticed in the recess between the pagas or pilasters as usual; it is found in *alto-relievo* on the two sides of the Rahapagas only both in the case of the Vimana and Jagamohana.

Some peculiarities of carving

Plate No. VIII indicates the state of the temple before

PLATE X.

Facade of Muktesvara showing the niche, tasselwork & scroll.

Photo by A Ghose, F. C. S. F. G. S.

Printed by K. V. Sayne & Bros.

the repair works were undertaken by the Public Works Department, The Kalasa was altogether wanting; the Amlaka Beki and Gh*ad* Chak*da* were in good order. The R*a*h*apa*ga on the east side of the sanctum had been threatening to come down. The Public Works Department at a total cost of Rs. 4,266 executed the repair works of the temples of Muktesvara and Siddhesvara with their appurtenances including the Torana, tank and 16 other minor temples. The outer compound wall (vide plate:—VI. A) is altogether a new one, and was constructed when the temples were restored. It should be borne in mind that although many portions of the temple and its appurtenances had to be wholly dismantled before they were restored, there were very few missing stones which had to be replaced by new ones. It will be seen at once that the new pieces of carved work cannot bear any comparison with the old ones.

Repair by the P.W.D.

The surface of the temple is again overgrown with moss which the Public Works Department should do well to remove at once, for it has already spoiled the surface fearfully.

Saptarshi.

There are seven figures carved on blocks or slabs of stone collected round a *bakula* tree (*Mimusops elengi*) on the raised terrace to the south of the temple of Muktes-

* Report with Photographs of the Repairs Executed to some of the Principal Temples of Bhubaneswara, Between 1898 and 1903 by M. H. Arnott.

vara. These go by the name of *Saptarshi*, or seven *rishis*. The most important of these is the standing figure of Surya, or sun-god incised on a slab of sandstone measuring 3′-10″ by 1′-6″ ; it is 11 inches thick. The slab faces the east. This representation of the sun-god is not usually met with. The figure is two-handed ; the hands are broken ; it has no head-dress ; a flat horizontal band having a disc in the centre passes round the head. It has no characteristic necklace with a central gem, nor has it any sacred thread. Two flat horizontal bands pass through the breast and waist respectively having buckles in the centre. The style of putting on the cloth is rather peculiar. The figure has no arm ornament. Arüna, or the legless charioteer of the deity is provided with thigh and leg ; he holds a stick in the right hand. The feet of the deity are not kilted as usual. The two attendant female figures standing on two sides are about to dart arrows from their bows ; they represent Usha, or dawn. The face of the pedestal is carved with the usual figures of seven horses.

Temple of Siddhesvara. This temple is shown in ground plan in plate VI. A. It is situated on the north-west of the compound of the temple of Muktesvara.

The temple of Siddhesvara is a plain Pancharatha dewl having a Jagamohana attached to it of the type called *Nadu-mohana* (vide page 115). The Konaka paga of the temple shows five *bhūmis* or divisions. This temple is not famous for any workmanship; but it has a grandeur of its own due to plain mouldings without any further decoration. It has been thoroughly repaired by the P. W. D. I give below the measurements of the different parts taken by me personally.

Vimana :—

Bada	...	16'-0"
Rekha	...	24'-0"
Upper Jangha	...	3'-10"
Upper Barandi	...	3'-6"
Bandhana	...	1'-3"
Lower Barandi	...	3'-6"
Lower Jangha	...	3'-11"
Ghad Chakda	...	1'-3"
Amla Beki	...	1'-11"
Amla	...	2'-3"
Tripata Dhara	...	0'-10"
Amla Karpuri	...	1'-6"
Kalasa pada (including dori)	...	1'-0"
Kalasa Handi	...	1'-11"
Kalasa Karpuri	...	0'-10"
Kalasa Ghadi	...	0'-4"

———

Gauri's Temple :—Plate—XI.

The temple of Gauri stands to the west of Kedara Künda and on a raised pavement, the height of which is 1'-6". It faces the east. The quadrangle, or court-yard of the temple is made up of flags of stone. The Jagamohana of the temple is completely broken and is being raised anew by subscriptions. The Vimana (Plate-XI) had its top broken long ago as gathered from local tradition ; it was repaired and sandplastered subsequently about a hundred years ago. The spire of the temple is quite different from the usual type.

The temple has been built of Rajarania variety of sandstone. The plinth or *pristha* of the temple is 1'-5" ; the *vimâna* is a Pancharatha Dewl, but the plinth resembles that of a Triratha Dewl. The face of the plinth consists of two parts :—(*a*) The topmost one called the Padma pristha somewhat resembling the *pâda* of *Janghâ*, (*b*) the lower part called the Vetala Pristha for being carved with the figures of *vetâlas*, or dwarfs, in panels separated by balusters. This is a characteristic feature of this variety of temples called Gauri Chara referred to on page 135. The Jagamohana is being made a Saptaratha Dewl, whereas the *vimâna* is a Pancharatha one.

The central niches of the *vimâna* are flanked by the carved figures of Ganga and Yamuna, and those only of the northern

PLATE XI.

'emple of Gauri, Bhubanesvara.

Photo by A. Ghose, F. C. S. F. G. S.

Printed by K. V. Sayne & Bros.

one stand on their respective vehicles of *makara* (capricornus) and *kūrma* (tortoise).

The pilasters for the *dikpâlas* are similar to those of Muktesvara already described, *i. e.* only the Jangha and the Barandi exist ; the Barandi terminates in a *rekha* separated by a vase or *kalasa* ; the upper *rekha* forms a part of the *rekha* of the Dewl.

The Jangha consists of the usual five elements ; some, however, contains only four, the *kani* being dispensed with.

The Gauri Chara type differs from the ordinary one in the following respect. From the point whence the rekha starts, small rekha representations rise up ; upon these rest other *rekhas* with a recess. The *rekhas* are surmounted by a big moulding all round the temple at a height equal to twice that of the *bâda*, or cube from the pavement. This moulding shows the leaves of the lotus ; over it comes a recess carved with *jâli* work. This is an important feature of this style. Over the recess there is a rectangular moulding, and next comes the curved top consisting of two parts ; representations of small heads of the lion are made to project from the centre of the *rahapagas* or central pilasters ; the *bhos* are also noticeable.

Peculiarity of Gauri Chara

Gauri Chara type has no *amlâ*, *sree*, etc. This is another characteristic feature of this style, and it is so pronounced that the representation of *amla* is nowhere to be found on the face of this temple. In a *rekha* or an ordinary *dewl*, the *dikpatis* are located in the Konakapagas, whereas in a Gauri-chara dewl, they are placed in the Anarthapagas.

It may be mentioned here that all the Dikpatis and Parsvadevatas have been removed. The Naga and Nagini columns are found in the recesses between the Konaka and the Anartha-pagas, and on the eastern and western faces only. The Nagini column is on the right hand side of the observer. The Naga, or Nagini column ends in the representation of *vetalas*, or dwarfish figures referred to already.

I give below the following measurements taken by me.

Height of Bada	= 7′-1″
" " Rekha	= 7′-3″
" " Jangha	= 2′-2¾″
" " Barandi	= 4′-10¼″
" " Moulding showing lotus leaves	= 1′-2″
" " Jali	= 0″-7″
Length of Vimana (north to south)	= 13′
" " " (east to west)	= 11′
" " Konak paga (on the nothern and southern faces)	= 1′-6″
" " Anartha paga (")	= 2′-9″
" " Raha paga (")	= 4′-6″

Length of Konak *paga* (on the eastern and western faces) = 1'-6"

„ „ Anartha *paga* („) = 1'-11"

„ „ *Raha paga* („) = 4'-2"

There are several points of resemblance between the temples of Muktesvara and Gauri; both show the female figures standing in front of opened doors. (2) As in Muktesvara, dwarfish figures struggling to uplift the structure are noticed in panels in the Konak-*pagas*. (3) The medallions enclosing heads of human figures, as in Muktesvara, are also noticeable here. (4) The *Sârdula* of Gauri's temple is similar to that of Muktesvara in many respects. (5) Profusion of *Kalasa* or final is a characteristic feature; the number is, however, much more than what is noticed in Muktesvara. (6) The *Bâda* of Gauri is similar to that of Muktesvara.

Muktesvara and Gauri compared

There are several unimportant temples in the vicinity of the temples of Muktesvara and Gauri. Their names with a short description are given below. Those within the compound of the temple of Muktesvara have bee shown on Pate VI. A.

Minor temples in the vicinity of Muktesvara.

(*a*) There is a small, nameless, ordinary temple to the south of Muktesvara and within its compound; it is a Pancharatha-dewl. Farther to the south, and about 20 ft apart from the former, is the temple of Vanesvara ; it is a Saptaratha-dewl. without any workmanship ; a little farther from it there are two small *rekha* dewls.

(*b*) To the north of the *vimâna* of Muktesvara, and within its compound are two small pida dewls containing Siva *lingam*.

(*c*) To the noth of the Jagamohana of Muktesvara, there is a small Rekha-Pancharatha dewl without any carving called Gokarnesvara : the *lingam* has been broken. To the north of the former, and about 4 ft apart, is situated a *pida dewl* without any name and containing no image.

(*d*) There is a small *pida dewl* about 3 ft. to the west of Gokarnesvara ; it is spoken of as the abode of Valmiki, the great epic poet.

(*e*) On the north-west of the temple of Muktesvara is situated the temple of Siddhesvara (vide Plate—VI. A)

(*f*) There are 6 small temples on the eastern edge of the raised terrace on the west of the quadrangle referred to already. The second and the third temples counted from the north contain the figure of Ananta, the rest do not contain any figure.

(*g*) Outside the compound of Muktesvara, and to the south of it, and also to the north of Kedaresvara, there is a *pida* dewl in a dilapidated state ; it was originally divided into two rooms one of which is now broken. This temple is described by local tradition as the birth place of Lava and Kusa.

(*h*) To the south of the above, is the temple of Kedaresvara which is a Pancharatha Dewl. This has a Jagamohana attached to it. This temple unlike others faces the south.

(*i*) To the west of Kedaresvara is the temple of Yukti-Kedaresvara which is a plain, Pancharatha-rekha-Dewl.

(*j*) To the south-west of Yukti-Kedaresvara, and about 18 ft. apart from it, is a plain *pida* Dewl. This is called the temple of Yukti-Kapilesvara.

(*k*) At the north-west corner of Gauri-Kunda, is situated an ordinar, pida-dewl containing the figure of Hanumana, the great monkey-god.

(*l*) Near the above is the clere-story *mohana* used as the cook-room of Kedaresvara.

The temple of Parasuramesvara :—Plates—XII, XIII.

The temple of Parasuramesvara one of the oldest at Bhubanesvara is on the west of the Siddhyaranya, and is at a distance of a little less than a furlong to the west of the sacred Kedara Kunda. This temple is unique from an architectural point of view, being a departure from the usual type. What strikes the most casual observer at first sight is the Jagamohana which does not present the usual shape of a stepped pyramid towering a cube. The plan of the Jagamohana is rectangular, the larger side being in the same line

Parasuramesvara

with the face of the Vimana,the rahapaga of which is 1'-4" ahead of the main body. The Bada of the porch 7ft. in height is a low rectangular parallelopiped having a door opening both on the south and west respectively. It is topped by a sloping roof formed by slabs of stone 6ft. long having in the centre, a sort of clere-story, or skylight of six windows in front, *i.e.*, on the west, and twelve windows on the sides, *i.e.*, south and north (Vide plate—XII).

This temple, unlike those of the usual type, faces the west. The interior of the Jagamohana presents the appearance of a nave, and two aisles characteristic of a Christian church, the roof being supported by two parallel rows of three rectangular pillars. The constructive peculiarity of the porch necessitated the use of pillars which were monolithic before the present restoration was effected. It may be mentioned here incidentally that the plan of the clere-story has also been resorted to in the case of the Vaitala Dewl which, again, belongs to a different class of architecture. The purpose of this is obviously to admit more light and air, but now after the restoration, the windows of the clere-story referred to have been blocked up.

Peculiarity of the temple.

Another peculiarity which strikes the attention of an observer is the absence of plinth. The level of the floor is that of the adjoining ground. The *Báda* of the Vimana starts

The Temple of Parasuramesvara, Bhubanesvara.

(showing the clerestory of the Jagamohan)

The Lakshmi Printing Works, 64-1, 64-2, Sukea's Street, Calcutta.

at once from the Talapattana or pavement. Departure from the usual type is also noticed in the Jangh*a*, the first element of the *Bâda*; for, instead of the five component mouldings, or projections, it consists of the following three, boldly executed, viz., P*a*da, Kümüda, and Basanta; the Padma or cyma reversa, or recta has been replaced by a flattened Kümüda, or or an astragal or torus.

The Vim*a*na is a Triratha dewl. The *Bâda* does not show the usual five elements; only the Jangh*a* and B*ara*ndi have been used, and the remaining three elements have been omitted. The *Bâda*, again, is not a cube but a rectangular parallelopiped. There is a sharp line of demarcation between the *Bâda*, and *Rekha* by a bold projection and a deep recess.

The height of the Vim*a*na does not bear the usual proportion to the width of the base; it is rather less than the proper height, and accordingly, the Vim*a*na looks more solid and compact than the usual type.

The peculiarity of the Jagamohana in respect of the general design has already been pointed out; it also deviates from the usual type by having a distinctly rectangular, or oblong plan instead of a square one.

No figure of the lion is seen to project from any face of the sanctum, and the characteristic Dewl Charanis are not found in the recess between the Amlaka-*sila* and the Gh*ad* Chak*da*.

The lions that are found in the recess stated above were placed there at the time of restoring the temple. The usual carving resembling a coat of arms and flanked by recumbent female figures is not seen on the R*a*h*a*p*a*gas of the dewl.

Credit is due to the P. W. D. for an effective restoration of the temple which cost them Rs. 3,465* ; much damage was caused to the temple by unequal settlement. The Jagamohana was most badly damaged, and it had to be almost entirely rebuilt with old and new materials ; the pillars supporting the roof of the Jagamohana have been replaced by new ones ; the Beki, *A*ml*a* and Karpuri have been effectively reconstructed, and a new *kalasa* has been substituted, for, on referring to plate XII made from a photograph before the restoration, we do not notice the *kalasa*.

Restoration by the P.W.D.

The eastern face of the *Bâda* contains three niches (vide Plate XIII), the two side ones being smaller than the central one. The side niches do not form a prolongation of the pilasters as is noticed in all the Orissan temples. The pilasters themselves do not exist in a striking manner. The central one, however, is a prominent r*a*h*a*p*a*ga extending right up to Gh*ad* Chak*da*. The face of the *Bâda* is very plain without any decoration except those around the niches (Vide Plate XIII).

* Report with photographs of the Repairs executed to some of the Principal Temples at Bhubanesvara. M. H. Arnott.

PLATE XIII.

Eastern facade of Parasuramesvara showing the details of carving.

Engraved & Printed by K. V. Sanye & Bros.

The images from the side niches have been removed (Plate XIII); they were the Dikpalas. The figure of Kartic seated on a throne carved with peacock killing a serpent has been placed in the central niche, the position of which in respect of the *Bâda*, is a little lower than in other temples; the Jangha or the first element of the *Bâda* is noticed here to be occupied by a portion of the central niche. The canopy over it projecting from the face does not show elaborate carvings, or tiers or series of projections. The niches are not flanked by the usual figures carved in *alto-relievo*; they are flanked in this case by plain bands containing panels enclosing human figures in *basso-relievo*; just below the moulding separating the Bada from the Rekha are placed two *A*mlas on the two sides of the *rahapaga* over the central niche. The Konak-*pa*gas seem to be accentuated by the introduction of *A*mlakas at regular intervals, three courses of stone intervening between them.

The arrangements of niches on the northern and southern faces are exactly similar to that on the eastern one; but unfortunately all the images have been removed from the northern ones and the side niches of the southern face; the central niche of the latter contains the figure of Ganesa seated on a pedestal. The position of Ganesa in respect of the sanctum has been reversed; it should have been placed in the central niche of the northern face. This is probably due to the carelessness and ignorance of the engineer of the P. W. D. in charge of the restoration of the temple.

The representation of the peacock is noticed abundantly for the decoration, specially, of the face of the topmost canopy of the niche, and the topmost frieze of the *Bâda*. The long horizontal recesses near the frieze contain panels enclosing standing male and female figures followed by panelled *jâlis* in succession. These are surmounted by tassels.

The bas-relief on the northern niche of the Vimana depicts a hunting scene. A man seated on a horse is spearing a lion; another, piercing the body of an elephant, another, again, defending himself from the attack of a lion with a shield. The entrance to the porch on the south has a bas-relief with Ganesa in the middle; on the left side is represented a Gandharva with an Apsara on his leg and bearing with both hands a reticulated basket containing fruits; on the right is represented a man taking out a garland from a reticulated basket resembling that for wastepaper; next to this, is a man carrying a jack fruit on his shoulder, then a man with palm, and last comes an ascetic counting the beads of a rosary with his legs tied with a piece of cloth.

The western doorway of the Jagamohana shows the characteristic figure of Gaja-Lakshmi; on the right side is represented the worship of Siva Linga; and on the left is depicted the scene of capture of a wild elephant by domestic ones. The wild elephant has one of his legs tied with a rope; a man on foot is cautiously attempting to tie the right hind leg of the wild elephant with the noosed end of a rope; and the animal is kept at bay with a long spear by the rider of an elephant in front. The elephants are very life-like, and seem to have been copied from nature.

The Western face of the Jagamohana

The western wall of the Jagamohana, as I have stated above, is provided with a door 4′-11⅜″ × 2′-7¼″, the door sill being at a height of 1′-1½″ above the level of the pavement. There is a lattice window of the type called *Chunkhanti-Jali-panjara* on each side of the door, the holes of the window being 2½″ × 3″. These two windows are decorated with the carvings of bands of musicians and groups of dancers in nice poses, some playing on *damaru* (a sort of drum resembling an hour-glass), some on *vinā* (a stringed instrument), and some on cymbals; the dancers are male; one of them is noticed to dance holding the ends of the scarf like an ordinary dancing girl of the present day. The frieze above the doors and windows stated above is nicely carved with artistic representations of elephants; it shows also the worship of the *Siva lingum* by the naked anchorites with only a *kaupina* (a small piece of cloth worn over the privities) on. The pilasters flanking the doorway are carved with representations of *Kümbha* and a floral device issuing out of it as shown on plate V. A. In the pilasters are two panels containing Nandi and Mahakala on the left and right respectively. Nandi and Mahakala have four and two hands respectively.

The Southern face of the Jagamohana

On the south side of the Jagamohana there is also a door (4′-10½″ × 2′-5½″) not in the middle, but more towards the east. There is one window (3′-2½″ × 2′-9″) of a type similar to those on the west.

It is rather strange that the doorways of the Jagamohana are not lined with the usual mouldings such as Barajhanji, Gelbai, etc. described on pages 180-181. There is another peculiarity that may be noticed here. Unlike the doorway on the west, the top sill of the southern one is carved with the figure of Ganesa and not Lakshmi as usual. Nandi and Mahakala are noticed on the sides.

The northern face of the Jagamohana has no door; but there is a widow (4′-½″ × 3′-4½″) of the type already described. At the north-west corner of this face is met with a peculiar figure of Ganesa to be seen nowhere else; close to this figure are those of Sapta Matrika in seven consecutive panels. They hold a *trisula* and some of them, a *trsula* and an axe. There are 9 panels on the right of the lattice window, and 6 bigger ones on the left side, but the figures contained in the latter could not be identified.

The Jagamohana starts at once from the pavement or *tala-pattana*; it has a plinth. The *Bâda* shows a Jangh*a* of three elements, the height being 1′-6″; next to the jangh*a* is a recess 1′-10″ high containing panels; the portion above is plain.

The floor of the Jagamohana measures 24′-11¼″ from east to west, and 18′-4″ from north to south. The Jagamohona has six rectangular pillars inside to support the roofing. The distance of the pillars from the north and south walls of the Jagamohona is 3′-8⅛″, that from the eastern wall, i. e., from the sanctum is 5 feet, and from the western wall is 3′-10″. The distance between the pillars across the width of the Jagamohana is 7′-9″; this is reduced to 5′-10″ between the pillars close to the western wall. The interval between the pillars along the length of the Jagamohana is 5′-3½″.

A sort of corbelling projects inside from the outer wall of the *Bâda* of the Jagamohana, and over it rest the slabs of stone placed at an angle. I give below the dimensions of the inclined length and rise of the slabs.

Angle of slope.

Inclined length = 3′-4″ (measured from the edge of the bracket).

Horizontal length = 3′-2″.

Rise = 1′-1″.

∴ Angle of Inclination of the slab

$$= \cos^{-1} \frac{3'\text{-}2''}{3'\text{-}4''} = \cos^{-1} \frac{38}{40}.$$

$$= \cos^{-1} \cdot 95 = 18^\circ\text{-}11'\text{-}40''.$$

The outside length of sloping slabs of stone of the first storey is 5′-7″, and that for the upper storey is 6 feet; the difference in height between the storeys is 1′-8″.

I give below the dimensions of the Vimana as measured by me.

The outside height of the *bâda* = 14′-3″.

The height from Ghad chakda to *Talpattana* – 35′-8″.

Rekha = 21′-5″.

Beki = 1′-3″.

Amla Dhara = 0′-4″.

Karpuri = 0′-4″.

Kalasa (newly restored) = 2′-10″.

Trisûla = 1′-8″.

Diameter of Karpuri = 10′-0″.

Diameter of Amla = 12″.

Outside length of Vimana from

east to west = 22′-6″.

(including the *râhâpâgas*)

" " (excluding ") = 19′ 9″.

Inside dimension of the Vimana (east to west) = 9'-9".

" " " (north to south) = 9'-10½"

Muktesvara and Parasuramesvara

On carefully comparing the Muktesvara and Parasuramesvara temples one is surely to conclude that their sanctums, roughly speaking, belong to the same type. The small Rekha representations on the Anartha-pagas of the sanctum are wanting in both Parasuramesvara and Muktesvara; those of the former are carved with a plain ornamental device containing three medallions, and those of the latter, with an elaborate carving of uniformly placed semi-circles noticed on the pagas of the Lingaraja temple at Bhubanesvara; both the temples face the west; there is a similarity of sculptures noticed on both, e. g., ascetics with emaciated ribs, the scene of worship of *Siva lingam*. In both the temples the *bāda* and *rekha* are separated from each other by a distinct projection and recess not to be seen in a temple of the usual type.

Foreign influence

The temple of Parasuramesvara is a bolder departure from the usual type than that of Muktesvara. The former one was evidently built by a class of architects not prevalent in the locality but hailing probably from the south. This receives corroboration from the carving of lion spearing noticed on the northern face of the Jagamohana; I have nowhere come across any scene of lion hunting in Orissa, the animal being considered an emblem of the royal dynasty; in this temple, the characteristic figure of lion projecting from the *rekha* is also wanting.

A most peculiar representation of Ganesa is noticed at the north-west corner of the north face. The figure has the well-defined features of a human form; and the characteristic proboscis of Ganesa has strangely been made to protrude from the chin. The lintel over the doorway separating the sanctum from the Jagamohana is carved with the figure of eight planets instead of nine, as is invariably met with. The jamb mouldings of the dooway are most peculiar. The figure of Gaja-Lakshmi usually noticed on the lintel over doorways is seen to have been replaced by that of Ganesa in the case of the southern doorway of the Jagamohana. This is most unusual. The Jangha of the Vimana consists of three elements, instead of five, as usual; the central one, again, is not *kümbha* but *kümüda* or torus. All these things tend to prove without doubt the existence of foreign influence in the Orissan art.

The temple of Muktesvara was built by a class of architects who were children of the soil, but who had before them a model illustrating an exotic Orissan type. They adapted this model as much as possible to the Orissan one, and built in its very vicinity a prototype, as far as the sanctum is concerned. It cannot be expected that the children of the soil should be equal to the foreigners or birds of passage in making an experiment on the same bold scale. Their boldness must have heen hampered by the national traditions to which they clung with tenacity. Another point in connection with this is that the temple of Parasuramesvara cannot be much older than Muktesvara, for the spirit of imitation naturally loses its force according as the model grows old, and in this case, the model, I have shown, has been closely followed. I cannot accordingly take the interval between their respective dates of construction longer than half a century at most.

It is very difficult to fix with anything like accuracy the date when the temple was built ; many theories are advanced

Date

as to its chronology based on evidences external and internal. I have examined them very carefully with the aid of observations made by me *in situ*. I have proved already at great length that the possible date that can be assigned to the temple of Parasuramesvara is the 5th or the 6th century A. D. at the latest. The temples of Muktesvara and Parasuramesvara may for all practical purposes be supposed to belong to the same period of architectural history ; as Muktesvara is an advance on the other, the former may be supposed fairly accurately to have been built in the 6th or 7th century A. D. Both Muktesvara and Parasuramesvara are obvious departures from the established type of which the great Lingaraja is the typical example.

The sculpture of Parasuramesvara is very peculiar; it resembles that of Muktesvara in many respects, and differs from it in many others; for instance, as in Muktesvara, no beaded tassel work is noticed anywhere here. Sardula and Naga representations, or Phandagranthi ornament (page 195) are also wanting. The carvings of Parasuramesvara are chaste and elegant; the figures are not lascivious; in this respect it is similar to Muktesvara. Some of the carvings of the temple of Parasuramesvara are peculiar and are not evidently of Orissan origin. I have noticed a fret ornament just below the third panel from below upwards in the recess between the *konaka* and *anartha-pāgas* at the south-west corner of the vimana. This is the only instance of fret noticed by me (vide pages 195-196) in Orissa. The ornamental device of showing the stem of a creeper at regular intervals is very striking; it resembles the Grecian guilloche to some extent. The profusion of *Bhos* (page 129) having various sorts of insets such as lotus, lion, Ganesa, Parasurama, etc., is a characteristic feature of this temple. A casual observer even can not but be struck with the *bhos*; the representation of *Kūmbha*, or a jar from which a floral device is made to issue forth is a characteristic of this temple and Vaitala to be described later on (vide Plate V.A). This is a decided piece of Buddhist sculpture.

Some peculiarities of Sculpture

The representations of pyramidal battlements and half or three-quarter discs of lotus, etc., are decidedly Buddhistic in character. In the temple of Parasuramesvara we notice a distinct reminiscence of Buddhist influence. Unlike other temples, the central niches of Parasuramesvara are bordered by nice carvings. The northern and eastern niches have a border characteristic of a door opening. In the case of the northern one, the similarity is marked, for we notice distinct ***Barājhānji*** and ***Dāli*** of intricate design ; the intermediate border is not ***Gelbāi***, strictly speaking ; it contains human figures in various poses. In the case of the eastern one, ***Barājhānji*** is noticeable, but ***Dāli*** and ***Gelbāi*** are wanting ; the ***Dāli*** has been replaced by projecting human figures in various postures of devotion ; the ***Gelbāi*** has been replaced by small panels containing insets of various floral designs and human scenes. In the southern one, it should be noted, all the three are wanting, and have been replaced by floral devices. A peculiarity noticed by me is worth mentioning here ; the course of stone just above the ***janghā*** shows ***alto-relievo*** representaions of rows of half elephants and half lions. Mention may be made of the elaborate floral devices issuing out of the tail of birds, a very few instances of which have also been noticed in the temple of Muktesvara. As in Muktesvara and other Orissan temples, we notice representations of female figures standing in front of opened doorway ;

scenes of worship of *siva lingam* by emaciated anchorites are also noticeable here.

Taking everything into consideration, the sculptures of Parasuramesvara have an elegance and chasteness nowhere to be seen in a purely Orissan style. In this case the captious critics have no reason to find fault with the so-called over-decorated ugliness they so bitterly complain of. It is not so elaborately carved as an ordinary Orissan temple is, but the sculptures with the arrangement thereof have a charm all their own nowhere to be seen.

Minor temples near Parasuramesvara :—

(*a*) There is a broken, dilapidated temple to the east of Parasuramesvara ; it has no name.

(*b*) To the south of Parasuramesvara is the temple of Kotitirthesvara ; it is a *pancharatha dewl* ; it has no jagamohana at present ; the one that existed originally being in a bad condition was dismantled by the P. W. D about 9 or 10 years ago, and the stone blocks of which it was made were utilized in the restoration of the temples of Ananta Vasüdeva and Sari dewl.

(*c*) The temple of Tirthesvara is to the north-east of Kotitirthesvara ; it is a small pida-dewl, and without any workmanship.

(*d*) About 170 feet to the north of Kotitirthesvara is situated a rekha-dewl without *mohana*, and exactly similar to the temple of Parasuramesvara. It is a Triratha dewl like Parasuramesvara ; it faces the east and contains a rather big *Siva lingam*. The western face of the temple is in a most dangerous condition and threatens to come down ; the temple is buried in the ground up to a certain portion of the jangha. ; it was constructed in a most unworkmanlike way as far as the interior filling in of the wall is concerned. This is clearly seen in the eastern wall ; no regard for bond, horizontality of courses and evenness of blocks seems to have been had when the work was going on. The bad condition of the temple is principally due to this.

All the Parsvadevatas of it have been removed except the figure of Parvati contained in the northern niche.

The same design, the same nature of carvings and the same details, as those of Parasuramesvara, are noticeable here. Pyramidal battlements, profusion of *bhos* and *kumbha* ornament noticed in the case of Parasuramesvara are also met with here. The same representation of half elephants on the course of stone blocks just above the *jangha*, and the carvings of birds with floral devices issuing out of the tails are noticeable here.

This temple may, under the circumstances stated above, be considered to be an exact prototype of the temple of Parasuramesvara and may reasonably be supposed to have been built in the same period.

I may mentión here that an exactly similar temple exists near the Vindüsorávara tọ be described later on.

(*e*) About 150 feet to the south-west of Kotitirthesvara are situated two small pida-dewls ; in nearly the same line with them there is a Pancharatha-rekha-dewl facing the east, and without any Jagamohona attached to it. This temple goes by the name of Suvarnesvara, and is without any workmanship.

(*f*) To the west of the above there is a small, unimportant Pancharatha-rekha-dewl without any workmanship.

RAJARANI TEMPLE :—

Nomenclature of the temple. This temple is a furlong to the east of the Siddhyaranya, and stands isolated from any temple near its vicinity ; it faces the east ; it is picturesque by reason of the expanse of green fields on its four sides. This magnificent, though picturesque, temple is without any idol in it ; it is said that this was meant as a pleasure resort of the king of Orissa and his consort. We reject this theory as utterly baseless ; for, in that case, out-houses, stable, &c., must have been attached to the structure ; the least vestige of any such thing is not traceable now, and on close examination it will be apparent that these were never under contemplation. The Vimana shows the characteristic Dikpalas, or deities presiding over the points of the compass, and niches for the Parsva Devatas.

PLATE XIV

The Temple of Raja Rani, Bhubanesvara.
(showing the balustraded window of the Jagamohan)

The Lakshmi Printing Works, 64-1, 64-2, Sukea's Street, Calcutta.

From these considerations I am inclined to think that it was meant as a veritable temple, though it is doubtful if the idol was ever installed; the installation ceremony might have been abandoned by some inauspicious event happening in the royal household.

The belief that it was a temple is confirmed by the occurrence of the characteristic Nava Grahas and the figure of Lakshmi over the doorway of the Jagamohana.

Rajarani, a Vaishnavite temple

That the temple was intended for enshrining an image and not a *lingam* in the sanctum will be evident from an inspection of its floor. On examining the *khüra pristha*, or upper plinth carved as it is with the petals of lotus, it appears that the temple was meant for being dedicated to Vishnü.

The nomenclature of the temple may, however, be explained by considering the fact that it is an edifice built almost exclusively of very fine-grained yellowish sandstone called R*a*jar*a*nia (राजरानिया) in common parlance. The temple has derived its name from the stones used in its construction. The sand stone blocks are noticed to contain long veins of quartz.

This temple consists of two parts, the Vim*a*na and the Jagamohana. The former is most elaborately carved, whereas the latter has been finished in haste, or it may be that it is a subsequent addition. We come to this conclusion by the glaring contrast presented by the two parts of the structure.

The temple is more massive and compact than Muktesvara. The Vimana which is a Rekha-Panchamunda Dewl, and hence presents the appearance of two storeys, rises from two tiers of plinth, the upper one receding back from the lower one by 8″ (vide plate XV). The upper and lower plinths measure 2′-7″ and 1′-11″ respectively in height, the total height of the plinth being 4′-6″. The second, or upper plinth contains P*a*da, Kani, and Pat*a*, the intervening recesses being carved with J*a*li, or perforated lattice work; from the centre of the P*a*da portion of the upper plinth, rises a stud or knob containing a medallion enclosing the head of a human figure, or the lotus. The basement of the temple has, of late, been repaired by the Public Works Department, and the stone blocks have been wisely connected together with stone dowels, instead of iron cramps.

The b*a*da consists of Jangh*a*, S*a*kkara or B*a*r*a*ndi (without S*a*kkar Ch*a*l), Sikkar consisting of two elements (instead of three), the second S*a*kkara, and the second Jangh*a* consisting of seven mouldings; the topmost and the central mouldings are unusually bigger than the rest. A miniature Rekha temple rests upon the *Sa*tk*a*ma, or the second Jangh*a*; thus terminate the end or salient corners; the vertical ribs or pilasters higher than the outer ones recede back from them, and thus present the appearance of a two-storeyed structure (*vide* plate XIV). This is peculiar with this temple. The Vimana, it should be noted here, is a Pancharatha Dewl having seven *bhûmis*.

Judging from the apparent red colour of the stones, Dr. Mitra erroneously came to the conclusion that the temple had been built of brick-red sandstone ; the temple, I have noticed before, was built of a yellowish variety of sandstone rendered red by an external coat of red ochre. The huge blocks of stone, exquisitely carved have been very accurately dressed and fitted in their respective places. No mortar seems to have been used and vertical joints have been regularly broken.

The upper plinth of the Vimana which is exquisitely carved has been replaced by a plain rectangular one in the Jagamohana.

Jagamohana. The jangha of the wall of the Jagamohana corresponds to that of the Vimana, and consists of four, instead of five elements. Kani is wanting. Much light is afforded to the interior of the Jagamohana by means of two balustraded windows consisting of 5 balusters each, like those noticed in the temple of Siddhesvara (Vide plate XIV). The windows of Muktesvara are latticed. The windows of Rajarani are flanked by two big pillars supporting a plain bracket projecting from the main wall, thereby causing a pleasing effect. The pillars are carved with the figures of Naginis standing with their entwined tails on three griffins mounted on elephant triplets.

The Naginis with their tails on the northern face do not exist at all, and those on the southern one have become much weathered and mutilated. The pillars flanking the entrance represent Nagas and Naginis surmounted by a canopy of seven hoods on the left and right respectively. The architrave over the front entrance on the east is carved with the characteristic figures of nine planets, or *grahas* having no attendant *dwârpâlas* commonly met with in big temples ; spaces seem to have been left for the location of the *dwârapâlas*. The lintel over the doorway contains the characteristic figure of Lakshmi. The figure of lion on the top of the Jagamohana on the east resembles that on the Muktesvara Jagamohana and is called Khepa-Sinha. There are 3 figures of lions on the north, east and south respectively. The carvings of the doorway of the Jagamohana are peculiar ; the characteristic element of the Barajhanji is wanting.

The door carvings of the Jagamohana

The carvings are noticed below in the following order from the edge farthest from the door opening—Dali, Padma-pakhuda, Dali, Gelbai, Dali. At the base of the side pilasters are two panels containing the figures of Nandi and Mahakala with a female figure.

The carvings of this temple are very beautiful and have been represented by Dr. Gustave le Bon in his monumental work, "Les Monuments de l' Inde." The carvings, simple and graceful as they are, indicate frequent repetitions of the same design. The base of the temple above the plinth contains small medallions with scroll borders, the inset being the face of some deity, or human figure. The medallions are followed by three-tier cornices supporting another projection with a perforated base of honeycombed pattern. This cornice is faced with scrollwork in relief. The top of the projection is covered with single petals of lotus with ornamental borders arranged side by side at an angle. This supports the main pilasters.

Representation of leafs shooting from a branch and terminating in flower, is found in the centre of the *kumbha* portion of the pilasters. This representation is copied from nature, and is more beautiful than what we come across on the temple of Muktesvara. The hook scroll or *Phand-granthi* of Muktesvara (vide plate VI) is noticed here in the Rekha portion of the Vimana; the floral device similar to that noticed below the beaded tassels on Muktesvara temple is noticed abundantly on the face of the Rajarani.

The statuettes of Rajarani

The Rajarani temple is famous for its statuettes projecting from the pilasters in *alto-relievo.* These statuettes are characterized by most natural and elegant expressions. These tempted the European explorers to remove them from their original position to garnish their drawing rooms at home; nature too, has wrought immense mischief by defacing the figures by her weathering action. Many of the statuettes have been rendered indistinct by the oxidising action of the atmosphere. What still remains, indistinct as it is, exacts the admiration of the critics of art who frequent this glory of Orissan Architecture. The figure that used to adorn the niche at the rear of the temple has probably gone across the seas. The two semi-octagonal columns that flank this niche are most artistically carved. The pilasters on the sides of the niches are usually carved with beaded tassels.

The central niches are each flanked by two octagonal columns very exquisitely carved with scrolls and ornamental devices; the columns terminate in portions resembling the *jangha* of the pilasters to some extent; but the number of mouldings is greater, for some out of the characteristic five mouldings of the pedestal are noticed to have been repeated. It may be mentioned here that all the P*a*rs*v*a Devat*a*s have been removed from the central niches. A peculiarity of the Vim*a*na is that the characteristic N*a*ga and N*a*gini columns are wanting; but the small figures of a N*a*ga and N*a*gini are seen projecting from the pilasters flanking the central niches, and at a certain height below the niches.

I give below a brief description of some of the important statuettes.

The standing and bearded figure of Agni on a lotus and having a ram as his *Vâhana* or vehicle is very significant;

PLATE XV

The Facade of Raja Rani temple showing plinth, Jangha, and Barandi

Photo by A. Ghose F. C. S. F. G. S.

flames, too, have been represented. The figure of *Siva* on a bull, and holding a club with the right hand and a noose of rope with the left, and flanked by two attendants is worth noticing. The male and female figures in various postures attract the attention of even a careless observer. They have been copied from nature with the colouring of an artist. On the southern face are seen the figures of females wearing finely plaited cloth, and standing under trees with monkey and peacock, the latter picking at their ornaments for the head. The figure of a female (vide plate VII) fondling her child held in her left hand and having her right one passing round its back and neck is full of grace and beauty. The tender look of the mother has been so nicely depicted as to leave a lasting impression on the minds of a casual observer. The figure of a female touching the head of her child with upraised hands is also significant. The terrific figure of a male on the west side, and holding a sword in the right hand and the chopped off head of a demon in the left, with the sacred thread encircled athwart his breast hardly fails to attract one's notice while going round the temple. This is Batüka Vairava, flanked by two attendants—male and female—on the right and left respectively.

From the stand-point of Orissan sculpture indecent statuettes have been sparingly used; but their number is more than what we see at Muktes*v*ara.

The Zoology of Rajarani is not varied, for animals have been most meagrely represented. Here, one comes across an infinite variety of scrolls and fantastic plants.

I give below the dimensions of the temple as taken by me personally.

Vimana :—

The outside length of the vimana from east to west	29′
" " " " " north to south	31′
The inside dimensions both from north to south and east to west	10′-3″
The total height of the two tiers of plinth ...	4′-6″
(*a*) the uppper plinth	2′-7″
(*b*) the lower plinth	1′-11″
The height from the plinth to Ghad-Chakda ...	45′-4″
The height of bada from plinth	18′-4″
The height of Rekha up to ghad-chakda ...	27′-0″
The height (from the plinth) of the rekha looking like the 1st storey measured on the konakapaga	26′-4″
The height (from the plinth) of the *rekha miluda* of the rahapaga	30′-8″
The height from plinth up to the bottom of the lion projecting towards Jagamohana ...	30′-0″

The elements of the *Bada* :—

(*a*) Upper Jangh*a*	3'- 9"
(*b*) Upper B*ara*ndi	3'- 9"
(*c*) Bandhan*a*	1'- 4"
(*d*) Lower B*ara*ndi	4'-11"
(*e*) Lower Jangh*a*	4'-11"
Beki	1'- 1"
*A*ml*a* Dh*a*ra	0'- 4"
*A*ml*a*	2'- 1"
Tripatadh*a*ra of Karpuri	0'- 9"
Karpuri (vertical height)	1'- 0"
*A*ml*a* (diameter)	14'-10"
*A*ml*a* Karpuri (diameter)	11'-0"
Kalasa (height)	4'- 5"
Kalasa (diameter)	2'- 4"

Jagamohana :—

The inside dimension of the Jagamohana both from north to south and east to west ...	17'-10"
The plinth of Jagamohana	4'- 6"
The B*a*d*a*	11'- 2"

Restoration by the P. W. D.

This temple has been fairly repaired by the Public Works Department at a total cost of Rs. 3,096. Plate XIV illustrates the condition of the temple before the repair works were executed. The Jagamohana has been repaired with old stones, the first four courses of *Pidas* from the top have been repaired with new stones. In this piece of repair work the height of the Jagamohana has been diminished by providing a different and flatter slope, and by doing away with the *Kânlis* or vertical recesses in respect of the four courses of *Pidas* referred to above. The Kalasa of the Jagamohana is altogether new. The eastern face of the sanctum has been much more repaired than any other face. The Beki, *A*mla and Karpuri of the *dewl* were in a bad condition, and have been thoroughly repaired. A low palisaded enclosure wall has been built round the temple.

The Temple of Bhaskaresvara ;—(Plate XV. A)

The temple of Bhaskaresvara is due west of Meghesvara, and not very far from it. It has no Jagamohana, and is two-storeyed, the lower storey forming a well-proportioned basement from the middle of which rises the tower. The basement referred to rests on a plinth 2 ft. high : its height exclusive of the plinth is 8 ft. The dimensions of the pavement = 47′-9″ square : the external dimensions of the tower = 31′-6″, and the internal dimensions = 13′-9″ square. Though the temple faces the west, the flight of steps leading to it is situated on the north, the tread and rise being 1′-9″ and 1′ respectively ; the steps are made of laterite, the length of each being 7′-3″.

The temple is a *pida* dewl having 9 *pidas* : the walls of the

Plate XV.A

Northern face of the temple of Bhaskaresvara, Bhubanesvara.

Engraved & Printed by K. V. Sevne & Bros

bāda present the usual five elements of Jangha, Sakkara, Sikkara, etc. The face of the first storey shows Jangha with the first four elements, Barandi, Bandhana and Upper Barandi. The temple as it indicates a departure from the established type as far as the constructive peculiarities are concerned, is also peculiar from the sculptural point of view. The architrave over the doorway is not carved with the figures of Nava Grahas or nine planets, nor does the door lintel show the characteristic figure of Gaja-Lakshmi. The central niches contain the Parsvadevatas ; but their usual position described in the sixth chapter seems to have been deviated from. The figures of Ganesa and Parvati are noticed in the southern and northern niches respectively ; their positions should be reversed.

The front of the temple presents a bare face ; the usual jamb carvings have been omitted. The usual figures of four lions on the four sides do not project forward so as "to float in the mid-air." They rest on the *rahapagas* ; in the recess between the *Amla* and the Ghad Chakda, four *dewl-charanis* are noticeable without the intermediate lions.

The huge lingam.

The height of the *Sivalingam* is 9 ft. from the level of the pavement below, and some portion of it is imbedded in the ground. The circumference of the *lingam* as measured by me is 12'·1", whence the diameter is deduced to be 3·10" (approx)

From the broken and tapering end of the *lingam*, Dr. Mitra surmised* that it must have been "the fragment of a huge monolithic column," or, in other words, a portion of "an Asokan lat." It is very difficult to accept this view unless some other cogent reasons are advanced in its favour except that the place was a stronghold of Buddhism.

The temple has no ornamentation of any kind, and although very plain in structure, it presents a somewhat imposing appearance. There are statues in the niches in the middle of each wall except the front (west) where the door is located. The door faces the west as in the temple of Meghesvara. The sandstone has become extremely weathered, and at places conchoidal weathering is seen prominently. The statues are also eroded by weathering action. The statues worth noticing in this temple are the figures of Ganesa, Mahadeva and Vishnu on the south, east and north walls respectively.

Repair by the P. W. D.

This temple had been in a bad state of preservation ; the Beki, *Amla*, Karpuri and Kalasa had entirely broken up. It has been repaired by the P.W.D. at a total cost of Rs. 3,798.†

* Antiquities of Orissa, Vol II. p. 89.

† Report with Photographs of the Repairs executed to some of the Principal temples at Bhubanesvara, M. H. Arnott (1903).

I cannot pass on to the next temple without expressing the sense of doubt naturally raised in my mind regarding the identity of the temple of Bh*a*skares*v*ara. I have accidentally come across the following lines in the Brahma Pur*a*nam regarding Bh*a*skares*v*ara.

Identity of the temple.

"तस्मिन् क्षेत्रवरे लिङ्गं भास्करेश्वर संज्ञितं
पश्यन्ति ये तु तं देवं स्नात्वा कुण्डे महेश्वरं
आदित्येनार्चितं पूर्वं देवदेवं त्रिलोचनं
सर्वपाप विनिर्मुक्ता विमानवरमास्थिताः ॥"

77th Sloka, 41st Chapter.

In the above lines it is enjoined that the *Lingam* of Bh*a*skares*v*ara, or the Lord of the solar god, is to be worshipped after bathing in the *künda* or spring near at hand; but there is no *künda* in the vicinity of the temple; moreover, it is locally called by the name of Meghes*v*ara. The reason why it is so called is inexplicable; such reversal of nomenclature of the temples very close to each other is rarely expected from local traditions which are unerring in these respects; moreover, the name has some significance. Meghes*v*ara means, the Lord of the clouds; the *lingam* being a huge one may appropriately be styled the god of the clouds floating high up in the air.

The temple of Meghes*v*ara, or the Lord of the clouds, has

not been noticed by Dr. Mitra ; it is a few hundred feet to the east of the temple of Bhaskaresvara. This temple is noted for an inscription which has been published in the Epigraphia Indica, Vol VI.

Megheswara Temple.

It faces the west unlike the usual type of temples, and consists of the *vimâna* and *Jagamohana* standing on a spacious paved quadrangle enclosed by a compound wall of laterite capped by a plain coping. There are signs to indicate that there was probably a wooden Bhogamandapa in front ; the stone structure was not probably built. There is a small pillar in front of the Jagamohana called the *Vrisha Stambha*, or the bull pillar ; the *brisha* or bull surmounting the pillar is lying scattered in a neglected state on the south side of the compound. The compound has a big tank to its north mentioned in the inscription to be referred to later on. The compound wall shows recesses by reason of its being doubled over. The dimensions of the quadrangle are given below.

The maximum inside length (north to south)			...	70'- 2"
The minimum	„	„	„ ...	63'- 7"
The maximum	„	„	(east to west) ...	161'- 5".
The minimum	„	„	„ ...	156'- 6"

The Vimana and the Jagamohana have no plinth ; they start from the pavement or *tala pattana*. The *bâdi* of the vimana which is a *saptaratha dewl* is 15'-10' high ; both the upper and lower *bârândis* are provided with niches, the lower ones containing the figures of *dikapâlas* many of which have been removed, and those remaining are much weathered. Some of the *dikpatis* are not seen in their respective positions assigned to them; for instance, the position of Indra has been reversed through inadvertence by the P. W. D while executing repairs to the temple.

The dimensions of the different parts of the temple are given below.

Lower Jangh*a* of five mouldings	3'-11"
Lower B*a*r*a*ndi	3'- 4"
Bandhan*a* of three mouldings	1'- 4"
Upper B*a*r*a*ndi	3'- 3"
Upper Jangh*a* of seven mouldings ...	4'- 0"
Total height of *bada* ...	15'-10"
Rekha	23'-10"
Pavement to G*had* Chak*da*	39'- 8"
Beki	1'- 9"
Aml*a* Dh*a*ra	0'- 5"
Aml*a*	2'- 3"
Tripata dh*a*ra	0'- 8"
Vertical height of Karpuri	2'- 0"
Kalasa	3'- 0"

Therefore the total height of the Vimana from the pavement to the top of the finial or *kalasa* comes up to 50′-2″.

The height from pavement to the bottom of central lion projecting from the Vimana = 27′-2″.

The outside length of the Vimana (north to south) = 24′-10″

" " " " (east to west) = 36′- 3″

Jagamohana.

The Jagamohana is a *pida* dewl existing up to the G*had* Chak*da* only. Its entrance is flanked by semi-cylindrical pillars carved with seven-hooded Naga and Nagini representations. The jamb mouldings are of the usual type. The doorway is surmounted by the characteristic Nava-graha lintel and the panel containing the figure of Lakshmi in relief.

The inside of the Jagamohana is a square, its sides being 21′-6″.

The Jagamohana has two plain balustraded windows. The only figure worth mentioning on the walls of the Jagamohana is a chlorite (?) figure of Hara-Gauri on the left; this is very exquisitely carved. Hara has three heads and six hands. On the right wall is noticed a weathered figure of Hanumana, the monkey-god carved out of sandstone.

The Jagamohana, a subsequent addition.

The Jagamohana is decidedly a subsequent addition to the Vimana; the following among other reasons are given below. There are distinct traces of addition. The Jagamohana is built of *khadia kanda* already described, the Vim*a*na, of *Bogdâkandâ*, both coarse and fine-grained. The Nava-graha architrave over the doorway of the sanctum is partially exposed to view. The western face of the Vim*a*na, now hidden, is complete in all its details, that of the Jagamohana is not so; this is due to its being hastily finished.

The Sculpture of Meghesvara.

The sculpture of Meghesvara is very elegant and cannot be charged with the defect of over-decorated ugliness. The statuettes in the recesses are very nice and stand in graceful poses. Their expressions are very natural. The *dâli* figures contain animal insets; this is a peculiarity of its sculpture. The zoology of the temple sculpture is rich and varied. Among others the following animals are seen represented:—rhinoceros, stag, monkey, peacock. The sides of the pilasters show various scenes from animal life. The sculpture representing foliage and floriage is rather poor; beaded tassels are very sparing. Another peculiarity of this temple is that indecent figures are not met with as usual in Orissan temples. As a good specimen of sculpture, the peacock of K*a*rtika, the war-god, placed in the central niche of the eastern wall of the Vim*a*na may be referred to.

From an inscription* incised on a slab of stone now stuck on the western compound wall of the temple of Ananta V*a*sudeva, the date of construction of the temple of Meghesvara

Epigraphia Indica, Vol. VI. (1900-01), p. 199.

can be fixed with sufficient accuracy. This inscription relates the history of the construction of the temple of Meghesvara with an amount of poetic license which may be appraised at its true value. General Stewart removedthe slab from its true position in 1810, and deposited it in the museum of the Asiatic Society; it was restored back, though not in its proper position, by Lieutenant Kittoe in 1837 at the solicitous request of the people of Bhubanesvara. The slab, in question, has been put in the compound wall of Ananta Vasudeva just to the left of another slab belonging to the latter temple and which shared the same fate as the Meghesvara slab.

Date of Meghesvara.

It is very surprising that this inscription escaped the attention of Dr. Mitra, for I could not find it out in his monumental volume on Orissa. He has quoted the inscription of Brahmesvara (page 88, vol. II.) as seen by him on a slab stuck on the compound wall of Ananta Vasudeva placed in the very place where the slab of Meghesvara is located now. The testimony of a careful scholar like Dr. Mitra can not forthwith be rejected. Is it the fact, which, of course, is not probable, that the slab of Brahmesvara did actually exist in the compound wall of Ananta Vasudeva when Dr. Mitra visited Bhubanesvara and that it was subsequently removed and replaced by the slab of Meghesvara? Anyhow the Brahmesvara slab is missing, and that for Meghesvara unnoticed by Dr. Mitra has taken the place of the former.

On referring to Babu Rakhal Das Banerjee, M. A., Assistant Superintendent of the Indian Museum, I am informed that the inscription of Brahmesvara is not a spurious one; but he, I believe, has not been able up till now to trace the whereabouts of the missing slab, for he was to let me know the result of his enquiry which has not been communicated to me as yet.

From the inscription* we learn that the temple was built under the auspices of Svapnesvara of Gautama Gotra, the Commander-in-chief (Mahasamantadhipati) of the Ganga kings of Orissa; we learn also that Surama Devi, the sister of Svapnesvara was married to Rajaraja Deva, the son of Chodaganga who inaugurated the Ganga dynasty in Orissa. The date of Rajaraja Deva, the elder brother of Anianka is known with sufficient accuracy. Anianka, according to Professor Kielhorn, ascended the Orissan throne in 1192 A. D.; and Rajaraja Deva ruled for 25 years; hence the ascension of Rajaraja Deva is dated in the year 1167 A.D. The temple may accordingly be supposed to have been built sometime towards the close of, or in the last quarter of the twelfth century.

Chronology fixed from another stand-point

We may consider it from another stand-point. From the 24th line of the *Prasasti* or eulogium contained in the inscription, in question, we trace the authorship to the poet Udayana, who according to Bhadudi

* J. A. S. B. Vol. LXVI, Part I. p. 11 (1897)

Vamsavali, was a contemporary of Küllüka Bhatta and Mayüra Bhatta ; he is the reputed author of Kusumanjali, a treatise on the Nyaya system of Hindu philosophy. According to Pandit Ganga Nath Jha*, Udayana, the author of Tatparya Parisuddhi, a commentary on Nyaya Vartika Tatparyam by Vachaspati Misra, flourished in the reign of Lakshmana Sena, the last Hindu king of Bengal ; hence the date of Udayana is fixed in the close of the twelfth century. Again, Vachaspati Misra is known to live in the last quarter of the 10th, or the beginning of the 11th century A.D ; and it is reasonable to suppose that one hundred years must have elapsed since the composition of the work by Vachaspati on which Udayana wrote the commentary. This also brings Udayana, the author of the Meghesvara inscription to the close of the twelfth century A.D. We may support the above date by another reference to contemporary literature. The author of Nyarasa Vijay has quoted from the work of Udayanacharya ; hence Udayana must have flourished at least before 1252 A. D ; and in those days when the art of printing was not known, it is most unlikely the case that a reference to a work by a contemporaneous author should be made ; Udayana accordingly was not a contemporary of the author of Nyarasa Vijay who flourished in 1252 A.D. Udayana

* Preface to the English Translation of the Tattva Kaumudi, Ganga Nath Jha, M.A. (1896).

may reasonably be supposed to have flourished 75 to 100 years before this date, or, in other words, he may be supposed to belong to the last quarter of the twelfth century.

Brahmesvara Temple :—

Nomenclature

The temple of Brahmesvara is not well-known by reason of its distance from the Lingaraja Temple; it is, however, situated within the sacred area of *Pancha Kosi*, being at a distance of about a mile to the north-east of the temple of Bhubanesvara. We learn from the Ekamra Puranam that Sankara requested Brahma to erect a temple at a certain distance to the north-east of the temple of Lingaraja; whereupon the temple was constructed by Visvakarma in obedience to Brahma's injunctions, and hence the name of Brahmesvara, or the Lord of Brahma. If not from the point of view of sanctity, its importance is due to the peculiarity of carvings, and dim reminiscence of history that may be gathered from an inscription carved on a slab of stone which was subsequently translated* to the western boundary wall of Ananta Vasudeva, according to Dr. Mitra, and which cannot be traced now. For the inscription, I refer my readers to the article in the Journal of the Asiatic Society by James Prinsep, or to the Antiquities of Orissa Vol. II, (p. 88) by Dr. Mitra.

* See my remarks on this on page 330.

Chronology of the temple.

The authorship of the inscription is ascribed to one Purushottama Bhatta, probably the court-poet of Udyotaka Kesari, the king of Kalinga under the auspices of whose mother Kolavati, the temple was erected. Udyotaka Kesari is stated to be seventh in descent from Janmejaya; it is not stated who this Janmejaya was; but from the description in the inscription, I am inclined to take him to be the father of Yayati; I have discussed at great length in the first chapter to establish the identity of Janmejaya, and the time when he flourished. I have placed him in the middle of the 8th century, and hence Udyotaka naturally belongs to the early part of the 10th century, or the latter part of the 9th century A. D. as he is the 7th in descent from Janmejaya. I may state here that Udyotaka does not certainly belong to the main line of Janmejaya. The temple accordingly is a work of the end of the 9th, or the beginning of the 10th century A. D; this will be apparent from the study of its architecture. This receives additional strength in the shape of corroboration from palæographic considerations, judging from which Dr. Mitra was inclined to place it between the 8th and the 9th century A. D.

The temple of Brahmesvara has a spacious compound surrounded both inside and outside by two walls; it will be seen that portions of the outer walls are still traceable now both

Plate XV.B

The northern face of the temple of Brahmesvara
showing the Jagamohana and the compound wall

on the east and south. The compound has a tank on the south side. The dimensions of the inner compound are 107′-9″ (east to west) and 71′ (north to south). The inner compound has four temples at the four corners. (*vide* plate—XV. B).

The temple is situated on a plinth 3′-9″ high ; as usual with most of the Orissan temples, it faces the east. It consists of a vimana and a jagamohana. Both the vimana and the jagamohana are *Pancharatha dewls*; the Konakapaga of the vimana shows five *bhümis* ; from all its *pâgas* just over the *bâda* and in the first *bhümi*, project the *rekha* representations. The middle of the konakapaga is carved with srcoll work surrounded by a beaded border with animal insets. Such an ornament in the konakapaga is nowhere met with. The recess between the konaka and anartha-pagas is not distinct. The rahapaga over the central projecting lion is carved with a central band of *vana latâ*. This is peculiar. The Ânartha-paga shows *bhos* and representations of temples containing male and female figures in their panels. The upper *bârândis* are provided with niches containing male and female figures in graceful poses. Their expressions are exquisitely beautiful. In the case of the temple of Meghesvara, the niches of upper *bârândis* contain the figures of gods and goddesses. All the Parsva Devatas have been removed from the central niches.

The Sardüla columns of the temple of Brahmesvara are

peculiar; those between the Konaka, Anartha and Rahapagas are all similar; the *Sárdulas* are represented with their heads turned back; they are standing on crouching elephants with no human figure in the vicinity.

I give below the dimensions of the different parts of the Vimana and Jagamohana as measured by me.

Vimana :—

Lower Jangha	4′- 8″
" Barandi	4′- 2″
Bandhana (one moulding only)	1′- 2″
Upper Barandi	4′- 2″
Upper Jangha	4′- 8″
Total ...	18′-10″

Bada	18′-10″
Rekha	28′-0″
Beki	2′- 2″
Amla Dhara	0′- 5″
Amla	2′-10″
Tripata Dhara	0′-10″
Karpuri (vertical height)	1′- 6″
Kalasa	5′- 6″
Total ...	60′- 1″

Height up to the bottom of the projecting lion on the *rahapaga* towards jagamohana ... 31′- 6″

Diameter of Karpuri ... ... 12′- 0″

Diameter of *Amla* ... ... 16′- 0″

Gh*ad* chak*da* from konakap*a*ga to konakap*a*ga ... 12′- 6″

Jagamohana :—

Jangh*a* ... ... 3′- 9″

B*ada* ... ... 12′- 2″

Beki ... ... 0′-10″

Dh*ara* of *Sree* ... ... 0′- 2″

Sree ... ... 1′- 1″

Vertical height of *Amla Sree* ... ... 3′ -0″

*A*mla Beki ... ... 5′- 0″

Amla Dh*a*ra .. .. 0′- 2″

Amla ... ... 0′-10″

Amla Karpuri including Dh*ara* ... ... 0′-11″

Kalasa ... ... 4′- 6″

Vertical height of pyramidal top of the b*ada* of Jagamohana ... ... 10′- 3″

Slant height ... ... 15′-10″

$$\text{Angle of inclination} = \sin^{-1}\frac{13'-3''}{15'-10''}$$

$$= \sin^{-1}\cdot 83684$$

$$= 56^\circ 48' 30''.$$

The Jagamohana is provided with two windows on the north and south sides consisting of plain columns carved on the outside with five figures many of which have been obliterated; the female figure on the north side looking up at a full-blown lotus is very striking.

Jagamohana

The face of the *bâda* of Jagamohana shows only Jangha and Barandi with its top. The *dikpatis* are noticeable in the niches of the *bârândis* referred to.

The Jagamohana of Brahmesvara is similar to that of Muktesvara by reason of having the ceiling of it most elaborately carved. The lowest part of the spire of the Jagamohana (inside) is carved by three tiers of animated friezes describing various scenes. The third, or the uppermost course of stone blocks has carved on it the serrated copings like those on the outer enclosure wall of the Puri Temple. The second course of stones contains the carvings of anchorites worshipping the *Siva Lingam*, and of rows of anchorites standing with folded hands in front of a *sâdhu* or ascetic in meditation. In this course there are small projecting statuettes of females suckling their babes. In the first or the lowest course are depicted the elephant procession, cavalry and armed foot soldiers. The three tiers of friezes already referred to enclose an exquisitely carved lotus hanging from the ceiling.

Interior decoration

The exterior of this temple contains numerous carved blocks and statuettes. Compared with those on Muktesvara, and Meghesvara, the workmanship is inferior, and details are wanting. Absence of purity in the representation of domestic scenes is patent everywhere except on the Jagamohana. Most of the blocks of the Jagamohana are plain, and the number of carvings is limited. On either side of the entrance of the Jagamohana, the outer face of the jamb contains in high relief the figure of a bejewelled man with a sword in hand in a striking attitude facing an enemy not represented, and riding on a griffin towering over a diminutive elephant in a crouching attitude. Just below the roof, herds of deer, elephants, and flocks of geese are depicted in a running order following close upon one another.

The main rectangular frieze on the south is set in a frame of scrollwork with beaded borders which has been much obliterated except in the lowest border. A man is seated on a throne supported on ornamental legs; below the seat, a *kamandalū* and a conchshell on a circular stand are depicted, probably indicating that the central figure on the seat is a sage. He is seated cross-legged, his right hand being partly supported on an ornamental pillow behind his back. The other hand rests on his left leg. There is an ornamenta awning over his head. Behind stands a servant with a *chowrie*.

For want of space, the artist has given a diminutive form to this individual. In front, and on the floor stands a young boy with his back against the principal figure; and facing him there are two figures in a kneeling attitude. By the side of these and in the background are five erect figures the foremost of which is richly attired; the rest except one are in a posture of praying; and among these, the foremost figure exhibits much fervour.

The pilasters of the Jagamohana entrance are carved with scrolls, flowers, and human figures with two Dw*a*rp*a*las, each supported by a couple of griffins. Lakshmi figures in the middle of the lintel.

The lowest tier of bass-reliefs of the temple shows gods (*S*iva, Bhairava, &c.) in the central niche of brackets with well-executed female figures in each of the double side-niches. The figure of Ch*a*mund*a* on the western face is striking. The central frieze on this face is a small one, and depicts an ascetic discoursing to his disciples who are all attentively listening to him. There are only 14 figures of gods, and goddesses as against innumerable male and female figures. The human figures are extremely important as depicting various musical instruments, domestic implements, garments, jewellery and toilet of the age they belong to.

The Vimana

There are 5 erect figures on the north and south faces;

Plate XVI.

(1) & (2) Statuettes of the Raja Rani Temple.

(1) to (4) Statuettes of the Bhubaneswara group.

Photo taken from the gallery of the Indian Museum, Calcutta by A. Ghose M. A. B. L.

they are much mutilated. They are the largest of all the figures in this temple. There are no Naginis, but on the north wall of the Jagamohana one of the above statuettes has a seven-headed snake over its head. It has a *kamandalu* in one out of the four hands; the other figures are of women, each having a lotus in full bloom over her head; I may refer in passing to a very nice female figure noticed in the recess between the anartha and *rahapagas* at the north-west corner of the western face just where the *bada* terminates. The figure is represented as about to put on an anklet resting her leg on a tiny statuette of a female figure. The female figure fondling a child is also worth mentioning.

The zoology of the temple

The zoology of the temple is rich and varied. The base of the central niche on the north is flanked by two small pilasters containing scrolls enclosing figures of the peacock, crab, elephant, fish, tortoise and *makara*. The top frieze of the Jagamohana shows rows of stags, monkeys and ducks.

The panelled statuettes of Brahmesvara are very graceful and expressive. The carvings of Brahmesvara are similar to those of Muktesvara in many respects; the anchorites or ascetics, the frequent repetition of the *Siva lingum*, the beaded tassels with scrolls of both the temples resemble one another in a very striking manner; the lion of the Jagamohana on the east is similar to that of Muktesvara.

"There were bad vertical cracks in the Dewl undoubtedly occasioned by unequal settlement".* The Public Works Department has thoroughly repaired the temple and its appurtenances including the four temples at the corners and the compound wall at a total cost of Rs. 5,192.*

Restoration by the P. W. D.

The Temple of Lingaraja—

The temple of Lingaraja is the biggest of all at Bhubanesvara; it ranks among the best of the group belonging to the Indo-Aryan style of Architecture. It is also important from the sculptural point of view, for some of the chlorite figures which I shall refer to later on indicate the climax of the decorative art reached by the old artists of Orissa.

The temple has a spacious compound (520′ × 465′)† enclosed by a boundary wall of laterite about 7′-6″ thick and surmounted by a plain, slant coping; alongside the inner face of the boundary wall there runs a terrace probably meant to protect the compound wall against the incursions of the Mahomedans; at the north-east corner of the wall and on it, rests a small structure called the *Bhet Mandapa* where an image of the consort of

* Report with photographs of the Repairs executed to some of the Principal temples at Bhubanesvara between 1898 and 1903 by M. H. Arnott.

† Dr. Mitra is responsible for this measurement. I have taken it from his Antiquities of Orissa. I may mention here that I have very rarely relied on the measurements taken by others; but in this case insuperable difficulties were presented to me in taking the measurement.

Plate XVII

Northern face of the Temple of Lingaraja, Bhubanesvara.

Engraved & Printed by K. V. Seyne & Bros

Lingaraja is placed to accord him a befitting reception on his return home after the car festival, or *Rutha Yâtrâ*.

The compound wall is provided with three gates on the north, south and east, that on the north being called the *sinha-dwâra* by reason of its being flanked by two rampant lions. The structure for *sinha-dwâra* is itself sufficient for a temple of ordinary proportions; it is a *pida-dewl*. It was customary in Orissa in the mediæval times to provide a structure for the entrance in the case of big temples, though it differs materially from the *gopurâm* or propyllon of the Dravidian style.

Access is gained to the court-yard through the eastern entrance by a descending flight of steps, for its level is lower than that of the road; on traversing the compound for some length, the terrace or the raised platform on which the temple with its appurtenances stands is reached by an ascending flight of steps.

The temple consists of the following four parts—the Vimana, Jagamohana, Natamandira and Bhogamandapa, of which the first two and probably the last in its original form are coeval.

Vimana :—

The Vimana which is a Pancharatha dewl stands on a paved quadrangle; the jangha, 10′-4⅜″ in height, and without any plinth starts at once from the pavement or *tala pattana*;

the *bâda* consists of the usual five elements; the upper jangh*a* shows ten mouldings, and is accordingly called *Dasakâma.*

The dimensions of the above five elements are given below.

Upper Jangh*a*	...	...	...	11′- 0″
Upper B*a*randi	...	...	...	9′- 3″
Bandhan*a*	...	...	...	3′- 0″
Lower B*a*randi	...	...	...	9′-10″
Lower Jangh*a*	...	...	...	10′-4½″

In the Konak-*pa*ga above the second Jangh*a* are noticed five similar mouldings surmounted by an *a*mlaka-*sila*; these comprise one *bhümi*; there are tiers of ten similar *bhümis* one above the other; next comes the course of stone called Gh*ad*-chak*da*. In the anartha-p*a*ga above the *bâda* are noticed nine projections of *kani* and *basanta*, and over them rests a rekha-dewl representation, the top of which corresponds with that of the fourth *bhümi* of the konaka-p*a*ga; over this, there are, again, six mouldings of *kani* and *basanta* surmounted by a similar rekha representation, the top of which is in the same line with that of the seventh *bhümi*; this is surmounted by a similar succession of four mouldings capped by a *rekha* the top of which corresponds with the ninth *bhümi*; over this is noticed one moulding with a *rekha* representation corresponding with the tenth *bhümi*; the b*a*randi of this rekha contains the figure of Lakshmi. On the r*a*hap*a*ga (north side) is

PLATE-XVII(A)

SCALE 32′=1″

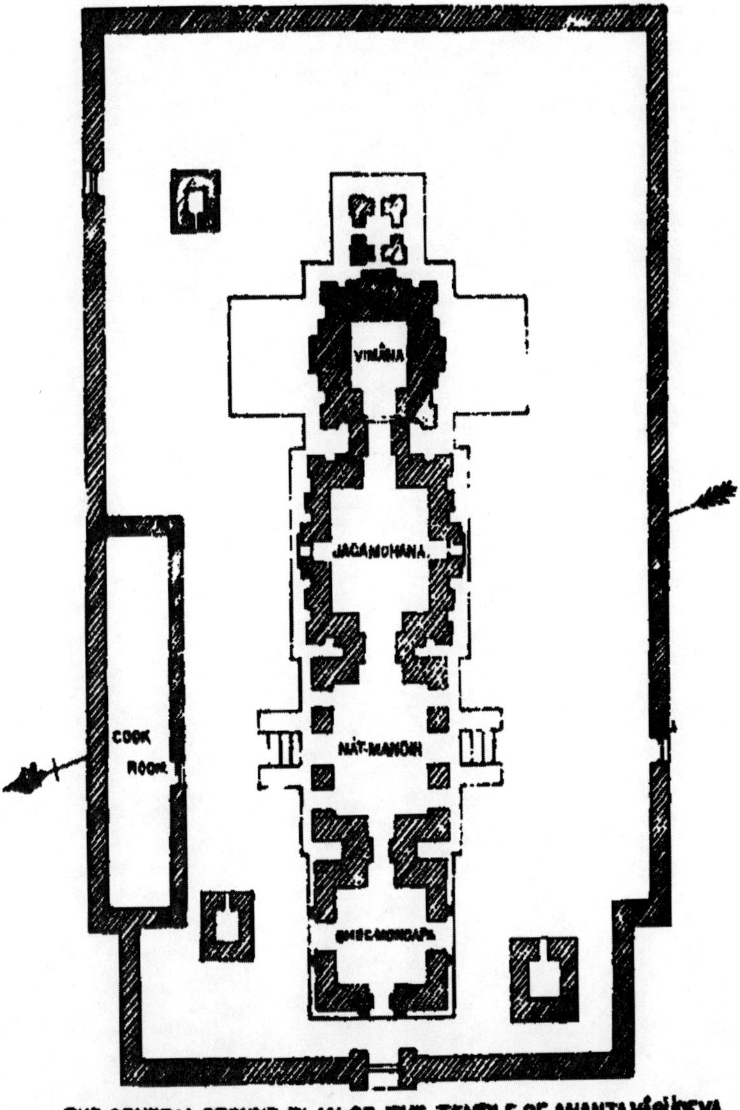

THE GENERAL GROUND PLAN OF THE TEMPLE OF ANANTA VÁSUDEVA.

noticed a small lion placed on a slab of stone projecting forward at the top of the *bâda*; over this is seen *Padma-bho* (page 129) flanked by two reclining male figures; the top of the *bho* corresponds with the top of the second *bhûmi*; over this is a slab supporting a *Jhâppâ-sinha* (p. 204) floating, as it were, in the mid-air; the top of this corresponds with the middle of the third *bhûmi*. The figure of *Udâ-guja-sinha* (p. 204) is placed at a height equivalent to the top of the sixth *bhûmi* and projects from the rahapaga facing the Jagamohana.

In the middle of the *janghâ*, there runs a vertical band terminating in a panel enclosed in a miniature *dewl*; these panels contain human figures which have been much obliterated by the weathering action of the atmosphere.

Side-structures. On the sides of the vimana except the east, abut three two-storeyed structures just close to the central niches containing the figures of the *Pârsva-devatâs*. The structures serve the purpose of *mohanas* of the niches which by reason of their containing the images of the *Pârsva-devatâs* resemble the vimenas or sanctums. The plan of these structures is nearly a square (21′ × 20″); the ground floor starts from a low plinth 11″ high; the height of the ground floor (south) is 9′-3″; over it rests a second plinth 2′-1½″ high from which rises the second storey.

The storeyed structures are obviously subsequent additions

to the vimana; the lowest *pida* of the first-floor has been made to abut skilfully on the top of the niche.

Parsva-devatas.

The figures of the *Pârsva-devatâs* placed in the niches mentioned above have been most exquisitely carved out of chlorite (?) blocks; the nice carvings showing among other things the folds of the garments register the high water-mark of the skill in the art of sculpture reached by the Uriya artists of a by-gone age. These may compare favourably with any master-piece of sculpture noticed in any part of the world; but for want of space I would have devoted a whole chapter to the description of the images. I would, however, content myself with giving a brief and general description of them conveying most meagrely the idea of their perfection in the art of sculpture.

The Western niche.

The figure of Kartika or war-god standing on a pedestal of lotus is noticed in the western niche, *i. e.*, that at the rear of the sanctum. The part of the pedestal below the lotus referred to presents a nice front carved with artistic floral devices. The figure has the characteristic arm ornament and a necklace with the central gem as usual. The peacock, the characteristic vehicle of the deity, has been nicely represented with plumes and tail; the head of the bird has been broken. The figure is flanked by side deities; there are two flying nymphs holding garlands on the two sides of the top; beaded tassels are represented as hanging from the mouth of a *kirttimükha* forming the background of the image.

The Northern Niche.

The northern niche contains the four-handed figure of Parvati standing on a pedestal of full-blown lotus supported by a figure of lion looking up in a peculiar pose towards the deity; the lion is moustached. There are the characteristic *Pârsva-devatâs* and *devis* flanking the sides of the figure; flying nymphs are also noticed at the top. The figure is also flanked by a group of musicians playing on stringed instrument, drums, cymbals, *damarü*, &c. There is a nice full-blown lotus on the right side springing up from the lotus pedestal already referred to. The background of the figure is capped by a trefoiled arch surmounted by a *kirttimükha*. The deity is evidently a *vaishnavi* for having a *vaishnava mâlâ* encircled round her neck; the image has the characteristic arm and ankle ornaments and also a necklace set with a central gem hanging from it.

I may mention in passing the following fact noticed by me which is worth mentioning; only the left leg of the image and the same of some of the attendants of this deity are provided with anklets; this is rather peculiar.

The workmanship of the figure of Parvati is so nice that it never fails to exact the admiration of the most captious critics of art. On referring to the best sculptor of Orissa who accompanied me in my sojourns there on several occasions, I learn that he would take more than a year to complete this piece of sculpture.

The southern Niche.

The southern niche contains the pot-bellied, four-handed figure of Ganesa standing on a full-blown lotus flanked by a saddled mouse and a *pâsa* or an axe carved with beaded tassels. The figure has a nicely carved cloth reaching up to the knee. Ganesa has his tusk and the tip of fingers of the left hand broken. The figure has a peculiar ornament formed by a representation of snake encircled round the ankle; the sacred thread shows the same device.

Dikpati.

The *Dikpatis* are noticed in the niches of the *bârându*. Enclosed in a panel carved with the floral devices seen abundantly at Rajarani and sparingly at Muktesvara, is seen the figure of Agni with a ram or sheep as his vehicle; the characteristic flames of Agni have been represented. The lower part of his body below the navel has been broken. The figure of Indra has been removed; the sides of the niche meant for Indra (south side of eastern face) are carved with medallions containing insets of animal figures such as the elephant, peacock, fish, mouse, monkey, dog, *makara*, etc. Yama with the buffalo as his vehicle is noticeable in the niche on the west side of the south face; the figure of the buffalo, however, resembles more a sheep than the horny ruminant of the ox family. Nirita sitting on a lotus has as his vehicle a reclining human figure; the niche (south side of west face) has its sides carved with scrolls containing animal figures such as the elephant, fish, sheep, stag, etc. Varuna with a *makara* as his vehicle is seen in the niche on the north side of the western face; the sides of the niche show floral devices usually met with at Rajarani. Pavana having as his vehicle a stag is seen in the niche on the west side of the north face; the sides of the niche are carved with scrolls containing animal figures such as the monkey, elephant and stag. Nothing is particularly noticeable regarding the figure of Kuvera. Isana with a bull as his vehicle is seen in a niche having a beautiful top surmounting it.

Measurement of the height of the temple.

I took a theodolite and other survey instruments with me for determining the true height of the temple of Lingaraja. I set up the theodolite in the school compound to the south of the compound wall of the temple, the site chosen being a comparatively level plot of ground. The distance between the two different positions of the theodolite was 100 feet. I took several readings the mean of which are given below.

A = Angle of inclination of the top of the metallic kalasa surmounting the stone kalasa; this angle is from the nearer of the two positions from the temple.

A′ = The same up to the base of the stone finial or kalasa.

B = The same; the angle in this case is that from the more distant of the two positions from the temple.

B′ = The same up to the base of the stone finial.

A = 25°-59′

B = 19°-49′

A′ = 24°

B′ = 18°-5

C = The vertical angle of the triangle having the top of the metallic kalasa as apex and the distance between the two positions, *i. e.* 100 feet as the base.

C′ = The same up to the base of the stone finial.

C = (25°-59′) − (19° 49′) = 6°-10′

C′ = 24° − (18°-5′) = 5°-55′

Sin A = Sin 25°-59′ = ·4381

Sin B = Sin 19°-49′ = ·3392

Sin C = Sin 6°-10′ = ·1074.

∴ Height of the temple up to the top of the metallic kalasa above the level of the theodolite

$$= \frac{100 \times \cdot 4381 \times \cdot 3392}{\cdot 1074}$$

= 138·37 feet.

The height of the instrument = 4′-8″

∴ The height of the temple *up to the top* of the metallic kalasa = 143·03 feet.

(2) $\text{Sin } A' = \text{Sin } 24^\circ = \cdot 4067$

$\text{Sin } B' = \text{Sin } 18^\circ\text{-}5' = \cdot 3103$

$\text{Sin } C' = \text{Sin } 5^\circ\text{-}55'' = \cdot 1030$

∴ Height of the temple up to the base of the stone kalasa above the level of the theodolite

$$= \frac{100 \times \cdot 4067 \times \cdot 3103}{\cdot 1030} = 122 \cdot 46 \text{ feet.}$$

The height of the instrument like the above is 4·66 feet.

∴ The height of the temple above ground level of the school up to the base of the stone finial = 127·12 ft.

$= 127'\text{-}1''$

Jagamohana :—

The same conventions of A, B and C have been used in this case also; the distance of the instrument between the two positions and the height of the instrument above ground are the same in this case as in the vimana.

The angles have been measured up to the top of the stone kalasa surmounting the Jagamohana.

$A = 16^\circ - 47'$

$B = 12^\circ - 32'$

$C = (16^\circ - 47') - (12^\circ - 32') = 4^\circ - 15'$

$\text{Sin } A = \text{Sin } 16^\circ - 47' = \cdot 2887$

$\text{Sin } B = \text{Sin } 12^\circ - 32' = \cdot 2170$

$\text{Sin } C = \text{Sin } 4^\circ - 15' = \cdot 0741$

∴ The height of the Jagamohana above the theodolite and up to the top of the stone kalasa $= \frac{100 \times \cdot 2887 \times \cdot 2170}{\cdot 0741} = 84 \cdot 5$ ft.

The height of the instrument $= 4' - 8'' = 4 \cdot 66$ ft.

∴ The height of the Jagamohana above the ground level and up to the top of the stone kalasa is 89·166 ft. or 89′ – 2″.

Jagamohana :—

The Jagamohana or the Audience Chamber or the Porch is a *pida dewl*, and is contemporaneous with the *vimána* or sanctum. The southern face is provided with a doorway 8′ – 9⅛″ × 3′ – 9″; a flight of three steps leads to this doorway, the tread and rise of the steps being 2′ – 9″ and 10″ respectively. The height of the terrace including the ledge in front of the doorway is 10′ – 6″; the terrace exclusive of the ledge is 8′ – 2″ high. On the left of the staircase referred to is a small *pida dewl* for Madan Mohana; on the right is a pillared *mohana* for the temple manager to sit in; this has recently been built.

The *pida* of the Jagamohana shows the usual five elements of jangha, barandi, &c. I give the dimensions below.

Upper Jangh*a* (This consists of 10 projections)	7′ – 1″
Upper Barandi	6′ – 1⅛″
Bandhan*a*	2′ – ⅛″
Lower Barandi	6′ – 6″

Lower Jangh*a* ... ... 7′–0″

Total height of *bâda* ... ... 28′–9″

The pavement of the quadrangle has buried part of the Jangh*a*.

The lower Jangh*a* contains the usual five elements of *pâda*, *kümbha*, *patâ*, *kani* and *basanta* ; it has a central band containing panels with standing human figures and miniature temples.

The southern doorway referred to above is not provided with the Nava Graha architrave, but the figure of Lakshmi is

Doorways

noticeable. There is a bold projection over the doorway which is very plain in execution and without any carving. The frieze between the projection and the figure of Lakshmi stated above contains scenes from mythology that could not be deciphered. The doorway is flanked on the right by two female figures standing by trees and on the left, by one female figure ; this has spoiled the symmetry, and rendered the frontage rather ugly.

The space over the doorway between the plain projection stated above and the first *pida* from below upwards is flanked by pilasters carved with beaded tassels, scrolls, etc. The central space is covered by three projections of *rekha dewl* supported on a projection of Basanta with Kani below it. There are four standing figures in the recesses between the pilasters and the rekha representations; the end figures are males, and the intermediate ones, females.

The Jagamohana has a balustraded window of five nicely worked balusters upon which female figures in various poses

Balustraded windows.

and standing under the shade of trees have been carved; some of the figures have been broken. The width of the window is 7′ – 5″, and the interval between the balusters is 3⅛″. The window is flanked by a frame of three bands, the first and second of which are carved with scroll work, and the third one shows medallions enclosing animal figures almost wholly obliterated; among the animals, the stag, elephant, duck and fish can be identified.

There is a figure of Lakshmi just above the window, and over it is a row of carvings among which that of a *rishi* who looks like a king is the most important; in front of the *rishi* are represented several standing and seated figures.

The pilasters at the two sides are surmounted by dwarfs, not pot-bellied as is usually met with, but rather graceful; they are represented as uplifting a projecting *pida* or canopy, the face of which is carved with figures of elephants. There are three *rekha* representations (similar to the southern face) in the intervening space between the *pida* or canopy stated above and the lowest *pida* of the pyramidal spire. The end pilasters are most exquisitely carved with beaded tassels, scrolls and medallions containing animal figures. The topmost figure just below the lowest *pida* of the pyramidal portion contains figures of elephants.

The pyramidal portion consists of 9 *pidas*, a recess and 7 *pidas* successively till the *beki* is reached. The faces of the *pidas* represent scenes of war processions consisting of infantry carrying bows and swords. well-caparisoned elephants and horses with or without riders. It is a matter of great regret that saltpetre action has already spoiled the faces of some of the *pidas* to a fearful extent, so much so that many of the figures cannot be recognised.

Pyramidal Spire

Just over the fourth *pida* rest several projections of small *pida dewls* containing panels in the space between them showing figures in *basso-relievo*; over these is the *bho* upon which rests the lion projecting from the Jagamohana; one of these panels on the north side contains a figure of *Siva lingum* worshipped by two anchorites in front. On the south side, however, there are 6 panels which show scenes from the Ramayana and the Mahabharata. The journey of the Pandavas to heaven has been depicted very faithfully. The lower right panel contains four human figures, two of which are armed with bows. The four figures represent Rama, Lakshmana, Sita and an attendant. Hanumana and Bibhisana are walking in front. This scene probably refers to the release of Sita from her captivity.

Natamandira.

The Natamandira resting on a plinth 2'-8" high is decidedly a later addition to the Jagamohana, and was not originally contemplated. Its construction is ascribed to the wife of *Salini* Kesari, a minor king of Orissa who is supposed to have reigned towards the close of the eleventh century A. D. That it belongs to a later age than that of the Vimana or Jagamohana is proved by its constructive peculiarities and artistic details.

The face of the Natamandira is not in the same vertical plane as that of the Jagamohana, which recedes back from the former; owing to this the width of the ledge in front of it is narrower than that of the Jagamohana. The sloping roof of the Natamandira formed by four tiers of *pidas* ends in a flat terrace surrounded by battlemented tiles, or crest tiles presenting a nice appearance. This structure comes under the class of *pida mohona* as defined by me in Chapter V; it resembles the Natamandira of Jagannath in this respect, and is likewise without *sree*, *amla*, kalasa, &c.

The Natamandira is a square, each side being 52 feet, and the height of the wall of *bada* 19'-4"; hence the structure may be spoken of as a rectangular parallelopiped surmounted by a frustum of a pyramid. The roof of the Natamandira is supported by four nine-foiled arches formed by corbelling and resting on four rectangular columns.

The columns rest on plain pedestals or *pristhas* 2'-3" high and consist of plain Jangha, barandi, bandhana, upper barandi and upper Jangha till the springing point is reached.

The base of the column is nearly a square, the sides varying from 4'-2" to 4'-3¼". The inside dimensions of the Natamandira are 38'-2" both from north to south and east to west. The space between the pillars stated above is 13'-10", and their distance from the walls varies from 7'-10" to 8'; so we see that the columns are symmetrically arranged on the floor. The walls consist of the usual five elements referred to already.

Inside columns.

The measurements of the *bâda* together with those of the usual five elements are given below :—

The *bâda* from plinth	...	...	19'- 4"
Upper Jangha	...	...	4'- 6¼"
Upper Barandi	...	...	4'- ¼"
Bandhana	...	...	1'- 8¼"
Lower Barandi	...	...	4'- ¼"
Lower Jangha	...	...	4'-11"

The Sikkara or Sikhara or upper Jhangha consists of 10 bands as in the vimana of the Jagamohana. The barandi or the second element from below upwards is flanked by two slender pilasters which have ensured grace to a great extent.

The face of the ledge contains plain representations of small dewls carved in rows.

Doors.

All the walls except the eastern one are provided with three doors, the two side ones being of less dimension than the central one. The eastern door leads to the Bhogamandapa, and the corresponding one on the west wall leads to the Jagamohana.

The measurements of some of the doorways are given below so as to convey an idea of their proportions.

South side :—

Central doorway	...	...	14′-9″ × 6′-7″
South-east ...	...	...	10′-1″ × 4′-2⅛″
South-west	...	...	Same as south-east

The dimensions of the doorways on the north side are the same as those on the south. The width of the end doorways on the west side is 3′-4⅛″ and that of the central one, 10′-5⅛″. The door-sill of the central doorway on the south is 7″ higher than the level of floor ; a flight of four steps leads to this doorway from the quadrangle outside. The side doorways on the west side lead to a sort of open terrace between Jagamohana and Natamandira. The floor level goes down by 11 inches just after the doorway separating it from the Jagamohana is crossed ; the thickness of the wall of the Natamandira on this side is 7′-8″; there is a straight vertical joint noticeable separating the walls of the Jagamohana and Natamandira; it proves without the least shadow of doubt that the latter is a subsequent addition to the former.

The north-eastern doorway on the north side leads to the room for the sacred bull.

The central doorways on the north and south have the characteristic Navagraha lintel over them flanked by two panels containing the figures of dwarfs or Bhūtas or Vetalas and Lakshmi. On the north face there are no statuettes worth the name except a few small ones over the right hand doorway. There are four female figures over this lintel, and over these, again, are two Bhūtas or Vetalas struggling to uplift the structure.

The flanks and tops of doorways are not carved but present a plain surface; the architrave over the central doorway only is carved with the figures of Navagraha capped by a plain awning or projecting band. There are thin vertical bands running in the middle of the jangha or the first element. The niches of the barandi or the second element are unlike ordinary ones that are commonly met with. The space between the fifth element and the architrave over the side door is occupied by plain bands representing three temples flanked by pilasters.

Though the face of the Natamandira is not at all carved with any floral device, or arabesque, the plain surface, I think, has a charm all its own by presenting a glaring contrast with the Jagamohana just close to it on the west. One's eyes are much relieved by a surfeit of carvings in the vicinity; and in this respect the structure has a special artistic effect.

The jamb mouldings of the doorway separating the Natamandira from the Jagamohana are peculiar in some respects. The usual *gelbâi* carving shows human figures in grotesque poses; then come a small recess and a moulding the like of which is never seen to decorate a doorway. The carving referred to shows small panels representing portions of *pidas* placed one above the other; these panels contain male and female figures in various poses of amour; below the *gelbâi* moulding are seen the figures of Ganga and Yamuna in *alto-relievo.* The vehicle of Ganga is existing, and that of Yamuna is broken.

Jamb mouldings of the Natamandapa.

The central doorway on the north side is flanked by *pida* representations containing the standing figures of Vishnu and Siva as *dwârapâlas* or guards on the left and right respectively. This is rather strange as far as the jamb mouldings are concerned.

The Bhogamandapa is coeval with the Natamandira, and is placed in the second quarter of the thirteenth century A. D.; the intervening open space between the Bhogamandapa and the Jagamohana has been subsequently filled up by the Natamandira. That the Bhoga-

Bhogamandapa.

mandapa is older than the Natamandira will be proved by examining some of the mouldings which had been evidently exposed to public view before the Natamandira was constructed. There are four columns in the middle of the Bhogamandapa supporting its ceiling; the base of the columns is nearly a square (7′-6″ × 7′-9″). The space between them is 10′-6″; the columns are plastered up to the height of 8′-9″ above the floor level, the thickness of the coat of plaster varying from 3½″ to 4″. The columns present three pilasters with two recesses on each side. The pilasters consist of the usual five elements of jangha, barandi, bandhana, etc. The jangha and barandi portions only of the columns have been covered with a coat of plaster. There were probably continuous openings on all its sides suggesting its adaptibility as a place for reciting texts from the *Sastras*, or holding *sâstric* discussions.

The Bhogamandapa is a *Ghantâ-sree-mohana*, and is provided with kalasa, karpuri, *sree*, and beki; five steps lead from the open terrace in front to the entrance on the east side, the tread and rise of the steps being 3′-5″ and 6″ respectively.

The structure rises from a plinth 3′-3″ high above the level of the terrace; the plinth is plastered over with a coating 1¾″ thick; it has two mouldings both at the top and bottom, and the intervening space between the two pairs of mouldings is carved with representations of balusters, and *pida dewl* representations containing panels enclosing male and female figures in various poses, and in many cases obscene. The topmost moulding has on its front edge carvings of various figures much obliterated by the weathering action of the atmosphere. It does not, however, contain a continuous length of carvings but it does so by fits and starts.

The outside length of the Bhogamandapa from north to south is 56'-2½"; it is a square. The length between the extremities of the pilasters flanking the central doorway of the eastern face is 16'-10½". The inside dimensions or floor area of the Bhogamandapa are 42'-½" (square). The outside height of the *bâda* is 13'-7" and the inside height, 13'.

Faces of the Bhogamandapa. The eastern face of the Bhogamandapa is provided with two plain windows on each side of the central doorway, the left and right hand ones consisting of two and three plain balusters respectively. Each of the northern and southern faces of the Bhogamandapa is provided with two windows consisting of three plain balusters and one central doorway. The doorway of the northern side has been blocked by a wall projecting inside by 1'-9". The dimensions of the doors and windows are given below :—

South side :—

Central doorway ... ... 7'-½" × 5'-6

The sill of the door is higher than the floor level by 7½".

South-eastern window ... ... 4'-½" x 2'-7"

North side :—

The central doorway has been blocked up.

North-eastern window ... 3'- 6" (height) x 3'-8"

North-western window ... 3'-10" (height) x 3'-6½"

West side :—

The door leading to the Natamandira

=10'-2" x 5'-8"

East side :—

Central doorway ... ... 7'-11" x 7'-1"

(the sill of the doorway is higher than the floor level by 8 inches.)

North-eastern window ... 4'-1" x 3'-1"

South-eastern window ... 4'-1" x 3'-2"

On the northern side is a plain staircase consisting of two dog-legged stairs of three steps leading to a small terrace in front of a small room which is a part of the Bhogamandapa and contains the figure of Lakshmi-Narayana alleged to be damaged by Kalapahar. One thing which is sure to strike the attention of an observer is the absence of the usual Navagraha lintel and the figure of Lakshmi over the doorway. A little to the south of the centre of the Bhogamandapa and in front of it, stands a monolithic cylindrical pillar capped by the figure of a bull and Garuda, the vehicle of Vishnü. The pillar stands on a pedestal 2′-4″ square and 1′-4¾″ high; its circumference is 7 feet.

Restoration by the P. W. D.

Owing to a crack, the roof and dome of the jagamohana leaked fearfully; there were cracks also near the junction of the vimana and the jagamohana. The kalasa of the vimana was entirely blown down by a thunder-storm breaking out in March, 1900, and the stones thereof lay scattered on the *karpuri* and the *amlā*. The lintels of the niches containing Kartika and Parvati were cracked. The faces of the vimana at the south-west and north-east corners were badly damaged. The chlorite lintel and supports of the doorway separating the natamandira from the jagamohana were in a very bad condition and demanded immediate repair. There were other minor cracks in several parts of the temple. The repair works were executed by the Public Works Department at a total cost of Rs. 2,861,* half of which was contributed by the Temple Committee.

The temples within the compound of the temple of Lingaraja.

There are many temples within the compound of the temple of Lingaraja; some of the above are in a bad state of preservation while others are in a good order. The following among them are worth

* Report with photographs of the Repairs executed to some of the Principal Temples at Bhubanesvar, etc., between 1898 and 1903 by M. H. Arnott.

mentioning :—the temple for the *brishava* or bul. oı *S*iva, the temples of Gop*a*lini or Bhubanesvari, S*a*vitri and Bhagavati.

Abutting on the north of the N*a*tamandira stands a small *pida* dewl with a floor 2 ft lower than the quadrangle of the main temple ; it is obviously a subsequent addition to the former ; it contains huge monolithic figure of a squatting bull. I have referred to it on page 207 as a well-proportioned and nicely carved example of the animal.

The temple for the *brishava*.

A small door of the n*a*tamandıra leads to this dewl. The eastern and western walls of it are provided with plain balustraded windows. Its eastern face shows the five characteristic elements of a *bâda* starting with jangh*a* ; on the right hand of the balustraded window of this face is carved in a panel, a *ratha* containing the figure of the sun-god with 4 horses and Arüna, the charioteer. The representation of four horses instead of seven is most peculiar ; I think this has not been noticed here by any one before me. The only instance of the sun-god driving a four-horsed chariot is noticed in a bas-relief of a pillar at Buddha Gay*a* regarding which General Cunningham writes as follows.

The sun-god driving a four-horsed chariot.

"In this treatment, I think, that there is a decided evidence of Greek influence in the restricted number of the *four* horses attached to the chariot, for the Indian Surya, from the earliest times down to the present day, has always been represented as driving a chariot with *seven* horses: In the Rig Veda he drives "seven bay" or bright-backed steeds, and in all Brahmanical sculptures that I have seen there are seven horses carved on the pedestal, which are being driven by Arüna, while two attendants on each side shoot downwards the golden arrows of the solar rays."

It is needless to add that I do not share the above view which I shall try to examine in the chapter on Konarka.

The figure of the sun-god carved on the *brishava* temple referred to by me deviates from the usual type by having two hands instead of four.

On the rahapaga of the northern face of the dewl are seen panels containing figures of Vishnü. The pilasters on the two sides of the window on the western face contain two panels on each side containing two four-handed figures of Kartika, the war-god with the peacock as his vehicle. The figure is represented as holding the following things :—*khadga* or a sacrificial scimitar, *kamandalü* or bowl, *trisula* or trident and *damarü* or a drum shaped like an hour-glass.

Temple of Gopalini or Bhubaneswari.

To the north of the jagamohana is a temple of the Gauri-chara type called the temple of Gopalini; the top dome has several pilasters on the four sides.

There is another temple of the above type situated to the south of the vimana ; the top dome shows pilasters on all sides. This is called the temple of Savitri.

The temple of Bhagavati is situated at the north-west corner of the compound of Lingaraja. It consists of the vimana, jagamohana, natamandira and bhogamandira ; although comparatively small in size, the temple contains carvings so nice and varied that they excite the admiration of the most fastidious critics of art ; the finest workmanship is noticed on the jagamohana. The carvings showing floral loops having animal insets are worth mentioning. The niches of the temple are surmounted by hoods or canopies most magnificently carved.

The temple of Bhagavati.

The position of the temple, however, is not such as to enable an observer to study it with advantage. All the *dikpatis* have been removed from the niches. The date of its construction is unknown ; but it is pretty certain that it must have been erected within two hundred years after the temple of Lingaraja came into existence.

We learn from the Madla Panji that the temple was constructed by Yayati Kesari ; I have proved at great length in the first chapter that Yayati flourished in the beginning of the 9th century A. D., and hence it has been stated by me on page 273 that the temple was

Date of Lingaraja

built in the beginning of the ninth century A. D. The vimana and the jagamohana are contemporaneous structures. The natamandira and the bhogamandapa in its original condition are works of the 13th century. From an inscription incised on the right jamb of the doorway of the *dewl*, we learn that the natamandira with the chlorite linings of its doorway were constructed by Nrisinha Deva, the great Ganga king of Orissa; the temple of Konarka was built in the reign of this Nrisinha Deva. We learn also from the very same inscription that the bhogamandapa was built in the 24th year of the reign of Anianka Bhima Deva, the son of Rajaraja Deva (राजराजतनुजः).* This Anianka is not the king of that name who made a systematic arrangement of the ceremonies of the temple of Jagannath. Anianka Bhima Deva, the builder of the bhogamandapa ascended the throne of Orissa in 1219 A. D.; hence the bhogamandapa was built in the 1243 A. D.

There is an inscription incised on the jamb of the western doorway of the natamandira leading to the jagamohana. From this we learn† that Kapilesvara Deva, the founder of the Surya Vansa Dynasty made an endowment of land and property for the systematic worship of Lingaraja; this inscription, however, does not throw any light on the date of construction of the temple, or any of its appurtenances.

* † See Visvakosa by Nagendra Nath Vasu.

A few hundred feet to the south of the compound of the temple of Lingaraja is seen a mound overgrown with wild vegetation. This plot of land was evidently the site of a big edifice now razed to the ground; the foundations only are noticeable giving indication of the stupendousness of the structure no longer existing. I walked along the foundations and am convinced that these were meant for some structure; but it cannot be ascertained whether it was a palace of Lalatendu Kesari, now considered a mythical person, or of Udyotaka Kesari under the auspices of whose mother Kolavati, the temple of Brahmesvara was built.

The ruins to the south of the temple of Lingaraja.

The Temple of Ananta Vasudeva :—

The temple of Ananta Vasudeva is a Vaishnavite one dedicated to Ananta and Vasudeva, or Balarama and Krishna, a dual image of whom is enshrined in the *vimāna*. On going through the eleventh chapter of the Kapila Sanhita, it will be seen that Ekamra-kanana, or Bhubanesvara had been already sanctified by the presence of Ananta and Vasudeva before the advent there of *Siva**. I have come across a reference to Ananta Vasudeva in the *Siva* Puranam also†.

* [illegible]

[illegible]

11th Chapter, p. 21, Kapila Sanhita.

(Manuscript of the Asiatic Society of Bengal).

† p. 276, M. S. copy of the *Siva* Puranam belonging to the Asiatic Society.

The entrance of the temple compound facing the west is in front of the central bathing *ghât* of the Vindü Sarovara. The temple consists of four parts like the great temple of Lingarâja, *i. e.* the vimâna, jagamohana, natamandira and bhogamandapa; the latter two are subsequent additions. The compound containing the kitchen and the corner temples is surrounded by a thick wall of laterite which is in a good order of preservation; the quadrangle is paved with irregular slabs of stone many of which are khondalite.

Both the vimâna and jagamohana are Panchratha Dewls; the plinth is made of *sarü kandâ*, the pilasters, of *khadiâ kandâ* and the columns flanking the niches are of *Phül-khadiâ*, all these being different varieties of sandstone described in Chapter VII.

The Vimana. The vimâna stands on two tiers of plinth receding from each other by about a foot. They are called *talaprishtha* and *khüraprishtha* respectively from below upwards.

The height of *talaprishtha*	...	...	1'- 6"
" " " *khüraprishtha*	...	...	3'-11"

As can be expected in a Vaishnavite temple the *khüraprishtha* is carved with the petals of lotus.

The *bâda*, 16'-1" in height, consists of the usual five elements, the dimensions of which are given below *ad seriatim*.

Janghâ ...	...	...	...	4'- ½"
Barândi ...	...	...	...	3'- 4"

PLATE-XVII(B)

SCALE 32'=1"

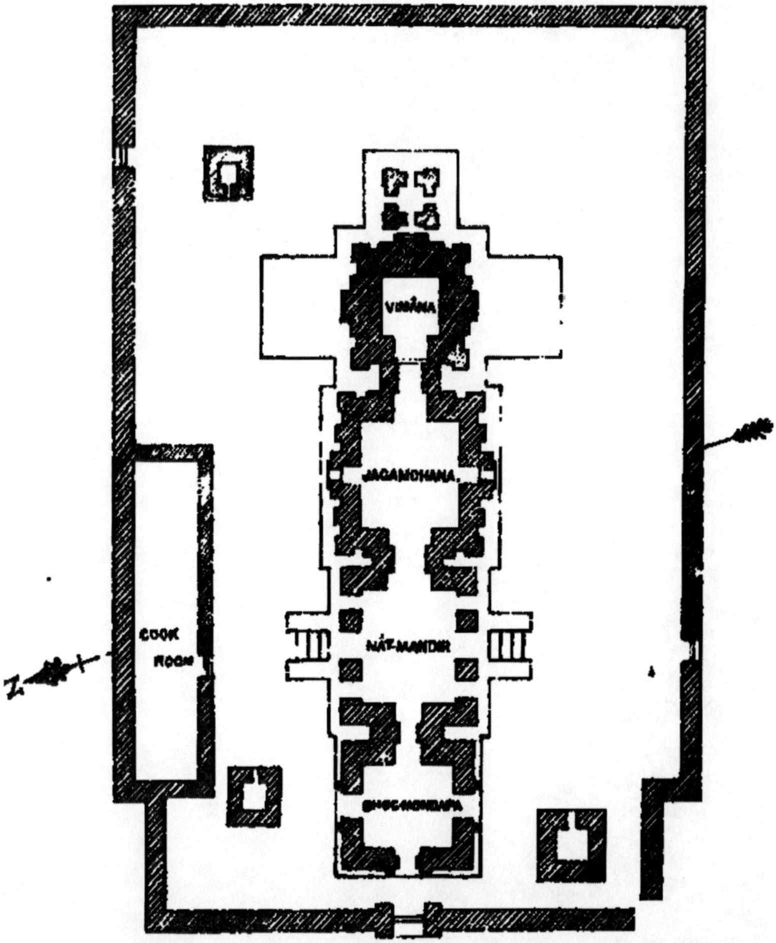

THE GENERAL GROUND PLAN OF THE TEMPLE OF ANANTA VĀSUDEVA.

[illegible] LITHD BY J. L. [illegible].

Bandhana	...	...	...	1'- 4"
Upper Barandi	...	...	...	3'- 4"
Upper Jangha	...	...	...	4'- ½"
The outside length of Vimana from east to west		...	...	22'- 1"
The inside length of the Vimana from east to west		...	...	10'- 7"
The inside length of the Vimana from north to south		...	...	10'-11"

On the *kūmbha* of the jangha, it may be noted, is seen a *dori* or bead similarly met with in the temple of Sapta-matrika near the temple of Lingaraja. The carvings of the vimana are very nice and chaste, and indicate a careful finish; but unfortunately as the face stones are a soft variety of sandstone, most of the carvings have been hopelessly obliterated by the weathering action of the atmosphere.

The niche of the northern *rahapaga* contains a standing chloritic (?) figure of Vamana, an incarnation of Vishnü, the head and legs of which have been broken. From what still remains, it appears that the right leg rested on the ground, and the left one pointed upwards. The figure has four hands, two of which are now broken; the upper and lower right hands holding *chakra* (discus) and *sankha* (conchshell) exist intact.

The Northern niche.

This arrangement of *chakra* and *sankha* in the case of the vimana coincide exactly with the text of the Agni, or Padma Puranam and the Siddhartha-Sanhita by Hemadri. The figure is flanked by two attendant female figures carrying a musical instrument and lotus respectively; flying nymphs with garlands are noticed at the top. A tre-foiled arch forms the background. The jambs of the niches are nicely carved with *jâli,* scrollwork consisting of *mâli*, *dâli* and *Nati*.

The Parsva-devata of the eastern niche is missing. This was certainly the figure of Nrisinha.

The southern niche contains the figure of Varaha, an incarnation of Vishnü bestriding Ananta seated with folded hands.

The southern niche.

There is the characteristic tre-foiled arch forming the background and having two geese at the springing and a *kirttimükha* at the top. The figure has curling tufts of hair covered by a peculiar head-dress.

A peculiarity is noticed regarding the *dikpatis*; they are

Dikpatis.

found with their respective vehicles in the niches of the lower *bârândi* of the anartha-pagas, those of the upper *bârândis* containing female figures having exactly similar features and vehicles. They are probably the consorts of the dikpatis; similar is the case with the jagamohana. This peculiarity has been noticed in the Sari-dewl, the temple of Sapta-matrika, &c.

The vimana like that of Lingaraja has three two-storeyed
Side structures. structures abutting on the north, east and south; these are all Ghanta-sree-pida dewls only the plinths of the structures on the north and south exist; these were originally meant as the jagamohanas of the central niches serving as veritable vimanas. The distance between the inner edge of the eastern compound wall and the outer edge of the side structure on the east is 21 feet. The width (east to west) of the structure referred to is 15′-6″, including the recess or offset of 3′-8″. The width of the temple proper, or the second storey on the east is 10 ft. from east to west, and 9′-3″ from north to south. The width (north to west) of this structure on the south is 15ft., and the distance between the inner edge of the southern compound wall and the outer edge of the side structure on the south is 22′-5″.

The jagamohana is a Pancharatha-dewl standing on
Jagamohana two tiers of plinth similar to that of the vimana. Their dimensions are given below.

Talaprishtha.................................1′-3″.

Khüraprishtha..............................3′-11″.

The *khüraprishtha* is provided with niches containing the figure of Lakshmi. The space between the projections contains *jāli* and small panels of dwarfs or *vetālas* at regular intervals.

The height of the *bāda* is 12′-1½″ made up of the five usual elements.

Jangha..................................3'-½"
Barandi.................................2'-6"
Bandhana................................0'-11½'
Upper Barandi........ ....2'-6"
Upper Jangha.........................3'-½"
The outside length of the jaga-
mohana from east to west.. .....27'-11"
The inside length...,,.........,,.........18'-6"
" " " from north to south...18'-6".
The height of the door leading to
the natamandira...........…..... 7'-7"
The width of the door
leading to the natamandira........4'-0"

On the *kümbha* of the jangha is noticed a *dori* or bead like that on the vimana.

Balusters on the north.

The rahapaga on the north contains nice balusters, 5 in number, showing representations in *alto-relievo* of standing male and female figures; on the jangha portion of the rahapaga there are nice balusters corresponding with the above and showing Naga and Nagini figures surmounted by canopies of five-hooded serpent. The pilasters flanking the balusters contain nice scroll and *galbâi* carvings; the portion of the rahapaga at the top of the balusters shows elephants in panels, horse procession and a palankeen carried by bearers.

Natamandira. The natamandira is an obvious addition to the jagamohana; the lintel originally meant for being exposed to view has been hidden by the natamandira abutting on it. The natamandira is a *Ghantī-sree-mohana* as already defined, having two storeys or tiers of *pidas* separated by a recess. The upper and lower tiers consist of 3 and 4 *pidas* respectively; next comes the *beki.* The inner and the outer faces of the structure are covered with a coat of plaster ¼" thick. Two flights of steps on the north and south lead to the natamandira; the north and south walls are provided with three doors each; the central ones are the biggest in size, the width being 4 ft.; that of the side ones is 2'-6"; the western wall has only one door leading to the bhogamandapa: its width is 4'-10".

The outside dimensions of the natamandira

from east to west	...	..	26'-5"
„ north to south	...	...	24'-7"
The inside dimension from east to west			19'-8"
„ „ „ „ north to south			17'-3⅛"
The inside height of the *bāda*		...	8'

The *bāda* of the natamandira is higher than that of the bhogamandapa and seems to belong to an earlier age than the latter.

The natamandira has on its floor a small pillar capped by a figure of Garūda, the vehicle of Vishnū.

The bhogamandapa is a *pida-dewl* containing kalasa, amlaka, etc. ; hence it is a *Ghantâ-sree-mohana* ; it has five *pidas* with crest tiles ; the *jhâppâ-sinha* projects from the north, west and south sides. A dog-legged staircase leads to it on the north. The structure stands on two tiers of plinth receding from each other by 2¼". The height of the *tala-prishtha* and *khürapriskhtha* are 2'-3½" and 3'-1¼" respectively. The *khürapriskhtha* shows 3 bold mouldings of *pâda*, *kani* and *basanta* provided with notched crenullations or small vertical projections resembling crest tiles.

Bhogamandapa.

The face of the bhogamandapa is sand-plastered and shows plain *janghâ* having no mouldings ; the space for the *bârândi* contains *pida-dewl* representations at intervals ; then comes the *bandhanâ* consisting of three mouldings ; the space above is for the upper barandi ; the upper *janghâ* consists of three mouldings similar to the *bandhanâ* ; the peculiarity with this element is that its lowest moulding shows notched crenullations.

Face of the bhogamandapa

The outside dimension from east to west ... 19'-11"
" " " " north to south ... 23'- 9"

There is a door on each side of the bhogamandapa. The door on the east is flanked by pilasters containing the *alto-relievo* figures of Vishnu standing on a pedestal of lotus. The figure on the left hand side is moustached, and has in his

Doorways.

upper right hand a *chakra* (discus), in his lower right hand, a garland, in his upper left hand, a *sankha* (conch-shell), and in his lower left hand, a *gadâ* or club. The head-dress of this figure is elaborate ; it has the characteristic necklace set with the central gem and has also ornaments for the arm, wrist and ankle. The figure on the right hand side is not moustached ; everything is similar to the former except that the right lower hand is placed just over the left lower one holding a *gadâ* ; the right lower hand is in a pose of benediction, or *Asirbâda-mudrâ*. The left hand figure flanking the doorway on the south is mutilated ; it is a standing figure without a head-dress, which seems to have been replaced by small heads of many serpents. This figure is more pot-bellied than the previous one ; all its hands are similar to those of the previous one except the lower right hand which holds a full-blown lotus. The right hand figure is similar to the left hand one ; the right lower hand holds a garland. The northern doorway is flanked by pilasters nôt carved with any figure.

The zoology of the temple.

The zoology of the temple of Ananta Vasudeva is very rich; the elephant has been most naturally depicted ; the monkey in the *hanumanta-latâ* on the right hand jamb moulding of the southern central niche of the jagamohana is very striking ; the figure of the goose by the side of the niche for the *Pârsva-devatâ* on the south is very nice.

Mention may also be made of the fish and *makara* represented in the arabesque on the right hand moulding of the central niche (south) of the jagamohana; a profusion of *Phula-latā* with various designs containing animal figures as insets is a characteristic feature of this temple.

Before I state anything regarding the date of the temple, I think I should mention here that the opinion recorded on page 273 and formed some three years ago that the temples of Ananta Vāsudeva and Meghesvara were constructed in the twelfth century A. D. has very recently undergone a change in respect of the temple of Ananta Vāsudeva only. That was the view of Prof. Kielhorn*, and I shared it as I had not then collected sufficient data to reject it as untenable. This change of opinion has been confirmed by a recent discussion with Mahāmahopādhyāya Pandit Hara Prasād Sāstri who again, as I understand, holds a somewhat different view regarding the date of construction.

Chronology of the temple of Ananta Vāsudeva.

I have already referred to the two slabs containing the inscription of the temples of Ananta Vāsudeva and Meghesvara stuck on the western compound wall of Ananta Vāsudeva. It is a comparatively easy task to fix the chronology of the temple with the aid of this inscription. We glean from it the following among other facts; that the inscription

* Epigraphia Indica, Vol. III.

was composed by Sri Vachaspati as a eulogium upon his friend Bhavadeva Bhatta, a Bengali Brahman of the *rádhya* class, and a minister of Harivarma Deva, the king of Bengal who exercised dominion for a long time "assisted by the force of his counsel"; that Bhavadeva Bhatta was an astronomer of great renown like Varaha Mihira by reason of his promulgating a new system of astronomy; that Bhavadeva Bhatta had the temple constructed and a tank excavated in front of it.

We learn from a copper-plate inscription composed by Raghabendra Kavi Sekhara* that Harivarma Deva was a king

Harivarma Deva

of Bengal, and the seat of his government was Vikrampura. During his reign several Brahmans of Kanauj headed by Gangagati Misra settled in Kotalipara near Vikramapura to get rid of the Mahomedan depredations; the whole country was in a state of confusion owing to the advent of the Moslems, and it was unsafe to live there with family; so Gangagati with his family and friends set out for Bengal and settled there. This signal fact furnishes a key to unravel the mystery in which the chronology of Harivarma Deva is enshrouded. It is a patent fact that Mahmud of Guzni came to Kanauj in 941 Saka, or 1019 A. D; hence it is settled that Harivarma must have flourished at least in the first quarter of the eleventh century A. D.

* Banger Jatiya Itihasa, Part II, by Nagendra Nath Vasu.

A doubt may naturally be raised in the mind of the reader that there is nothing to show that this Hari-varma Deva is identical with his namesake mentioned in the inscription of the temple of Ananta Vasudeva.

Bhavadeva Bhatta.

The inscription of Raghabendra Kavi Sekhara referred to above is also conclusive on this point. From the inscription we learn that Harivarma Deva had seven ministers including Vachaspati and headed by Bala Bhatta*. It is needless to point out that this Bala Bhatta was no other than the famous Bala-balabhi-bhüjanga Bhavadeva Bhatta. In the Ananta Vasudeva inscription, Vachaspati has declared himself a friend of Bhavadeva; here also we see Vachaspati as a colleague and hence a friend of the latter. There is even a direct reference in the inscription to the Ekamra Kanana, or "mango grove", another name for Bhubanesvara, where Harivarma Deva constructed 108 temples. From the above considerations I feel inclined to place Bhavadeva and Vachaspati in the last quarter of the 10th century, or the beginning of the 11th century A. D.

Let me examine the above from another stand-point. Vachaspati Misra, the great author of the Sankhya Tattva Kaumudi was a Bengali Brahman, though there was a philoso-

* [illegible] बालभट्टमहामात्यो [illegible] प्रमुख [illegible] ।

राघवेन्द्रकविशेखर[illegible]

pher of that name in Mithila.* It is natural that Bhavadeva Bhatta, the minister of the king of Bengal should have requisitioned the services of an eminent scholar like Vachaspati Misra, in composing the eulogium referred to already. The date when Vachaspati flourished is known with sufficient accuracy. Vachaspati wrote the Nyaya Nibandha Süchi, a treatise on Logic in 898 saka or 977 A. D.

Vachaspati Misra, the author of Tattva Kamudi.

It is reasonable to suppose that Vachaspati must have been at least 30 years old when he wrote the above work. This brings us to the middle of the 10th century A. D.; again, Vachaspati was a contemporary of the great king Bhoja Deva, who routed in battle the Mahomedan invader Mahmud of Gazni. Bhoja Deva, according to M. M. Pandit H. P. Sastri, ruled from 1006 to 1032 A. D. This fact also renders possible the existence of Vachaspati in the first quarter of the 11th century; I have shown above that the birth of Vachaspati is dated sometime in the middle of the 10th century, and it is reasonable to suppose that he must have been at least 40 years old when he composed the inscription of Ananta Vasudeva. So the temple, in question, belongs to the end of the 10th century A. D.

* Here I may mention that I differ from Dr. Ganga Nath Jha in thinking that Vachaspati, the author of the Tattva Kaumudi was a Maithili Brahman and flourished sometime in the 9th century A. D. See the preface to the translation of the Tattva Kaumudi by Dr. Ganga Nath Jha.

From the thirty-first line of the inscription we learn that Bhavadeva had a tank excavated in front of the temple of Ananta Vasudeva. This is clearly the Vindu Sarovara.

THE SARI-DEWL :—

The Sari-dewl facing the west is a temple situated by the side of a small alley leading to the Vindu Sarovara and branching off from the main road that passes by the north side of the temple of Lingaraja. It is too obvious to mention that the real name of the temple is not Sari-dewl but something else which it is difficult to ascertain. The temple was dedicated to Siva; the *lingam* of the deity does not exist now, the *yoni* or the phallic symbol only is noticeable.

The temple consists of two parts—the vimana and the jagamohana, both of which are *saptaratha dewls*; the vimana shows seven *bhumis*. The structure is now buried in the ground for a few feet, *i. e.*, up to the jangha. The *mohana* shows the characteristic Navagraha lintel, Gaja-Lakshmi and the usual jamb mouldings of barajhanji, &c.

The temple has been built of the following varieties ot sandstone :—*(a) saru-bogdâ-kandâ*, *(b) khadiâ-kandâ*, *(c) Phulkhadiâ-kandâ*.

Materials used.

The *bâda* of both the vimana and jagamohana consists of the usual five elements of jangha, barandi, &c.

The Jagamohana has nice balustraded windows on the north and south; the balusters show projecting figures now in a much dilapidated state; the windows are bounded by nice carvings very simple in execution. The workmanship of the niches above is most exquisite; they are flanked by representations of *kalasa* and *phūla-latā*, the niche on the south face is very beautiful and surpasses description.

Windows of the Jagamohana.

The pyramidal top of the jagamohana consists of two tiers of *pidas* separated by a recess; the lower and upper ones contain 6 and 5 *pidas* respectively.

The *dewl charunis* of the vimana do not exist, and their places have been occupied by slabs containing figures of some deities; these were probably placed when the restoration of the temple took place.

The sculpture of the temple is very rich and varied; the figure of the *mohana* shows rows of animal figures in succession, such as the duck, deer, elephant, &c.; one is surely to be struck by the abundant representations of *hamsas* or geese in small panels and following close upon one another. The barandis, both upper and lower, contain niches enclosing the figures of *dikpatis* and their consorts. The sculptural representation of foliage is very nice and simple and shows various patterns of *phūla-latā*. There is

Sculpture.

noticed a resemblance between the sculptures of the Sari-dewl and Ananta Vasudeva.

The roofstones of the jagamohana were displaced owing to unequal settlement; all the *pidas* were dismantled and restored; some other minor repair works were executed at a total cost of Rs. 231.

Restoration by the P. W. D.

The Vaitala Dewl :—

I have referred to the Vaitala dewl on page 133 as exotic in origin; on looking at the figure of the temple it will be at once apparent that architecturally speaking, it forms a distinct group having very little in common with the Indo-Aryan style. This is the only example of its class noticed at Bhubanesvara. The *báda* is the only portion that bears some resemblance to the Indo-Aryan type.

The Vaitala Dewl.

The peculiarities of the Vaitala-dewl have been described by me in detail on pages 133-135, and the reader is requested to go through the following lines along with what I have already mentioned there.

The temple with its *mohana* stands on a raised quadrangle paved with flags of stone; a low enclosure wall surrounds the, compound. The *torana* in front of the compound is not an old structure; it was set up, I learn, some 30 years ago.

The temple with the *mohana* facing the east is an *ekaratha* or *chaurasa dewl* made of *rangdálimá* and *khadiá kandá*.

PLATE VIII

The Vaital Temple, Bhubanesvara.

(showing the Mastak of Vaital and the clerestory of the Jagamohon)

The Lakshmi Printing Works, 64-1, 64-2, Sukea's Street, Calcutta

varieties of sandstone. Although a *chaurasa dewl*, it bears a faint resemblance to a Pancharatha dewl showing five *pâgas* or pilasters in the same vertical plane; the widths of the *pâgas* are equal.

The jangha of the vimana shows four out of the usual five elements, the *kani* being dispensed with. The *bâda* consists of the jangha and barandi; there is no bandhana and its place has been occupied by the top of barandi niche; representations of pairs of maned lions placed end to end are noticed above the barandi top; in the recesses at the level of the lions referred to there are noticed elephants in rows of two; these have been nicely carved. Above the lions are two projections of *basanta*; the lower of these contains medallions enclosing heads of the sun-god; the upper one is carved with tassels; above them there is a deep recess containing human figures in *basso-relievo* and in various attitudes of amours. Above the recess are noticed three projections at the corners surmounted by an *âmlâ* forming a *bhûmi*; this is repeated; panelled recesses containing nice *jâlis* (*chaurasa jâli*) are found in the line of the *âmlâ*; the vimana resembles a rekha dewl so far, and from this point begins the Vaitala proper.

The Vaitala.

The Vaitala portion consists of (1) the *Vaitâla-pâda* and (2) the *Vaitâla mastaka* (vide plates XVII and XVIII). The *vaitâla pâda* is carved at the bottom with bas-reliefs of war-procession of elephants with riders.

There is a recess (Plates XVII, XVIII) between the *vaitâla-pâda* and *mastaka* where panels with *jâli* works are noticed with floral representations at regular intervals. The *vaitâla-mastaka* is set off with 3 *amlas* capped by 3 kalasas provided with *trisulas* or tridents. The *vaitâla-mastaka* does not present a carved appearance; it is plastered on all sides. The *vaitâla-pâda* presents ornamental faces at the two ends on the north and south, and shows sparing representations of elephants on the east and west faces also.

The dimensions of the vimana with its different parts are given below.

Length of the vimana from north to south	...	20′- 0″
" " " " " east to west	...	17′- 6″
Height of *prishtha* on which the vimana stands		0′-10″
Jangha	...	4′- 4″
Barandi exclusive of top ...	...	4′- 2″
Barandi top	...	1′- 3″

I give below the rough proportions of the different parts of the vimana.

Proportion.

Jangha = Barandi

First *bhûmi* = Second *bhûmi*

= ¾ Barandi or Jangha.

Vaitâla-pâda = Jangha = Barandi

Vaitâla-mastaka = ½ Jangha

PLATE XIX

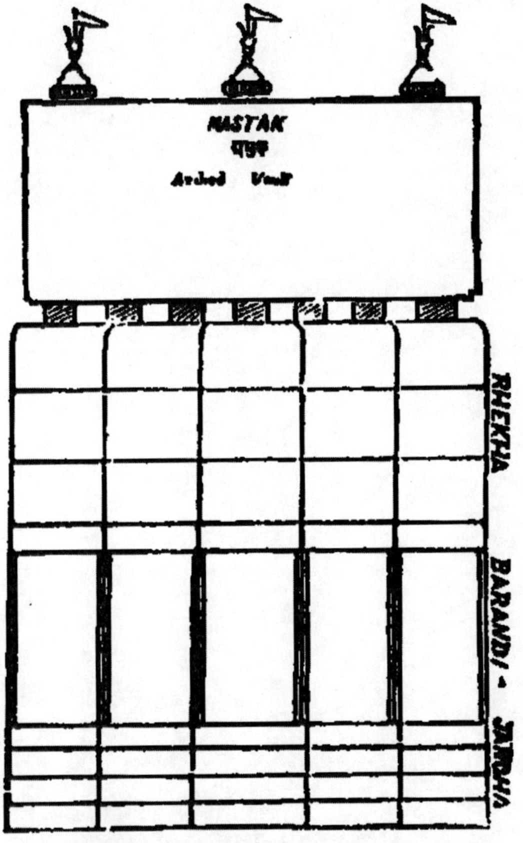

Rough Sketch of the elevation of the Vaital Temple.

Sketch by M. Gangulv.

The jagamohana of the Vaitala dewl resembles that Parasuramesvara except that the former contains four *triratha-rekha* temples at the four corners (Plate XVIII) so as to form part of it. The walls of the jagamohana on the north and south sides are provided with slabs containing square perforations of the type called *jāli-panjara*. In front of the jagamohana and to the east of it is a small *pida dewl* containing a sacrificial post or *yūpa* which belongs to the period when the image was installed in the temple.

The jagamohana.

The interior of this temple unlike those of the usual Orissan type shows ornamental decoration.

The vimana has five niches on the western face, the central one of which contains the dual figure of Hara and Parvati; the figure has four hands, the right upper hand holds a rosary, the lower right one, a *kamandalū* or bowl which has been broken; the upper left hand holds a mirror, the lower one, a corner of the piece of cloth worn by Parvati. The figure of Mahisa Mardini in a niche of the north face is worth mentioning; it is an eight-handed figure holding the following weapons in her eight hands :—sword, shield, trident, snake, spear, bow, arrow and a sacrificial scimitar or *khadga*. The central niches of the southern and northern faces contain the figures of Bhairavi and Ashtabhūja

Sculpture of Vaitala.

Dürga; the full-blown lotus represented in two of the niches on the north face hardly fail to attract an observer's attention.

The eastern face of the vimana is magnificently carved with the *bhos* (Plate XVIII). This representation of *bhos* on a forward vertical projection resembling a *gopurâm* as shown on plate XVIII is not met with in the Indo-Aryan style prevalent in Orissa. There are two *bhos* noticeable; that at the bottom is the *Narâyana-bho* and the one at the top is the *Tândava-nritya-bho* depicting the frantic dance of Siva; these *bhos* are not flanked by the usual standing or recumbent human figures. The lintels over the doorways of both the vimana and the jagamohana do not show the usual figures of Lakshmi and Navagrahas. The architrave over the doorway is provided with 6 small panels or holes intended to contain images. The jambs and doorways do not show the characteristic carvings.

Peculiarities of carving.

That there is a distinct reminiscence of Buddhist influence noticeable in the sculpture of the Vaitala dewl is proved by the presence of pyramidal battlements just at the bottom of the *basanta* of the jangha; half or three-quarter discs of lotus as at Sanchi or Bharhüt are noticeable here. The representations of pairs of maned lions placed end to end in a recumbent posture are striking. The ornamental design of the *kümbha* with floral devices

Buddhist influence.

issuing out of it (Plate V. A) is a distinct piece of Buddhist sculpture.

Kapalini.

The image enshrined in the temple is called Kapalini ; it is a terrific figure of Dürga. It is really fearful to look at the emaciated figure of the deity. It resembles the figure of Chamünda as described in the Sarada-tilaka-Tantram.

Date of the temple.

I have traced the Buddhist influence in the sculpture of this temple ; the outward form has been taken from the Dravidian style. I have shown on pages 134-135 that the form is derived from the *rathas* of Mahavellipore, the earliest date of which is the 4th century A. D. There is also a similarity in sculpture noticed in both the temples of Parasüramesvara and the Vaitala ; there are also many points of architectural similarity. From the above it may be surmised that the Vaitala temple is probably dated in the 5th or the 6th century A. D. like Parasüramesvara when there was a fellow feeling between the Hindu and Bauddha Tantrikas. The temple, I need hardly add, belonged to the former school of the Tantrikas.

It may be mentioned here that there is a temple containing a *siva lingam* called the Nanda dewl to the north of the Vaitala dewl. It is a *triratha rekha dewl* having a clere-story *mokana* attached to it, the upper storey of which does not exist.

This temple is similar to the temple of Parasuramesvara in general design and execution.

THE TEMPLE OF RAMESVARA :—

The temple of Ramesvara is of no especial interest or importance from the architectural point of view except that it forms a member of the outlying group of temples. It is at a distance of a little more than a mile from the great temple of Lingaraja and by the side of the road leading to the station; I have come across a reference to Ramesvara in the Kapila Sanhita.

Ramesvara temple.

Near the temple and on the other side of the road are noticed the ruins of a great structure the foundations only of which are in existence. Dr. Mitra considered the ruins as belonging to the palace built by Yayati Kesari.

The ruins near Ramesvara temple.

On going through the inscription of Raghabendra Kavi-Sekhara referred to on page 379, I am convinced that the palace with the temple of Ramesvara was built by Harivarma Deva, the king of Bengal in the beginning of the eleventh century A. D. We learn from the inscription that Harivarma Deva built 108 temples of Hara, Hari, Rama, Sita, Lakshmana and Hanümana in Ekamra Kanana and laid out flower gardens, etc. The site, now in a ruinous state, was occupied by his gardens and garden-houses. The temples of Sit*a*, Lakshmana and Hanüm*a*na still cluster round the temples of R*a*mesvara. I quote a portion of the inscription in the foot-note.

Temples by the sides of the Vindu-Sarovara tank :—

East side of the tank :—

(1) Three *pida* dewls just on the bank.

(2) The temple of Ananta V*a*sudeva already described.

(3) A small, unimportant *pancharatha rekha dewl* to the north-west of Ananta.

(4) To the south of Ananta is situated a small *pida dewl* with a discus at the top and containing the figure of Hanümana ; this is called the Chakra-Hanüm*a*na-mandira ; it has no workmanship.

South side :—

On the south side of the tank are situated, one *pida* and six rekha dewls ; out of the latter, one is only worth mentioning ; it is called the temple of Mohini Th*a*kur*a*ni.

* विजयलक्ष्मीहामकामश्रीरैकाम्रकाननप्रतिष्ठापित-हरिहरविरिञ्चिवेदेशोराघव-लक्ष्मण-हनूमदाद्यष्टेश्वर-यन्ताभृतवैजयन्तो विभाषितामन्दगन्धप्रसूनप्रसून-पटल-सौन्दर्यादिन्दुकृत-नन्दनकाननवैभवपरमामोदमवोदारमसमवसृतहरपवनंसर्पि-सुन्दरमन्दिर-मन्दाकिनीविमलजलैकासकमल-कह्लारेन्दीवर......................

राघवेन्द्रयतिविशेषर-रचित-भवभूमिकास्तायाम्

This temple facing the east is similar to Parasürameśvara; it is a *triratha* rekha dewl with five *bhümis* having a clere-story jagamohana attached to it; the upper storey of the mohana does not exist now; in consequence of this there is an opening in the centre. It has six pillars—four big and two small—dividing it into two aisles and one nave, like a Christian church. The temple is exactly similar to Paraśürameśvara as far as the general outward shape and design are concerned. It does not, however, present a carved appearance; the carving work was not started; fine lines were drawn preliminary to carving. This affords a proof that the carving work used to be executed *in situ*; this temple is not provided with any lion projecting towards the jagamohana.

Mohini Thakurani's temple.

There is another temple just at the south-west corner of the tank which is exactly similar in design to Paraśürameśvara. This is called the temple of Paschimeśvara; it faces the west; it is a *triratha dewl* with five *bhümis* having a jagamohana attached to it. The characteristic carving of a *kümbha* with a floral device issuing out of it is noticeable here as in the temple of Paraśürameśvara and the Vaitala dewl.

Temple of Paschimeśvara.

West side of the tank:—

On the west of the tank and at its south-west corner is

situated the temple of Markandeyesvara; it faces the east. It is a *trirathu dewl* with a clere-story jagamohana attached to it; the upper storey of the *mohana* does not exist now, in consequence of which a central opening exists; the jangha with the niches of the Parsvadevatas is buried in the ground. The carving of the temple is exactly similar to that of Parasürāmesvara. There are noticeable the same *kümbha* ornaments (plate V. A), the same half or three-quarter lotus discs, the same profusion of *bhos* and *jâlis* and the same ornament of half elephants on the jangha as we notice on the temple of Parasuramesvara. The *dewl chavanis* and the projecting lions are not noticeable here. This temple shows two magnificent scroll works with foliage and floriage on the two sides of the southern niches containing the Parsvadevatas.

The temple of Markandeyesvara.

There is a *pidu dewl* just on the west bank meant as a resting house for the pilgrims; it is called the *Visrâma-dewl.* To the west of it is situated an unimportant temple called the Nilkantha dewl.

North side of the tank :—

On the north side is a group of temples of which Uttaresvara is the most important. It is a *pancharatha rekha dewl* and is without any workmanship; its jagamohana is similar to that of Parasu-

Uttaresvara temple.

*ra*mesvara or the Vait*a*la. It is surrounded by a compound wall.

There was a *triratha* temple within the compound of the last named one and to the north of it; the jagamohana of it does not exist now; portions of the dewl still exist.

There are eight other rekha temples to the south of Uttaresvara. I have come across references to Uttaresvara in the Kapila Sanhit*a** and the Siva Pur*a*nam. †

The temples near Lingar*a*ja:—

(1) To the north of the temple of Lingra*a*ja and to the west of the north gate is situated the temple of Chitrakarini in a comparatively good state of preservation; it is a *saptaratha dewl* having a saptaratha jagamohana attached to it. It has a spacious compound surrounded by a compound wall and having four temples at the four corners. The temple does not show any good carving; there is some workmanship, however, on the *bāda*.

(2) There are three rekha dewls to the west of the former; a broken rekha dewl farther to the west and having no kar-

* बिन्दुसरसो विभागे सरसो मुनिसत्तमाः । सर्वपापहरं रम्यमाश्रमं श्रीमदीश्वरं ॥
[illegible] ।

Chapter. 15th, p. 32. M. S. copy of the Kapila Sanhita of the Asiatic Society of Bengal.

† p. 278, M. S. copy of the *Siva Puranam* of the Asiatic Society of Bengal.

puri, kalasa, etc. is the temple of Yamesvara. It is a pancharatha-dewl with a pancharatha mohana attached to it; the mohana has only the *Sree* existing and nothing above it. There is a *Siva lingam* in the temple.

(3) There is a rekha temple farther to the north-west and within the compound of the Bharati math.

(4) There are 2 temples outside the compound of Lingaraja and near its north gate; they are the temples of Kasi Nath and Bhubanesvara respectively.

Temples near Sahasralinga tank or Devipadahara :—

There are several temples of no significance near the Devipadahara tank, and out of these, that at the north-east corner is striking; it is somewhat similar to Rajarani in general design; it has a jagamohana attached to it, but there is no *lingam* inside it; the kalasa is wanting; the *Amla* and *karpuri* only exist. About 175 ft. to the north-east of the eastern gateway of Lingaraja there is a pretty big temple, the *karpuri* of which is in a broken state; the *phandgranthi* ornament similar to that of Lingaraja is visible on it: this temple is similar to the temple of Lingaraja in many respects such as general design, execution and carving. It has no mohana attached to it, and no *lingam* exists here.

While going southward along the way passing by the eastern gateway of the temple of Lingaraja, one comes across the huge *lingam* of *Kharâkhiyâ* Vaidyanath about 2 furlongs to the south-east of the great temple. *Kharâkhiyâ* Vaidyanath is a huge *siva lingam* standing on a raised stone platform having no structure above it; it is in an exposed situation by the side of a great banyan tree. Mention of this temple has been found in the Siva Puranam, Uttara Khanda.*

Kharakhiya Vaidyanath.

About 50 ft. to the south of the above, is the compound of Maitresvara. The temple of Maitresvara is a plain *pancharatha* temple having a *pancharatha* jagamohana attached to it. It opens on the west; the mohana is overgrown with wild shrubs. There is a raised platform in front of the jagamohana that was intended to be the *prishtha* or plinth of a wooden structure which does not exist now. The vimana is not provided with any niche for the *dikpati*; those for the *pârsva-devatâs* only exist; the temple was probably repaired and the *pârsva-devatâs* have, in consequence, been wrongly placed. The jagamohana has two plain balustraded windows. The compound containing three hopelessly dilapidated temples is surrounded by a stone wall. Two out of the above three temples are rekha dewls with *pida* jagamohanas, and the remaining one is a *pida-dewl.*

Maitresvara.

Going further in a southward direction one meets with the

* Ch. 28, p. 280 Siva Puranam, Uttara Khanda, M. S. copy of the A. S. Bengal.

temple of Kapilesvara surrounded by a compound wall of laterite. It consists of the following four parts :—the vimana, the jagamohana, the natamandira and the bhogamandira. It stands on a raised platform within its compound. The carvings are most simple, and there is nothing peculiar to study here. The only interesting feature of it is that it contains all the four appurtenances of an Orissan temple.

The temple of Kapilesvara.

The vimana and the jagamohana were primarily built to which the nata and bhogamandiras were subsequently added. There are some temples of no importance within its compound. There is a tank attached to it on the south side. I have found the mention of this in the Kapila Sanhita* and the Siva Puranam† (Uttara Khanda).

* कपिलेशं परं लिङ्गं ईशान्यां स्वयम्भुवं ।

कपिलसंहितायाम् ।

M. S. copy of the Asiatic Society of Bengal, Chapter 14, p. 31.

† M. S. copy of the Siva Puranam of the Asiatic Society of Bengal, Ch. 28, p. 290.

CHAPTER IX.

THE TEMPLE OF JAGANNATH AT PURI.

Topography of the place.

Puri (Lat. 19°18′17″ and Long. 85°51′39″) is mentioned in the Puranas as Nilachala,* Purushottama Kshetra, Sri Kshetra. The area of the place was far greater than what obtains at present; in the Kapila Sanhita, the length is stated to be 10 *Yoyanas* or 80 miles, and the height, as it is called the "Blue Mountain," 4 miles; or in other words, it is stated to be as high as Darjeeling. I need hardly point out that this exaggerated statement of the length and height proceeds from the over-rich imagination of the poet which, of course, exceeds the natural bounds of poetic license to an unpardonable extent.

References regarding its antiquity and sanctity.

Puri is the seat of Jagannath, the Lord of the Universe; the sanctity of the place exists from a pre-historic period where traditions cannot reach. I have referred to the antiquity of Kalinga in the second

* [illegible] ।
[illegible] ।

Chap. III, p. 4. M. S. copy of the Asiatic Society of Bengal,

† [illegible] ।
[illegible] ॥

Chap. III, p. 4. M. S. copy of the Asiatic Society of Bengal.

PLATE XX

The Temple of Jagannath, Puri.

(showing the appurtenances, the eastern propylaeum and the monolithic column in front)

chapter. In the Mahabharata, Van Parva,* I have come across a reference to the site of the Purushottama Kshetra which has been described as the "vedi"; this vedi of the Mahabharata is considered to be identical with the *vedi* or the raised platform of the temple upon which the image of Jagannath has been placed.

The *vedi* or the raised platform is even now considered as equal in sanctity to the image itself. Puri has a pan-Indian influence; people from all parts of India resort to this place to worship the deity and to die† perchance, being "lulled to their last sleep by the roar of the eternal ocean". Puri is considered by some to be the most sacred place in India, even more sacred than Benares‡. There is no doubt, that the sanctity of the

* ततः [illegible] पृथिवी [illegible] पाण्डव ।
पुनरुत्थाय सलिलाद्वेद्याकृतिर्बभौ ॥
सैषा प्रकाशते राजन् वेदीसंस्थानलक्षणा ।
आरुह्यात्र महाराज वीर्यवान् वै भविष्यसि ॥
सैषा सागरमासाद्य राजन् वेदी समाश्रिता ।
एतामारुह्य भद्रं ते त्वमेकस्तर सागरम् ॥

Vana Parva, 114th Chapter, slokas 22-24.

† यस्मिन् क्षेत्रे [illegible] ।
[illegible] ।

Chap. III p. 4. M. S. copy of the Asiatic Society of Bengal.

‡ [illegible] ।
[illegible] ॥

The same, Chap. IV. p. 9.

place is dated anterior to the growth and rise of Buddhism; but it must be admitted here that Buddhism has wrought an immense change in the details of worship and religious rites.

The introduction of Buddhism, I have shown in the second chapter, is connected with the tooth-relic of Buddha; and the consecration of the tooth-relic has much in common with the installation of the image of Jagannath.

It is beyond the scope of this book to deal with the legendary account of the place and the deity for which I refer my readers to the Utkala Khanda of the Skanda Puranam, Brahma Puranam, Narada Puranam, Padma Puranam, Kapila Sanhita, Niladri Mahodaya, etc.

Puri and its presiding deity Jagannath have given rise to a rich literature in several languages, such as Uriya, Bengali, and Telegu, and are hence important from a literary point of view. Puri is particularly dear to us by reason of the association with it of Sri Chaitanya, the Prophet of Nadia, who revolutionised the religious and social life of Bengal. His journey to Nilachala and sojourn there for several years have been most graphically described by the Bengali Vaishnava poets, the descriptions forming a rich treasure of the Vaishnava literature.

It is very difficult to ascertain with accuracy the exact date when the temple was constructed; it is believed by many that it was built on the site of an old Buddhist temple where the tooth-relic of Gautama Buddha had been preserved. In an article of the Journal of the Asiatic Society,* Rev. Long has briefly described how the tooth-relic was for some time removed from Puri to P*a*talipütra in the 4th century B. C., brought back and eventually carried to Ceylon in 311 A. D.

Date of the temple of Jagannath.

Puri seems to me to have been an intermediate place of pilgrimage where the pilgrims from Ceylon used to stop en route to Bihar; it was, as it were, a connecting link between Bihar, the birth place of Buddhism, and Ceylon; pilgrims used to go hence to Bhubane*s*vara and T*a*mralipti, and thence would proceed to Bihar by boats along the Rupn*a*r*a*yaṇa and the Ganges.

There cannot be any doubt as to the sanctity of the place existing for a long time anterior to the construction of the present temple. The popular belief ascribes the construction of the temple to Anianka Bhim Deva, the 5th king of the Gang*a* dynasty; but the copper-plate grants of the later kings as unearthed and deciphered, place it in an earlier period. In the Gang*a* Vansa Copper-plates containing an inscription of Nrisinha Deva IV, the 14th king of the Gang*a* dynasty, we come across

* J. A. S. B., Vol. XXVIII, Nos. I-V (1859), p. 186.

the following couplet which throws a great flood of light on this dark and murky corner of Orissan history.

"प्रासादं पुरुषोत्तमस्य नृपतिः को नाम कर्तुं क्षम ।
स्वस्वे त्याद्य नृपैरुपेक्षितमयं चक्रेऽथ गङ्गेश्वरः ॥"*

This work which had been neglected by previous kings was done by Gangesvara.

Gangesvara is otherwise called Chodaganga whose accession to the throne took place according to Sewell, in 999 *Saka*, and according to Dr. Hultzsch, in 997 *Saka*. If we accept the earlier date, *i. e.*, 997 *Saka* or 1075-76 A. D., it is certain that the construction of the temple cannot be earlier than 1075 A. D, and hence not later than 1075*+70, or 1145 A. D., for Chodaganga is said to have reigned for 70 years.†

The important facts that can be gathered from the couplet quoted above are the following, *viz.*, (1) that the temple was built by Gangesvara, (2) that the sanctity of Pürüshottama had existed before the present temple was constructed, and perhaps there had been a temple in a dilapidated state which was completely overhauled and replaced by the present one by Gangesvara, (3) that there were kings before Gangesvara, or in other words there were lines of kings before the Ganga Dynasty.

* J. A. S. B. Vol LXVII, part I, (1898), M. M. Chakravarty.

† J. A. S. B. Vol LXXII, part I, (1903) p. 120.

That there was originally a temple at Puri for Pürüshottama Deva supplanted by the present one is too obvious; for the place had been attracting devotees and pilgrims for a long time before the present temple came into existence. I am tempted to go so far as to hold that the present one is but a restoration of the former. That the name of Pürüshottama Deva had reached far and wide before the present temple was built receives ample corroboration from the Nagpur Prasasti of the Malava ruler dated 1104 A. D., in which mention is made of Pürüshottama. In the Govindapura inscription edited by Prof. Kielhorn and dated 1137 A. D. it is said that one Manoratha went to the sacred Pürüshottama Kshetra. This does not, however, tend to prove that the temple of Pürüshottama did actually exist at that time as the author of the article on page 330 of the J.A.S.B. Vol. LXVII believes; it only establishes the sanctity of the place at the time when the inscription, in question, was composed. It may be mentioned in passing that the great Bengali poet Jayadeva passed the closing years of his life at Pürüshottama Kshetra. We know that Jayadeva flourished in the time of the last Hindu king Lakshmana Sen whose reign terminated in 1198 A. D.; hence Jayadeva must have gone there towards the close of the twelfth century, and it is certain that Pürüshottama was then one of the most sacred places of pilgrimage established for a long time, or else the old poet would not have gone there in those days of inadequate means of communication.

Cho*d*aganga did not build all the appurtenances of the temple ; I noticed three inscriptions on the left wall of the P*atu*les*v*ara temple written in three different characters. The second inscription refers in eulogistic terms to Ananga Bhima Deva and begins thus,

स्वस्तिश्रीअनङ्गभीमदेव महाराजराजस्विस्तु श्री…

The construction of the temple of P*uta*les*v*ara within the precincts of the main temple is ascribed to Ananga Bhima, the fifth king of the Gang*a* dynasty who is supposed to have. ascended the throne in 1192 A. D.*

The name of Ananga or Aniyanka has been handed down to posterity as the builder of the temple ; this is probably due to his having built the important appurtenances and having made systematic arrangements and endowed property for the daily worship of the deity.

The palm leaf records give a detailed account of the structures built and repaired in successive reigns. The bhogamandapa and the inner enclosure wall are ascribed to Pürüshottama Deva flourishing from the middle to the end of the 15th century A. D. The Arüna-stambha was brought from Kon*a*r-

* Kielhorn, Epigraphia Indica, Vol. III, p. 200.

ka to Puri by the *Mahratas* at the instance of their *guru* or spiritual preceptor at the end of the 18th century A. D.

Buddhistic influence.

Opinion is not divided as to the theory that Buddhism is at the root of the conception of Jagann*a*th. Let us briefly analyse the theory. The Buddhist triad of Buddha, Dharma, and Sangha seems to appear in disguise in the Hindu triad consisting of Jagann*a*th, Subhadr*a* and Balar*a*ma. In the Buddhistic conception, Dharma was supposed to belong to the female sex ; this has evidently been replaced by, Subhadr*a*.

Jagannath and Subhadra.

There is another thing which is very striking, and should not be lost sight of. .In the Hudu Pantheon the male and female gods invariably represent the creative principle and the creator (Purusha and Prakriti), and are worshipped as husband and wife and never as brother and sister, as in the case of Jagann*a*th and Subhadr*a*. We should pause here to ascertain the source whence this idea has been derived.

Resemblance to Bauddha stūpa.

The figures of Jagann*a*th, Subhadr*a*, etc. do not bear the least resemblance to any deity of the Hindu Pantheon ; many theories have been advanced to trace the origin of these peculiar forms. To some, they have been copied from the Bauddha Stūpa indicative of the five elements, Kshiti, Apas, Tejas, Marüt and Vyoma.

We agree with Colonel Sykes in thinking that "the uncouth figures of Jagannath were more like Chaityas than beings with human form;" he even goes so far as to identify the site of the temple with that of an older Buddhistic shrine; there are some who hold that the tooth-relic of Buddha as described in Datha-dhatuvamsam had been preserved here till it was removed for some time to Pataliputra in the 4th century A. D. The individual figures of the triad bear definite resemblance to the Tri-ratna or the "Disc-Crescent" symbol of the Buddhist system, and this has been very ably pointed out by General Cunningham in his "Bhilsa Topes," and the "Stupa of Bharhut". General Maisey comes to the same conclusion on an examination of the remains at Sanchi; the "Tri-ratna", or the "Disc-Crescent" symbol is very prominent there. Prof. Wilson, Colonel Sykes and Prinsep viewed the symbol as representing Buddha, Dharma, and Sangha; so we see that each individual figure of the Brahminical triad is a combination, as it were, of the members of the Buddhistic group.

Tri-ratna of the Buddhists.

There are many, I am afraid, who are loth to believe that this conception of Jagannath has been derived from the Buddhist system; they seem to forget that Buddhism is an offshoot of the Hindu religion, and is based on it. The idea of the Tri-ratna might have been taken from the

The figure of Tri-ratna traced to Pranava.

parent stock., and communicated back to it. I believe the figure of Tri-ratna has been copied from the triliteral syllable *aum* (ॐ), and hence is due the resemblance of the figures of the Brahminical triad of Jagannath, Subhadra and Balarama to the holy Pranava. We cannot, however, establish with accuracy the exact process of transition from the Brahminical symbol to the human figure.

There are other reasons which lead me to assign to it a Buddhistic origin.

Car procession of Jagannath.

The car procession of Jagannath is very significant; we find in it a dim reminiscence of the car procession of the Buddhist triad as noticed by Fa-Hian at Khotan in Central Asia; we cull the following from the Travels of Fa-Hian by Prof. Legge, which speaks for itself.

"At a distance of 3 to 4 li from the city they made a four-wheeled image car, more than 30 cubits high, which looked like the great hall moving along. The seven precious substances were gradually displayed about it, with silken streamers and canopies hanging all around. The (chief) image stood in the middle of the car, with two Bodhisattvas in attendance on it."*

In this case, too, I think that the car procession of Jagannath has been borrowed from the Bauddha religion, which in its turn has taken it from the Brahminical one, as is held by the Buddhists of Ceylon. I may draw, in this connection, the attention of the readers to the car procession of the tooth-relic of Buddha.

The absence of caste distinction within the precincts of the temple of Jagannath proves conclusively that the idea of Jagannath must have had some definite relation to Buddhism at some unknown period. The low class Brahmins claiming their descent from Vasu Savara (who was a veritable Savara) are in charge of the image. The Hindus partake of the Maha-Prasada from the same dish without any caste prejudice. This seems a paradox when we consider that Hinduism or more properly Brahmanism, is based on Varnasrama or caste system. This paradox can be best explained by reference to the Buddhist origin.

Absence of caste distinction.

On referring to the Uriya literature we see that the Buddhist tradition has been well preserved. The two following passages from Magunia Das will bear me out regarding the Buddhistic origin of Jagannath. A transliteration of the Uriya verses in Deva Nagari is given below.

Reference to Uriya Literature.

"बुद्ध बउद्ध-रूपधर ।
कलियुगरे बिजे करि ।
सुवर्ण बात नीड़धारि ।
गड़ाबि देव दक्षधारि ।"

* Legge, Travels of Fa-Hian (1886), Chap. III., pp. 18—10.

"देखिले सिंहासनोपरे ।
बिजे बउद्ध रूपरे ।
पद पहुंचि नाहि हात,
श्रीदारुब्रह्म जगन्नाथ ।"

The preceding stanzas relate graphically what the King Indradyumna saw when he opened the doors of the temple to see how far the carving work of the images had progressed at the solicitous request of his wife, Gundicha ; the king saw the figure of Buddha on the Sinhasaṇa, sans leg,. toes, hand, a veritable stump.

We have in the first chapter referred to the Datha-dhatu-vamsam wherein the legend of Buddha's tooth-relic has been

Buddha's tooth-relic.

described ; it gave rise to dissensions among the neighbouring kings,one of whom Danta Kumar by name,the prince of Malwa concealed it on the banks of a river in order to elude the grasp of the king of Swastipura. The image of Jagannath, too, was kept buried in the swamps of the lake of Chilka. These two incidents seem to draw their inspiration from the same source.

Considerations of Architecture furnish the key to unravel

Consideration of Architecture.

the mystery of its origin. All the Hindu temples are constructed so as to face the south or west. It is a surprise to see the temples of Jagannath, in fact almost all the temples of Orissa facing the east contrary to the strict Hindu principles of temple building.

The temple of Jagannath and its compound

The temple of Jagannath stands within an enclosure (Vide plate XX.A) abutting on the main road or the Baradanda, surrounded by two lines of walls built of laterite. The external dimensions of the outer wall are 665 ft. by 640 ft.; it is not uniformly high, the height varying from 20 ft. to 24 ft.; it is topped by serrated battlements.

The outer enclosure is provided with four gates on the four sides, that on the east being considered the most important; it is called the *Sinha-dwâra* or the Lion Gate. This entrance is flanked on two sides by two huge figures of lion.

The gates on the north, west and south are called the *Hasti-dwâra*, the *Khânjâ-dwâra* and the *Asva-dwâra*.

The Arüna stambha

The portion in front of the eastern entrance is paved with flags of stone, and from it rises a monolithic column called the Arüna-stambha (Vide plate XX) with a nicely carved pedestal resting on a basement with two offsets. The pedestal consists of pada, kani, basanta and padma or cyma showing representations of lotus leaves. The height of the basement referred to is 11′-4″ and that of the pedestal is 2′-11″; the face and the corners of the elements comprising the pedestal show crest tiles. The pillar is 16-sided and is built of

PLATE-XX(

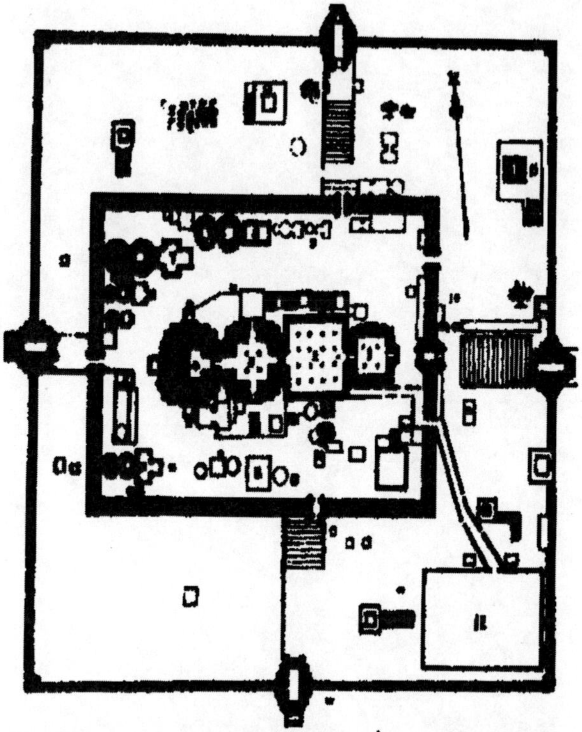

THE CENERAL CROUND PLAN OF THE TEMPLE OF JACANNÂTI
AT PURI.

chlorite or *mugni*. The capital is elegant; it shows two beads surmounted by a *padma* and flat tiles capped by a squatting monkey. The total height of the pillar is 34 feet.

This pillar used to grace the front of the temple at Konarka whence it has been shifted to its present position by the Mahrattas in the beginning of the 18th century.

The inner enclosure is not symmetrically placed in respect of the outer one; nor do the four entrances with which it is provided face the outer ones exactly (Vide plate XX.A). This irregularity or want of symmetry in ground plan does not, however, strike one's attention while strolling about the compound, for the huge proportions of the sanctuary towering in grandeur stop one's breath so to say. The dimensions of the inner enclosure are 420 ft. by 315 ft.; 15 steps lead from the eastern entrance to the paved quadrangle enclosed within the inner walls. The width of the tread varies from 5'-10½" to 6'-3" and the rise is 6" to 7"; the steps are made of felspar and khondalite. From the paved quadrangle rise almost all the temples with their appurtenances.

The propyllon at the eastern entrance of the inner enclosure wall has been built about 30 years ago; this is perhaps a work of the Ramat Vaishnavas.

The Vimana (No. 4, plate XX. A) starts from a plinth

Vimana

5'-2" in height and plastered all over with

cement; the height of the jangh*a* is 11'-6". It is a pancharatha dewl, the konakap*a*ga showing 9 *bhūmis*; a peculiarity noticed here is that there is a band in each *bhumi* of the konakap*a*ga dividing it into two equal portions. The recess between the konaka and anartha-p*a*gas is wholly plain except at its base where it shows a rekha representation reaching in height the projection or central band just below the lowest *a*ml*a* of the konakap*a*ga. The anartha-p*a*ga shows three rekha representations till the Gh*ad*chak*da* is reached; the lowest of the above three is unusually high, its top being on the same level with the fourth *a*mlaka of the konakap*a*ga.

The *bāda* has the usual five parts; the jangh*a* shows the characteristic five elements; the b*a*r*a*ndi contains *pida* representations; the bandhan*a* consists of three elements as usual; the upper b*a*r*a*ndi is similar to the lower one; the upper jangh*a* shows eight mouldings; the lower b*a*r*a*ndi is provided with niches for containing the *dikpatis*. Three heads of Asūras or R*a*hūs are noticed in the centre of each jangh*a*.

The S*a*rdūla between the konaka and anartha-p*a*gas is a figure of lion standing over a crouchant elephant with its head

Sardūla turned back; it is maned and moustached and has erect and leafy ears; its tail passes through the hind legs and is shown in front. It is a Ult*a*-gaja-vir*a*ja-sinha as described on page 179. The S*a*rdūla between the anartha and the r*a*h*a*p*a*ga is an Ulta-gaja-sinha (page 179); it has an elephant's head. On the outer face of the lobby separating the vimana from the jagamohana is noticed the *Chhidā-udā-gaja-sinha* (p. 179) standing over a crouchant elephant and mounted by a human figure holding the bridle passing through its mouth.

Decorations on the face of the Vimana

The faces of the vimana are carved with the figures of the deities of the Hindu Pantheon. I shall describe in detail the southern face only in a descending order as an illustration of the type of decoration noticed on the faces. The figure of Rahu is seen at the top of the rahapaga; the figures of Jagannath, Balarama and Subhadra are noticed below it; about 30 ft. further down is seen Hanumana, the monkey-god holding a branch of a tree; a little below and on the right of the above is depicted the scene of Kaliya-damana; on the left is seen Narayana on the shoulder of Garuda, his vehicle; in the centre is seen the figure of Garuda; from about this height the huge figure of the lion over a crouchant elephant projects in the mid-air; below the elephant stated above is noticed the figure of Nrisinha with Lakhmi flanked by two *dwārapālas*; below Nrisinha comes the dual figure of Hari-Hara provided with eight hands and flanked by Balarama; further on the right is seen Krishna with two cow-herd boys holding aloft the *Govardhana-Silā*. Below the figure of Hanumana described above projects another lion over a crouchant elephant flanked on both sides by two rekha dewl representations. Below these, comes the scene of the monkeys with R*a*ma, their lord; on the right and a little higher up is noticed the figure of Das*a*nana in a flat niche with two *Dwârapâlos* or guards on the two sides. There is a small solitary figure of Sit*a* on the same level with the monkey scene. Hanum*a*na is represented as making obeisance to her.

The figures of *S*ri Chaitanya and Gane*s*a are noticed in the niches of the southern face of the *bâda*. The heads of Asūra are met with on the vertical bands of the jangh*a* of the vim*a*na.

The north face of the vim*a*na shows the figures of R*a*ma with Hanum*a*na and his large following of monkeys. The figure of Nrisinha flanked by Brahm*a* and N*a*rada on the right and left respectively is striking; the image of Hanum*a*na is noticeable above the projecting lion. The western face does not show any important figure.

On the three sides—north, south and west—of the vim*a*na

Side structures

are three two-storeyed *pida* dewls meant as jagamohanas to the niches of the r*a*hap*a*gas containing the figures of V*a*m*a*na, Var*a*ha and Nrisinha respectively. The height of the first storey of these structures is 11'-6".

The standing figure of Vamana (see glossary) is noticed in the southern niche of the *rahapaga* ; it stands with one leg on the ground and the other stretched upwards ; the figure has four hands and a long conical head-dress. The cut of the face is nice except the nose which is rather tapering and protuberant. There is noticed the *kirtti-mukha* at the top ; beaded tassels represent the ornaments for the waist.

Vamana

The figure of Varaha (see glossary) standing on two lotuses is seen in the southern niche of the *rahapaga* ; it is a four-handed figure with the *chakra* or discus and a female figure in the left and right upper hands respectively ; the left lower hand is in a pose of benediction ; the lower right hand is broken. The garments of Varaha show nice carvings like those noticed on the Parsvadevatas of Lingaraja at Bhubanesvara. This figure has a *kirttimukha* at the top.

Varaha

The figure of Nrisinha or Man-lion is seen in the western niche at the rear of the sanctum. It is represented as four-handed, taking out the entrails of Hiranya Kasipu with two hands ; the left upper hand holds a *chakra* or discus, and the right upper one, *gada* or club. The figure has a rosary of *rudraksha* (see glossary) passing round his neck and dangling in front. The garments of the deity show

Nrisinha

nice carvings ; the figure strangely, has no kirttimukha at *the top.*

Height of the Vimana

Having no suitable ground in the vicinity of the temple where I might set up the theodolite for the determination of the height of the temple, I had to choose the compound of the Uttara-parsva Math to the north of the temple as the best site available. The compound, however, is not very even. I drove pegs on two comparatively even plots of land ; the distance between them was 131-8" or 131·66 ft.

I give below the angles of inclination measured by me with the instrument.

A—Angle of inclination of the top of the stone finial at the nearer of the two positions from the temple = $19°$-$8'$.

B—Angle of inclination of the top of the stone finial at the farther of the two positions from the temple = $15°$-$53'$.

∴ The vertical angle C = ($19°$-$8'$)-($15°$-$53'$) = $3°$-$15'$.

Sin A = sin $19°$-$8'$ = ·32776

Sin B = sin $15°$-$53'$ = ·27367

Sin C = sin $3°$-$15'$ = ·05669

∴ Height of the Vimana

$$= 131{\cdot}66 \times \frac{\text{Sin A}}{\text{Sin C}} \text{Sin B.}$$

$$= \frac{131{\cdot}66 \times {\cdot}32776 \times {\cdot}27367}{{\cdot}05669}$$

= 204·59 ft.

The height of the instrument = 4′-10″.

= 4·83 ft.

∴ The height of the vimana above the compound of the Uttara-parsva Math to the top of the stone finial = 209·42 ft.

The height of the compound of the Uttara-parsva Math above the road level is 5′-3″ or 5·25.

∴ The height of the vimana above the road level to the top of the stone finial.

= 214·67 ft.

= 214′-8″.

Jagamohana of Jagannath. The jagamohana (No. 3 of Plate XX. A) is a pancharatha pida dewl, the *anartha-paga* of which is not much developed ; this is a pseudo-pancharatha dewl. It may also be called a triratha-pida-dewl. The jagamohana stands on a plinth 6′-3″ high (north). Architraves of rolled mild steel beams support the lowest *pida* of the *mohana* all round, being themselves supported by columns made of old rails connected together by distant pieces. A staircase consisting of two flights of 5 and 4 steps connected by a landing step leads to the southern doorway of the jagamohana. The face of the *mohana* is plastered ; the *bada* consists of the five usual parts of jangha, barandi, &c. The height of the lower jangha is 8′-1⅜″.

The eastern doorway of the jagamohana leads to the natamandira, the western one to the vimana. The southern doorway is flanked by two cylindrical pilasters or columns supporting the Navagraha architrave; the doorway is not worthy of the jagamohana. The characteristic figure of Lakshmi is not seen over the doorway.

The pyramidal spire consists of 2 tiers of *pidas* separated by a recess and surmounted by the *Sree*. The tiers contain 7 and 6 *pidas* from below upwards.

The jangha of the *bâdu* shows projections representing rekha representations; the bandhana does not show any moulding; it presents a plain plastered appearance; the barandis, both upper and lower, show representations of *dewls*. The upper jangha shows 10 mouldings. The face of the mohana has been plastered in such a way as not to leave an indication of any sculptural work. The recesses between the *pâgas* contain the *Sârdûlas* and most obscene figures, of which the less said the better. It may be stated here that the vimana does not show a single indecent figure.

The room containing the treasures of the temple covers a part of the jagamohana on the north side.

The natamandira (No. 2 of Plate XX. A) is a subsequent addition to the jagamohana, for the courses of stone of the former do not correspond with those of the latter; its constructive peculiarities are similar to those of the natamandira of Lingaraja which is a *pida mohana* as defined in Chapter V.

Natamandira of Jagannath.

The roof is supported by horizontal arches springing from each of the four rows of four columns. I have been able to take the measurements of the room near the row of pillars situated close to the eastern wall. The dimensions are given below.

The distances of the pillars from the northern and southern walls are 7'-2" } 4'-7" }

The intervening open space between the first and second pillars	... 10'-6⅛"
" " " second and third pillars	... 14'-8⅛"
" " " third and fourth "	... 10'-6⅛"
The width of the first column from north to south	... 6'- ⅛"
" " " second column "	... 4'-2⅛"
" " " third column "	... 4'-2⅛"
" " " fourth column "	... 6'- 6"
TOTAL ...	... 68'- 6"

The width of the natamandira from east to west is very nearly 67 feet.

The width of the nave from east to west ... 14′

" " " " aisle on the east and close to the nave ... ... 10′-7″

" " " " aisle on the east and farthest from the nave ... ... 8′-4″

Two doors on each of the two sides—north and south, lead to it: but one of the two doors on each side has a flight of steps leading to it; there are two small doors at the south-east and south-west corners; the former is connected with the kitchen by means of the covered gangway to be referred to later on.

The roof is flat containing five rain water spouts shaped like the mouth of the *makara*.

Bhogamandapa :—

Bhogamandapa of Jagannath.

The bhogamandapa (No. 1 of Plate XX.A) is a pancharatha pid*a* dewl like the jagamohana; its anartha-p*a*gas are not of a pronounced type; it is really a triratha dewl. The bhogamandapa is made of yellowish sandstone rendered red by ochre. It stands on a plinth 6′-4″ high resting on a raised platform or *pâda-pitha* 1′-5″ high. The *pâda-pitha* consists of two tiers; the upper one 8½″ high shows weathered representations of a procession of elephants with intermediate riders on fiery horses (C. F. Kon*a*rka, Ananta V*a*sudeva).

Some portion of the plinth on the eastern face is covered with a red coat of plaster. The plinth has a drip moulding 1 foot in height at the top; this is carved with the figures of crocodiles, geese, etc. The drip stone presents a plain face and a cyma reversa of flat inflection. From the drip moulding project gargoyles of the shape of the mouth of a *makara*. The face of the moulding below the drip stone has the three following parts from below upwards;—Jangh*a*, b*a*r*a*ndi and sikkar, the dimensions of which are as follow.

Plinth

Jangh*a*	...	...	...	2'-4¾"
B*a*r*a*ndi	...	...	...	1'-8"
Sikkâr	...	...	...	1'-4¼"

The plinth distinctly shows the elements of jangh*a*, b*a*r*a*ndi, &c. at the ends where it has been doubled over to indicate the *pâgas*; the jangh*a*, again, has the characteristic five elements of *pâda*, *kümbha*, etc.; the b*a*r*a*ndi shows a bridled *sârdüla* mounted by a human figure having kilted legs. The *Sârdülas* at the corners of the plinth are very peculiar; they are called *düpichchâ* or "placed back to back".

The jangh*a* portion of the plinth contains *pida-dewl* representations, *nâga* columns, etc. The niches in the b*a*r*a*ndis contain chlorite figures of the deities and obscene figures, too; the narrow recesses in the b*a*r*a*ndi portion contain lascivious or obscene figures. J*a*li works are noticeable in them. The niches stated above are flanked by pilasters on each side, those on one side of the niches being Nagini columns capped by seven-hooded serpents.

The *bâda* consists of the five usual elements of jangha, barandi, etc.; the jangha is of the usual type. There runs

Bada of the bhogamandapa

a vertical band showing scroll work in its middle; the jangha portion of the *bâda* shows jangha proper, naga pilasters, fanciful rekha representations and thin pilasters containing panels; small figures of *kirtti-mûkha* project from the rekha representations just described. The barandis, upper and lower, are similar to each other; they show 16-sided columns exquisitely carved with scrolls, beaded tassels and niches containing chlorite figures.

The usual method of constructing a pida-dewl is to start the *pidas* just where the upper jangha ends; this method has been deviated from in the present case; over the upper jangha are noticed three ordinary plain projections receding from one another; the pidas have been placed over them.

The pyramidal spire of the bhogamandapa presents three

Pyramidal spire.

tiers of pidas separated by recesses; the lowest, middle and uppermost tiers consist of 6, 4 and 3 *pidas* respectively. Three figures of lion project from each face at the top of each tier. There is a niche below the projecting lion on the lowest tier.

The bhogamandapa is bounded on the south by a covered gangway leading to it and the part of the natamandira from the cook-room; this is a subsequent addition to the refectory. The eastern and northern sides of this bhogamandapa are provided with chlorite doorways the carvings of which are similar to those of the *mokana* at Konarka. There are 6 carvings on each side of the door on the south and east, five of which are very bold. The doorway is flanked by two pilasters in front supporting the Navagraha architrave built of sandstone, and supported by an iron lintel. The gargoyles on both sides of the pilasters are nicely carved.

The *pidas* of the pyramidal spire have recently been supported by columns made of old rails.

The chlorite figures contained in the niches of the barandi are very important as they depict various scenes from the Indian mythology. I shall attempt at describing them as briefly as possible. Starting from the left side of the eastern face, one comes across the scene of *dol-jātrā* or swinging festivities of *S*ree Krishna in the niche of the upper barandi. The seat on which Krishna sits is made to swing by means of an iron chain very nicely carved; the tassels at the top are striking. The figure of *S*iva on a bull is worth mentioning; the scene of the grazing of kine with their calves by *S*ree Krishna and the cowherd boys has been nicely depicted; *S*ree

Chlorite figures

Krishna is represented as playing on a flute, and the calves as hearing with their upraised heads. The scene of Rama's installation on the throne of Ayodhya or Oudh is striking; below the niche last stated is noticed the scene of the rowing of boat containing Krishna; the rowers are all milk-women, who are making strenuous efforts in rowing; in a niche of the lower barandi on the left is seen the figure of Indra with a row of celestial elephants. While passing on to the northern face, I may mention the 16-sided columns or pilasters flanking the niches; these are most magnificently carved. The figures of the northern face are also very beautiful, among which the scenes of Sita's marriage with Rama Chandra, the ascension of Rama on the royal throne, and Indra with his Airabata are worth mentioning.

Temples within the compound of Jagannath.

The temples within the compound of the temple of Jagannath have been shown in the general ground plan drawn on plate XX. A. None of the temples except one or two has any pretension to architectural importance, and I shall mention the names of the important ones only. On referring to plate XX A. it will be seen that some of the temples have been numbered which I state below with the respective number against each.

1. Bhogamandapa of the main temple
2. Natamandira " " "

3. Jagamohana of the main temple
4. Vimana " " "
5. Mükti-mandapâ
6. The temple of Vimala Devi.
7. The temple of Lakshmi.
8. The temple of Dharmaraja.
9. The temple of Patalesvara.
10. Ananda Bazar.
11. The Snana Vedi.
12. The kitchen of the temple.
13. Vaiküntha.

Mükti-mandapa.

The Mükti-mandapa is a pillared structure, square in plan, and is situated to the south of the jagamohana of the main temple; it measures 38 feet both in length and width. Pandits and Brahmins are noticed here to recite sanskrit texts, or to hold *sâstric* discussions. The pyramidal top of the structure rests on 16 pillars of chlorite; the Mükti-mandapa was built in the first quarter of the 16th century by Pratâprudra Deva, the king of Orissa.

It may be mentioned in passing that a nice central lotus pendant is noticed in the Jala-krida-mandapa to the south of the vimana and to the west of the Mükti-mandapa.

The temple of Vimala is situated at the south-west corner of the inner enclosure. It seems to be an old structure and has nothing striking in it from an architectural point of view except that it consists of four parts. It is a temple usually resorted to by the T*a*ntrikas who attach greater importance to it than to the main tower. They hold that Vimal*a* is the presiding deity of the Pürüshottama Kshetra, and Jaganna*a*th is merely her Bhairava. Mention of the temple is noticed in the Matsya Pur*a*nam* ; reference is also met with in the Kapila Sanhit*a*† and Utkala Khanda‡.

The temple of Vimala.

A sacrifice of goat is offered to the deity only once in a year, *viz.* on the eighth day of full moon in the month of *As*vina ; this is perhaps the only instance of animal sacrifice in the whole of Pürüshottama Kshetra.

The Temple of Lakshmi :–

The temple of Lakshmi is the most important of all the temples within the precincts of the main temple. It consists of the four usual parts of the vim*a*na, jagamohana, n*a*tamandira and bhogamandapa. The temple is supposed to have been built by Cho*d*aganga, the founder of the

The temple of Lakshmi.

* गयायाम् मङ्गला नाम विमला पुरुषोत्तमे ।

मत्स्यपुराणे ।

† वटस्य पश्चिमे भागे विमला विमला सदा ।

मलादर्शनमात्रेण विमलायाम् जायते नरः ॥

कपिलसंहितायाम् ।

*M. S. copy of the Asiatic Society of Bengal. Chap. 4, p. 9.

‡ मङ्गला वटमूले तु पश्चिमे विमला तथा ।

Ganga dynasty, and hence is contemporaneous with the main temple of Jagannath.

The lower part of the jagamohana consists entirely of an exquisitely carved series of pilasters and niches unique in the Puri group. The walls have been built entirely of blocks of a highly lateritoid sandstone fitted with great precision. The stone shows great susceptibility to weathering, and honeycombed appearance is frequent.

The central portion of one of the walls shows two well carved pilasters in which scrolls with beaded borders predominate. Statuettes of two female figures in artistic pose relieve the monotony of the decorative work. Enclosed between the pilasters is an inset consisting of a broad outer border and three inner ones displaying scrolls encircling diminutive human figures in various postures. The inset has been partly obliterated and shows a group of four female figures supporting a series of carvings of animals which ultimately terminate in the innermost frame which bears elegant floral patterns distinct from the scrollwork which predominates throughout the work. The inset is surmounted by a frieze depicting three large elephants and a young one, all mounted by riders or *mâhûts*. These are preceded by two men going in rapid strides and carrying some peculiar shaped arms on the right shoulder. These again are preceded by a horseman who has disappeared. The horse is well-equipped; the leafy branches of a tree are seen just behind the horse which is preceded by three female and two male figures, each carrying probably a club. This group is faced by a man sitting on a four-legged throne with a pillow at the back. This apparently important personage in the frieze is succeeded by a group of seven figures in vaious postures and bearing umbrellas, *chowries* and other royal insignia which, however, cannot be clearly recognised. The frieze supports a group of three statuetes in niches and two statuettes represented as female *dwárapálas.* The figure of Lakshmi with elephants pouring water over her from a *kalasa* or pitcher is represented in a protruding bracket which forms the centre of the three inner frames. Pillars with entwining N*a*ga terminating in N*a*gini with six hoods supported on griffins over crouching elephants are repeated on every face.

The Temple of Dharmar*a*ja or Surya N*a*r*a*yana :—

The temple of Dharmar*a*ja (No. 8 on plate XX. A) is of no architectural value except that it contains three parts contiguous to each other; this is rarely met with. The curve of the outer contour is very little in comparison with the height; and the elevation is consequently rather ugly. A peculiarity with the temple is that the figure of projecting lion is not noticeable here as is usually met with in the

The temple of Dharmar*a*ja or Surya N*a*r*a*yana.

temples of Orissa; the figure of a crouching elephant on a horizontal slab of some projects from the temple. The importance of the temple is due to the nature of the deity enshrined therein. In the vim*a*na are noticed the brass or bronze figures of the sun and moon gods with a lotus in each hand; the right hand figure is made of a mixture of eight metals or *ashta-dhātu*; between them and on a higher elevation is seen the figure of Dharma or Surya N*a*r*a*yana; and behind the stone back ground of this figure is seen a beautiful image of a mutilated Buddha in a sitting posture with several carved figures—all in black stone. The figure of N*a*r*a*yana stands on a pedestal of stone carved with the figures of 7 horses; this is evidently the figure of the Sun or Surya N*a*r*a*yana. I enquired of the priests as to whence the image of Buddha came; they hold that it has been there from time immemorial and that the figures of the Sun, and Moon and N*a*r*a*yana have been imported from Kon*a*rka. The general belief is that the images were brought from Kon*a*rka and placed in their present position in the reign of Narasinha Deva, the son of Purushottoma Deva, in the 17th century A. D. This temple, however, renders the problem of the Buddhistic influence on the conception of Jaganne*a*th easy of solution.

The Temple of P*a*t*a*lesvara :—

The temple of P*a*t*a*lesvara is important from an architectural point of view. It has been so built as to make the lower portion look buried in the courtyard of the temple. A descending flight of steps leads to the floor level of the sanctum where the *lingam* of the deity has been enshrined.

The temple of Patalesvara.

This temple is famous for an inscription incised in three different characters on the left jamb of the temple; it has not yet been published. The place where the inscription is located is very dark, and it is very difficult to stay there for a great length of time, for the damp air coming out is suffocating. I give below the first line of the second inscription which may throw some light on the date of the temple.

"स्वस्ति श्रीधनञ्जभौमदेवं महाराजराज स्वस्ति श्रीकुञ्ज—"

There is a somewhat similar temple noticed on the left side of the gate of the inner enclosure near the temple of Patalesvara; this has been shown in plan on plate XX. A.

The Ananda Bazar is the site marked 10 on plate XX. A. where the *Prasāda* or offerings made to the deity are sold.

Ananda Bazar.

The Snana Vedi (No. 11 of plate XX. A.) or the bathing platform is to the north of the Ananda Bazar on which the images of Jagannath, Subhadra and Balarama are placed during the Snana Yatra festival.

The Snana Vedi.

The kitchen of the temple (marked 12 on plate XXA) is an ordinary building connected with the natamandira by means of a covered gangway.

The Vaikūntha

The Vaikūntha (No. 13 on plate XX. A.) is a two-storyed building "intended for the dwelling of some of the priests. Rich pilgrims, who propose to grant a permanent endowment, are brought here, and made to undergo a ceremony called *Atkiabandha* whereby the endowment is ratified."*

There are lots of temples within the enclosure some of which are mentioned below :—The temples of Sarasvati, Nilamadhava, Gopinath, Sarva Mangala, Radha Krishna, Vata Krishna, Markandeyesvara, Indrani, Ganesa and a host of others.

Temples near the great Tower.

There are several temples scattered here and there outside the precincts of the temple of Jagannath ; they are not at all important from the architectural point of view, and hence I shall content myself with a brief description of some of the important ones.

The Temple of Lokenath.

The temple of Lokenath is a *sivite* temple of comparatively recent date situated on the western boundary of the town of Puri at a distance of nearly two miles from the great temple. There is nothing striking in the

* Dr. R. L. Mitra, The Antiquities of Orissa, Vol. II, p. 115.

temple except the *lingam* which is always under water of a spring.

At the extreme end of the main road passing by the main temple is situated the Gundichabari; one comes across the temple on his way to and back from Konarka and the tank called the Indradyumna tank. Gundicha, according to traditions and the Narada, Brahma and Samba Puranam, was the wife of Indradyumna, the great king at whose instance the temple of Jagannath was built. Reference to the tank is found in the fourth chapter of the Kapila Sanhita*

Gundichabari.

The temple compound is surrounded by a wall 432 ft. long and 321 ft. wide and 20 ft. high; the wall is provided with gates on the west and north sides called the *Sinha-dwara* and *Vijaya-dwara* respectively. The temple has the four usual appurtenances, *e. g.*, the vimana, jagamohana, nata-mandira and bhogamandapa. The vimana is 55 ft. by 46 ft. in general ground plan and 75 ft. in height The vimana and the mohana seem to be coeval. There is a raised platform in the vimana on which the images of Jagannath, Subhadra and

* गुण्डिचाख्यं महावाप्यां ये पश्यन्ति सुदान्विताः ।
सर्वपापविनिर्मुक्ता यान्ति ते भवनं मम ॥

4th chapter. p. 28 of the M. S. of the Kapila Sanhita of the Asiatic Society of Bengal.

Balarama are placed at the *ratha-yâtrâ* festival when they are driven in their respective cars from the main temple.

The temple of Markandeyesvara.

The temple of Markandeyesvara is situated on the south of the Markandeya tank; it consists of the four usual parts. The niches of the temple contain nice images of Kartikeya, Ganesa and Parvati.

I may passingly mention the names of the temples of Yamesvara, Kapala-mochana and Alabukesvara which are of no importance except that attached to them by tradition in respect of their sanctity.

I refer my readers to the treatises on Orissa by Drs. Mitra, Hunter and others dealing with the sacred places of the Purushottama-kshetra, *e. g.*, Svargadvara, Chakra-tirtha, etc.

Sacred tanks.

There are several tanks at Puri considered very sacred, *e.g.*, the Markandeya tank, Narendra tank, Indradyumna tank, Sveta-Ganga, Siva-Ganga.

The Markandeya tank.

The Markandeya tank is situated on the north of the temple of Markandeyesvara. It is lined with stone on all sides. Mention of this tank is found in the Kapila Sanhita.*

The Narendra tank is about half a mile to the north-east of

* मार्कण्डेय तटेच तीर्थं त्रैलोक्यपावनं

4th Chapter, p. 8, M. S. copy of the Kapila Sanhita of the Asiatic Society of Bengal.

the main temple; it is a very large tank having flights of stone steps leading to it on all sides. The tank measures 834 feet by 873 feet; it has an island in the centre with a few temples on it. I noticed crocodiles in the tank.

The Narendra tank.

The Indradyumna tank is situated on the north-east boundary of the sacred city; it measures 485 feet by 396 feet. A reference to it is met with in the Kapila Sanhita*.

The Indradyumna tank.

The *S*veta-Gang*a* is a comparatively small tank (254′×184′) to the south of the temple of Jagann*a*th; although considered sacred, its water is very impure.

The Sveta-Ganga.

The temple of Loken*a*th is situated by the *S*iva-Gang*a* tank.

The *A*th*a*ran*a*l*a* is a bridge of 18 spans built on the principle of horizontal corbelling over the river or waterway called the Muti*a*nadi or Madhupura; the total length of the bridge is 290 feet and its date is fixed in the 13th century A. D. I quote below what Mr. Stirling wrote in the Asiatic Researches, Vol. XV. in 1824, regarding the bridge. "It was built of a ferruginous coloured stone, probably the

Atharanala bridge.

* इन्द्रद्युम्नसरस्तत्र यत्रैव समपूरितं ।
तत्कालाच्च नदी सिप्रा यत्रैव सह सीदती ।

iron clay, early in the fourteenth century by Raja Narsinha Dev, the successor of Langora Narsinha Dev, who completed the black pagoda. The Hindus, being ignorant how to turn an arch, substituted in lieu of it the method, often adverted to above, of laying horizontal tiers of stones on the piers, the one projecting slightly beyond the other in the manner of inverted stairs, until they approch near enough at top to sustain a key-stone or crossbeam ; a feature so remarkable in Hindu Architecture that it seems strange it should not have been hitherto particularly noticed in any description of the antiquities of the country. The bridge has eighteen nalas or passages for the water, each roofed in the way described. Its total length is 290 feet, and the height of the central passage eighteen feet and its breadth fourteen feet ; of the smallest ones, at each extremity, thirteen and seven respectively, and the thickness of the piers, which have been judiciously rounded on the side opposed to the current, eight and six feet ; the height of the parapet, which is a modern addition, is six feet."

The temple of Satyavadi.

The temple of Satyavadi is situated near the Railway station Sakshi-Gopala on the branch line from Khurda to Puri, the terminus station. It is a Vishnuvite temple ; the legend connected with it is very interesting for which I refer the readers to the Chaitanya Charitamritam and the Bhaktamala. The temple consisting of two parts, the vimana and the jagamohana has no architectural value ; the sculptures besides being meagre are not at all interesting. The full-size image of Gopala enshrined in the temple is very nice and is of black stone ; the image of Radha is below full size. The compound of the temple is picturesque and makes up its architectural deficiency.

CHAPTER X.

THE TEMPLE AT KONARKA.

Konarka, commonly called Konarka, (Lat. 19° 53′ and Long. 86° 6′) is one of the four principal *kshetras* mentioned in the Kapila Sanhita; it is otherwise called Arka-Kshetra or Padma-kshetra. It is situated at a distance of 21 miles, north-east of the town of Puri. The term Konarka is derived from the words "kona" and "arka" meaning corner and the sun respectively; hence it means the "corner sun" The term corner or *kona* has been used with reference to the position of the Padma-kshetra in respect of the Chakra-kshetra or Puri, being situated at the north-east corner of the latter. Here there is a magnificent temple dedicated to the sun-god or Surya, standing in ruins which still testify to its former grandeur unrivalled by any temple in the world.

Konarka.

The sea is about 2 miles to the south-east of the temple site, and the dried up river Chandrabhaga is half a mile to its north. The Chandrabhaga was originally a branch of the Prachi river. On going through the Prachi Mahatmyam, it will be seen that the river had on its banks flourishing towns and villages containing massive temples; so Konarka by reason of its close proximity to the Prachi and by

Konarka, a prosperous town.

reason of its being an important *kshetra* or sacred place containing the magnificent temple the world has ever seen, might be reasonably supposed to be the site of a big and prosperous town whose name reached far and wide. It may be noted here that the town of Che-li-ta-lo-ching described by Hieun Tsang is not this place as some are inclined to believe.

The sun-god of the Arka-kshetra bears the name of the place, Kon*a*rka; he is otherwise called Kon*a*ditya in the Brahma Pur*a*nam, both the terms having the same meaning. I quote below in the foot-note* the couplets referring to it. There is a mention of the healing powers of the Sun to which I shall refer later on.

* कोणादित्य इति ख्यातस्तस्मिन् देवो व्यवस्थितः ।
यं दृष्ट्वा भास्करं मर्त्यः सर्वपापैः प्रमुच्यते ॥

* * * *

लवणस्योदधेस्तीरे पवित्रे सुमनोहरे ।
सर्वत्र वालुकाकीर्णे देशे सर्वगुणान्विते ॥
चम्पकाशोकबकुलैः करवीरैः सपाटलैः ।
पुन्नागैः कर्णिकारैश्च बकुलैर्नागकेसरैः ॥

* * * *

क्षेत्रं तत्र रवेः पुण्यमास्ते जगति विश्रुतम् ।
समन्तात् योजनं साग्रं भुक्तिमुक्तिफलप्रदम् ॥
यत्रास्ते सततं देवः सहस्रांशुर्दिवाकरः ।
कोणादित्य इति ख्यातो भुक्तिमुक्तिप्रदायकः ॥
ब्रह्मपुराणे अष्टाविंशोऽध्यायः ।

In the Kapila Sanhit*a* the place has been called the Maitreya Forest*, which has, again, been called the Ravi-kshetra a few lines below. While going through the description of the pilgrimage of Skanda in the *S*iva Pur*a*nam, I have come across a reference to this place which has been styled the Surya-kshetra†

The legendary account of the temple and the kshetra.

The legendary account regarding the sanctity of the place and the construction of the temple is described in the Kapila Sanhit*a* which has adapted the description in the S*a*mba Pur*a*nam in an abridged form. S*a*mba, the son of Krishna by J*a*mbavati, incurred the displeasure of Devarshi N*a*rada for some frolicksome pranks played on him‡. N*a*rada revenged himself by getting S*a*mba into a predicament which cost him his personal charms for which he was noted. N*a*rada by some means or other led S*a*mba to a

* [illegible] ।
[illegible] ॥
[illegible] ।

M. S. copy of the Kapila Sanhit*a* of the Asiatic Society of Bengal, Chapter 6th, pp. 11-12.

† [illegible] ।
[illegible] ॥
[illegible] ।
[illegible] ॥
[illegible] ।

M. S. copy of the *S*iva Pur*a*nam of the Asiatic Society, Bengal, Chapter 22, p. 251.

‡ Kapila Sanhit*a* is silent about N*a*rada.

place where 1600 wives of Krishna were bathing; on seeing him they were charmed with his beauty and became enamoured of him. *Samba* was betrayed by *Narada* who played him false and brought Krishna to the place. On seeing *Samba* there he flew into a fit of rage and cursed him to be a leper so that he would lose his youth and personal beauty. *Samba* proved his innocence; but the ball had been already set rolling, and it was futile now to crave for the withdrawal of the curse which had its inevitable effect, and he accordingly became a leper. Being convinced of his innocence, Krishna relented and advised him to repair to the Maitreya Forest and to practise penances there for twelve years for propitiating Surya or the sun-god for being cured of this loathsome disease. He acted accordingly, and after the expiry of the prescribed period, the sun-god being propitiated appeared to him and asked him to recite the twenty-one different names of the deity on doing which he would recover from the disease. He did so, and the next morning while bathing in the Chandrabh*aga* he discovered an image of the sun-god on a lotus pedestal in the clear water of the river; he took it out of the water, had a temple constructed and installed the image therein*. Then he was cured of the fell disease.

* [illegible]

[illegible]

PLATE XXI

The Jagamohan of the temple at Konaraka (showing the ruins of the Vimana on the left.)

With the kind permission of

The Hon'ble Mr. Justice J. G. Woodroffe.

Printed by K. V. Sayne & Bros.

The holy places within the confines of the Arka-kshetra as mentioned in the Kapila Sanhita* are the following, none of which except the great temple can be traced now :—the Maitreya Forest, the temple of the sun-god, the tanks of *Srimangala* and *Srisalmalibhanda*, the Surya-Ganga, the Chandrabhaga, the sea, the temple of Ramesvara situated on the sea-side and the Kalpavata, or the great banyan tree which fulfilled the desires of those frequenting it.

Sacred places in the Arka-Kshetra

The temple consists of the vimana, jagamohana and the bhogamandapa, there being an intervening open space between the last two. The vimana is in a ruinous state ; it was buried in heaps of sand, covered with debris and overgrown with wild shrubs before the restoration work was taken up in hand in right earnest in 1902. Babu Purna Chandra Mukerjee of the Archæological Survey laid open in 1893 about half of the plinth of the vimana and a portion of the bhogamandapa.

The temple of Konarka.

When Stirling and Fergusson visited the temple in 1822 and 1837 respectively, some part of the *rekha* to the height of nearly 120 feet had been still existing ; Dr. Mitra did

[illegible] पुनः पुनः ।
[illegible] पुरी ॥
[illegible] ।

M. S. copy of the Kapila Sanhita of the A. S. of Bengal, Chapter 6, p. 11.

* Ibid, Chapter 6, p. 12.

not see it when he went thither in 1869. We shall refer to it later on.

The compound of the temple is 857 ft. by 540 feet; it used to be surrounded by an enclosure wall which does not exist now; it was 14 feet high and 5′-4″ thick.

Direction of the temple. The direction of the temple was very accurately determined by the architects, and the result of my survey has been already recorded on page 138.

Vimana. The vimana exists at present in a dilapidated state; but the P. W. D. has restored the still existing portion to a tolerably good state. It exists up to a portion of the *bāda*. The inside of the vimana is a perfect square, the inner dimensions being 32′-10″; the walls rise straight up vertically, the present existing height being 30 feet above the level of the floor which is paved with slabs of chlorite, the thickness thereof being 5⅛″. The floor slopes perceptibly towards the north side where there is an outlet to drain the temple washings. The only door of the vimana leading to the mohana attached to it has been blocked up; its width is 9′-10½″.

Sinhasana or the pedestal for the image. There is on the floor near the western wall a nicely worked Sinhasana or pedestal of chlorite 4′-8″ in height intended for the image enshrined in the sanctum. A flight of chlorite steps leads to the pedestal on the

Plate XXII

The southern face of the Jagamohana of Konarka showing the Vimana in a dilapidated state.

Photo by A Ghose B. A *Printed by K. V Sayac & Bros.*

south. The Sinhasana has on its top a broken fragment of a block of stone meant for the direct support of the image.

The base of the Sinhasana shows panels with beaded borders enclosing rows of beautifully carved elephants. The top consists of three bold projections; next comes a deep recess containing niches flanked by pilasters representing columns of the Indo-Aryan type. The niches stated above contain figures from various scenes of life. Some female figures are just carrying offerings to the deity, some are about to wave the *chowrie*; some are carrying musical instruments or are standing in groups with folded hands. The expressions of the female figures are life-like. In some niches moustached and bearded figures are carrying offerings, or are standing with folded hands. All these figures indicate religious fervour and devotion. The figures of lions at the corners of the recess are very artistically represented. The face of the projection just below the recess is carved with scrollwork containing animal insets such as the hare, frog, deer, elephant, etc.

The inner face of the wall.

The inner face of the cella was originally plastered; I scraped off the coat of plaster, and on examination I found it to consist of two coats; the lower one is finely polished and over that another coat has been applied like stucco plaster (see page 259). The lower coat contains rather large grains of sand and the upper one, finer grains; the face of the wall presents a glistening surface. The thickness of the two coats taken together is $^1/_{16}$″ and that of the outer coat is $^1/_{16}$″. The first or the lower coat was applied by filling up the depressions or unevenness of the face of the stone blocks by a reddish mortar made of powdered laterite.

The inner face of the walls of the cella though not consisting of ashlar courses presents a smooth appearance. The blocks of stone are not set in mortar; the vertical joints of the consecutive courses are too close to one another so that they are not "broken" properly. This is defective; the joints, however, are very fine and look like hair-cracks.

Three cornices run round the inner face of the wall, the lowest one being situated at a height of 4′-10″ above the floor level; the forward projection of the cornices is 6 inches and the height of the wall occupied by them with the intervening recess is 2′-6″.

Both the vimana and the jagamohana stand on two tiers of plinth provided with a basement 1 foot high and carved with nice representations of elephants. I give below the dimensions of the two parts of plinth from below upwards.

Plinth.

The lower plinth or *tala prishtha*	...	... 13′-2″
The upper plinth or the *khura prishtha*		... 2′-4″
	Total	... 15′-6″

Plate XXII.A

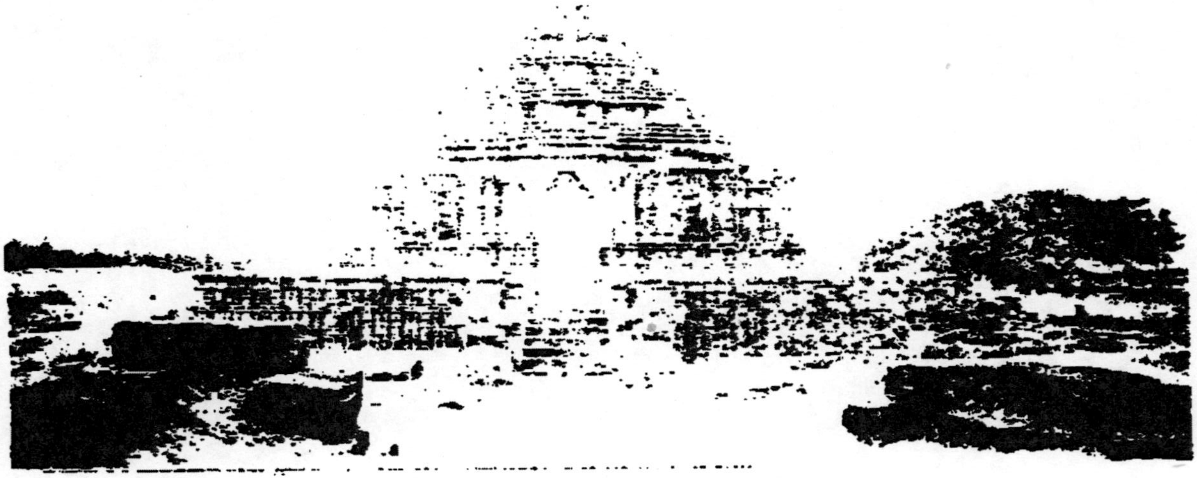

The eastern face of the Jagamohana at Konarka showing the Bhogamandapa in front.

With the kind permission of The Hon'ble Mr. Justice J. G. Woodroffe.

Printed by K. V. Seyne & Bros.

Therefore the top of the upper plinth is 16′-6″ high above the ground level. The superstructure rests on the *khurapriskha* or the upper plinth leaving an open terrace or berm all round varying in width from 8 to 12 feet.

The lower plinth consists of the five usual divisions of jangha, barandi, bandhana, upper barandi and upper jangha. The dimensions are given below.

The tala prishtha or lower plinth.

Lower jangha...	...	...	...	2′-11″
Lower barandi	...	..	...	2′-9″
Bandhana ...	...	...	...	1′
Upper barandi	...	...	...	3′-10″
Upper jangha	...	...	...	2′-9″
		Total	...	13′-3″

The jangha contains the five usual elements of pada, kümbha, etc. The pada shows continuous panels enclosing figures nicely carved in relief; *bhos* are noticeable in the pada, these being in continuation of the central bands of leafy representation running vertically down the jangha; the faces of the *patâ* and *basanta* are carved. The lower barandi contains panels at intervals flanked by pilasters representing temples and enclosing female figures, the *Sârdula* and *nâga* columns. The scenes represented in the panels of the

The face of the Plinth.

upper *barandi* are most indecent; the intermediate slender pilasters of the lower *barandi* have been dispensed with in the upper one, and the pilasters representing temples have been replaced by rectangular and recessed ones most magnificently carved with scrolls and various floral devices having animal insets in the centre. The upper *jangha* consists of two projections, the lower one containing scenes of war procession and the upper one showing *jâli* work.

The wheel of Konarka.

The face of the plinth is carved with magnificently carved representations of wheels (Vide plate XXIII) justifying the description of the temple as a *ratha* or chariot of the sun-god. The chariot of the deity is usually provided with one wheel, whence the name *Ekachakra ratha* or the one-wheeled *ratha*. The number of the wheels carved is 24; their location and number are given below.

	Number of wheels.
On the south face of the vimana	6
" " north " " " "	6
" " north " " " jagamohana ...	4
" " south " " " "	4
" main staircase facing south	2
" " " " north	2
Total ...	24

PLATE XXIII

The wheel carved on the plinth of the Jagamohan at Konarak

With the kind permission of

The Hon'ble Mr. Justice J. G. Woodroffe.

The diameter of the wheels is 9′-8″; the width of the rim =8″; the nave of the wheel in which the spokes are inserted, and the axle which projects forward by 11 inches are 1′-10″ and 9″ in diameter. Each wheel has a set of eight thick spokes having eight intermediate ones which are thinner than the former. The length of the spokes between the rim and the nave is 3′-3″.

The wheel is most elaborately carved all over; the thicker spokes show circular medallions 5⅝″ in diameter on the widest part of the face enclosing obscene figures; the medallions on the axles contain the figure of Lakshmi flanked by two elephants pouring water over her head. The face of the wheel is carved with scroll works enclosing animal figures; the rim has beaded borders.

There were originally figures of seven horses representing those for driving the chariot of the sun-god.

Surya and the side structures.

There are three huge figures of Surya or the sun-god noticeable in the niches of the *rahapagas* of the *vimana*; in front of the niches stretch forward open terraces which are the roofs of three structures below the level of the figures of the sun-god.

The central niche of the North face.

Two narrow staircases 2′-5″ wide lead to the niche on the north side; there is an open terrace or berm just in front of the niche and 16 feet long up to the farthest or the northernmost edge; below this terrace is a room through which the washings of the cella are drained out. The inner dimensions of the room are 6′-9″ by 10′-11″; it is provided with a door with a Navagraha architrave over it.

The statue in the central niche represents the heroic figure of the sun-god seated on a nicely decorated horse provided with a saddle showing the pommel and cantle distinctly; the deity is kilted. The stone block out of which the figure has been carved has been oxidised badly. The figure of Arüna, the legless charioteer of the deity, with his seven horses is not noticeable here. The statue is flanked by two male figures having their hands broken and standing by the side of rekha representations; judging from what still remains of the two figures, it is apparent that they were armed with a sword and shield with two studs and coats of arms in the centre. There are two tiny, bearded figures standing between the two above statuettes and the sun-god. Just over the rekhas already mentioned there are two standing female figures in peculiar poses and surmounted by canopies of three projections in which those of the trefoiled arch surmounting the head of the statue in the background terminate. Above the canopies referred to are seen the figures of the four-headed Brahma and four-handed Vishnü on the left and right respectively, both being seated on lotus pedestals. There are female figures noticeable at the top of the trefoiled arch playing on various musical instruments such as flute, *vinâ* (stringed instruments), cymbals, drums, etc.; over these are seen the flying nymphs carrying human figures and holding garlands. The trefoiled arch is surmounted at the top by a *kirttimükha* flanked by two recumbent male figures blowing conchshells.

Two narrow staircases on the east and west lead to an open terrace in front of the niche on the south side containing a huge chlorite statue of Surya. The open terrace measures 19′-7″ up to the extreme southern edge; the inner dimensions of the room below are 11′-5″ by 6′-9½″. The figure of the sun-god is kilted and has the characteristic ornaments for the arm, neck and ear; and it has also a peculiar head-dress; the waist band has a central stud and is provided with beaded tassels hanging down from it. The piece of cloth worn by the deity and reaching up to the knee is exquisitely carved. There is placed a dagger on the pedestal on the left side. The hands of the statue are broken; they used to carry two full-blown lotuses one of which still exists on the left. The pedestal of the statue is nicely carved with panels separated by thin beaded pillars; these panels contain groups of female figures, some playing on musical instruments and others dancing in a peculiar gait. The pedestal is also carved with the figures of 7 horses

The central niche of the south face

driven by Arüna, the charioteer of the sun-god sitting in front near the feet of the statue. The reins of the horses are exquisitely beautiful. Two standing figures about 3 ft. in height flank the statue on each side ; the right one holds a sword and shield and the left one, a bow. The figures of Brahma and Vishnü are noticed here also as in the case of the statue in the northern niche.

I measured the different parts of the statue the dimensions of which are given below.

Height from crown of head-dress to foot	...	8′-2½″
" " crown of head to foot	...	7′-7½″
" " Foot to centre of knee-cap	...	2′
" " Knee to navel ...	...	2′-6½″
" " Knee to hip ...	...	1′-10½″
" " Navel to breast ...	...	1′-1⅛″
" " Navel to shoulder ...	...	1′-7⅛″
" " Shoulder to elbow ...	...	1′-6″

Two narrow staircases on the south and north lead to the terrace in front of the niche ; the terrace is 17′-3″ in length ;

The central niche of the western face

the inside dimensions of the room below are 11′-1″ (east to west) by 6′-9″ (north to south). The room as is proved by the niche on its wall was intended for some image. The door of it has the characteristic Navagraha architrave over it.

The length from the inner edge of the wall of the sanctum to the extreme western edge of the terrace in front is 40′-1″

In the central niche of the western face is seen a huge chloritic statue of Surya wearing kilts or boots reaching a little below the knee-cap. The figure has long conventional ears with pendulous ear rings, characteristic armlets, &c. The piece of cloth worn by the deity is nicely carved. The statue stands on a pedestal, the face of which is carved with the figures of horses; Arūna does not exist. The carvings and workmanship are similar to those in the niches on the north and south.

I measured the different parts of the statue, the measurements of which are given below.

The height from foot to the crown of the head-dress...			9′-6″
"	"	foot to centre of knee-cap ...	2′
"	"	centre of knee to navel ...	2′-7″
"	"	centre of knee to hip ...	2′
"	"	navel to breast ...	1′-9½″
"	"	shoulder to elbow ...	1′-6″
The length of the foot with the boot ...			1′-1½″

The jangha of the *bâdu* of the vimana is 13′-6″ high; the approximate height of the vimana can be ascertained from this. Let me compare my

The height of the vimana

figure with that given in the temple records and quoted by the author of Konarka.*

I have given in the 5th chapter the proportions of the different parts of the bâda ; on referring to that it will be seen that the height of the bâda is the height of the jangha multiplied by $^{13}/_{3}$. The height of the jangha in the present case is 13′-6″ ; therefore the calculated height of the bâda is 58′-6″ ; now, I have shown also in the fifth chapter that the rekha portion of the tower is twice as high as the bâda. or the vimana is three times the bâda in height ; hence the height of the vimana is 175′-6″. The height quoted from the records is 174 feet† ; thus it approximates very nearly the figure that I have arrived at.

The height of the amla, kalasa, etc, was "20½ kathis or 36 ft."‡ The total height of the vimana above the level of the plinth is 175′-6″+36′=211′-6″ ; and that above the ground level is 211′-6″+2′-3″+13′-3″+1′=228 ft. On comparing this figure with that of the temple of Jagannath actually measured and recorded on page 417, it will be seen that the temple of Konarka was higher than the temple of Jagannath.

A few iron beams lie scattered near the jagamohana ; one

* † Bishan Swarūp, Konarka, p. 26.

‡ The same.

of the above seems to have belonged to the vimana for supporting its roof; the sections of this beam are not the same at both ends. The length is 35′-9″; the bearing of the beam on each side is 1′-6″.

Ironbeams

Some very nice statues carved out of chlorite were discovered in the vimana where they lay buried in the debris and sand. These have since the restoration of the temple been placed on the floor of the bhogamandapa; I shall give a brief description of some of them while describing the bhogamandapa.

Chlorite figures

The fall of the tower is a problem, the solution of which has given rise to several theories all of which are purely speculative in character. The popular belief is that the temple by reason of a huge loadstone or *kümbhapāthara* at the top used to draw ashore the vessels passing near the coast; the Mahomedan "crew of a ship landed at a distance and stealing down the coast, attacked the temple, scaled the tower and carried off the loadstone."* The priests, alarmed at this desecration left the temple and removed the image to Puri. We shall see later on that this legend has embalmed a bit of truth which it is difficult to detect.

The fall of the vimana

There are some who hold that the temple was never consecrated, and the collapse took place just after completion.

* A. Stirling, Asiatic Researches Vol. XV., p. 329.

Mr. M. H. Arnott, the Superintending Engineer, P. W. D. writes as follows in the District Gazetteer, Puri. "It is nearly certain that the *dewl* fell from the same cause, viz., that when the sand was removed from the interior, the weight above was not great enough to resist the tendency of the corbelling to fall in. The heap of stones is direct proof that the result of the catastrophe, when it did take place, hurled the stones inwards and not outwards; had it been the latter, the heap would have been a scattered one, instead of which it is a remarkably compact one."†

The above view seems to be erroneous; for, on clearing the interior of the sanctum filled with the debris of the temple, a nicely worked *Sinhâsana* referred to already was discovered; it lay buried in the debris. How could then the Sinhasana for the image of the sun-god gain access there? Moreover, from the description of Abul Fazl quoted already, it appears that so late as the middle of the 16th century, the main temple with all the minor ones was in a good condition. Even Dr. Fergusson saw a portion of the vimana, about 120 ft. in height existing in the second quarter of the 19th century. Mr. Bishan Swarûp has referred in his treatise on Konarka to some "marks on the *sinhâsana* to show that worship had been going

† District Gazetteer, Puri, p. 279.

on there for some time."* During my brief sojourn there on two occasions I could not detect any such mark; yet it is my firm belief under the circumstances stated above that the image of the deity must have been duly installed and must have received systematic worship for centuries.

There are some, again, who hold that the collapse of the temple is due to a sinking of the foundation. I examined the temple very carefully and did not notice anywhere the least trace of the subsidence of the soil. This would have, as a matter of course, occasioned vertical cracks in the structure and a horizontal one in the floor of the sanctum; the floor, I have noticed, is without any crack; moreover, the collapse due to the subsidence of the soil would have tumbled down the temple on one side which did not occur actually. The debris formed a uniform heap around the temple filling the cella completely. There are some other causes which must be sought to account for the collapse. Some ascribe it to seismic disturbances. It is idle to imagine for a moment that the shock of an earthquake brought about the break-down in respect of the vimana only keeping intact the jagamohana, a structure just close to the former. I admit, of course, that the chance of collapse of a vimana by reason of its constructive peculiarities is greater than a jagamohana, but still it is not

* Bishan Swarūp, Konarka, pp. 95-96.

so little as to make it stand undisturbed in its original condition while a sister structure just close to it comes down not being able to withstand the shock of an earthquake. Lightning, as some imagine, could not effect the collapse of such a stupendous structure, and the reasons stated above would also apply in this case.

The collapse of the vimana may, however, be best explained if we consider for a moment the method of construction and the means devised to ensure the stability of a structure of the Orissan type. I have explained at full length in the fifth chapter that the method of corbelling was resorted to by the Uriya architects in respect of large spaces which being reduced to reasonable proportions were covered by flags or blocks of stone supported on iron lintels. These, again, were topped by the *âmlaka silâ*, *karpuri*, etc. The last blocks of stone help the statical equilibrium of the structure to a considerable extent, for, if they be removed, the stone corbels would have a tendency to be displaced. In order to prevent these corbelled walls from tumbling inside the device of weighting them was found necessary. The force of friction exerted by the blocks of stone employed for weighting the corbels all round would counterbalance their ever-acting tendency to topple over ; hence it is easy to understand that as soon as they are removed, the tendency to fall in would preponderate; and the fall would be instantaneous or will be hastened according as the projection of the corbels goes beyond the safe limit. I may mention here that I have seen temples existing *in situ* after the removal of the *âmlaka silâ*.

We learn from the records* of the Puri temple that the temple of Konarka was attacked by Kalapahar in the middle of the 16th century; he tried to raze it to the ground; but being unable to do so he dislodged the copper kalasa, took it away and damaged the temple. The army of the vandal must have damaged the top of the temple including the *âmlaka, karpüri*, etc. The temple was profaned by the Mahomedans; it was accordingly abandoned. The image ceased to receive worship as before; it was perhaps removed before the advent of the Mahomedans and hidden in some place. In consequence of the abandonment of the temple it was never repaired afterwards. Nature commenced henceforth to hasten the displacement of the stone blocks already existing on the summit. The top stones were gradually displaced and the tower came down. The huge figure of the lion projecting forward from the vimana towards the jagamohana fell on the roof of the latter, and rolling down along it fell on the north side; in consequence of this, the roof of the jagamohana was badly damaged.

* Bishan Swarüp, Konarka, p. 97.

Fergusson saw only a small vertical portion existing in 1837 which was entirely blown down by a gale that swept over that part of Orissa in October, 1848.*

The Jagamohana of Konarka : Plates XXI, XXII, XXII.A

The Jagamohana stands on the very same plinth as the vimana. It is a pancharatha structure; its bada consists of the five usual elements of jangha, barandi, bandhana, etc. The bandhana shows five projections instead of three, the upper jangha, 10 projections instead of 7. I give below the dimensions of the above four parts.

The jagamohana

Jangha	...	...	...	...	10′-11″
Barandi	...	...	...	...	8′-10″
Bandhana	...	...	...	...	2′-7⅝″
Upper barandi	...	...	...	8′-1″½
Upper jangha	...	...	...	9′-4″
			Total	39′-10″

The jangha portion of the bāda shows temple representations at regular intervals; these are flanked by slender pillars on each side, the nearest one being the nāga column very gracefully carved; the farthest one is recessed at the ends and presents an ornamental surface being carved with scrolls. The

* Bishan Swarūp, Konarka, p. 98.

PLATE-XXIV

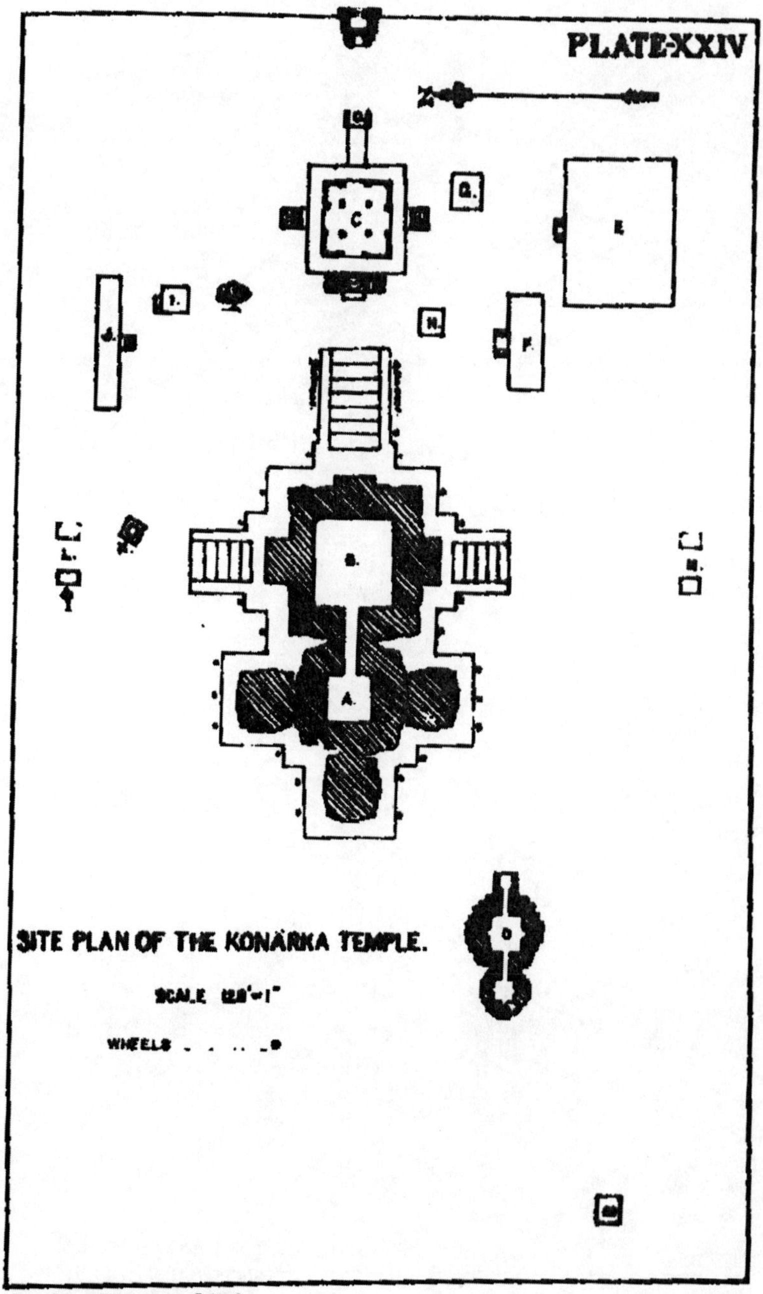

SITE PLAN OF THE KONÄRKA TEMPLE.

SCALE 128'=1"

WHEELS . . . . . . o

SURV & LITHO. BY J. L. GHOSE

top of this pilaster is elegant. The barandi shows the *sârdûla* columns and some thin pilasters nicely carved but containing obscene figures.

The roof, as usual, is pyramidal and consists of three tiers of *pida* or cornices separated by recesses. The lower two tiers consist of six, and the upper one, of five *pidas*.

The Pyramidal spire.

The measurements are given below.

The height of the first tier from below upwards		15'-8"
,, first recess	,, ,, ,,	7'
,, second tier	,, ,, ,,	10'-6"
,, second recess	,, ,, ,,	5'-7"
,, third tier	,, ,, ,,	7'-4"
	Total	46'-1"

The recesses between the tiers of pidas contain female figures playing on musical instruments such as *khol* (a sort of drum) and a sort of clarionet. They also contain the figures of Siva just over the central doorway. The faces of the two lower tiers of pidas are carved with the scenes of war processions, elephants, horses, etc.

The pyramidal roof of the jagamohana is surmounted by the beki, sree, karpuri, amla, etc. The kalasa is not noticeable

The total height of the *amla*, *sree*, etc. comes up to 25′-9″

Pyramidal roof

Therefore the total height as measured becomes 128′-2″ by adding up the following figures.

The *pada*-pitha	1′
The lower plinth	13′-3″
The upper plinth	2′- 3″
The *bada*	39′-10″
The pyramidal roof	46′- 1″
The *amla*, beki, *sree*, etc.	25′- 9
	128′-2″

Determination of the height of the Jagamohana.

Let me compare it with the figure that I got by measuring the height with the theodolite.

The distance between the two different positions of the theodolite is 100 ft.

A—Angle of inclination of the top of the jagamohana at the nearer of the two positions of the theodolite from the jagamohana ; this is equal to 19°-59′.

B—Angle of inclination of the top of the jagamohana at the farther of the two positions of the theodolite from the jagamohana ; this is equal to 15°-44′.

C—Angle at the apex of the triangle having the distance of 100 ft. as the base ; this is the supplement of the angles A and B.

Height of the instrument $= 4'\text{-}7\frac{1}{2}''$

$= 4{\cdot}62$ ft.

$\text{Sin A} = \sin 19^\circ\text{-}59' = {\cdot}3417$

$\text{Sin B} = \sin 15^\circ\text{-}44' = {\cdot}2711$

$\text{Sin C} = \sin (19^\circ\text{-}59' - 15^\circ\text{-}44')$

$= \text{Sin } 4^\circ 15' = {\cdot}0741$

∴ Height of the temple above the level of

$$\text{the theodolite} = \frac{\text{Sin A}}{\text{Sin C}} \times \text{Sin B} \times 100$$

$$= \frac{.3417 \times {\cdot}2711 \times 100}{{\cdot}0741} = 125.04 \text{ ft.}$$

∴ The height of the temple above the

ground level $= 129{\cdot}66$ ft

$= 129'\text{-}8''$

The calculated height is greater than the added up height by a foot and a half. It may be that the level of the ground where the theodolite was set up was lower than the ground level of the jagamohana ; the reason is not far to seek ; for the whole locality there being formed of drift sand had not the same uniformity of level as could be expected. The ground was undulatory. There might probably be an error in taking the measurements of the different parts of the temple with the tape

The jagamohana is provided with four doorways on the

four sides, the western one leading to the *vimana* ; they have all been blocked up at the time of the restoration of the temple, so I had no opportunity to study the interior of the jagamohana. The way in which the doorways have been blocked up will be apparent on referring to plates XXI, XXII; the carvings lining the doorway on the east side only are visible now ; they are somewhat similar to the figure No. II on plate V. A. They have been executed in chlorite and hence are so beautiful that any attempt at describing them will hardly convey an adequate idea of their grace. I quote below what Mr. Stirling wrote in the Asiatic Researches in 1824 regarding the finely worked frame of chlorite decorating the doorways of the jagamohana.

Doorways.

"The skill and labour of the best artists seem to have been reserved for the finely polished slabs of chlorite which line and decorate the outer faces of the doorways. The whole of the sculpture on these figures, comprising men and animals, foliage and arabesque patterns, is executed with a degree of taste, propriety and freedom, which would stand a comparison with some of our best specimens of Gothic architectural ornaments. The workmanship remains, too, as perfect as if it had just come from the chisel of the sculptor, owing to the extreme hardness and durability of the stone."†

† Asiatic Researches, Vol. XV., p. 332.

The eastern doorway had over it a Navagraha architrave supported on two iron beams or lintels resting on two forward projections no longer existing. It was in its original position when visited by Drs. Mitra and Hunter. It was dislodged and cut into two parts in 1893 in order to reduce its weight for easy transit to Calcutta; one of the two parts is lying on the way from the *dak*-bunglow to the temple site, and the other containing the figures of the planets is lying at a distance of about a quarter of a mile from the temple. The idea of taking it to Calcutta had to be abandoned for insufficiency of allotment, heavy weight and difficulty of manipulation; and the piece was left behind to take care of itself. I am sorry to note that this has happened in an age when the art of mechanical contrivance has reached its culminating point, whereas the entire block weighing about 26·5 tons had to be brought from a quarry many scores of miles distant from the temple site and several centuries ago when there was hardly any means of efficient communication. A thatched shed has been built over the portion of the architrave meant to be brought to Calcutta; and the figures of the *grahas* or planets are receiving worship from the local Br*a*hmins.

The Navagraha Architrave.

The dimensions of the portion of the block meant to be transhipped to Calcutta are 19′-10″ × 3′-9″ × 1′-6″*

* Out of the total width of 3′-9″, that of 3′-1″ is only exposed, the remaining portion being in the ground.

The dimensions of the rejected portion

$$= 19' - 10'' \times 3' - 9'' \times 3' - 3''*$$

Therefore the dimensions of the original entire block were $19' - 10'' \times 3' - 9'' \times 4' - 9''$; and hence the cubical contents are 353 c. ft., the weight accordingly being 26·5 tons.

The architrave is divided into nine panels containing the figures of the nine planets beginning with the Sun on the left. I give below the names of the figures *ad seriatim* starting from the left :—Ravi (the Sun), Chandra (the Moon), Mangala (Mars), Budha (Mercury), Vrihaspati (Jupiter), *S*ukra (Venus), *S*ani (Saturn), R*a*hü (the ascending node), Ketü (the descending node). Each of the figures except R*a*hü has a pointed. head-dress, and each of them except Ketu sits cross-legged or a lotus. The figures of R*a*hü and Ketü are the most interesting out of the whole lot; R*a*hü has been represented as a "grinning monster"; the lower part of the body of Ketü terminates in the tail of a serpent.

I had no opportunity to see the interior of the temple as all the doors had been blocked up. The roof was supported by iron beams resting on horizontal arches springing from four pillars.

* Out of the total depth 3-'3", that of 2'-6" is exposed and about 9" is imbedded in the ground.

Jagamohana.

Several iron beams lie scattered near the jagamohana. These were either lintels or beams supporting the ceiling and the architrave. I give the dimensions of a few of them.

(*a*) An iron beam on the south-east of the jagamohana :—

Length = 20′ – 10″.

It has hammer marks at the two ends up to a length of 2′ – 6″ on each side ; these marks indicate the portions to be inserted in the walls. The clear length accordingly is 25′ – 10″, and hence the beam was meant as a lintel for supporting an architrave. The depths of the beam at the two ends are 8 and 11 inches respectively ; the central depth is 11 inches. This is indicative of great engineering skill. I have referred to it in Chapter V.

(*b*) Another beam on the south-east side :—

Length = 21′ – 7″

Bearing on each side = 2′ – 11″.

∴ The clear length = 15′ – 9″.

The depths at the two ends are 8 inches and that at the centre is 9 inches.

(*c*) A beam on the south-east side of the Jagamohana :—

Length = 23′

Bearing = 3′ – 6″

Clear length = 16′.

From the clear length it appears that this beam was probably meant as a lintel for supporting the architrave over the southern entrance. The depths at the ends are 9″ and that in the middle is 11 inches. The beam has cracked in the middle,

The Bhogamandapa of Konarka:—(Vide Plate XXIV).

Opinion is divided as to the name of the structure in

The Bhogamandapa of Konarka.

front of the jagamohána, and to the east of it; on comparing it with that at Puri, and judging from the intervening open space; one is inclined to take it for the bhogamandapa. It is, no doubt, a subsequent addition, and sufficient room was left for the natamandira for being built afterwards. If the structure, in question, be supposed to be the natamandira as some would wish it to be called by that name*, the bhogamandapa, when built, would just approach the outer enclosure wall, and the flight of steps may even go beyond. This must never have been intended. The open space in front of the jagamohana would present a paradox, an anomaly, if it not be supposed to be the site of some structure, apparently the natamandira.

The bhogamandapa is square in plan, each external side being 74′, exclusive of the staircases appertaining to it. Four

* Annual Report, Archæological Survey of India, 1902-03.

PLATE XXV

Southern Facade of Bhogamandap, Ko ıaraka.

flights of steps lead to it on the four sides. I give below *ad seriatim* the dimensions of the staircases as noted by me in the general ground plan.

Staircases.

Western staircase	42′–8″	(north to south) × 7′–10″	(east to west).
Northern staircase	20′–9″	(do) × 14′–3″	(do).
Eastern ,,	15′	(do) × 25′	(do).
Southern ,,		12′–2″	(do).

The staircase on the west is rather peculiar, it consists of a pair of flights of side steps on the north and south joined together by segmental steps facing the west. This staircase may be styled a "dog-legged" one. The tread of the steps varies from 22″ to 23″; the rise is 10″. The staircase on the north consists of a series of segmental steps, the maximum length of the ordinate being 2′–4″; the rise is 10″. Those on the east and south consist of ordinary rectangular steps. The eastern staircase has got attached to its side walls two huge monolithic figures of lions placed on a low pedestal, it being part of the same block out of which the figures have been carved. The stone pavement supporting the figures of the lion is still buried under sand; I exposed a depth of 1′–6″; the bottom, however, could not be reached. The lion is rampant over a crouching elephant holding a prostrate human figure with its trunk. The elephant is girdled with a representation of iron chain from which dangles a bell. The claws of the lion are clearly depicted. The external dimensions of the figures are 8′–4″× 4′–8½″×9′–2″ (height), the cubical contents being accordingly 360 c. ft. (approximately). The weight of each block is 27·48 tons or 750 maunds, the average weight of a cubic foot of sandstone being 171 pounds.

I have come to learn from my esteemed friend Rái Sáhib Prasanna Kumar Pál, L. C. E., who was in charge of the restoration of the temple of Konarka, that the huge figures of the lions had been erroneously placed with their faces turned towards the west by Mr. Davies, Sub-Engineer of the P. W. D. in the early eighties of the last century on the heap of sand which buried the structure altogether before the present restoration was effected ; these were removed by means of a crane and inclined plane to their present position in 1903. These were originally placed on the two sides of the eastern staircase of the jagamohana and their positions may still be clearly identified.

The bhogamandapa starts from the *talapattana* or pavement on the ground level and surrounding the whole structure. This is made of flags of sandstone projecting by 2′-7″ from the face of the plinth. The plinth consists of 3 parts ; the first or the lowest one is 2′-1″ high and consists of 3 mouldings ; the second or the middle one recedes a little back from the former, and is 9′-7″ high ; the corners

Plinth.

or salient angles of the second plinth consist of jangha, barandi, bandhana, sikkar and second jangha: the second jangha, however, contains three, instead of seven mouldings. The interval between the janghas stated above is made up of pilasters showing representations of pida dewls containing female figures playing on musical instruments. These pilasters have a regularity in their arrangement. A thick pilaster is followed by a slender one. The recesses between the pilasters contain a profusion of jali or lattice work. The bandhana, however, runs round the plinth true to its etymological significance; it acts as a veritable bandhana or binding course. The second jangha runs along the four sides of the structure, and contains gargoyles or water spouts at regular intervals. The topmost moulding has its front face carved with rows of elephants.

The first and the second plinths form, as it were, a basement upon which the third one rests. The third plinth recedes back from the lower one by a little more than 11 ft., and is 4′-5″ high; steps on all sides lead to this plinth. The topmost course consists of three mouldings, basanta, kani and pata in a descending order. The basanta has panels carved on its front face containing elephants in procession. The above three mouldings are separated by a nice lattice work or jali; below these is the sakkar or barandi portion containing panels enclosing standing female figures in various poses. The *sukkar* shows the representations of temples at regular intervals; the panels stated above are separated by *jali* works; below the *sakkar* is the portion consisting of the three following elements, viz. basanta, pata and pada in a descending order. The pada represents lotus petals, the basanta and floral devices.

The top of the third plinth forms the floor level of the structure, the walls of which rise with a recess of 1'-9" from the edge of the plinth. The area enclosed by these outer walls is a square 48'-10" x 48'-10". The internal dimensions of the *bhogamandapa* are 36'-5½" (east to west) by 36'-4⅓" (north to south). Four pillars rise from the floor level, and were intended to support the roof. They rise with a plain surface without any decoration or moulding to the height of 2'-10"; this portion may be spoken of as the pedestal of the pillars; it has only rectangular projections. Then follow three mouldings 2'-¼" in height, forming the jangha; the three mouldings stated above are pata, kani and basanta, from below upwards. The face of the basanta or the topmost moulding contains panels enclosed by a beaded border containing figures of nicely carved elephants; a vertical band with nice scrollwork connects the three elements; over these rest five slender pilasters with intervening recesses, 3'-8" high. These form the *barandi* containing female figures in graceful poses standing in front of the pilasters on full-blown lotuses; the top of the barandi is carved with finely worked beaded tassels; then comes the bandhana 1'-2¼" in height; it is carved with nice scrollwork, the component elements being connected together by a vertical band similar to the jangha already described; hence the total height from the basement up to the basanta of the bandhana comes up to 9'-8½". I did not think it worth my while to take any further measurement higher up, for the sikkara portions over the bandhana do not exist in their entirety.

The intervening space between the pillars varies from 10' to 10'-3½", and that between them and the outer walls varies from 6'-2½" to 6'-4". The pillars are nearly square in plan; their dimensions are given below.

Pillar on the south-west 6'-9½" × 6'-10½"
" " " north-east 7' × 7'-1"
" " " north-east 7' × 6'-11"
" " " south-west 7' × 7'-3"

The outerwalls of the structures are provided with the characteristic jangha of five mouldings, barandi, bandhana of 3 mouldings, sikkar and second *jangha of 9 mouldings.* The openings where the steps *lead* have two *circular columns* in front.

The figures carved on the outer walls have badly weathered. The figures, especially in the *sakkar* and *sikkar* portions, are mostly females playing on *pakhoâj* (a sort of drum); abundance of full-blown lotuses is noticeable on the outer walls.

The roof supported by the pillars and the outer walls does not exist, and there is no evidence to show that it ever existed; from the plan and position of the structure it is certain that it was meant to be a pi*d*a dewl; but if we are to judge from the number of pi*d*as lying scattered in the vicinity, our doubt as to its completion would be confirmed. Mr. P*a*l saw only portions of the roof in existence at the north and south-east corners. It is worth mentioning that the central lotus pendant intended for the ceiling lies scattered near the site of the bhogamandapa.

The Temple of R*a*machandi :—(Fig D. of Plate XXIV)

The temple of R*a*machandi is situated to the south-east of the temple of Kon*a*rka. This has been called M*a*y*a*-devi by Mr. Bishan Swarüp. The temple consists of the vim*a*na and jagamohana.

The inside dimensions of the jagamohana are 28′-1″ square; on the north and south walls there are niches inside at a height of about, 5 ft above the floor level. The jagamohana has the inner face of walls decorated with pilasters the like of which has not been noticed by me anywhere; the pilasters show the characteristic mouldings of jangh*a*, etc. decorating the corners, the sides of doorways and niches.

Plate XXVI

The huge elephant on the north of the temple at Konarka.

With the kind permission of the
Hon'ble Mr. Justice J. G. Woodroffe.

The roof of the jagamohana does not exist, nor is it known if it was ever finished. The stone blocks placed at the corners over the main walls at right angles to each other have on them represented the scenes of war procession consisting of elephants, horses; the warriors have in their hands long rectangular shields.

The janghas of the vimana and the mohana are 6′-9″ and 5′ high; and their difference in height has been made good by the mouldings of the structure separating the two.

Both the vimana and mohana show nicely carved gargoyles of chlorite. The statue of the sun-god noticed on the floor of the bhogamandapa and to be described at full length later on, was in the western niche of the vimana and was removed thence to the bhogamandapa; it was subsequently buried in heaps of sand.

It cannot be ascertained as to what the structures marked E, F, G, H, I and J on Plate XXIV indicate. There are some pillars scattered near the sites of E, F, G and H; the kitchen of the temple was perhaps situated here. Heaps of broken stone are collected on the floor of the structure marked J; K represents an old well. M is the site of some unknown temple probably not finished; this is made of badly burnt bricks, and I have referred to it on pages 255-256. L and N represent the pedestals of pairs of huge monolithic elephants and horses on the north and south respectively. The plate XXVI illustrates the elephant, and I have referred to it already on pages 204-205; the horse is well caparisoned and led by a warrior walking in front.

I quote below what Prof. Havell has written in respect of the horse of Konarka. "Had it by chance been labelled "Roman" or "Greek" this magnificent work of Art would now be the pride of some great metropolitan museum in Europe and America......................Here Indian sculptors have shown that they can express with as much fire and passion as the greatest European art the pride of victory and the glory of triumphant warfare; for not even the Homeric grandeur of the Elgin marbles surpasses the magnificent movement and modelling of the Indian Achilles, and the superbly monumental war-horse in its massive strength and vigour is not unworthy of comparison with Verocchio's famous masterpiece at Venice."*

The chlorite figures on the floor of the Bhogamandapa.

I shall briefly describe here some of the chlorite statuettes recovered from the debris of the vimana and kept on the floor of the bhogamandapa. The way in which they have been preserved is objectionable; for some of the figures have already weathered fearfully being placed in an exposed situation. It is extremely desirable that some sort of structure should be built to

* Prof. Havell, Indian Sculpture and Painting, pp. 146-147.

preserve them, as in a museum, similar to the one built at Saranath.

Ganga

The slab containing the figure of Ganga measures 2'-5" × 1'-3". The deity is represented as sitting on a nicely carved *makara*; the fins, claws and canine teeth of the animal have been shown. The figure has a pointed head-dress and the ornaments usually noticed on the images of Orissa. The figure is already covered with a coat of rust.

Agni

Agni is a moustached figure with a nice head-dress and seated on a ram, the vehicle of the deity. The figure is pot-bellied and has a flowing beard of the Mahomedan type. There are four incense pots on the two sides from which flames are issuing. Mr. Bishan Swarūp has taken the figure to be Vrihaspati; but the flames, the characteristic vehicle and personal featūres have confirmed me in my belief that it is the veritable figure of Agni. Some take it to be Vibhandaka Muni. The slab measures 2'-10½" × 1'-5½".

Mahisa Mardini, Jagannath, &c.

The slab containing the figure of Mahisa Mardini measures 2'-10" × 1'-6½". On the extreme left, Parvati is represented as killing Mahisasūra; next come the figures of Jagannath and a Siva lingam; a gorgeously dressed king with a coiffure is standing before the deities with folded hands; between the king and the figures of the deities stands another figure whose head does not exist. All the figures are surmounted by a canopy of two tiers. The lower section of the slab contains rows of standing figures. The figure of Parvati has been oxidised very badly; this is due to the neglect of those who are in charge of the temple. The statuettes should be more carefully preserved.

Teaching scene.

The slab containing this scene contains a seated figure without head represent ed as reading a book and explaining the contents to his disciples standing in front; below this, is a scene of seated figures. The lowest section shows a few standing figures with an elephant and a well caparisoned horse.

Nothing is interesting in the next slab which shows an archery scene, except that it contains in the lower section a well caparisoned horse and some foot soldiers.

Sita's marriage.

The slab containing the scene of the marriage of Sita is interesting. It is divided into three sections containing different scenes. The first section represents the marriage of Sita Devi; the king Janaka offers her in marriage to Rama Chandra; Vasishtha is noticed in the middle. The second section represents a dancing scene; four girls are dancing with their arms resting on one another's shoulder; a few monkeys are enjoying the scene. The lowest section shows a group of female musicians playing on Pakhoaj (a sort of drum), cymbals, and clarions. The scene represents a

Plate XXVII.

The Sun-God found in the Bhogamandapa at Konarka.

marriage procession, and an elephant and a horse are marching with it. The horse is caparisoned, saddled and provided with stirrups. The horse and the elephant have been most naturally represented.

The slab containing the standing figure of Vishnu measures 3′-1″ × 1′-7½″. It is a four-handed figure holding in the right and left upper hands *Sa*nkha and Chakra, and in the right and left lower hands, gad*a* and a lotus. The hand holding the lotus is in a pose of benediction. It has the characteristic mark on the left lower palm. The figures of Brahm*a* and Mahesvara are noticed on the right and left respectively. The pedestal has a floral work carved on it flanked by female devotees kneeling with folded hands.

Vishnu

The slab in which the figure of Surya is carved is 6′-1⅛″ × 2′-11″, and is made of a variety of chlorite called *S*ankhamala in common parlance. The figure is 4′-10″ in height. The lower portion of the slab is cut into a pedestal with Arüna, the charioteer of the sun-god represented as driving seven horses depicted on the face of the pedestal; the horses are harnessed. The reins are gathered together and are held in the left hand of Arüna seated at the feet of the deity with a whip in his right hand.

Surya.
Plate XXVII.

The standing figure of the sun-god is flanked by two figures holding a sword and a shield. There are two small figures of *rishis* or sages in the spaces between the main image and the standing figures referred to. Further up, there are two female figures standing in peculiar poses on both sides of the image; there are two flying nymphs at the top. The image has two full-blown lotuses on the two sides near the level of its ear; it held them in two of its hands which are now broken. Near the lotus on the right hand is seen the figure of a rider about to strike with his sword and having his kilted legs inserted in the stirrup.

The image of the sun-god has an elaborately worked head-dress of a conical shape; the deity has the characteristic ornaments for the arm, ear and neck. One thing worth noticing in connection with this is that the eyes of the image are not finished.

The slab was originally in the western niche of the temple of Ramachandi described above, whence it has been removed to the bhogamandapa.

The historical records that we may fall back upon for ascertaining the chronology of the temple are the following, *viz.*, (a) the Madla Panji, (b) the copper-plate inscriptions of the Ganga kings and (c) the Ain-I-Akbari.

Date of the temple

The Madla Panji has very little historical value; it also contains contradictory statements in many cases; but one of such statements would serve our purpose of fixing the chronology. Dr. Mitra has quoted the following from the *Madla Panji* in his Antiquities of Orissa, Vol. II. I do not understand the cogency of the reason which has led Mr. Bishan Swarūp to reject it as "utterly incorrect."* It runs thus :—

सुपुच्छ नरसिंहेन श्रीमदंशुमालिनः ।
प्रासादः कारितो राज्ञा शके द्वादशके शते ॥

The temple for the "ray-garlanded god" was built at the instance of the tailed king Narasinha in the year 1200 *Saka*, *i. e.* in the year 1278 A. D. This date of the *Madla Panji* receives corroboration from the copper-plate inscription of the Ganga kings wherefrom we learn that the temple of Konarka was built in the 18th year of the reign of Narasinha Deva.

There is a little difference of opinion regarding the date of accession of king Narasinha to the throne of Orissa.

According to Babu M. M. Chakravarti, Nrisinha Deva I. ascended the throne in 1160 *Saka*†, and reigned up to 1186 *Saka*, *i. e.* from 1238 A. D. to 1264 A. D.; hence the construction of the temple is dated in the year 1256 A. D.

The year of ascension that is deduced from the reading of the copper-plates is 1258 A. D, if we take the date of Chodaganga's accession to the throne in 999 *Saka*, or 1075 A. D.

* Bishan Swarūp, Konarka, p. 71.
† J. A. S. B. Vol. LXXII, p. 120.

I give below the tabular statement of the names of the Ganga kings headed by Chodaganga with the date of accession to the throne against the name of each.

	Date of accession.
Chodaganga	999 Saka or 1075 A. D.
Kamarnava Deva II.	1145 „
Raghava	1155 „
Rajaraja II.	1170 „
Aniyanka-bhima Deva I.	1195 „
Rajaraja III.	1205 „
Aniyank-bhima Deva II.	1225 „
Nrisinha Deva I. ... ... or Narasinha Deva	1258 „

Thus we see that Nrisinha Deva ascended the throne in 1258 A. D., and hence the temple was constructed in 1276 A. D; this very nearly coincides with the date of the Madla Panji, *i.e.* 1278 A. D.

An account of the temple of Konarka is found in the Ain-I-Akbari which apparently tends to upset the conclusion arrived at from the inscription and the Madla Panji. I quote below the portion of the account having a bearing on the date of construction. "It is said that somewhat over 730 years ago, Raja Narasing Deo completed the stupendous fabric and left this mighty memorial to posterity."* From the above

* Ain-I-Akbari, translated by Colonel Jarrett, Bibl. Ind. Vol. II., p. 128.

statement of Abul Fazl, the general belief is that the temple of Konarka was built in 850 A D. Fergusson has supported the above date by advancing a theory, which, of course, has no sound basis, that the temple of Konarka indicating a climax of the art of architecture could never have been built after the temple of Jagannath showing distinct signs of decadence. In his own words, "it seems impossible—after the erection of so degraded a specimen of the art as the temple of Puri (A. D. 1174)—the style ever could have reverted to anything so beautiful as this...In all this uncertainty we have really nothing to guide us but the architecture, and its testimony is so distinct that it does not appear to me doubtful that this temple really belongs to the latter half of the 9th century."* The argument of Fergusson seems to me fallacious; the abstract theory of evolution or involution has not a universal applicability without any consideration for circumstances. I have already touched upon this point in considering the chronology of the caves at Udaygiri.

The account of Abul Fazl is clear on the point of chronology; he refers to Narasinha Deva as the builder of the temple; and I have shown above the time when Narasinha Deva flourished. It is too much to expect accuracy in that remote period regarding the date of a king whose seat of

* Fergusson, History of Indian and Easern Architecture, (1876), p. 426.

government was situated so far from the place where the statistical account was compiled.

I may passingly refer to the figure of Jagannath (see page 475) noticeable on a slab recovered from the debris of the vimana of Konarka. From this it is evident that the temple of the sun-god must have been built long after the temple of Jagannath at Puri was constructed, *i. e.* after the twelfth century A. D. at least.

Restoration of the mohana.

The mohana has been filled with sand after closing the doorways and lining the walls with masonry 15 feet wide. The lining of masonry was necessary to counteract the lateral pressure exerted by sand. The first stage of sand filling as far as possible was done through the northern door which was subsequently blocked up, a 3-inch hole was bored through the *amla*, and sand was dropped through it by means of a funnel attached to the hole; a good deal of repair works has been done in addition to that of sand filling. The southern doorway had to be strengthened by providing a sort of buttress (vide plate XXII).

The huge lions were removed from the floor of the bhogamandapa and placed at the two sides of its entrance on the east; the bhogamandapa was also cleared of sand, debris, etc. All this was completed in 1905; the work of repairing the vimana and removing the debris was taken up in 1906; in course of the removal of the debris, the temple of Ramchandi was discovered. We should express our thanks to the government for spending nearly a lakh of rupees for doing the above works. From this it can be imagined what a fabulous sum must have been spent in constructing the temple. I conclude this chapter by quoting from the Ain-i-Akbari, the portion giving us an idea of the cost incurred for the construction of this temple.

"Near Jagannath is a temple dedicated to the Sun. Its cost was defrayed by twelve years' revenue of the province. Even those whose judgment is critical and who are difficult to please stand astonished at its sight"* The annual revenue of Orissa at that time was 3 crores of rupees or £2000000 nearly.

* A n i-Akbari translated by Col. Jarrett, Bibl. Ind., Vol. II, p 128.

APPENDIX—I

BIBLIOGRAPHY.

Aesthetics by Hegel, translated by Kedney.

Agni-Puranam.

Ain-i-Akbari translated by F. Gladwin.

Ain-i-Akbari (Bangabasi edition).

An Account, Geographical, Statistical, and Historical of Orissa Proper, A. Stirling.

Analysis of Ornament, R. N. Wornum.

Ancient Geography of India, Vol. I., General Cunningham.

Ancient India as described by Megasthenes and Arrian, Mc. Crindle.

Ancient India as described by Ptolemy, Mc. Crindle.

Ancient Khotan, Dr. M. A. Stein.

Antiquities of Orissa, Vols. I and II. Dr. Rajendra Lal Mitra.

Archæological Survey of India, Vols. II, V, XIII, XVII.

Archæological Survey of India (Annual Reports). 1902-1908.

Archæological Survey of Southern India, Vol. XXI.

Architecture as a fine Art (1853). Lieut. Col. H. Goodwyn.

Architecture of Ancient Delhi. Lieut. Cole.

Arithematical Tables, Chambers.

Arya Jatir Silpa Chaturi, Syama Charan Sreemani.

Banger Jatiya Itihasa, Vols. I and II., Nagendra Nath Vasu.

Bhavishya Puranam.

Bhilsa Topes, General Sir Alexander Cunningham.

Bombay Gazetteer, Vol. I, Dr. J. F. Fleet.

Brahma Puranam.

Brihat Parasara Sanhita.

Brihat Sanhita edited by Jivananda Vidyasagara.

Buddha Gaya, Dr. Rajendra Lal Mitra.

Buddhist Art in India, Grünwedel, (edited by Burgess).

Buddhist Stupas of Amaravati and Jaggyyapeta, J. Burgess.

Buildings in the Neighbourhood of Agra, Cole.

Calcutta Review, Vol. LXXXVII.

Catalogue and Hand-book of the Archæological Collections in the Indian Museum, Parts I and II, J. Anderson (1883).

Cave Temples of India, Fergusson and Burgess (1880).

Chalukyan Architecture, Alexander Rea.

Chronology of India, C. M. Duff.

Corpus Inscriptionum Indicarum.

Cyclopædia of India (1885), E. Balfour.

Daru Brahma, Kailasa Chandra Sinha.
Dictionary of Architecture and Building, R. Sturgis.
Dictionary of Terms in Art, F. W. Fairholt.
District Gazetteer, Puri. L. S. S. O'Malley.
Dynasties of the Kanarese Districts, Dr. J. F. Fleet.

Early History of India, V. Smith.
Early History of the Dekkan, R. G. Bhandarkar.
Encyclopædia Britannica, 10th edition.
Epigraphia Indica, Vols. I-VII, Bühler.
Essays in National Idealism, Dr. A. K. Coomarswamy.
Essay on the Architecture of the Hindus, Ram Raz.

Geographical Dictionary of Ancient and Mediæval India, N. L. Dey.
Grammar of Ornament, Owen James.

Hand-book of Ornament, Meyer.
History and Chronology of the Myth-making Age, J. F. Hewitt.
History of Achitecture, B. Fletcher.
History of Art in Chaldæa and Assyria, Perrot and Chipiez.
History of Art in Persia, Perrot and Chipiez.
History of Art, W. Lübke.

History of Art in Sardinia and Judæa, Perrot and Chipiez.

History of Indian and Eastern Architecture (1876), James Fergusson.

History of Indian and Eastern Architecture (1910), edited by Burgess.

History of Science, (edited by Routledge).

India in Greece, Pococke.

Indian Antiquary, Vols. V. XI, XVIII, XXII,

Indian Mythology, V. Fausboll.

Indian Sculpture and Painting, E. V. Havell.

Indische Alterthumskunde, C. Lassen.

Indo-Aryans, Vols. I and II, Dr. R. L. Mitra

Influence of Materials on Architecture, B. F. Fletcher.

Journal of the Asiatic Society, Vols. VI, XXVIII. LVIII, LXII, LXIV, LXVI, LXVII, LXIX.

Journal of the Royal Asiatic Society, Vol. VI.

Kalika Puranam.

Kapila Sanhita, M. S. copy of the Asiatic Society of Bengal

Konarka, Bishan Swarūp.

Lalita Vistara.

Lectures on Architecture, E. M. Barry.

Lectures on Architecture, Vol. I., E. Viollet-Le-Duc.

Lectures on Art, John Ruskin.

List of Ancient Monuments in Bengal corrected up to 1895. (a govt. publication).

Mahabharata.

Mahanirvana-tantram.

Manual of Indian Buddhism, H. Kern.

Memoirs of a map of Hindustan, Major James Rennel.

Memoirs of the Asiatic Society of Bengal, Vol. III, No. 1, H. P. Sastri.

Memoirs of the Geological Survey of India, Vol. I.

Natural History of Pliny, translated by Bostock and Riley.

Numismata Orientalia, Vol. III., Part II., Coins of Southern India, Sir Walter Elliot.

Orissa, Vols. I and II, Dr. W. W. Hunter.

Padma Puranam.

Painting, Sculpture and Architecture, Raymond.

Physical features of the districts of Bankura, Midnapur and Orissa.

Picturesque Illustrations of Ancient Architecture in Hindustan, James Fergusson.

Preservation of National Monuments in India, W. Griggs.

Raghuvamsam.

Rajatarangini translated by Dr. M. A. Stein.

Ramacharita edited by H. P. Sastri.

Ramayana.

Report on the Elura Cave Temples, James Burgess.

Report on the Repairs executed to the Principal Temples of Bhubanesvara and Udaygiri Caves, M. H. Arnott.

Rig Veda, F Max-Muller.

Sanchi and its Remains, General F. C. Maisey.

Sankhya Tattva Kaumudi translated by Dr. Ganga Nath Jha.

Savda Kalpa Drüma, Rajah Radhakanta Deva.

Sculptures of the Parthenon, A. S. Murray.

Seven Lamps of Architecture, John Ruskin.

Siva Puranam, M. S. copy of the Asiatic Society of Bengal.

Skanda Puranam.

Sketch on the Geology of Orissa, Blanford.

South Indian Inscriptions, E. Hultzsch.

Sri Chaitanya Chandrodaya Mahakavyam, Kavi Karnapur.

Srimâtbhagavatam.

Statistical Account of Bengal, Cattack, Balasore, Dr. W. W. Hunter,

Statistical Account of Bengal, Puri, Dr. W. W. Hunter.

Stones of Venice, Vols. I-III, John Ruskin.

Stupa of Bharhut, General Cunningham.

Styles of various countries and periods, T. Bury.

Sukra Niti edited by Jivananda Vidyasagara.

Surya Siddhanta, edited by Girija Prasada Dvivedi.

Travels of Fa Hian, H. A. Giles.

Travels of Fa Hian, Professor J. Legge.

Tree and Serpent Worship, Dr. J. Fergusson.

Two Paths, John Ruskin.

Utkala Khanda of Skanda Puranam.

Vachaspatyavidhanam, Taranath.

Vishnumürti Parichay, Vinode Vehary Kavyatirtha.

Visva Kosha, Nagendra Nath Vasu.

APPENDIX—II.

GLOSSARY OF INDIAN TERMS.

*A*di Parva—One of the eighteen sections of the Maha-bharata.

Agni—the god of fire and regent of the south-east.

Airavata—the celestial elephant, the vehicle of Indra, the king of the gods.

*A*mlaka *Sila*, or *A*mlakà, or *A*mla—the block of stone having a ribbed appearance and presenting the form of an oblate spheroid ; this is placed over the *beki* or the cylindrical block of stone placed over the last course of the rekha portion of the temple. Illustrated on plate II.

*A*nanda—a disciple of Gautama Buddha.

Ananta—the prince of snakes. Ananta is another name of Balarama.

Anartha-paga—is the pilaster of a temple next to the corner one. Illustrated on plates II., IV.

Andhras—These people occupied the portion of India between the deltas of the Krishna and the Godavari ; they became powerful after the death of Asoka. Kalinga came under the Andhras in the second century A. D.

Anga—the Indian principality mentioned in the Mahabharata and other works corresponding with the modern district of Bhagalpur.

Apas—Water.

Apsara—nymph or heavenly maiden; the figure of it is noticed as an ornamental representation, both Brahminical and Buddhistic.

Arka—the Sun.

Arka-kshetra or Surya-kshetra—the sacred place of pilgrimage assigned to the Sun; another name of Konarka.

Arüna—the charioteer of Surya or the sun-god. Arüna is the name of the god of the Dawn. Arüna and Garüda were Casyapa's son by Vinata. Arüna is represented as thighless.

Arüna-stambha—a pillar dedicated to Arüna or the Sun; the monolithic stone pillar in front of the temple of Jagannath; it was originally in front of the temple of Surya or the sun-god at Konarka. Illustrated on plate XX.

Ashta Sakhi—eight maidens or female figures carved in the barandi of the anartha-paga.

Ashta Sakti and Ashtashtaka-Sakti—explained on page 170.

Ashta-tala—a standard of measurement for carving images

according to which the length of the image is eight times the length of the head from the crown to chin. (Ashta = eight ; *tala* = standard of measurement). This measurement has been referred to in *Sukra Niti*.

Asura—the common name for all the antagonists of the *Suras* or gods. They consist of several classes. Asura is also a Buddhist demi-god.

B*ada*—the term for the cubical portion of a temple up to the pyramidal or curvilinear spire. Illustrated on plates II, III.

B*alia*-kha*dia*—a variety of sandstone.

Bandhan*a*—the third element from below upwards of the b*ada* ; it usually consists of three mouldings and is accordingly called Tinkarma or Tink*a*ma. Illustrated on plates II, IV.A.

B*a*nk*a*-j*a*li—A sort of j*a*li or lattice or honey-combed work described on page 196.

Bar*a*jh*a*nji—a sort of carving lining the doorway of an Orissan temple illustrated on plates V, Fig. 3 and V.A Fig III.

B*ara*ndi or *Sa*kkar or *Si*kkar—the second and the fourth elements out of the 5 elements of the b*ada* from below upwards. They contain niches for the dikpatis. Illustrated on plate II. The lower b*ara*ndi usually contains the dikpatis and is called *Sakkar*; and the upper one is called *Sikkara*.

Basanta—the fifth element of the jangha from below upwards. Illustrated on plates II. IV. A.

Bauddha—belonging to Buddha.

Bauddha *Sramana*—See *Sramana*.

Bauddha Stüpa—See Stüpa.

Bauddha-trisula—See trisula.

Bauddha Vihara—See Vihara.

Beki—the cylindrical piece of stone just below the *amla* or just over the top of the curvilinear portion illustrated on plate II.

Bhairava—a terrific figure of *Siva*.

Bho—defined on page 129.

Bhogamandapa or Bhogamandira—the refectory; one of the four appurtenances of an Indo-Aryan temple farthest from the vimana or sanctum; here the offerings for the deity are kept.

Bhumi—defined on page 129.

Bhüta—a Jaina demi-god. It also means a demon or a dwarf, the figure of which is usually found in panels near the top of the bada; it is represented as a pot-bellied dwarf struggling to uplift the superstructure.

Bilkhüja-jali—A sort of jali work described on page 196.

Bodhica—the Indian name for the capital of a column.

Bo-tree or Bodhi-tree or Bodhi-drüma—the great banyan tree (Ficus Indica) under which Siddhartha is said to have attained Buddhahood or enlightenment at Gaya.

Brahma—"the personal form of the impersonal Brahma which comprises all existence. As such he is the first creator."* He is designated as Prajapati, Lord of the creation.

Brahma-Kanda—the rectangular column belonging to the IndoAryan style.

Brishava—bull, the vehicle of Siva.

Campa—fillet.

Casyapa—A treatise on Architecture by Casyapa.

Chaitya—an assembly hall of the Buddhists corresponding with a Christian church.

Chakra—discus; a weapon of Vishnu called Sudarsana; chakra is also called the Dharma-chakra of the Buddhists, or the wheel of the Law. Buddha is said to have turned the Dharmachakra or the wheel of the Law at Sarnath near Benares.

Chamunda—a terrific figure of Dürga.

* V. Fausboll, Indian Mythology, p. 69.

Chhi*da*-u*da*-gaja-sinha—explained on page 179.

Chitr*a*ngad*a*—the daughter of Duryodhana, the king of the Kürüs, the seat of their government being at Hastin*a*pur or Delhi.

D*a*li— a scroll-work ; a sort of carving lining the door-way. Illustrated or Plates V., V. A.

D*a*tha-dh*a*tu-vamsam—A legendary account of the tooth-relic of Gautama Buddha.

Deerghatam*a*—a müni or Indian sage through whose grace, Sudeshn*a*, the wife of Bali bore him five sons—Anga, Banga, Kalinga, Pündra and Sümba.

Deva—god,

Dewl—structure ; the vim*a*na is sometimes called dewl or baradewl.

Dh*a*na-müdr*a*—explained on page 195.

Dharma—religion ; virtue ; quality.

Dhy*a*ni Buddha—Buddha in meditation.

Dikp*a*la or Dikpati—Regent of one of the eight points of the compass ; there are eight dikpatis.

Dikpati-y*a*ga—A religious ceremony performed for the propitiation of the dikpatis.

Dupichch*a*—placed back to back (Du = two ; pichch*a* = pitha = back) ; lions are represented as *dupichcha* (vide page 204).

Dürga—the wife of Siva,

Dwarapala—guard; the figures of Dwarapala are usually *noticed in the panels flanking the doorway.*

Ekachakra—One-wheeled; the chariot of the sun-god is *supposed to have one wheel* (eka = one; chakra = wheel).

Ekamra-kanana—another name for Bhubanesvara; it literally means a garden of one mango tree. There is a Puranam called the Ekamra Puranam.

Ekaratha—a class of structure which does not show any pilaster on its face. (Eka = one; ratha = chariot); this is otherwise called "chaurasa."

Gaja-Lakshmi—a representation of Lakshmi or the goddess of fortune (Vishnu's wife) flanked by elephants on each side noticed usually in a panel carved in the middle of the lintel over the front doorway.

Gandharva—the heavenly musician. Gandharvas usually play on the stringed instrument. Gandharva is also a Jain or Buddhistic demi-god.

Ganesa—the god of success; he is the eldest son of Siva. He is represented as a *Parsva-devata* of the *Sivite* temples of Orissa, and is found in the central niche of the right hand wall of the vimana, the observer standing at the rear of the sanctum

Ganga—the most sacred river of the Hindus, otherwise called the Ganges. She is Himavat's eldest daughter and a wife of Siva. The figures of Ganga and Yamuna are noticed in panels on both sides of the doorway.

Ganga-dynasty—a dynasty founded by Chodaganga who ascended the Orissan throne in 1075 or 1077 A. D.

Garbha-müdra—a block of stone carved with the figure of lotus placed on the topmost course of corbels of the rekha. See page 175.

Garüda—the king of birds; one of the two sons of Casyapa by Vinata, the other son being Arüna. Garüda is the vehicle of Vishnu.

Gelbai—a sort of carving lining the doorway. Illustrated on plate V. A. Fig. II. 4.

Gauri—The wife of Sankara or Siva.

Gauri-chara—a type of Orissan architecture described on pages 135 and 291-292. Illustrated on plate XI.

Ghad-chakda—the last course of stone of the rekha; the beki starts from the ghad-chakda (Ghad = shoulder; chakda = piece).

Ghadi—the upper part of the Kalasa. Illustrated on plate II.

Ghanta-sree-mohana—a sort of pida dewl explained on page 115.

Girivraja—old Rajagriha.

Gümpha—cave.

Hamsa—goose.

Hara—Siva. "As the devastating power which sweeps away and destroys all things, he (Siva) is named Hara and is identified with sickness and death as well as with that all sweeping power which at last destroys all the universe"[1]

Hari—another name of Vishnu.

Hati—elephant (Hati is a contraction of Hasti). c. f. Hati-gümpha.

Indra—the chief of the gods,

Isana—a name of Siva; the regent of the north-east direction.

Jagamohana or Mohana—Audience Chamber or Porch; it is the structure next to the vimana or sanctum. It is made of a cubical portion surmounted by a pyramidal spire formed of *pidas* or cornices. Illustrated on plates III,, XXI, XXII.

Jali—a work of honey-combed pattern; there are several classes of jali-work.

[1] V. Fausboll, Indian Mythology, pp. 154-155.

Jangha—the first part of the five elements from below upwards forming the *bada* or the rectangular portion of a temple. Jangh*a* is sometimes called Panchakama or *Panchakarma.* Illustrated on plates II, IV.A.

J*a*taka—the birth story of Buddha.

Jh*a*pp*a*-sinha—a variety of rampant lion used as an ornamental device.

Kalasa— finial; it literally means a pitcher. Illustrated on plate II.

Kalasa-beki—Illustrated on plate II.

Kalasa-karpuri—explained on page 125. Illustrated on plate II.

Kalasa-p*a*da—the base of a finial (p*a*da = base). Illustrated on plate II.

Kalinga—described in detail in Chapter II.

Kand*a*—sandstone, as in R*a*jar*a*ni*a* kand*a*, Bógd*a* kand*a*, khad*i*a kand*a*, etc.

Kani—the fourth element from below upwards of the jangh*a*. Illustrated on plates II and IV.A.

K*a*nti—a Uriy*a* term for the recess between the pid*a*s.

Karpuri—the stone surmounting the *a*ml*a*. Illustrated on plate II.

K*a*rtikeya or K*a*rtika—the war-god; a son of *S*iva; the

figure of Kartikeya is noticed as a *Parsvadevata* in the niche at the rear of the *vimana* of a *sivite* temple.

Kathchalia—a type of pida-deul explained on page 114.

Ketü—the descending node ; it is one of the navagrahas or nine planets.

Khadia-kanda—a variety of sandstone.

Khadi-prastara—a red and tough variety of quartz found as an inclusion in a variety of sandstone.

Khüra-prishtha—the upper of the two tiers of which a plinth is usually composed. (c. f. the temples of Ananta Vasudeva, Konarka, etc.).

Kimpürüsha—a Jaina demi-god.

Kinnara—a sort of Gandharvas (p. 178); a Jaina and a Bauddha demi-god (p. 72).

Kirttimukha—a sort of ornamental device explained on page 187.

Kona—corner.

Konakapaga—the corner pilaster of a temple (paga = pilaster ; konaka = of the corner). Illustrated on plates II., IV.

Konarka—the corner Sun (kona = corner ; Arka = the Sun) one of the four *kshetras* mentioned in Kapila Sanhita.

Kshepa-sinha—the mad lion, a variety of the representation of the lion used as an ornamental device. c. f. the jagamohana of Muktesvara.

Kümbha—the second element from below upwards of the jangha. It means a water-jar; the moulding, in question, resembles a jar in shape. Illustrated on plates II and IV, A. Kümbha in kümbha-pathara means a load-stone.

Kümüda—an astragal, or torus resembling a semi-circle projecting from a vertical diameter; this moulding is chiefly employed in bases and cornices.

Künda—tank (c. f. Kedara-künda).

Kuvera—the king of the Yakshas; he is the god of riches and regent of the north direction (p. 172).

Lakshmi—the wife Vishnü; the goddess of fortune.

Lingaraja—the chief of the *lingas*; the *siva lingam* installed in the great Tower of Bhubanesvara is so called. (Linga = Phallic symbol).

Madla Panji—the archives or records of the temple of Jagannath at Puri.

Mahakala—a bhairava of *Siva*; the figures of Nandi and Mahakala are noticed in the panels on the sides of the doorway of a *saivite* temple as sentries; Mahakala is referred to as a guard in the Kalika Puranam.

Mahalakshmi—the figure of Lakshmi without the attendant elephants found in the niche of the lintel over the front doorway like Gaja-Lakshmi.

Mahavira Swami—the 24th Tirthankara of the Jainas.

Mahoraga—a demi-god both of the Buddhists and the Jainas.

Makara—capricornus; crocodile or an alligator. This is used as an ornamental device at the springing of arches (c. f. the *torana* or gateway of Muktesvara); the gargoyles are shaped like the mouth of a makara. This is seen as a piece of decoration in the old Buddhistic architecture (c. f. Bharhut sculpture).

Mali-phüla-phadika—explained on page 192.

Marüt—one of the five primary elements, meaning air.

Mastaka—head.

Mayamata—a treatise on Indian architecture.

Mlechchas—explained on page 97.

Mohana—see Jagamohana.

Mükti—salvation.

Nandi—the servant of Siva; the figures of Nandi and Mahakala are carved in panels on both sides of the doorway of a temple as its sentries. Nandi as a dwarapala or sentry is mentioned in the Agni Puranam.

Nadumohana—a pida dewl, the pidas of which coalesce.

Naga—one of the eight classes of Buddhist demi-gods resembling a semi-ophide human figure. The naga is also a

Brahminical demi-god ; he is the chief of the serpents. The naga has his consort called the Nagini.

Naha-chalia—a type of pida dewl explained on page 114.

Naminath—the twenty-first Jain tirthankara.

Narayana-bho—a bho having the figure of Narayana as its inset.

Natamandira—the dancing hall ; it is the structure third in order from the vimana and is situated between the jagamohana and the bhogamandapa. The plan of a Natamandira is illustrated on plates XVII.A, XVII.B, XX. A and XXIV.

Navagraha—nine planets according to Hindu astronomy ; they are, the Sun, Moon, Mars, Mercury, Jupiter, Venus, Saturn, the ascending and descending nodes. The figures of the navagrahas are shown in the architrave over the front doorway.

Nava-Khanda-prithivi—the world of nine parts. (nava = nine ; khanda = parts ; prithivi = world).

Kalinga was one of the nine such parts according to the Tamil lexicons.

Navaratha dewl—a structure showing nine pilasters on one face. (nava = nine).

Nava-tala—a standard of measurement for carving images according to which the length of the image is to be

64

nine times the length of the head from its crown to chin. (Nava = nine; tala = standard of measurement). It has been referred to in Sukra-niti.

Nati-lata—a class of scroll work explained on page 192.

Neminath—the twenty-second Jain tirthankara.

Nirita.—The regent of the south-west direction.

Nrisinha or Narasinha—Vishnu's incarnation as Man-lion; the figure of Nrisinha is seen as a Parsvadevata in a Vishnuvite temple. C. F. the temples of Jagannath, Ananta Vasudeva, etc.

Odra—a name for Orissa.

Pada—The first element from below upwards of a jangha illustrated on plates II and IV.A. It literally means a foot or base.

Padma—lotus; it has got a technical meaning derived from the curve or inflection of the petals of lotus. It means a cyma reversa or cyma recta.

Padma-bho—the bho containing padma or lotus as its inset.

Padma-pani—a Bodhisattva.

Paga—pilaster.

Pancharatha dewl—a structure that shows five pilasters on one face. Illustrated on plates II, IV. (Pancha = five).

Para-ghar—explained on page 114.

Parsva-devata—means literally the deity of a side. The central niches of the three sides of a vimana contain the figures of the parsva-devatas which vary according to the creed of the temple. (Parsva = side ; devata = god or deity).

Patra-lata—a class of scroll work explained on page 192. (Patra = leaf ; lata = creeper).

Pata—the third element from below upwards of a jangha illustrated on plates II and IV.A

Pata-jali—a class of jali work described on page 196.

Pavana—wind ; the regent of the north-west direction.

Phüla-jali—a class of jali work described on page 196.

Phüla-khadia-kanda—a variety of sandstone.

Phüla-lata—a class of scroll work explained on page 192. (Phüla = flower ; lata = creeper).

Pida—a projecting cornice or bracket of the pyramidal spire of a temple. Illustrated on Plate III.

Pida-dewl—A structure, the pyramidal spire of which is formed of pidas. Illustrated on plate III.

Pida-mohana—a class of pida dewl having no amla, kalasa, &c. Illustrated on Plate XX. The natamandiras of the temples of Jagannath, Lingaraja are pida-mohanas.

Parvati—wife of Siva; the figure of Parvati is noticed as a parsva devata in a Sivite temple. (c. f. the temple of Lingaraja).

Pisacha—a Jain demi-god (p. 72).

Pitha—Plinth. (It is a contraction of prishtha).

Raha-paga—the central pilaster of a face. Illustrated on Plates II and IV.

Rahü—the ascending node; it is one of the navagrahas or nine planets usually represented on the architrave over the front doorway of a temple. The head of Rahü is also used as an ornamental device; Rahü is represented as a grinning monster.

Rahür-mükher-mala—the garlands hanging from the mouth of a Kirttimukha. See page 187. For Rahü see above.

Rajarani—the king and queen.

Rajarania Kanda—a variety of sandstone.

Rakshasa—a monster hostile to the rishis, devas, etc.; a class of Buddhist demi-gods.

Rani—queen.

Ratna-müdra—the block of stone with a cavity for containing the jewels or treasures belonging to a temple; it is placed below the beki.

Rekha or rathaka—the curvilinear part of a structure

surmounting the cubical portion. Illustrated on Plate II.

Rekha dewl—a towered sanctuary illustrated on Plate II. It is a structure consisting of a cubical portion surmounted by a curvilinear tower. Illustrated on Plate II.

Rüdra-kanda—the 16-sided column of Indo-Aryan style is called Rudra-kanda (Rüdra = *S*iva; Kanda = trunk of a tree). The monolithic pillar in front of the temple of Jagannath is a rüdra-kanda.

Sagara—a prince of the Surya dynasty.

Sakkar—another name for lower barandi.

Samahita Buddha—Buddha in a state of super-consciousness.

Sambhavanath—the third Jain tirthankara.

Sangharama—a Buddhist monastery.

*S*ankü—gnomon for determining the north line.

Santinath—the sixteenth Jaina tirthankara.

Sapta—seven.

Saptakama or Satkama—a work of seven parts or mouldings; the upper jangha usually consists of seven mouldings and hence is called saptakama. Illustrated on Plates II, IV.A.

Saptaratha dewl—a structure showing seven pilasters on a face.

Saptarshi—seven rishis (Marichi, Angira. etc.) forming the seven stars of the constellation Great Bear.

Sapta-tala—A standard of measurement for carving images in which the length of an image is seven times the length of the head from its crown to chin. See pages 209-214.

Sardüla—lion ; a sort of ornamental representation described on pages 179-180.

Saura—belonging to the Sun.

Shada-tala—Similar to sapta tala ; the length of the image in this case is 6 times the head.

Sikkara—another name for upper barundi. Illustrated on plate II. It is a contraction of Sikkara.

Siva-kanda—a pentagonal column is technically called a Siva-kanda, the analogy being to the five heads of Siva. (kanda = trunk of a tree).

Skanda—another name of Kartikeya.

Skanda-kanda—a hexagonal column is technically called a Skanda-kanda, the analogy being to the six heads of Skanda or Kartikeya.

Sramana—mendicant ; an order of the Buddhists.

Sreansanath—the eleventh Jaina tirthankara.

Stūpa—"a tower erected to commemorate some event or mark some sacred spot dear to the followers of the religion of Buddha".

Sukra-niti—the book on polity written by *Sukracharya*, the preceptor of the Asuras.

Sumatinath—the fifth Jaina tirthankara.

Swastika—a mystic symbol or figure of the Hindus Buddhists and Jainas. See page 57.

Talapattana—pavement.

Talaprishtha—the lower of the two tiers of plinth. (Tala = bottom; prishtha = plinth).

Tamralipta or Tamralipti—another name of Tamlūk in the district of Midnāpur.

Tandava-nritya-bho—a bho having the scene of the tandava-nritya or frantic dance of *Siva* as its inset.

Tantrikas—a religious sect worshipping the *Sakti* or female energy or creative energy.

Tathagata—a name of Buddha.

Tinkama or Tinkarma—a work showing three works or three mouldings (tin = three; kama = work); the bandhana is otherwise called tinkama. Illustrated on Plates II, IV.A.

Fergusson, History of Indian and Eastern Architecture (1876), p. 50.

Tirthankara—a perfect being according to the Jaina scriptures having perfect vision (*Samyak darsanam*), perfect knowledge (*Samyak jnânam*) and perfect character (*Samyak charitram*). There were twenty-four such tirthankaras, the last one being Mahavira Swami who was a contemporary of Buddha and flourished in the time of Bimbisara, the king of Magadha.

Torana—gateway. (c. f. the Torana of Muktesvara).

Trikalingadhipati—lord of the three Kalingas. See page 21. (Tri = three ; adhipati = lord).

Tripatadhara—the short cylindrical portion over the *amla*. Illustrated on Plate II.

Triratha-dewl—a structure showing three pilasters on one face.

Trisûla—trident ; it is a weapon of *S*iva. Trisûla is also a Buddhistic symbol.

U*da*-sinha—flying lion ; a variety of the representation of lion as a decorative device. See page 204.

Ultagaja-sinha—explained on page 179.

Ulta-gaja-viraja-sinha—explained on page 179.

Upana—plinth of a column.

Upapitha—pedestal of a column or a structure.

Uttira—entablature of a column.

Vaishnava – a follower of Vishnü.

Vaitala dewl – described on pages 133-135. Illustrated on Plates XVIII, XIX.

Vajrapani – a Bodhisattva.

Vana lata—a kind of scroll work (see page 192). It literally means a creeper of the forest or a wild creeper. (Vana = forest ; lata = creeper).

Varüna—the god of water ; the regent of the west.

Vasishtha—a rishi ; the spiritual preceptor of the kings of Ayodhya.

Vasudeva—a name of Vishnü.

Vetala—it is an ornamental representation showing a dwar fish monster struggling to uplift a structure.

Vihara—monastery. The Buddhists used to have monasteries, *e. g.*, the vihara of Nalanda. The Vihara forms one of the five classes of Buddhist Architecture, *viz.*, Stambha or lat, Stüpa or tope, Rails, Chaityas or Assembly Halls, Viharas or monasteries.

Vimana—the towered sanctuary in which the image of the deity is enshrined. Illustrated on Plates XVII.A., XX.A, XXIV.

Yama—the god of the nether regions corresponding to Pluto of the European classic. A regent of the south.

Yamūna—the sacred river called the Jumna. The figures of Yamūna and Ganga are noticed in panels on both sides of the front doorway.

Yavana—described on page 97. It ordinarily means a Mlechcha or people other than the Hindus. See Mlechcha.

Yudhisthira—the head of the Pandavas.

INDEX.

C

D

G

H

I

J

L

M

N

O

R